Story and Art by Arina Tanemura

SAKURA HIME

The Legend of Princess Sakura

6

SAKURA HIME
The Legend of Princess Sakura

....

C O N T E N T S

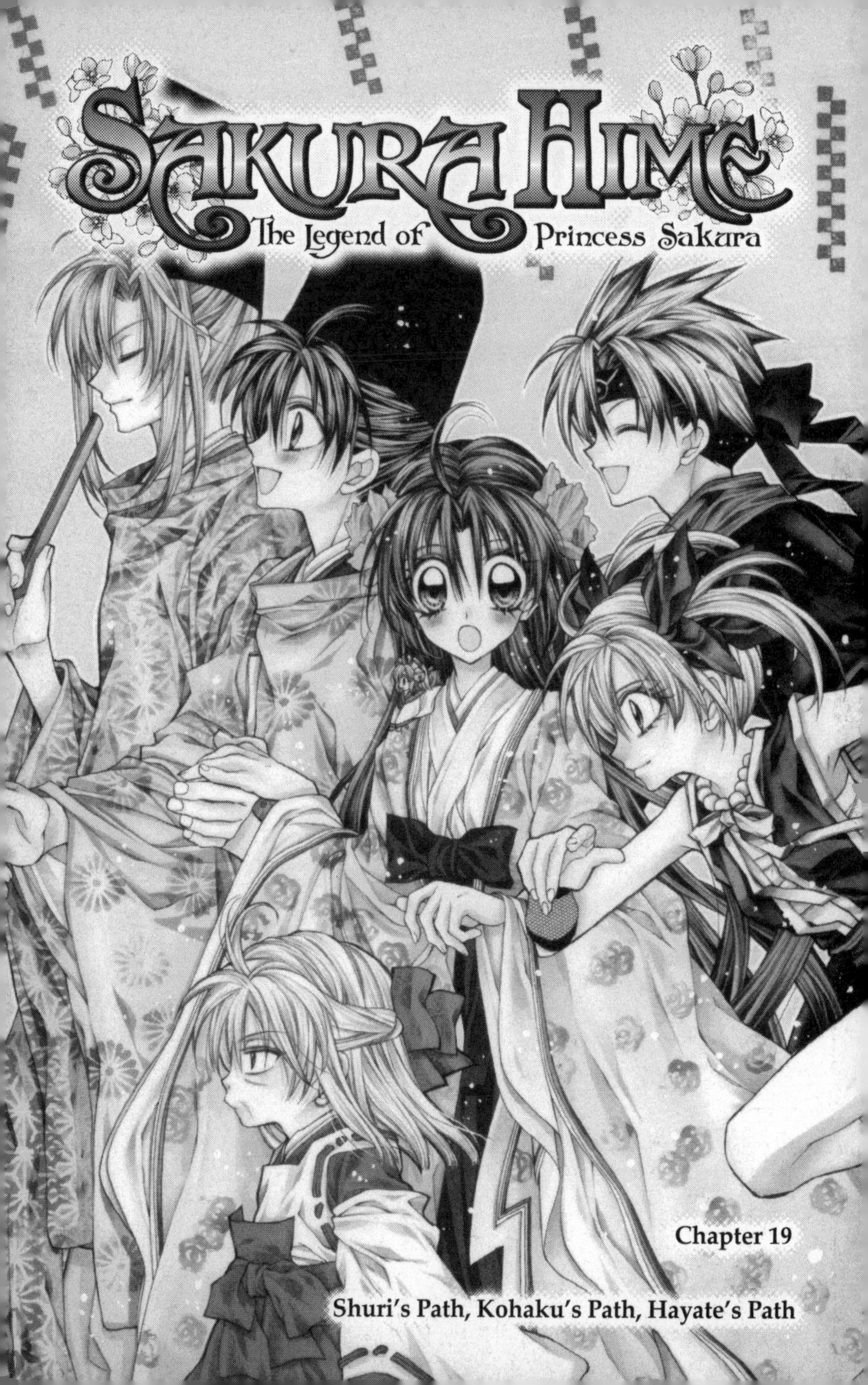
SAKURA HIME
The Legend of Princess Sakura
Chapter 19
Shuri's Path, Kohaku's Path, Hayate's Path

ONCE I FULFILL MY MISSION AND STEAL THE MOON SPRING WATER...

...THAT WATER MAY BREAK THE SPELL UPON HAYATE.

THEN KOHAKU MAY FINALLY SMILE FOR ME.

I'VE LOST EVERY-THING I WANTED TO PROTECT.

THIS IS THE ONLY WISH LEFT INSIDE ME.

THAT'S HOW I KNOW I'LL BE FINE.

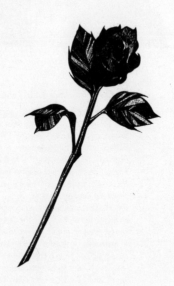

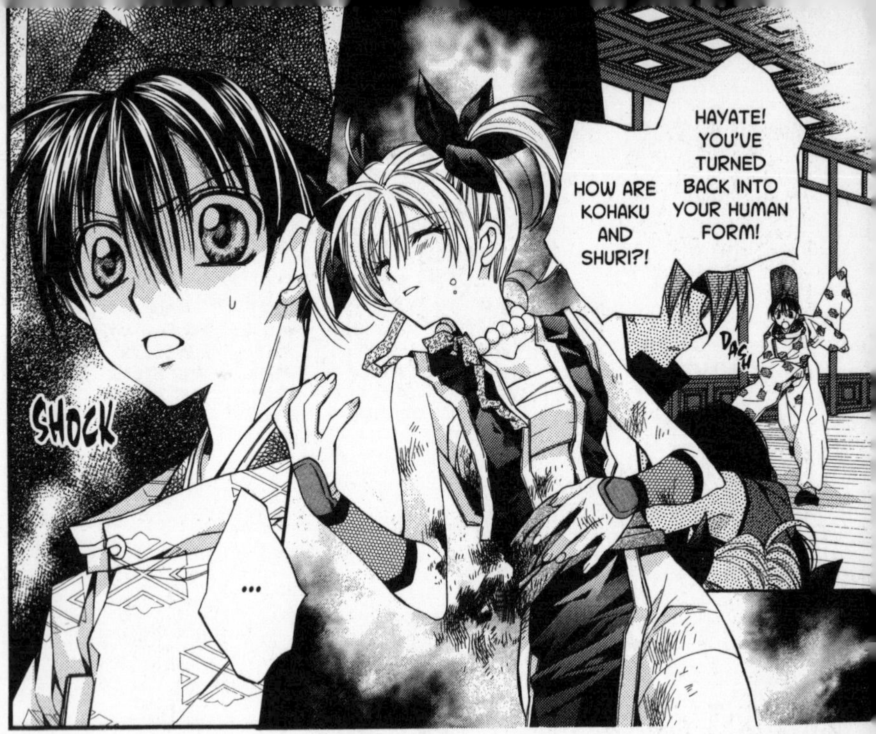
HAYATE! YOU'VE TURNED BACK INTO YOUR HUMAN FORM!
HOW ARE KOHAKU AND SHURI?!
DASH
SHOCK
...

Chapter 19: Shuri's Path, Kohaku's Path, Hayate's Path

※I'm giving away the story.

This chapter brings back memories for me because it ran in the magazine together with chapter 20. No matter how hard I worked, it never seemed to end, and I was forced to realize once again how time-consuming it is to draw manga.

Anyway, this is the final chapter for the Shuri versus Kohaku arc. Shuri is—how can I put it?—like a jack-of-all-trades who is never rewarded for what he does. On the other hand, Hayate is the guy who steals the spotlight even though he hasn't really done anything. To tell the truth, the secret main character (?) of this arc (or the one whom I wanted to write about) is Aoba. I wanted to write about a muddled, wishy-washy relationship like that of close childhood friends that never truly develops into a romantic one. There were those who asked, "Isn't Kohaku in love with Aoba?" but I don't think it's really love. The only person she has been in love with is Hayate, I think. Kohaku and Hayate's relationship totally depends on Kohaku, so I too am thinking, "Will you two hurry up and get together?!" (laugh) Kohaku is a rather stubborn person. That's what's good about her, but she does need to learn to give in a bit too...

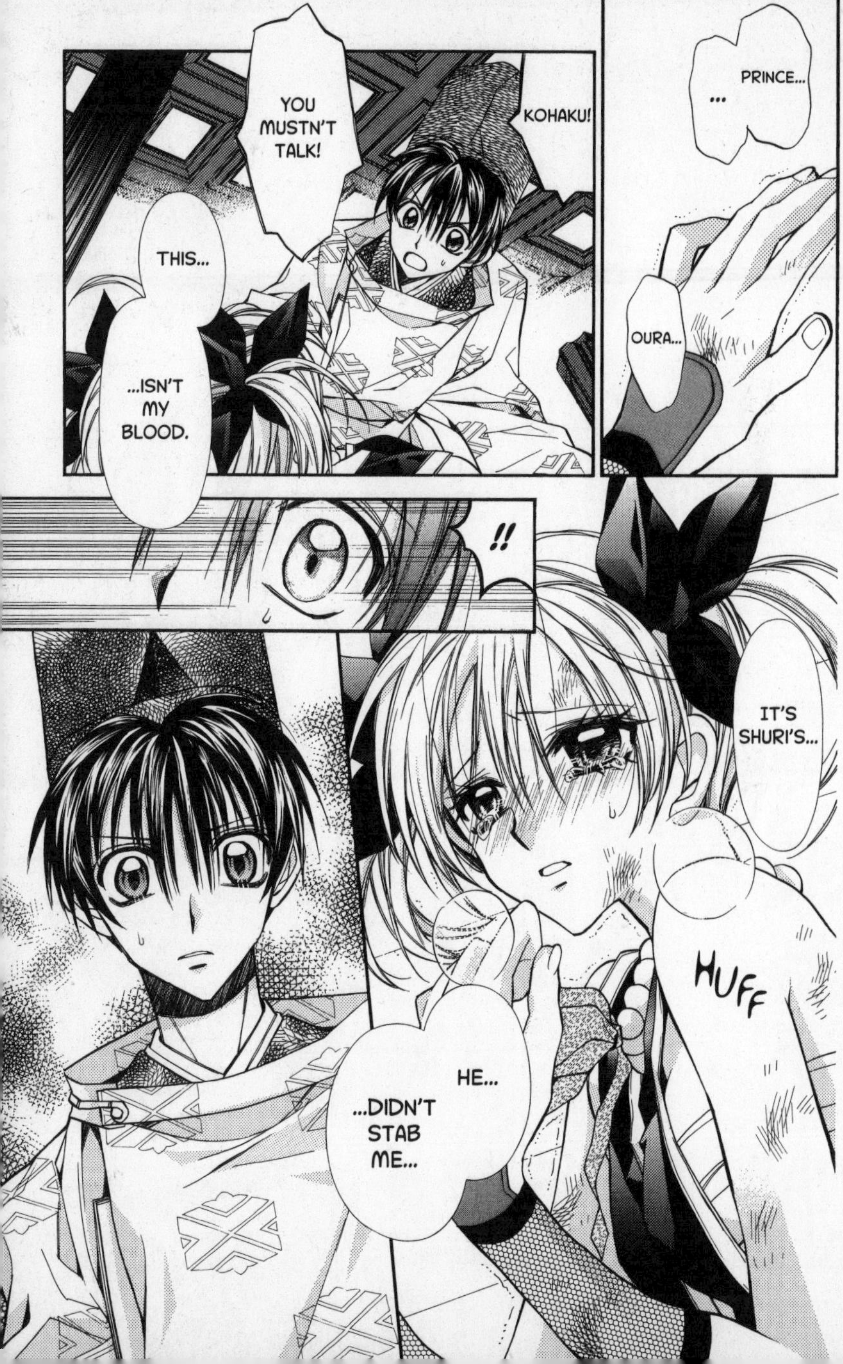
PRINCE...
...
OURA...
KOHAKU!
YOU MUSTN'T TALK!
THIS...
...ISN'T MY BLOOD.
!!
IT'S SHURI'S...
HUFF
HE...
...DIDN'T STAB ME...

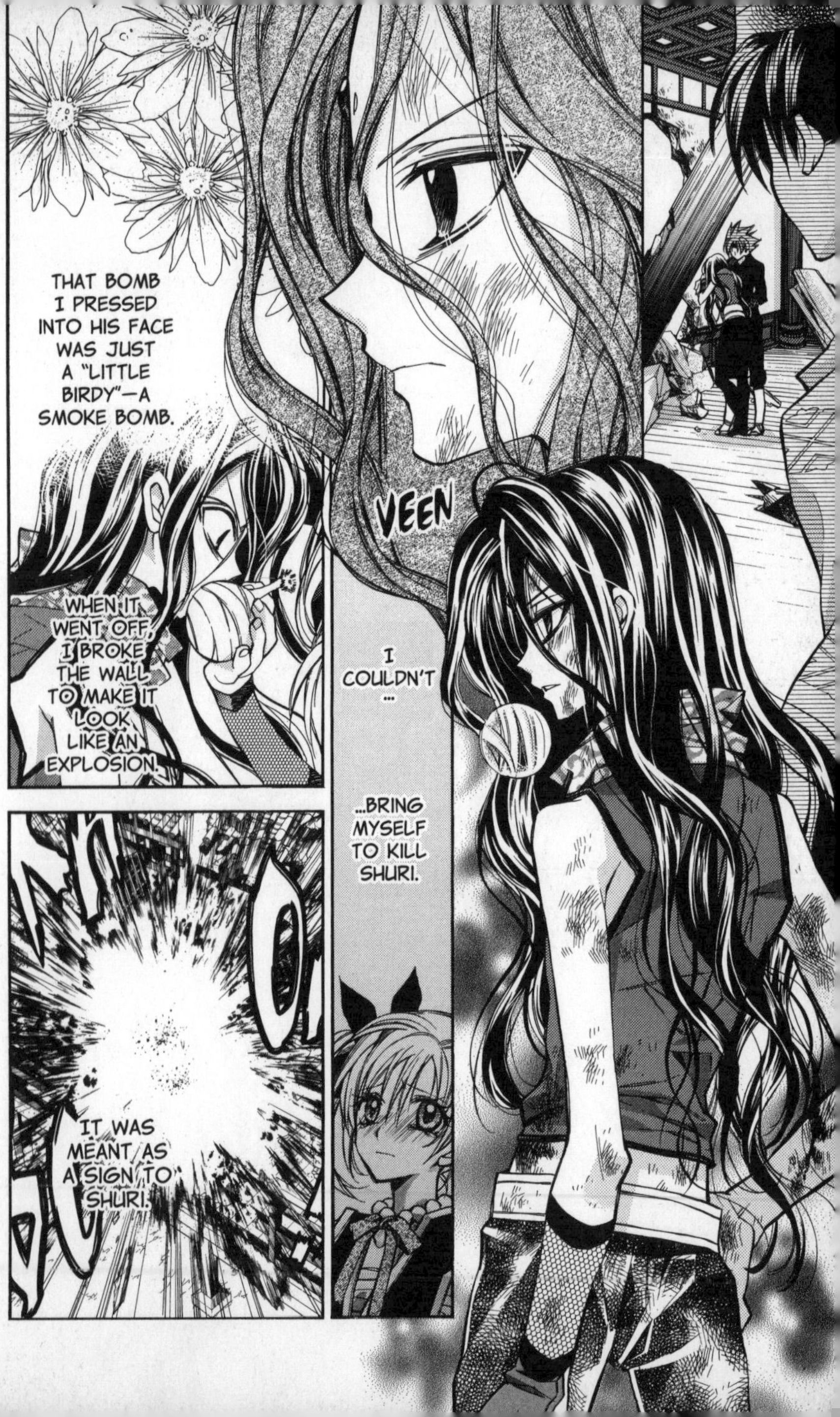
THAT BOMB I PRESSED INTO HIS FACE WAS JUST A "LITTLE BIRDY"—A SMOKE BOMB.
VEEN
I COULDN'T ...
...BRING MYSELF TO KILL SHURI.
WHEN IT WENT OFF, I BROKE THE WALL TO MAKE IT LOOK LIKE AN EXPLOSION.
IT WAS MEANT AS A SIGN TO SHURI.

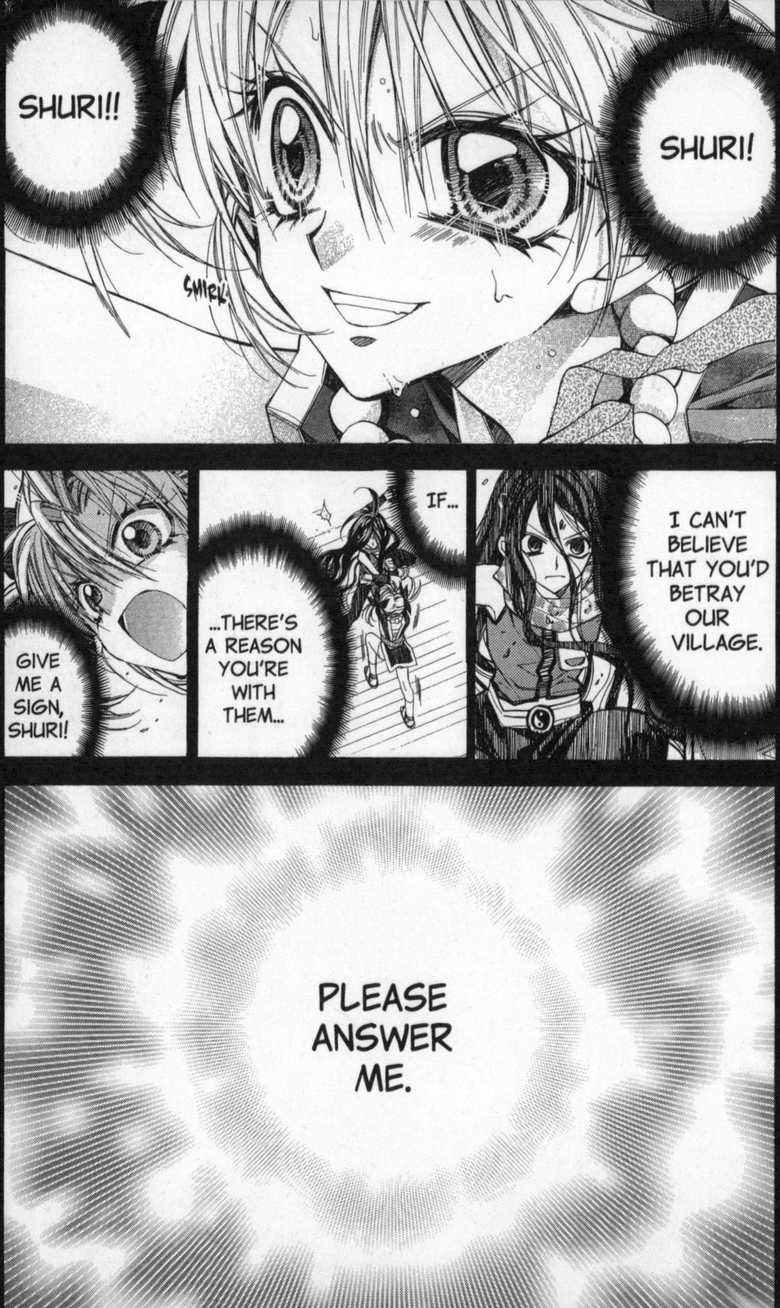
SHURI!
SHURI!!
SMIRK
I CAN'T BELIEVE THAT YOU'D BETRAY OUR VILLAGE.
IF...
...THERE'S A REASON YOU'RE WITH THEM...
GIVE ME A SIGN, SHURI!
PLEASE ANSWER ME.

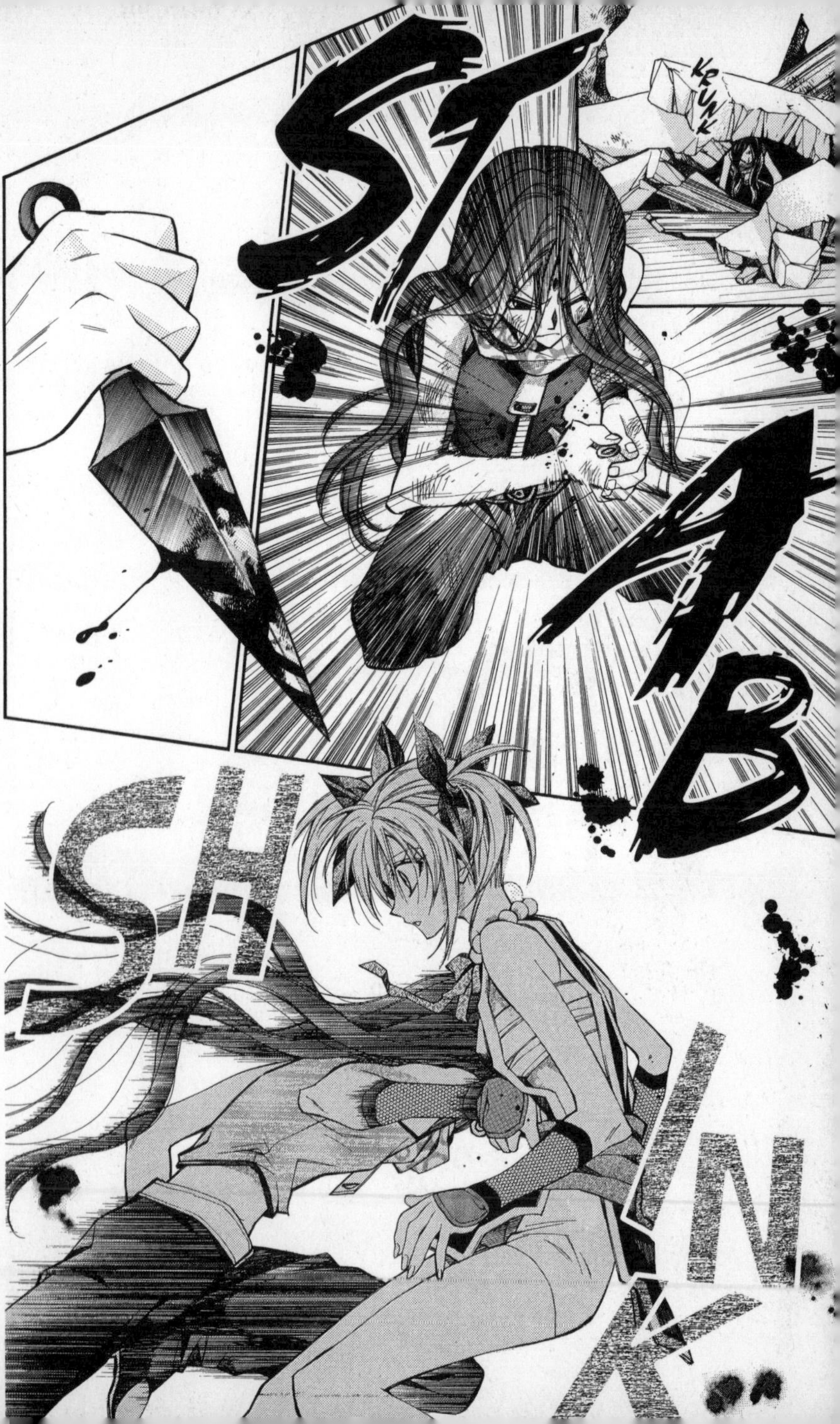
KRUNK
STAB
SHINK

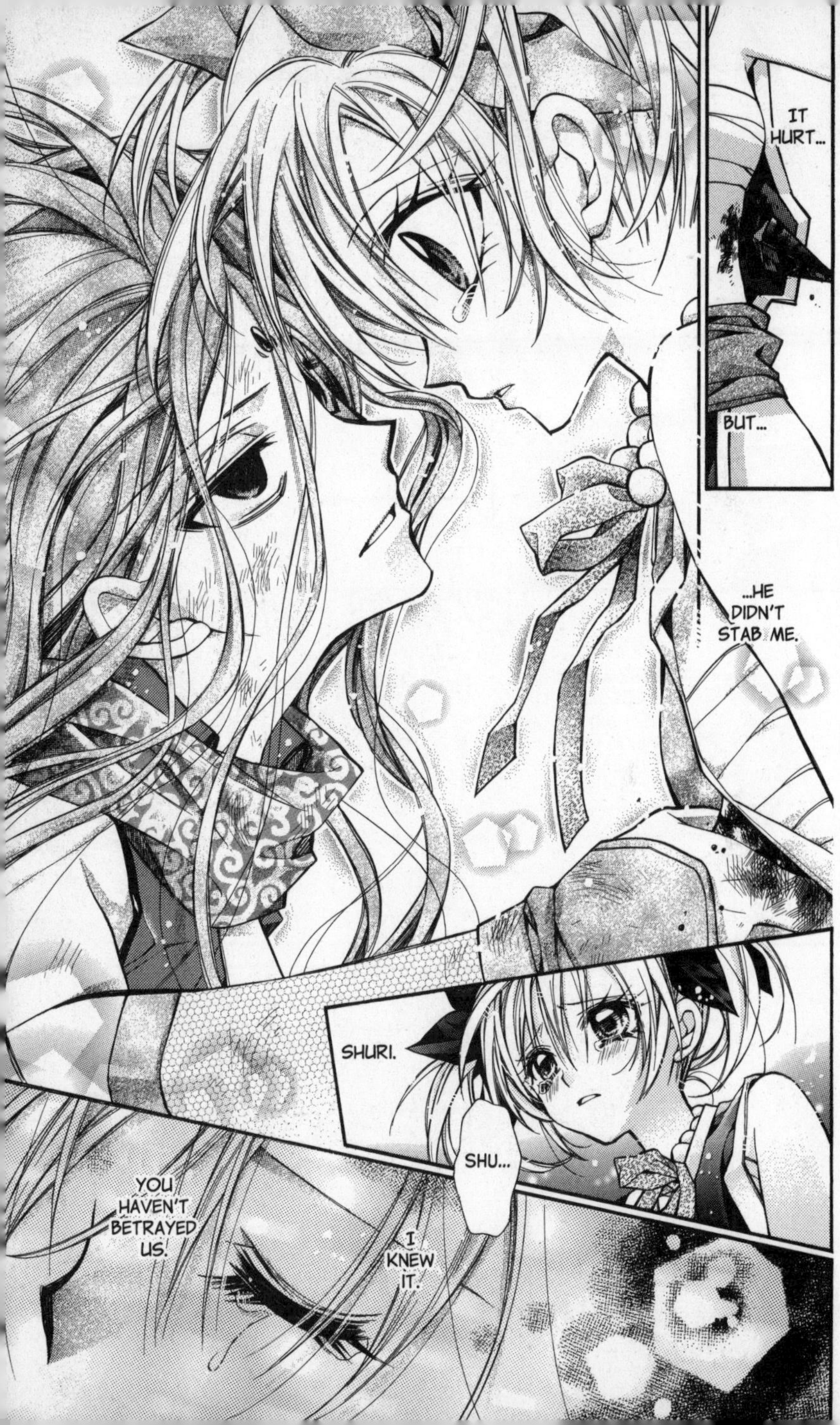
IT HURT...
BUT...
...HE DIDN'T STAB ME.
SHURI.
SHU...
I KNEW IT.
YOU HAVEN'T BETRAYED US.

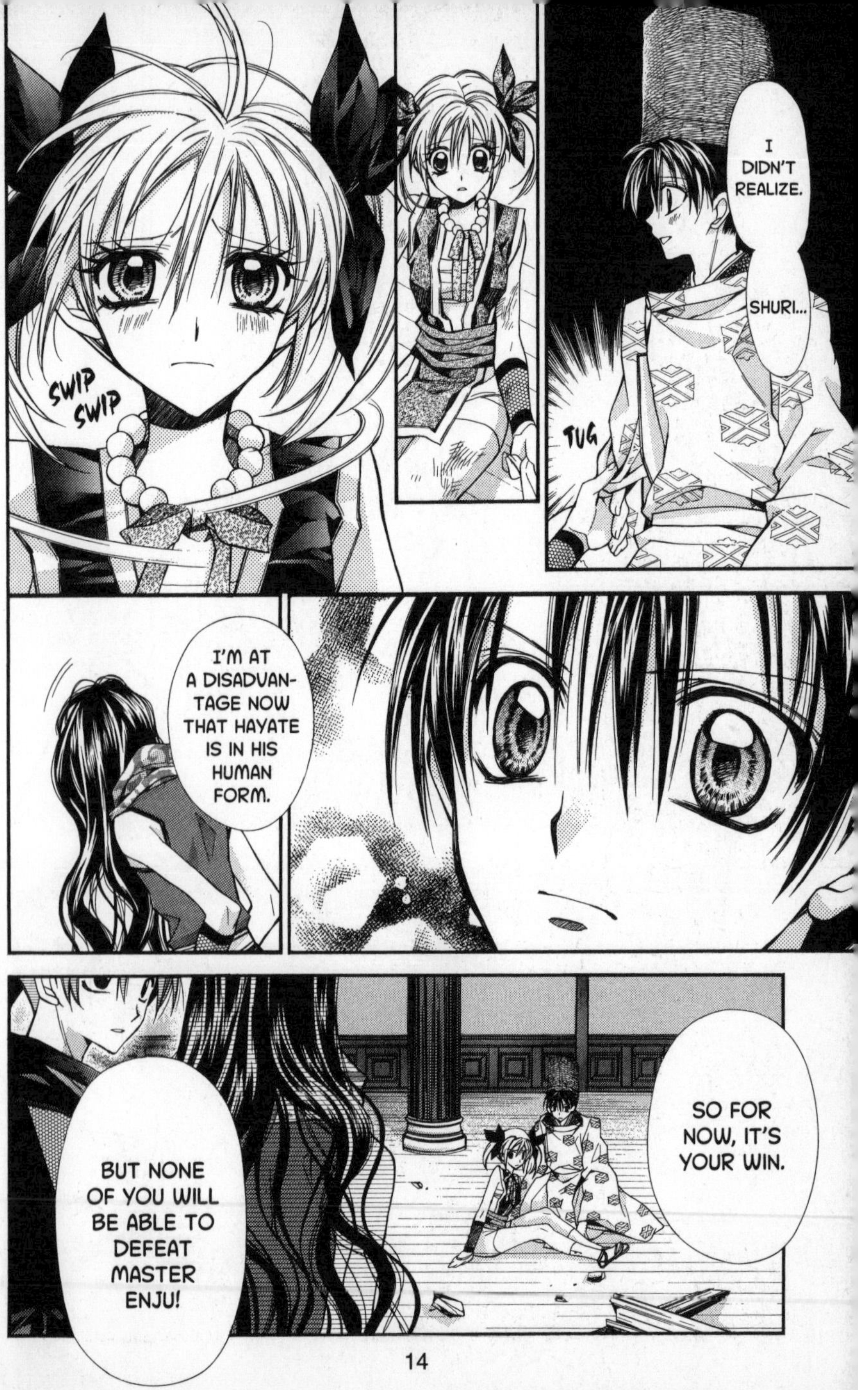
I DIDN'T REALIZE.
SHURI...
TUG
SWIP SWIP
I'M AT A DISADVAN-TAGE NOW THAT HAYATE IS IN HIS HUMAN FORM.
SO FOR NOW, IT'S YOUR WIN.
BUT NONE OF YOU WILL BE ABLE TO DEFEAT MASTER ENJU!

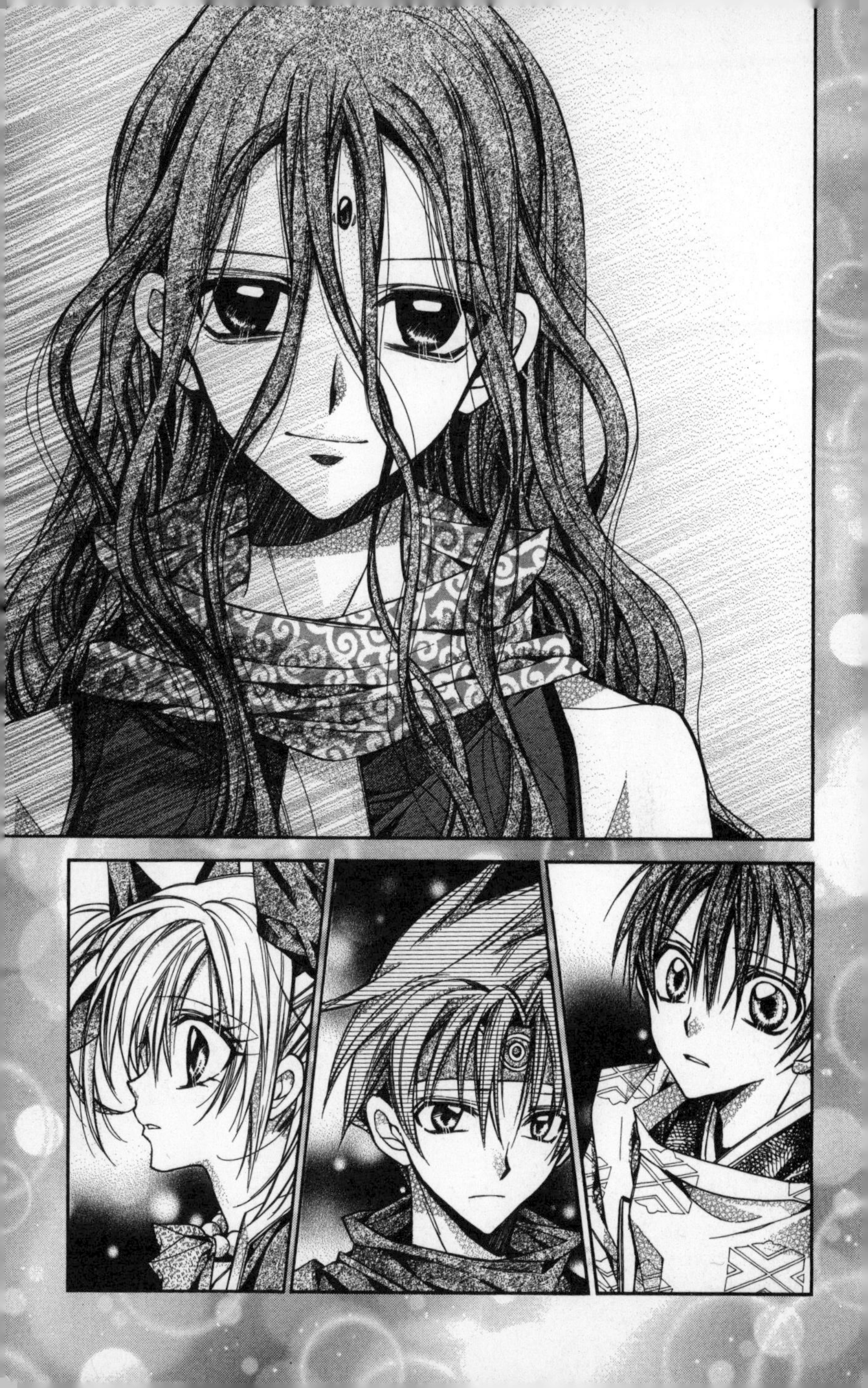

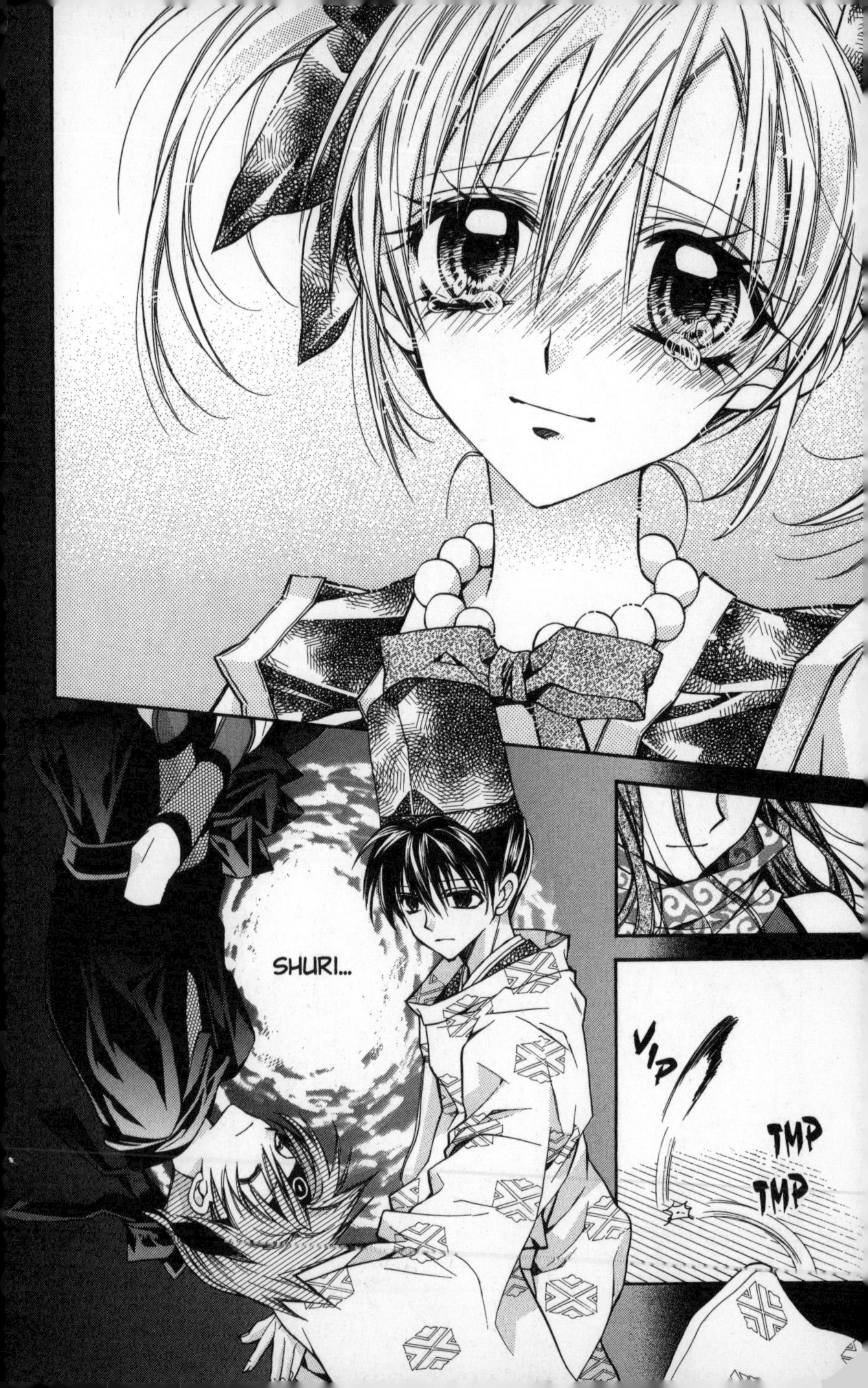
VIP
TMP
TMP
SHURI...

HELLO ✿

Hello! Arina Tanemura here. ✿ I bring to you *Sakura Hime: The Legend of Princess Sakura* volume 6!

Those who bought this manga as it came out in Japan bought two volumes in two months. (This came out right after volume 5.) Thank you very much for your continued support! ✔

Sakura Hime has more pages than my usual series, so the volumes can be published faster. ♪

The Shura Yugenden arc has reached its middle point, and I've been presenting the story to you in a rather unique way for a shojo manga.

I enjoy drawing stories about the past, so I wanted to present the Shura Yugenden arc with battles + stories about the past. Actually, I'm not even a quarter of the way into the whole series yet. I often get questions asking me how long the series will run for. It looks like we've still got quite a long way to go.

I also have urges to draw ordinary love stories too... (So I intend to include those every now and then.)

But this will surely become my longest running series so far. (I cannot fall ill while I'm working on a series, so I feel slightly nervous when the series will run for a long time.)

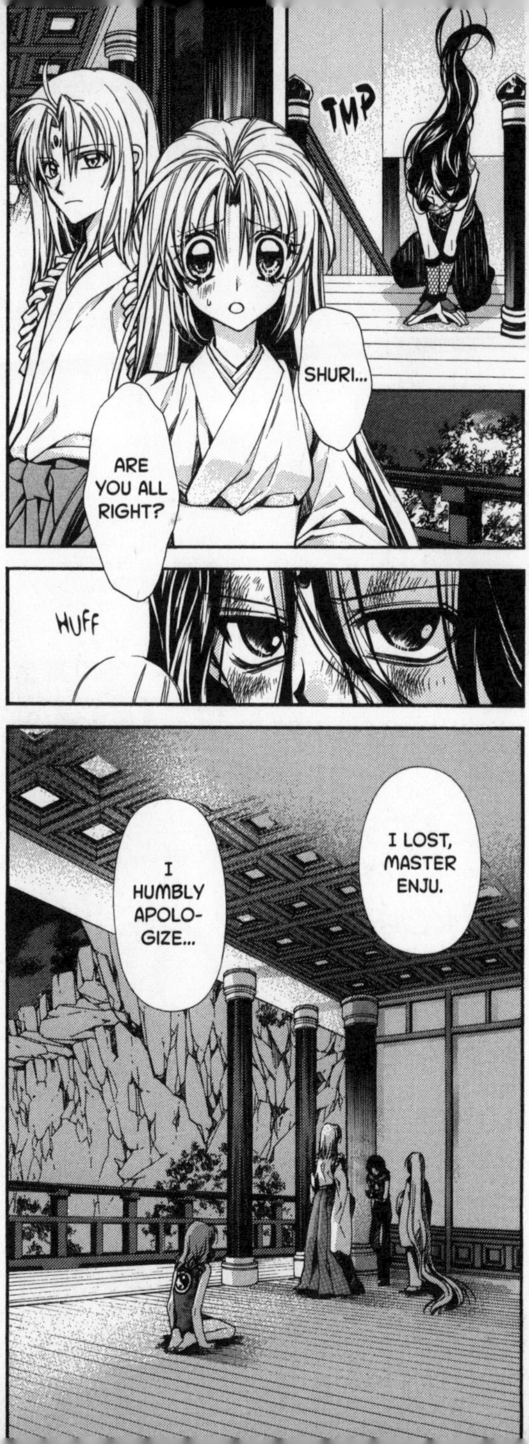
TMP
SHURI...
ARE YOU ALL RIGHT?
HUFF
I LOST, MASTER ENJU.
I HUMBLY APOLOGIZE...

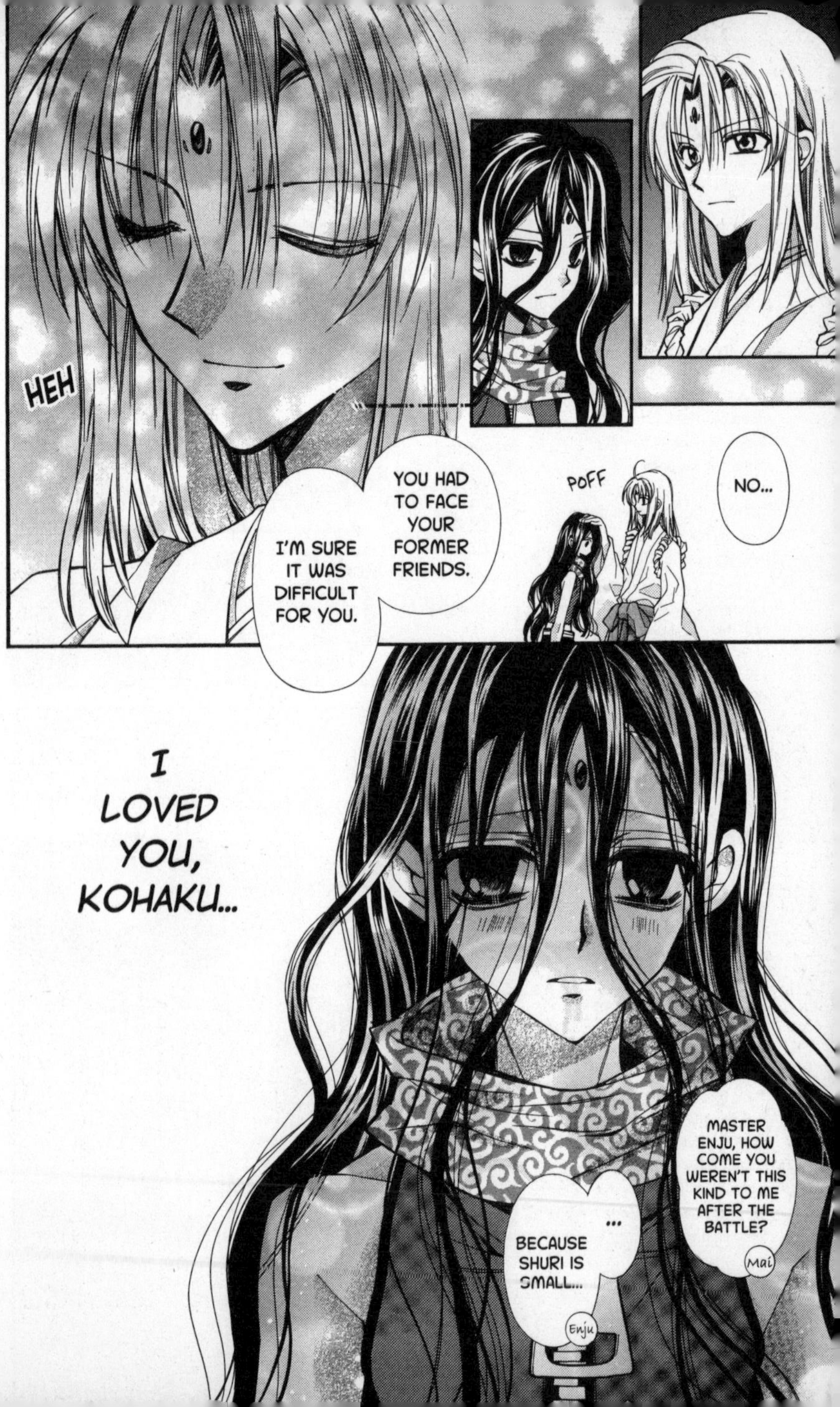
NO...
POFF
YOU HAD TO FACE YOUR FORMER FRIENDS.
I'M SURE IT WAS DIFFICULT FOR YOU.
HEH
MASTER ENJU, HOW COME YOU WEREN'T THIS KIND TO ME AFTER THE BATTLE?
Mai
...
BECAUSE SHURI IS SMALL...
Enju
I LOVED YOU, KOHAKU...

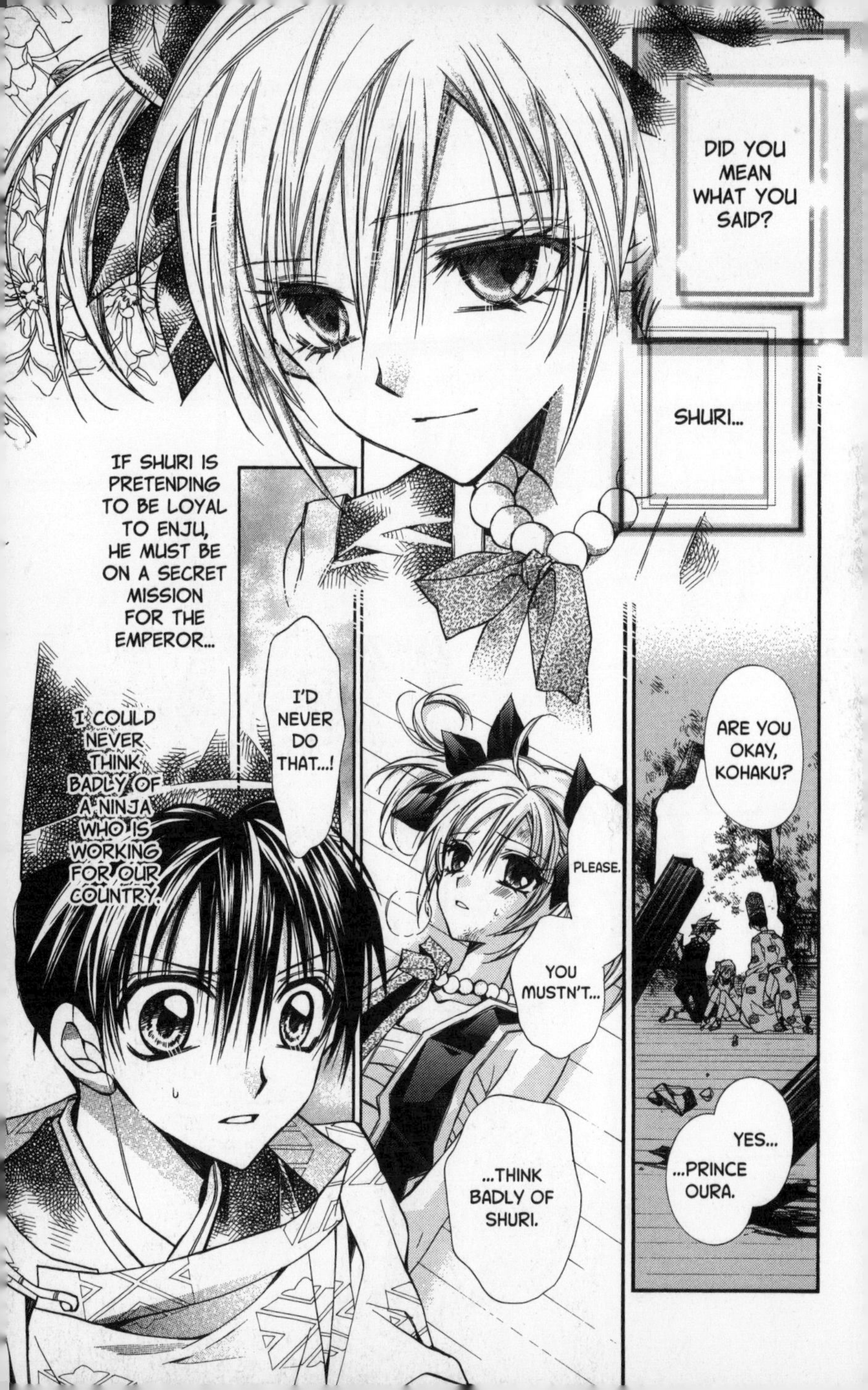
DID YOU MEAN WHAT YOU SAID?
SHURI...
ARE YOU OKAY, KOHAKU?
YES...
...PRINCE OURA.
PLEASE.
YOU MUSTN'T...
...THINK BADLY OF SHURI.
I'D NEVER DO THAT...!
IF SHURI IS PRETENDING TO BE LOYAL TO ENJU, HE MUST BE ON A SECRET MISSION FOR THE EMPEROR...
I COULD NEVER THINK BADLY OF A NINJA WHO IS WORKING FOR OUR COUNTRY.

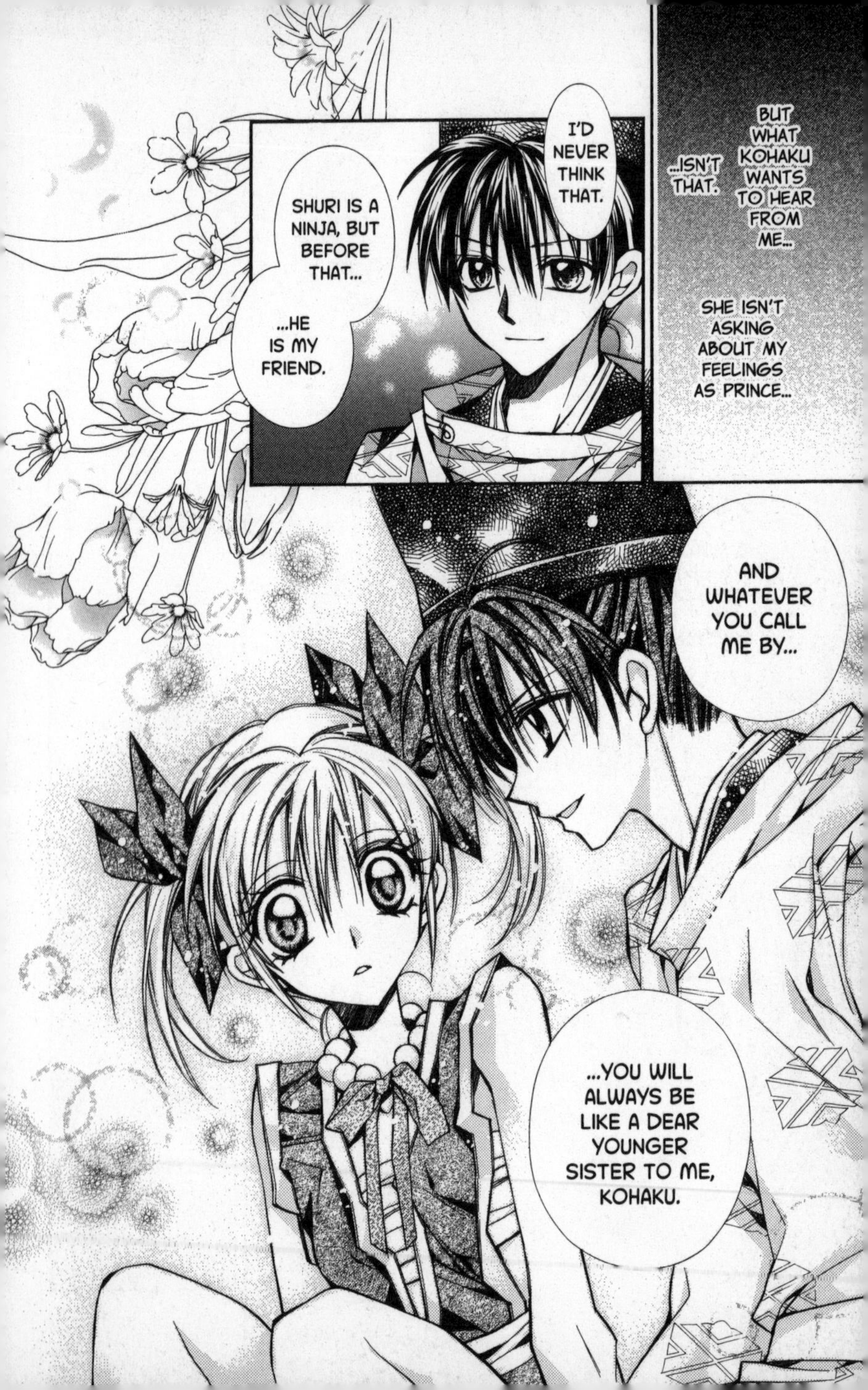
BUT WHAT KOHAKU WANTS TO HEAR FROM ME...
...ISN'T THAT.
SHE ISN'T ASKING ABOUT MY FEELINGS AS PRINCE...
I'D NEVER THINK THAT.
SHURI IS A NINJA, BUT BEFORE THAT...
...HE IS MY FRIEND.
AND WHATEVER YOU CALL ME BY...
...YOU WILL ALWAYS BE LIKE A DEAR YOUNGER SISTER TO ME, KOHAKU.

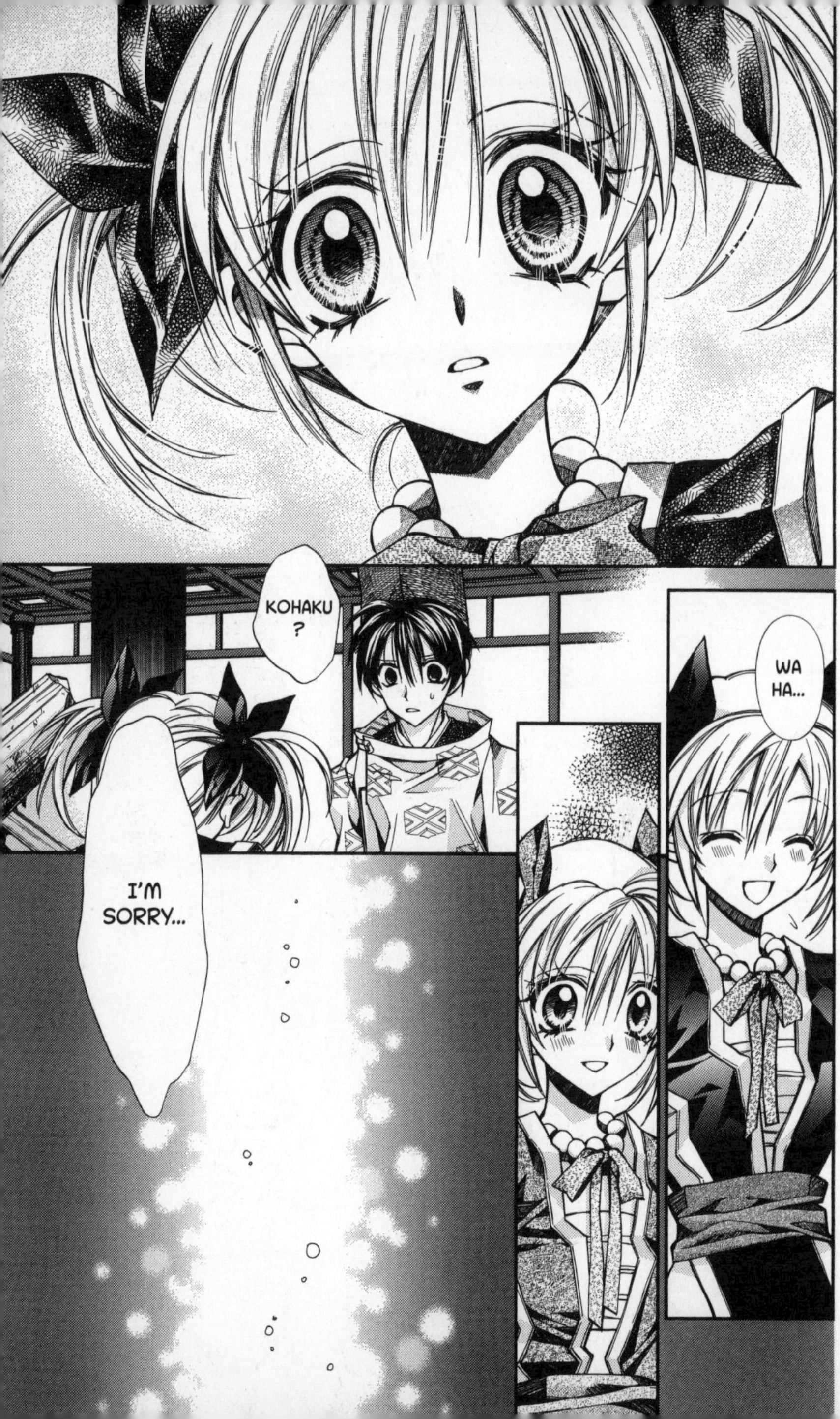
WA HA...
KOHAKU ?
I'M SORRY...

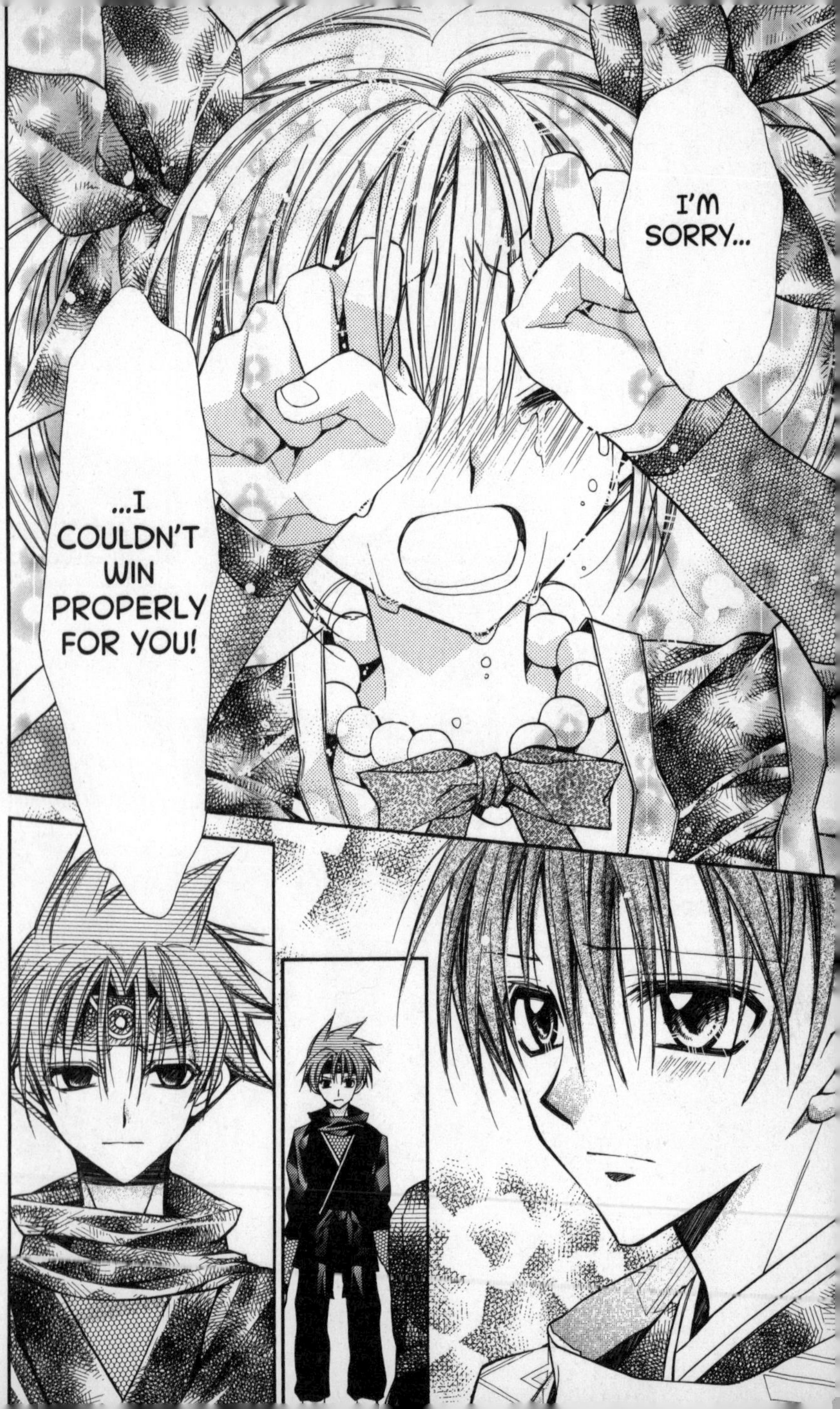
I'M SORRY...
...I COULDN'T WIN PROPERLY FOR YOU!

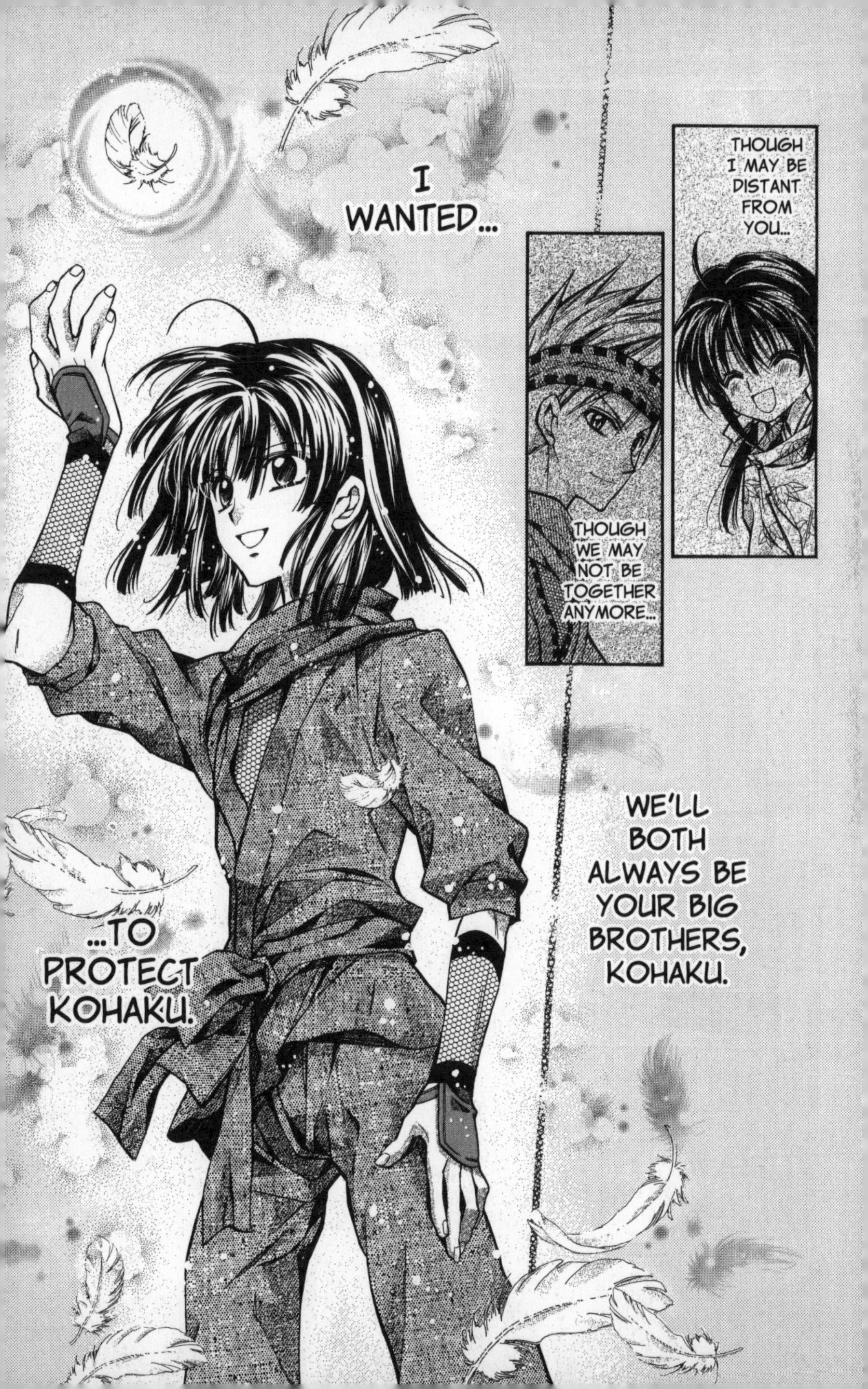
THOUGH I MAY BE DISTANT FROM YOU...
THOUGH WE MAY NOT BE TOGETHER ANYMORE...
WE'LL BOTH ALWAYS BE YOUR BIG BROTHERS, KOHAKU.
I WANTED...
...TO PROTECT KOHAKU.

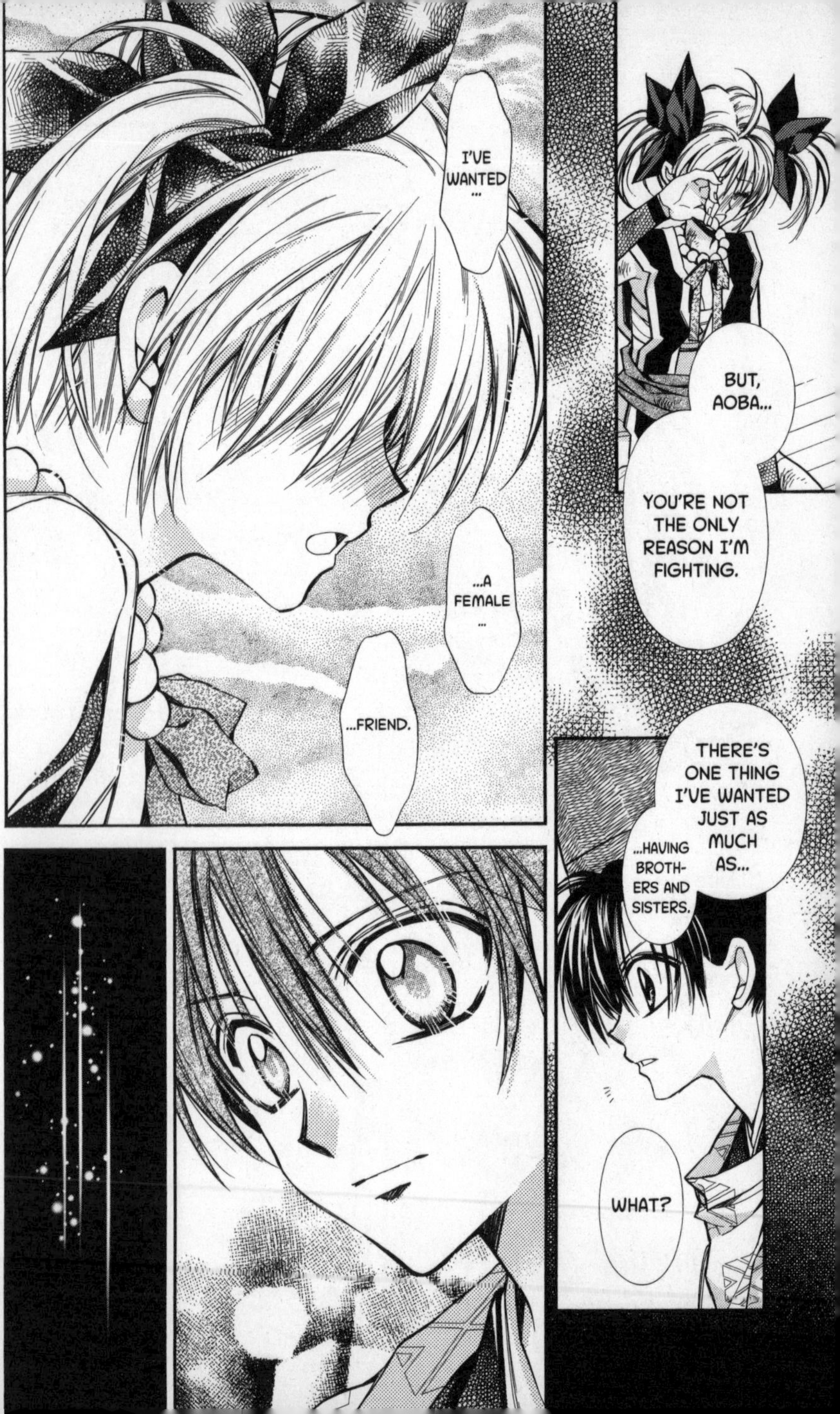
BUT, AOBA...
YOU'RE NOT THE ONLY REASON I'M FIGHTING.
I'VE WANTED ...
...A FEMALE ...
...FRIEND.
THERE'S ONE THING I'VE WANTED JUST AS MUCH AS...
...HAVING BROTHERS AND SISTERS.
WHAT?

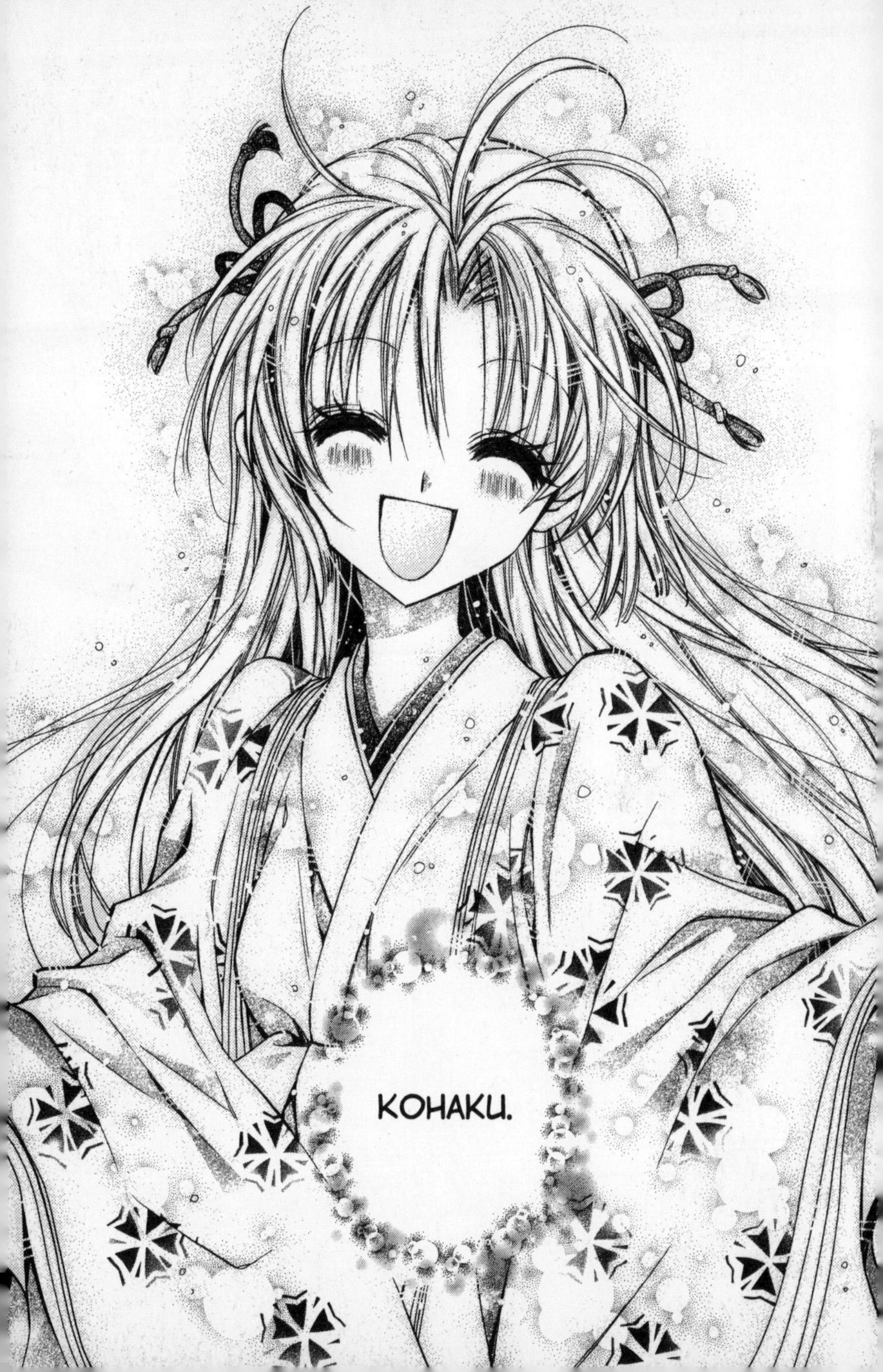
KOHAKU.

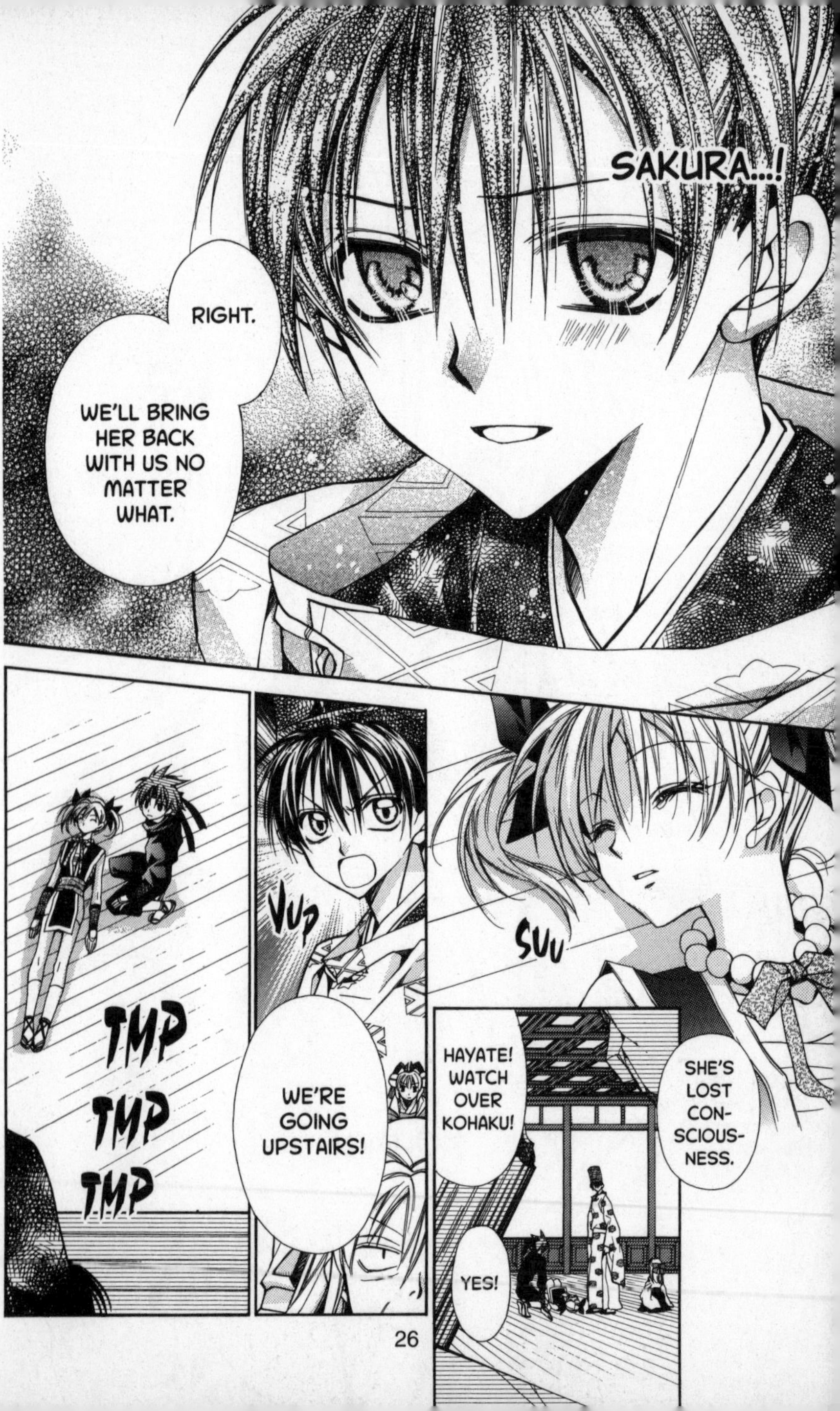
SAKURA...!
RIGHT.
WE'LL BRING HER BACK WITH US NO MATTER WHAT.
SUU
SHE'S LOST CONSCIOUS-NESS.
HAYATE! WATCH OVER KOHAKU!
YES!
VUP
WE'RE GOING UPSTAIRS!
TMP
TMP
TMP

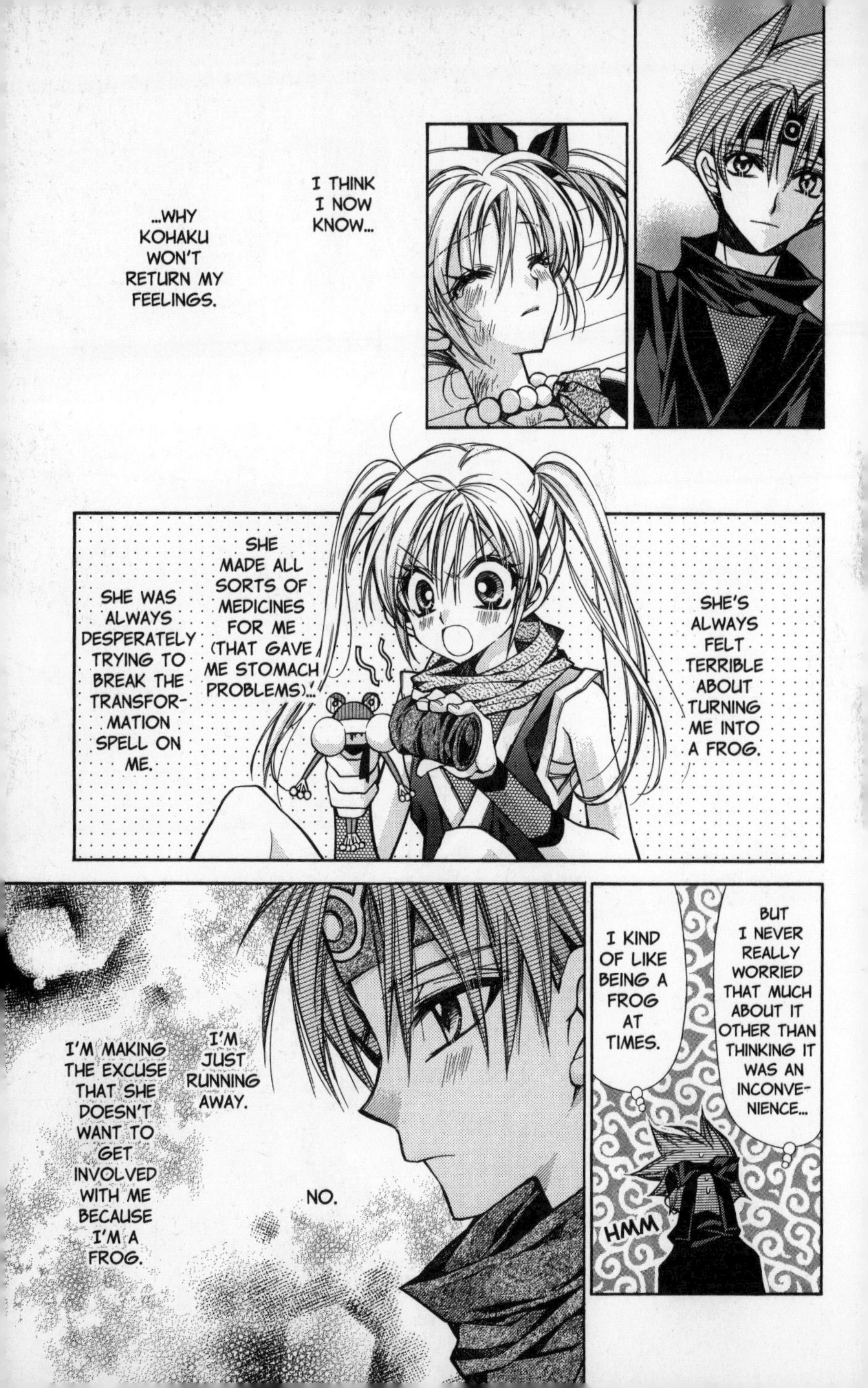
I THINK I NOW KNOW...
...WHY KOHAKU WON'T RETURN MY FEELINGS.
SHE'S ALWAYS FELT TERRIBLE ABOUT TURNING ME INTO A FROG.
SHE MADE ALL SORTS OF MEDICINES FOR ME (THAT GAVE ME STOMACH PROBLEMS)...
SHE WAS ALWAYS DESPERATELY TRYING TO BREAK THE TRANSFORMATION SPELL ON ME.
BUT I NEVER REALLY WORRIED THAT MUCH ABOUT IT OTHER THAN THINKING IT WAS AN INCONVENIENCE...
I KIND OF LIKE BEING A FROG AT TIMES.
HMM
NO.
I'M JUST RUNNING AWAY.
I'M MAKING THE EXCUSE THAT SHE DOESN'T WANT TO GET INVOLVED WITH ME BECAUSE I'M A FROG.

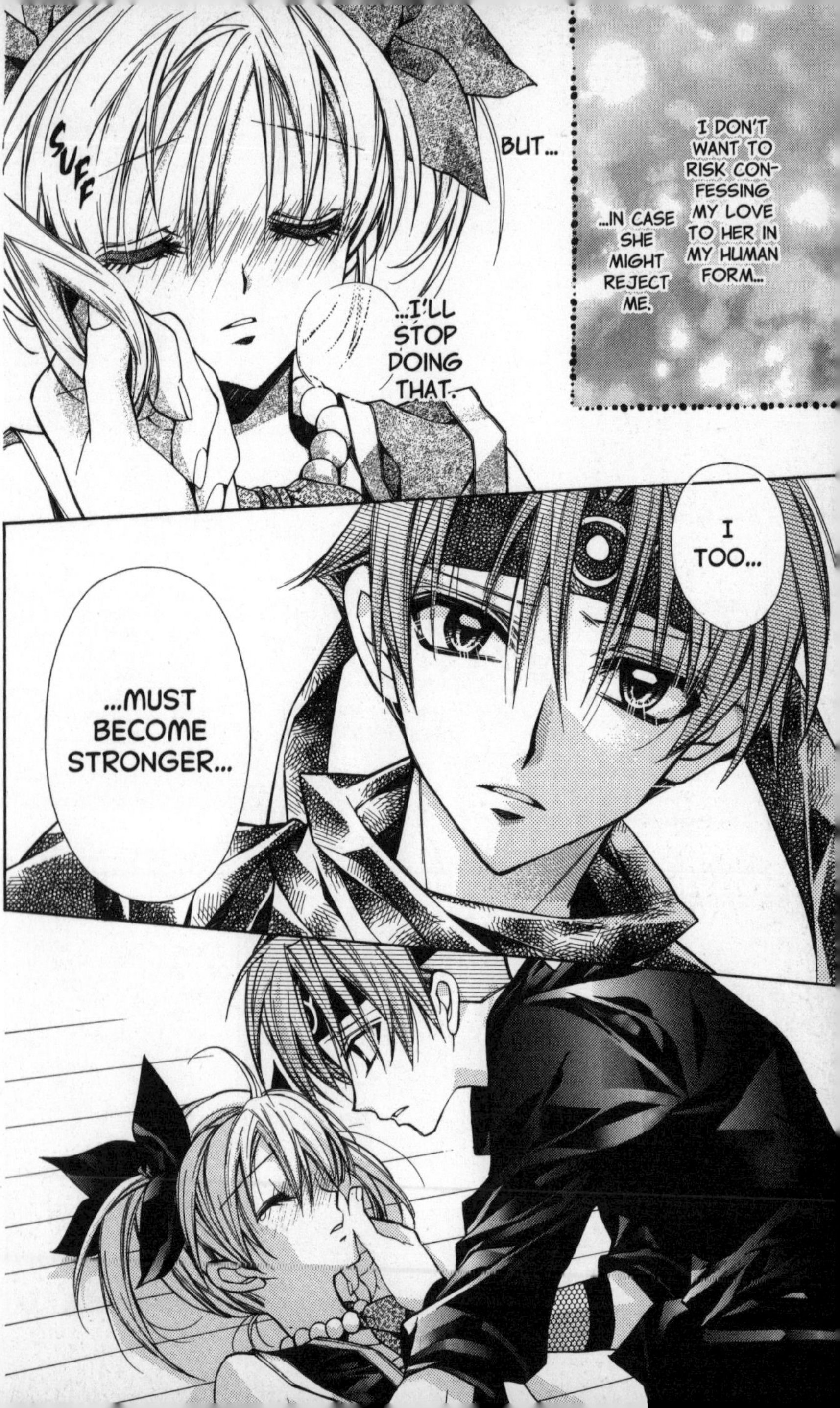
I DON'T WANT TO RISK CON-FESSING MY LOVE TO HER IN MY HUMAN FORM...
...IN CASE SHE MIGHT REJECT ME.
BUT...
SUFF
...I'LL STOP DOING THAT.
I TOO...
...MUST BECOME STRONGER...

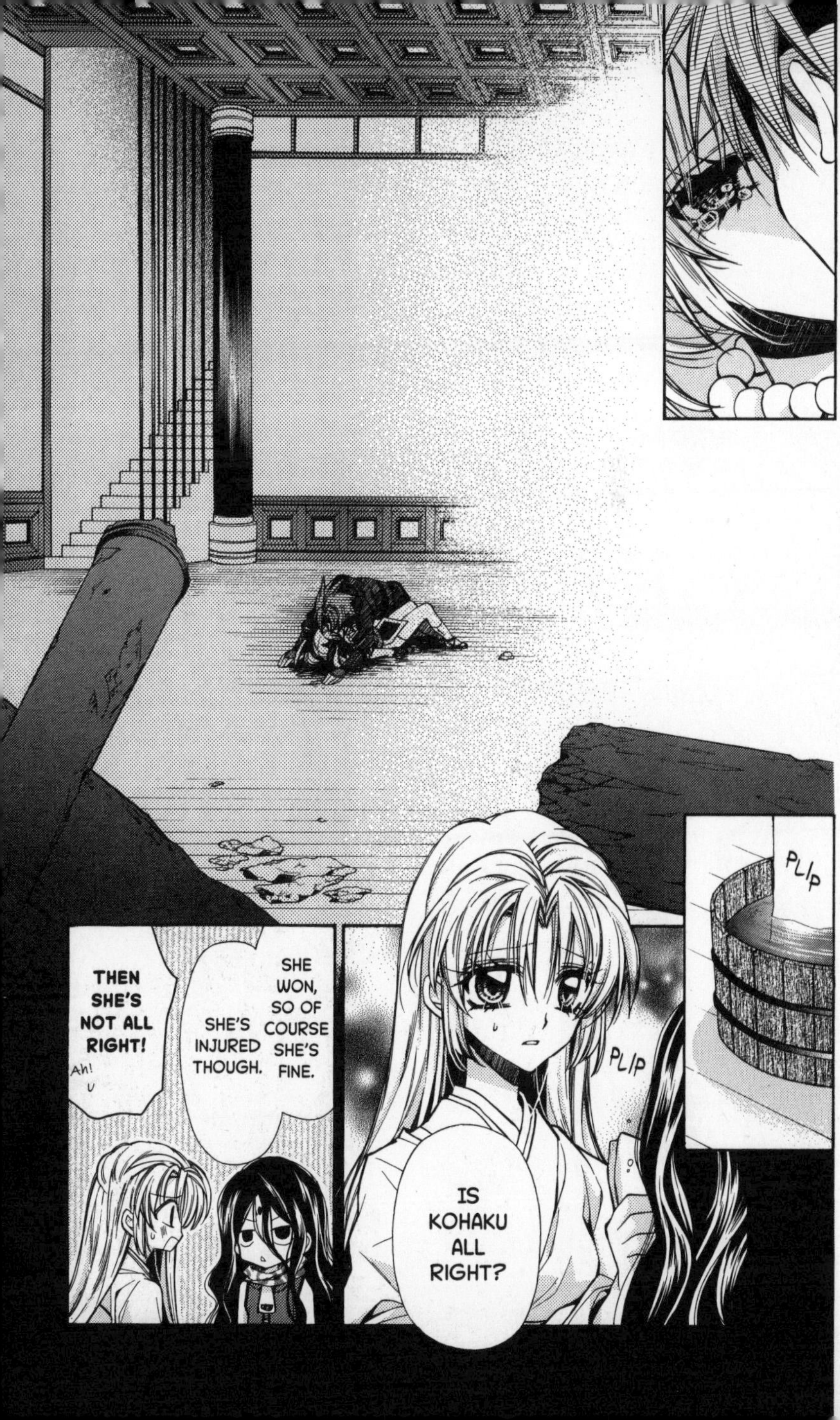
PLIP
PLIP
IS KOHAKU ALL RIGHT?
SHE WON, SO OF COURSE SHE'S FINE.
SHE'S INJURED THOUGH.
THEN SHE'S NOT ALL RIGHT!
Ah!

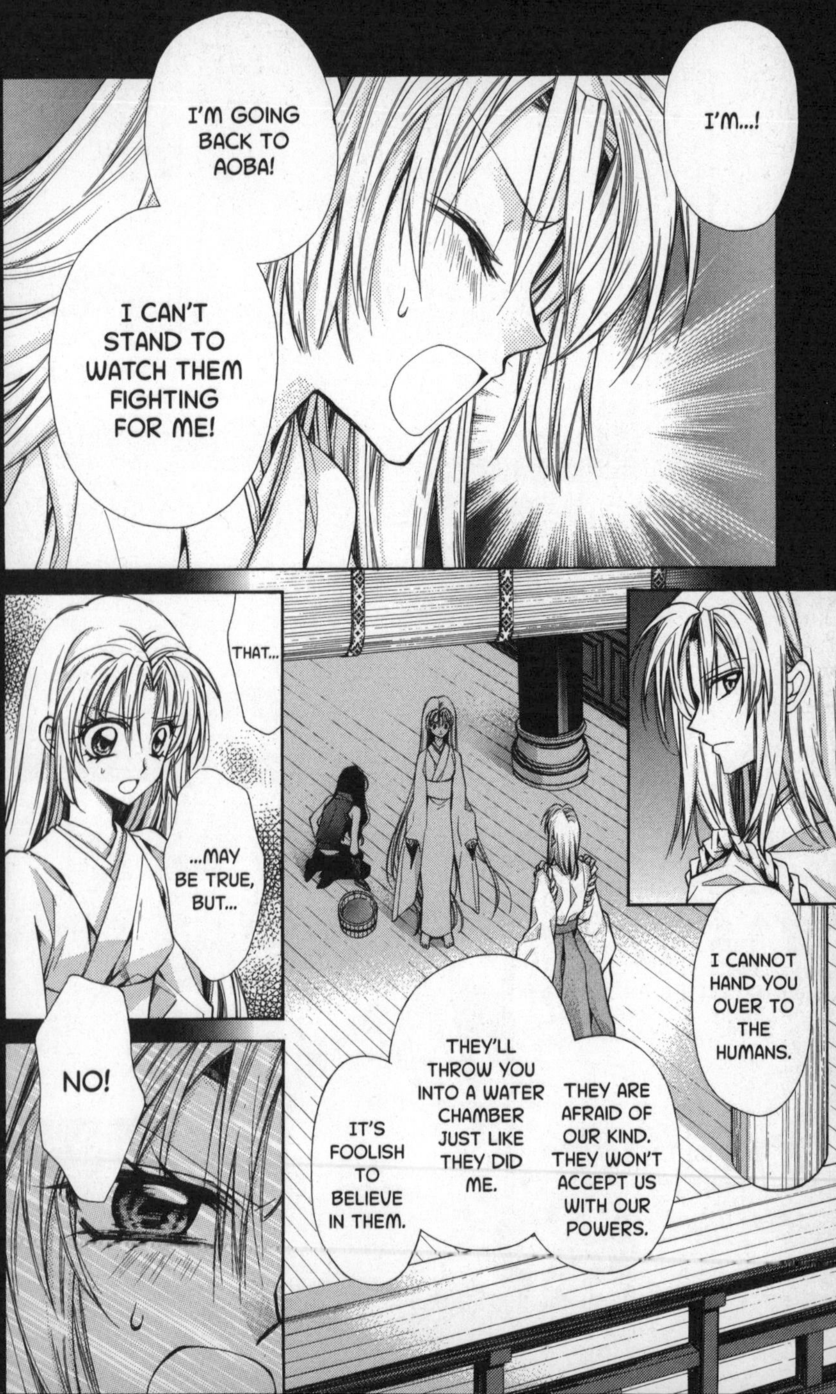
I'M...!
I'M GOING BACK TO AOBA!
I CAN'T STAND TO WATCH THEM FIGHTING FOR ME!
I CANNOT HAND YOU OVER TO THE HUMANS.
THEY ARE AFRAID OF OUR KIND. THEY WON'T ACCEPT US WITH OUR POWERS.
THEY'LL THROW YOU INTO A WATER CHAMBER JUST LIKE THEY DID ME.
IT'S FOOLISH TO BELIEVE IN THEM.
THAT...
...MAY BE TRUE, BUT...
NO!

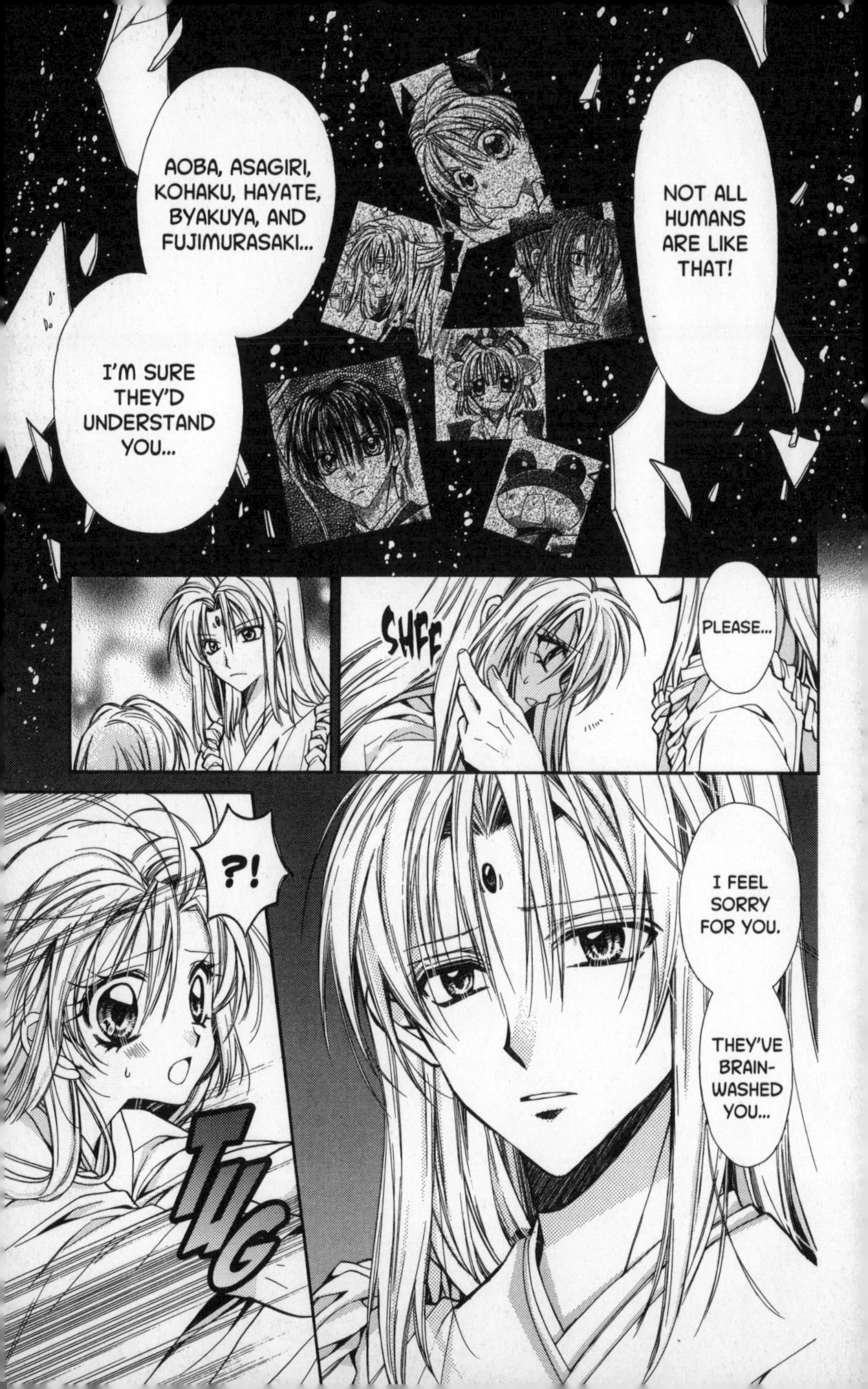
NOT ALL HUMANS ARE LIKE THAT!
AOBA, ASAGIRI, KOHAKU, HAYATE, BYAKUYA, AND FUJIMURASAKI...
I'M SURE THEY'D UNDERSTAND YOU...
PLEASE...
SHFF
I FEEL SORRY FOR YOU.
THEY'VE BRAIN-WASHED YOU...
?!
TUG

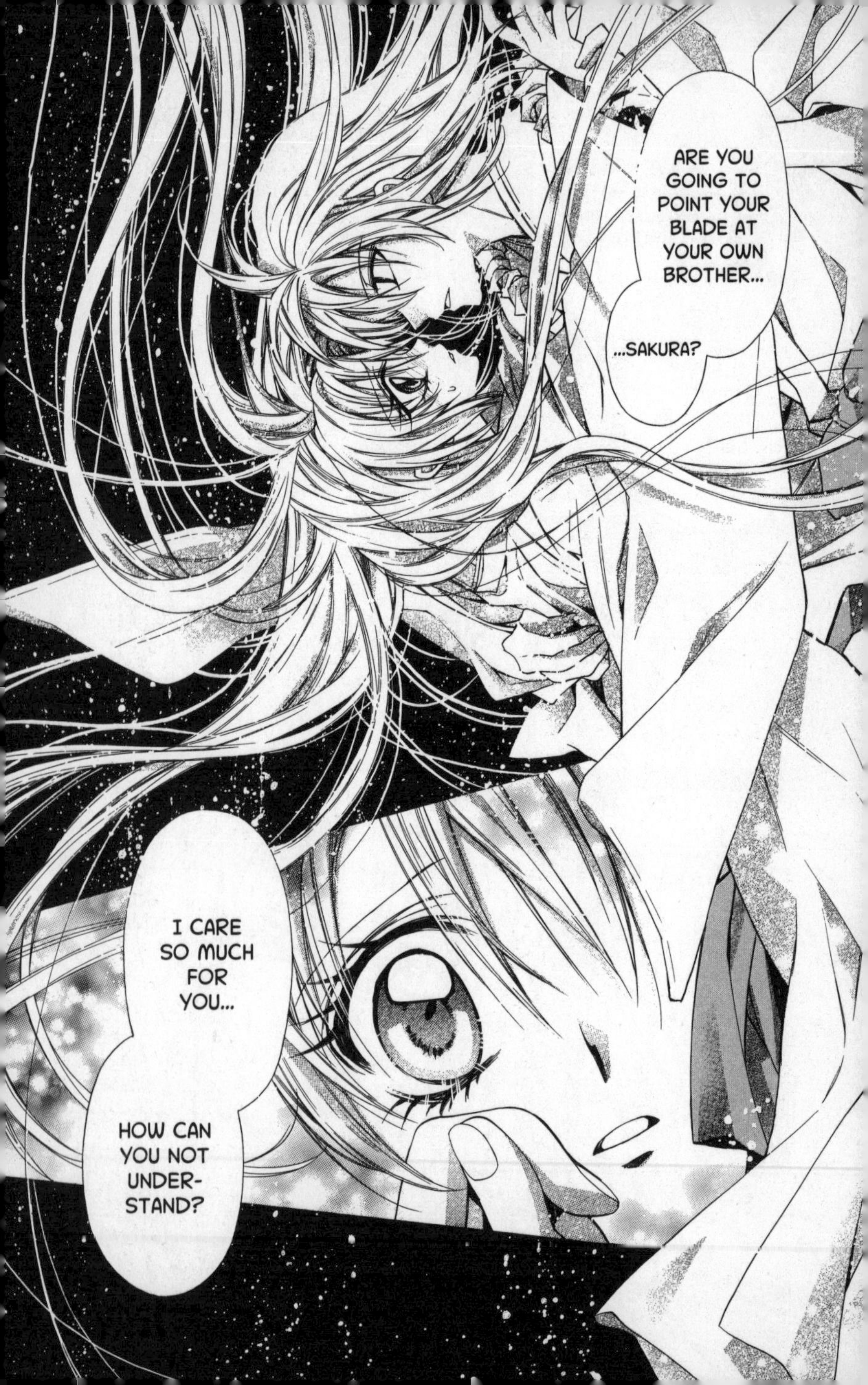
ARE YOU GOING TO POINT YOUR BLADE AT YOUR OWN BROTHER...
...SAKURA?
I CARE SO MUCH FOR YOU...
HOW CAN YOU NOT UNDER-STAND?

Tokimeki Memorial Girls' Side 3

I played the Nintendo DS game *Toki-Memo GS*...!! (I had been looking forward to it so much that I apparently preordered it twice.) I was sure surprised when I received two of them! (laugh) Thankfully a friend of mine bought one off me.

※ I may be giving away part of the story, so don't read this if you haven't played it yet.

For this game, Ruka was so cool! I actually hadn't played 2 (I played this after playing 1!), so I didn't know about the "Close Encounter Mode." I was playing it with bloodshot eyes. (laugh)

I was holding my breath around the end (around February?) when the story takes an unexpected turn! I even mumbled to myself, "I can't believe something like this is happening in GS..."

Ooh, but GS is so great!
I feel like such a girl! We're all girls!!

I have yet to try out the triangle relationship mode and whatnot, so my summer still hasn't ended.

These days I'm so hooked on playing GS that I've started thinking each time I have a conversation with someone, "Hurray! I've left a great impression on that person!"

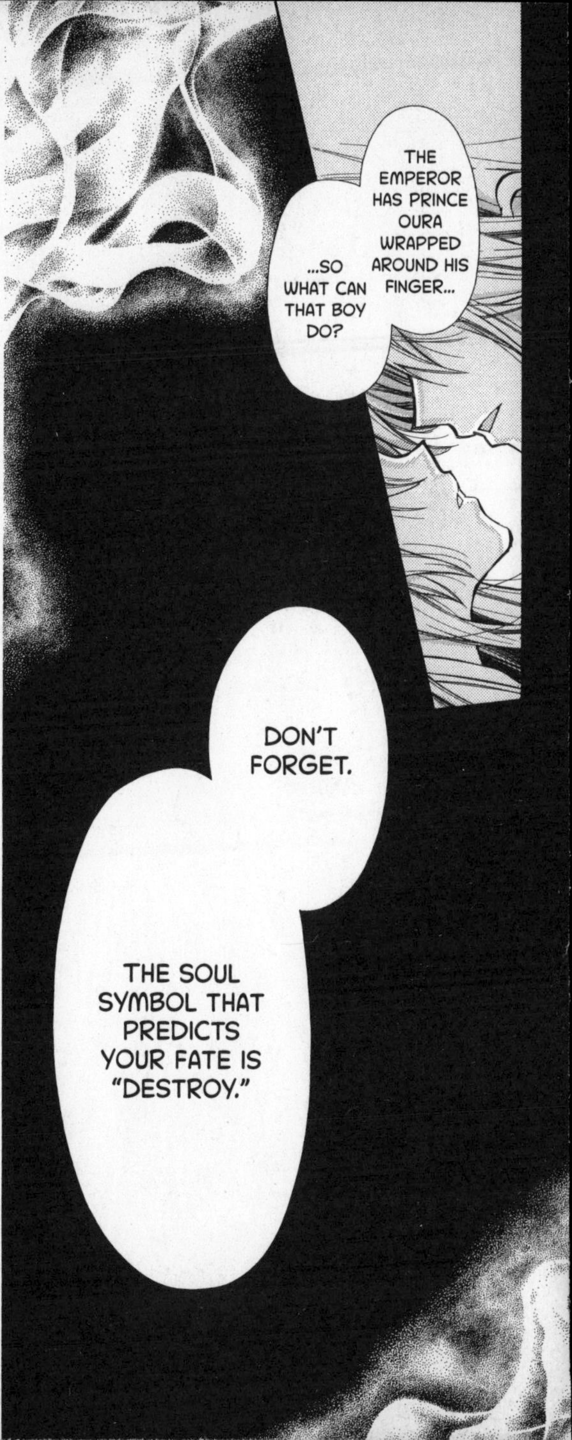
THE EMPEROR HAS PRINCE OURA WRAPPED AROUND HIS FINGER...
...SO WHAT CAN THAT BOY DO?
DON'T FORGET.
THE SOUL SYMBOL THAT PREDICTS YOUR FATE IS "DESTROY."

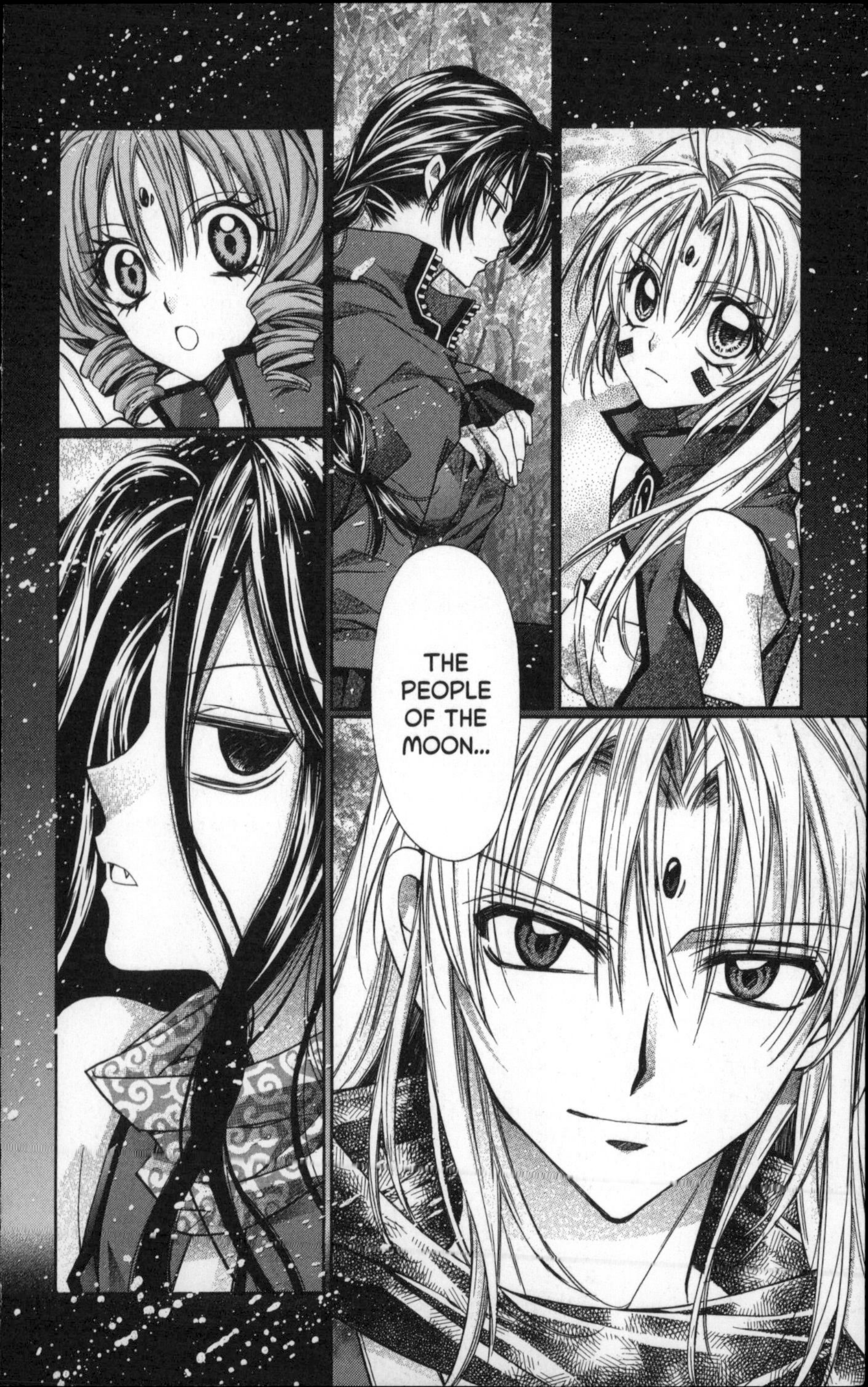
THE PEOPLE OF THE MOON...

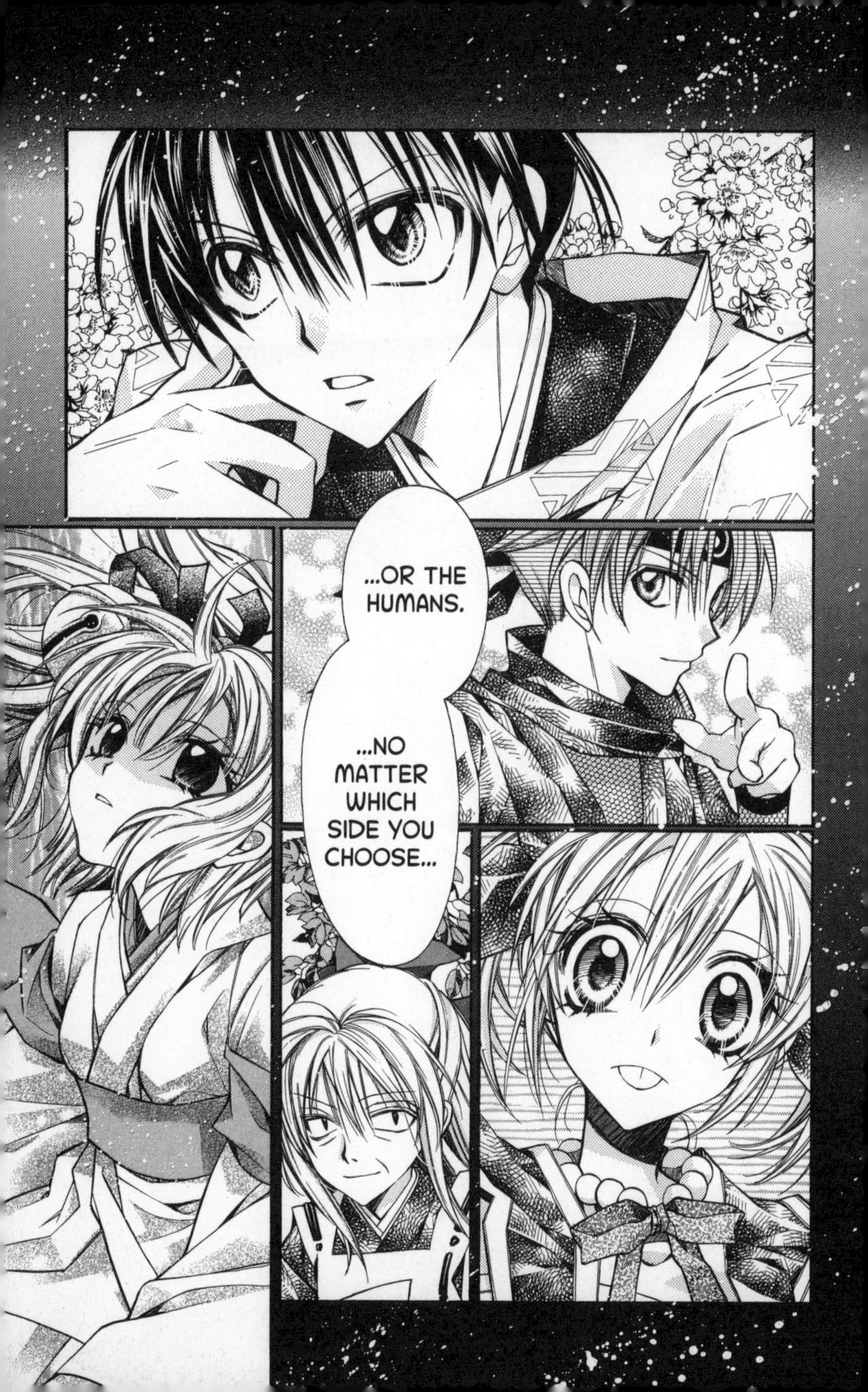
...OR THE HUMANS.
...NO MATTER WHICH SIDE YOU CHOOSE...

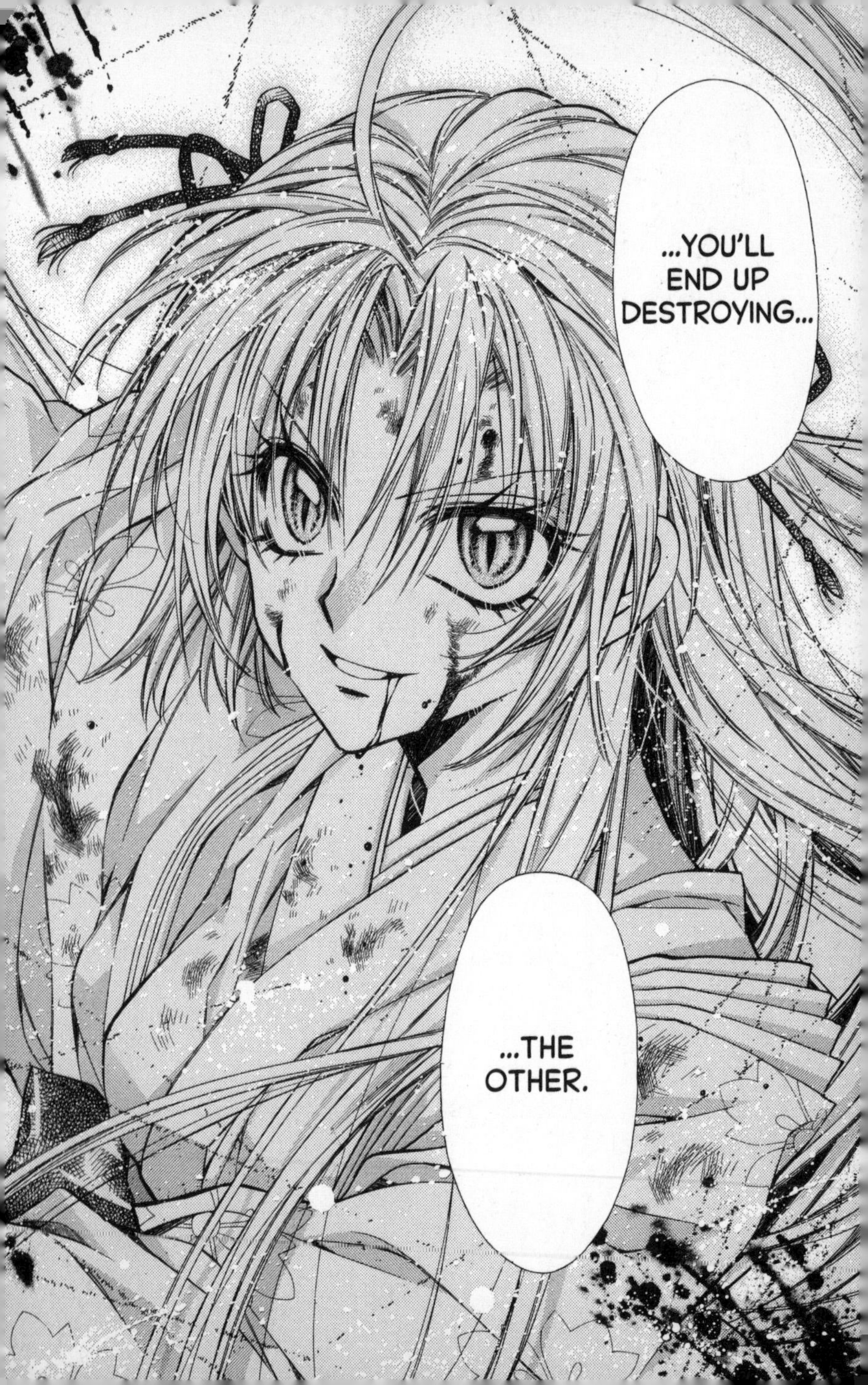
...YOU'LL END UP DESTROYING...
...THE OTHER.

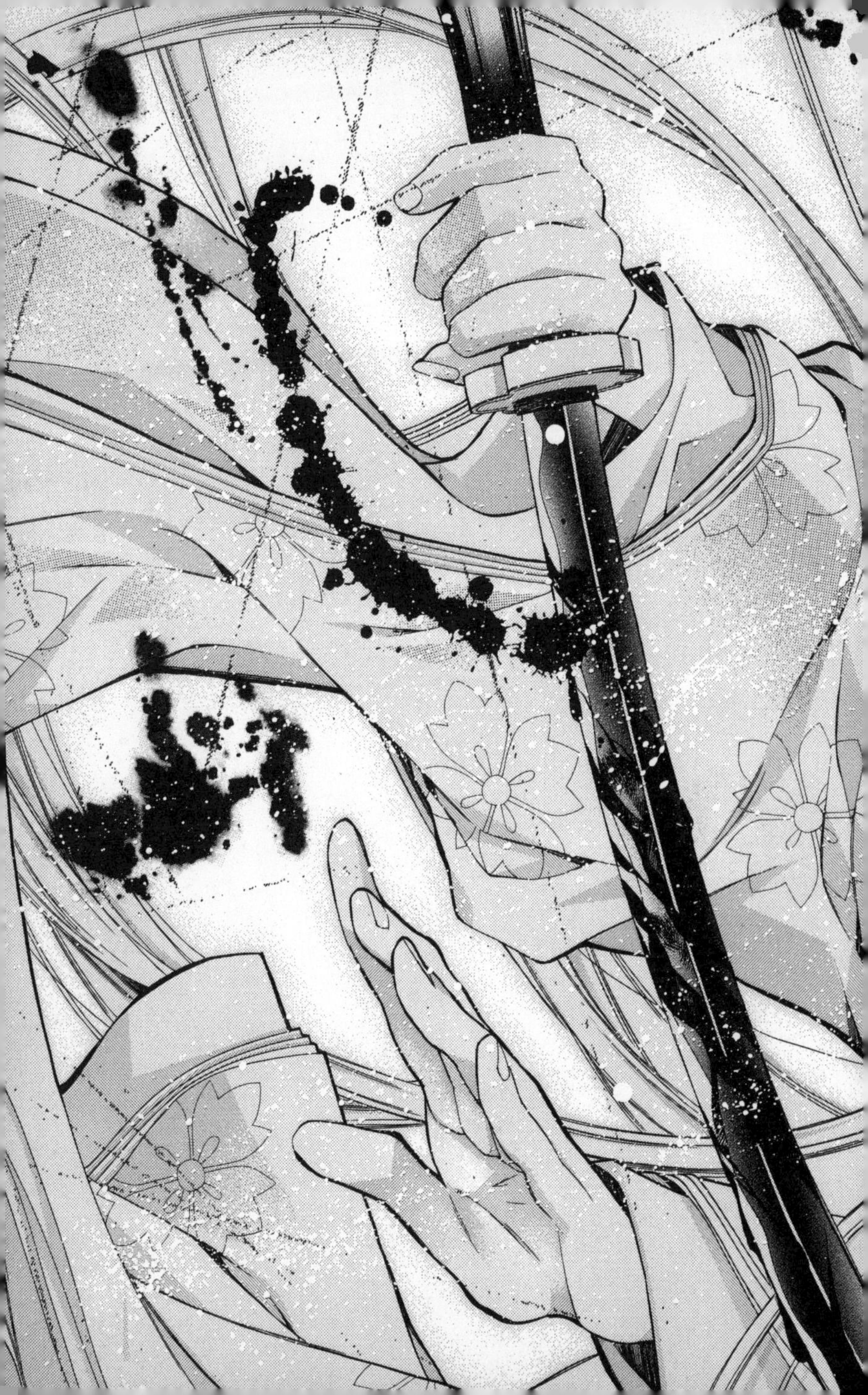

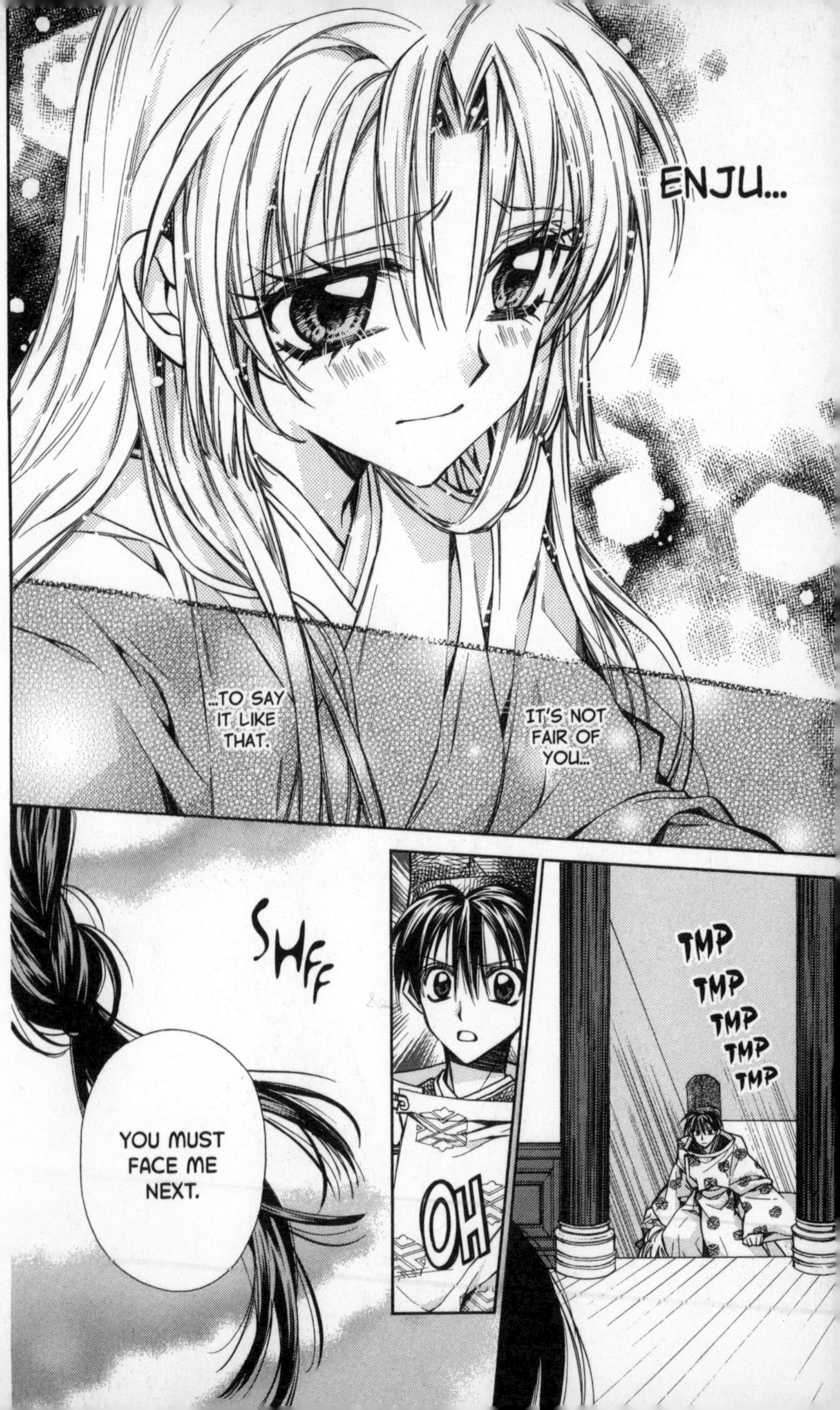
ENJU...
IT'S NOT FAIR OF YOU...
...TO SAY IT LIKE THAT.
TMP TMP TMP TMP TMP
OH
SHFF
YOU MUST FACE ME NEXT.

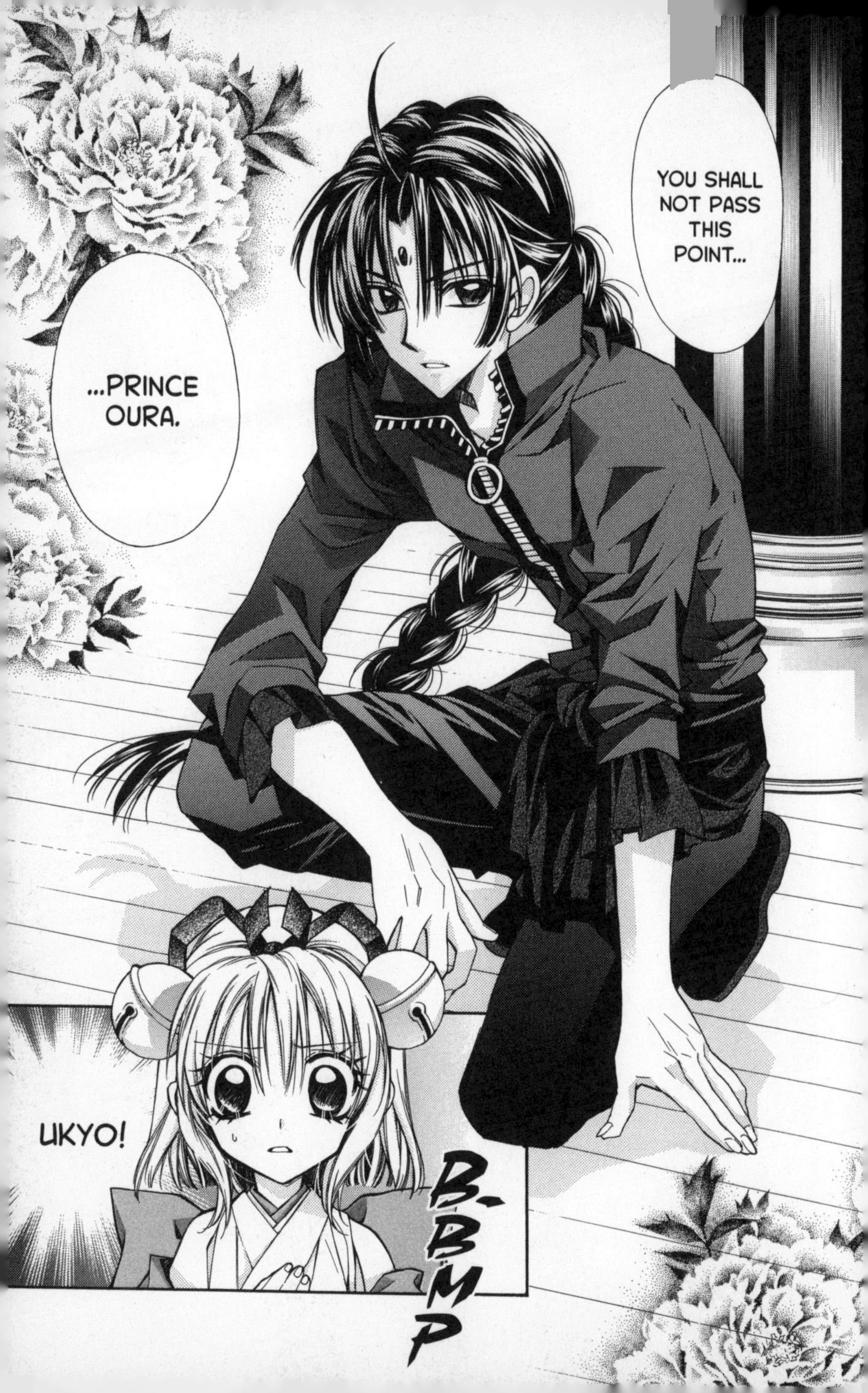
YOU SHALL NOT PASS THIS POINT...
...PRINCE OURA.
UKYO!
B-BMP

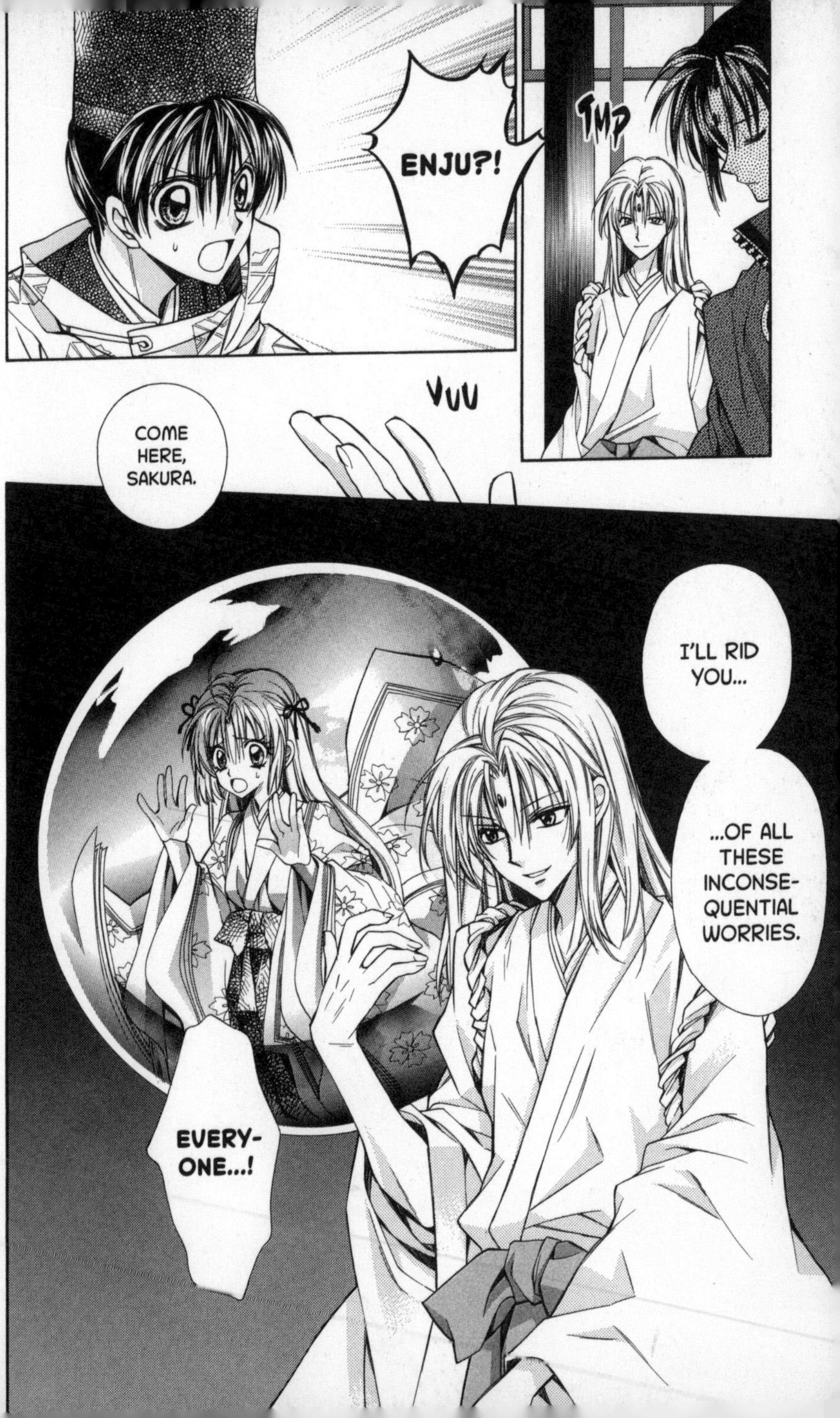
TMP
ENJU?!
VUU
COME HERE, SAKURA.
I'LL RID YOU...
...OF ALL THESE INCONSE-QUENTIAL WORRIES.
EVERY-ONE...!

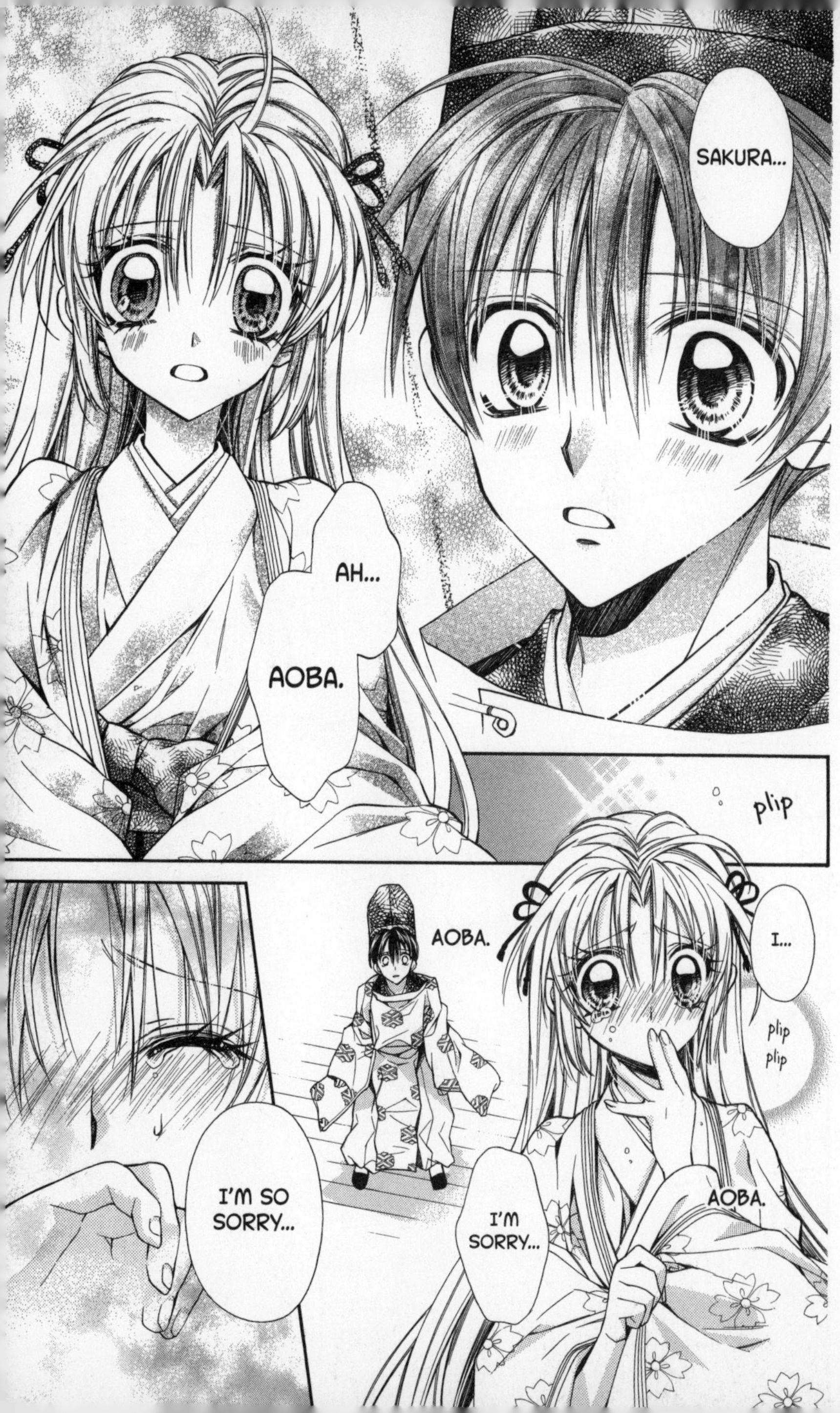
SAKURA...
AH...
AOBA.
plip
I...
AOBA.
plip
plip
AOBA.
I'M SORRY...
I'M SO SORRY...

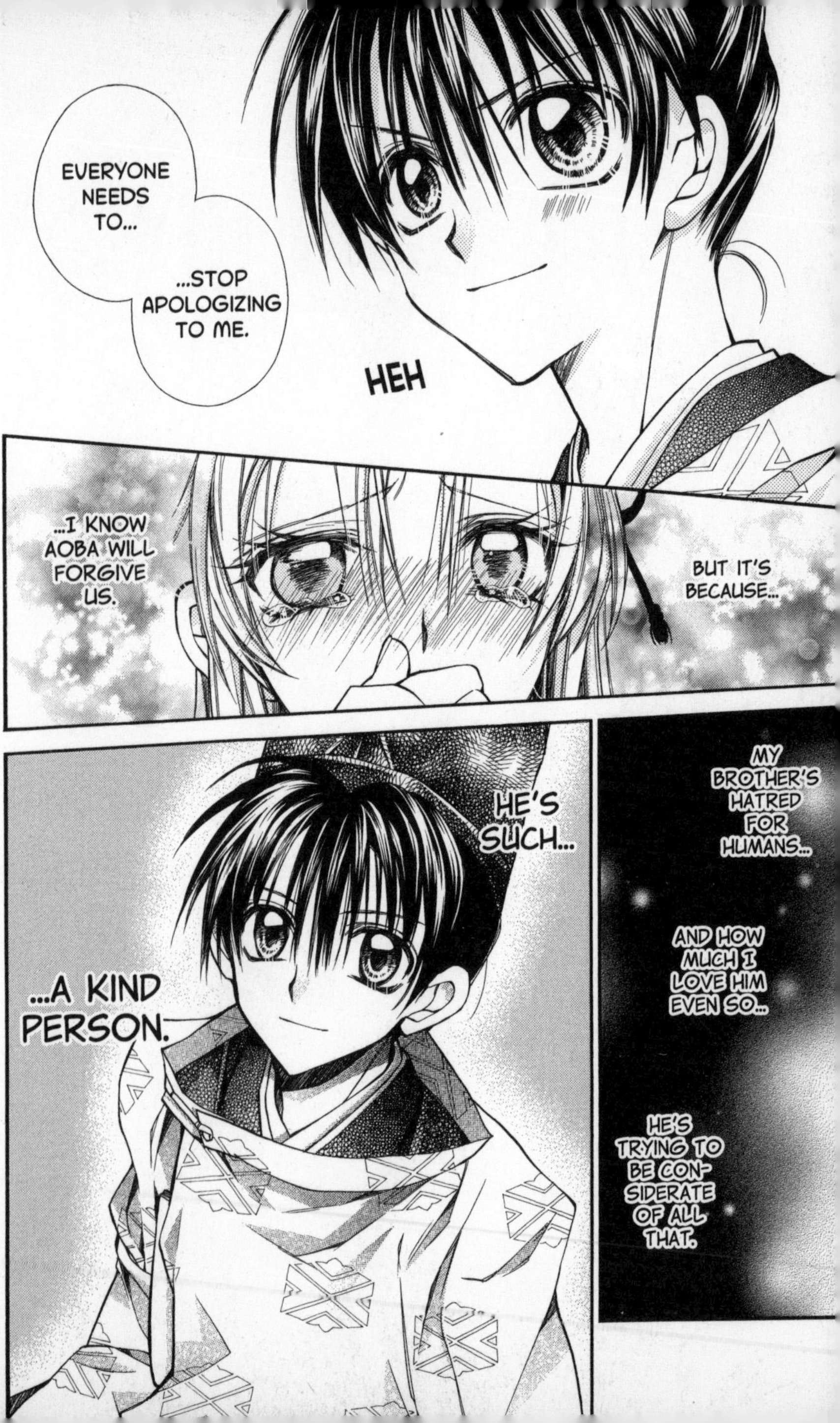
EVERYONE NEEDS TO...
...STOP APOLOGIZING TO ME.
HEH
BUT IT'S BECAUSE...
...I KNOW AOBA WILL FORGIVE US.
MY BROTHER'S HATRED FOR HUMANS...
AND HOW MUCH I LOVE HIM EVEN SO...
HE'S TRYING TO BE CON-SIDERATE OF ALL THAT.
HE'S SUCH...
...A KIND PERSON.

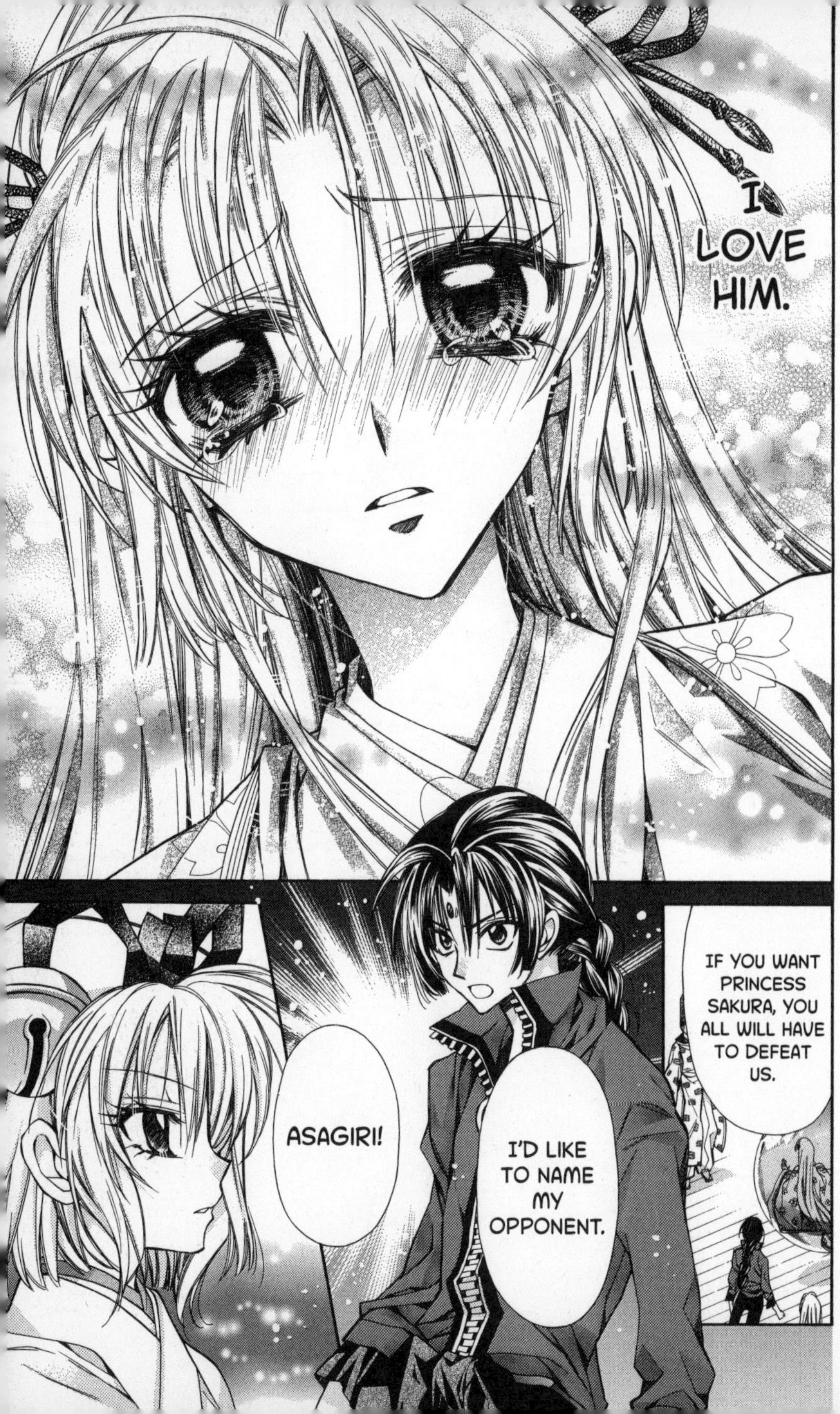
I LOVE HIM.
IF YOU WANT PRINCESS SAKURA, YOU ALL WILL HAVE TO DEFEAT US.
I'D LIKE TO NAME MY OPPONENT.
ASAGIRI!

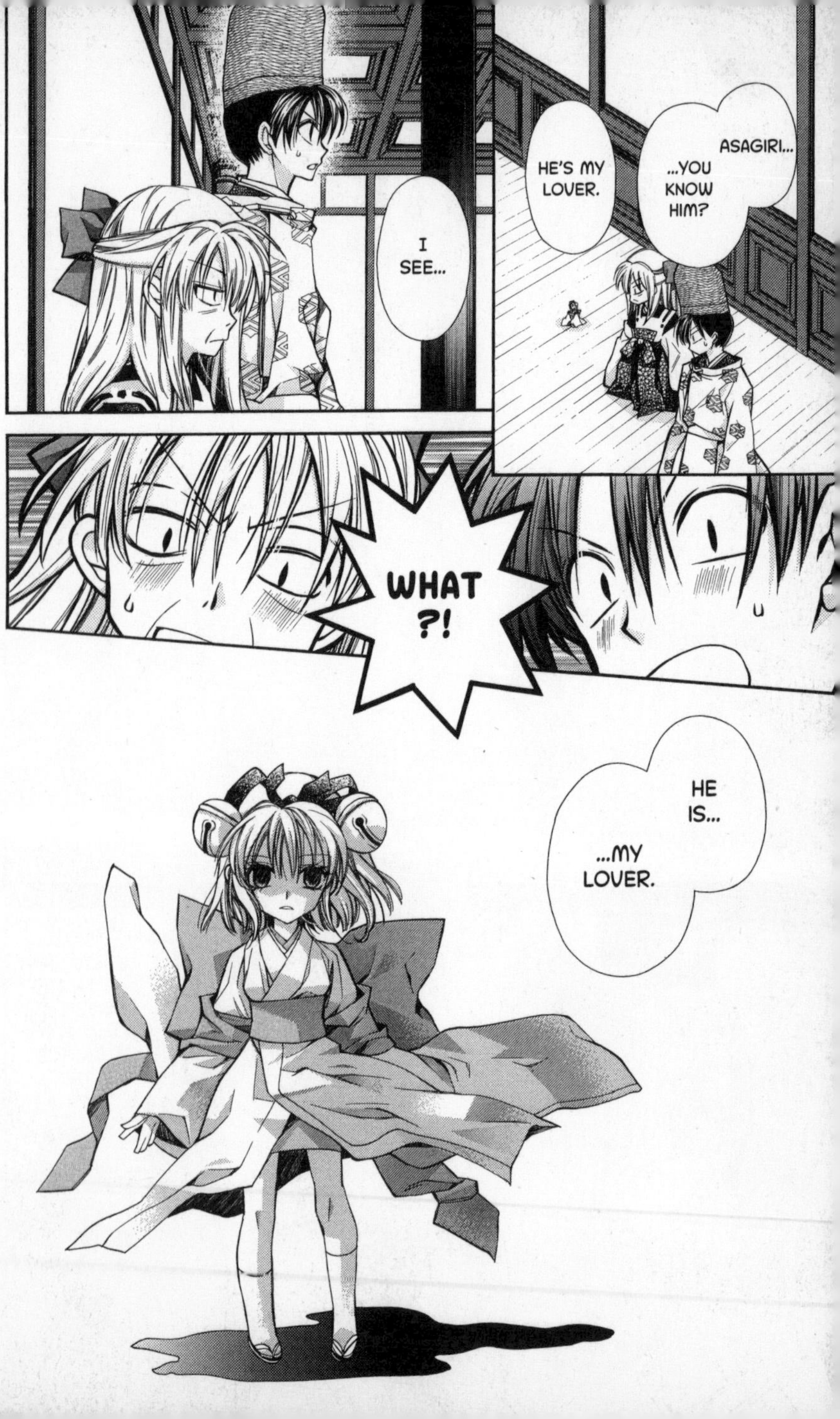
ASAGIRI... ...YOU KNOW HIM?
HE'S MY LOVER.
I SEE...
WHAT?!
HE IS... ...MY LOVER.

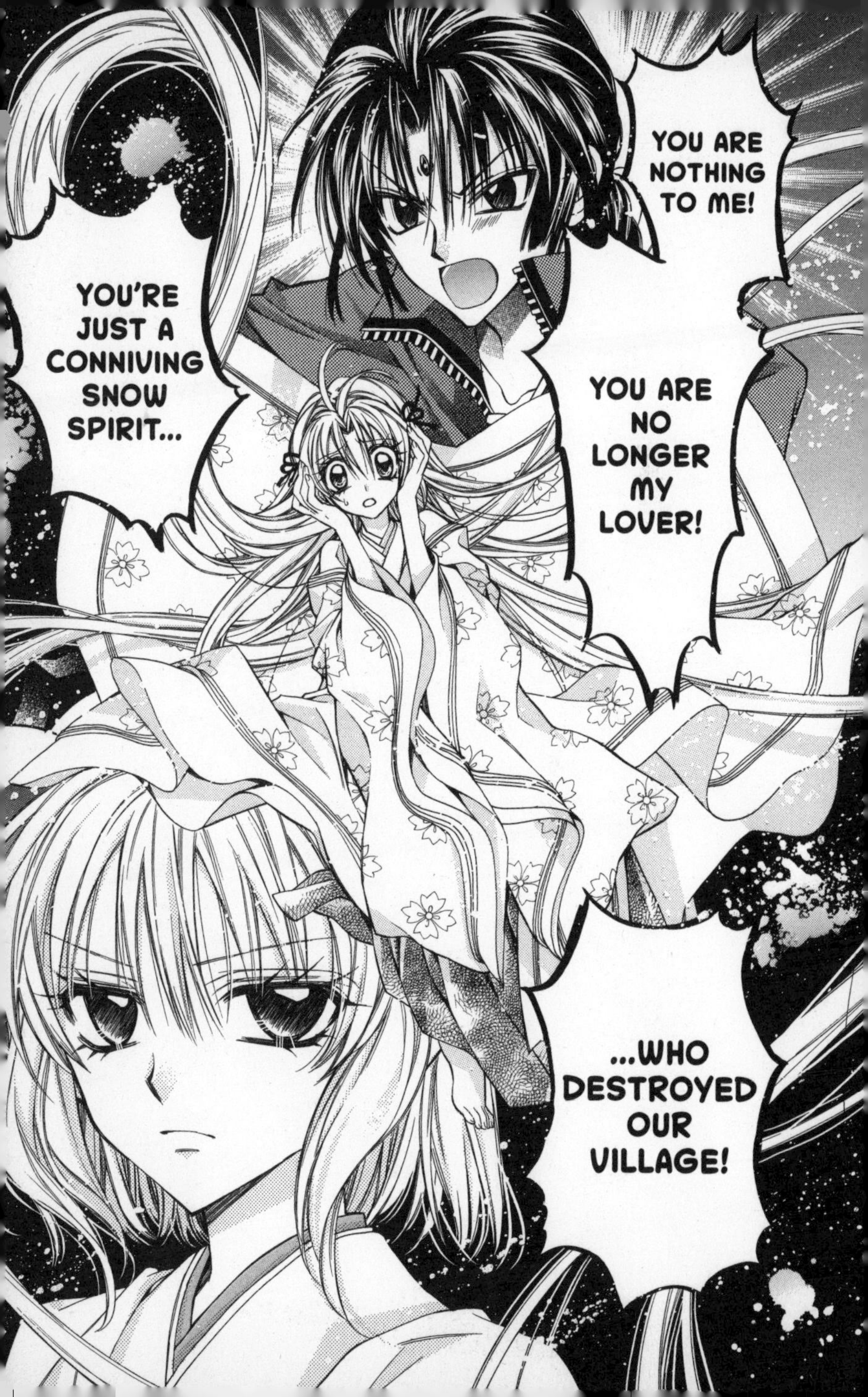
YOU ARE NOTHING TO ME!
YOU ARE NO LONGER MY LOVER!
YOU'RE JUST A CONNIVING SNOW SPIRIT...
...WHO DESTROYED OUR VILLAGE!

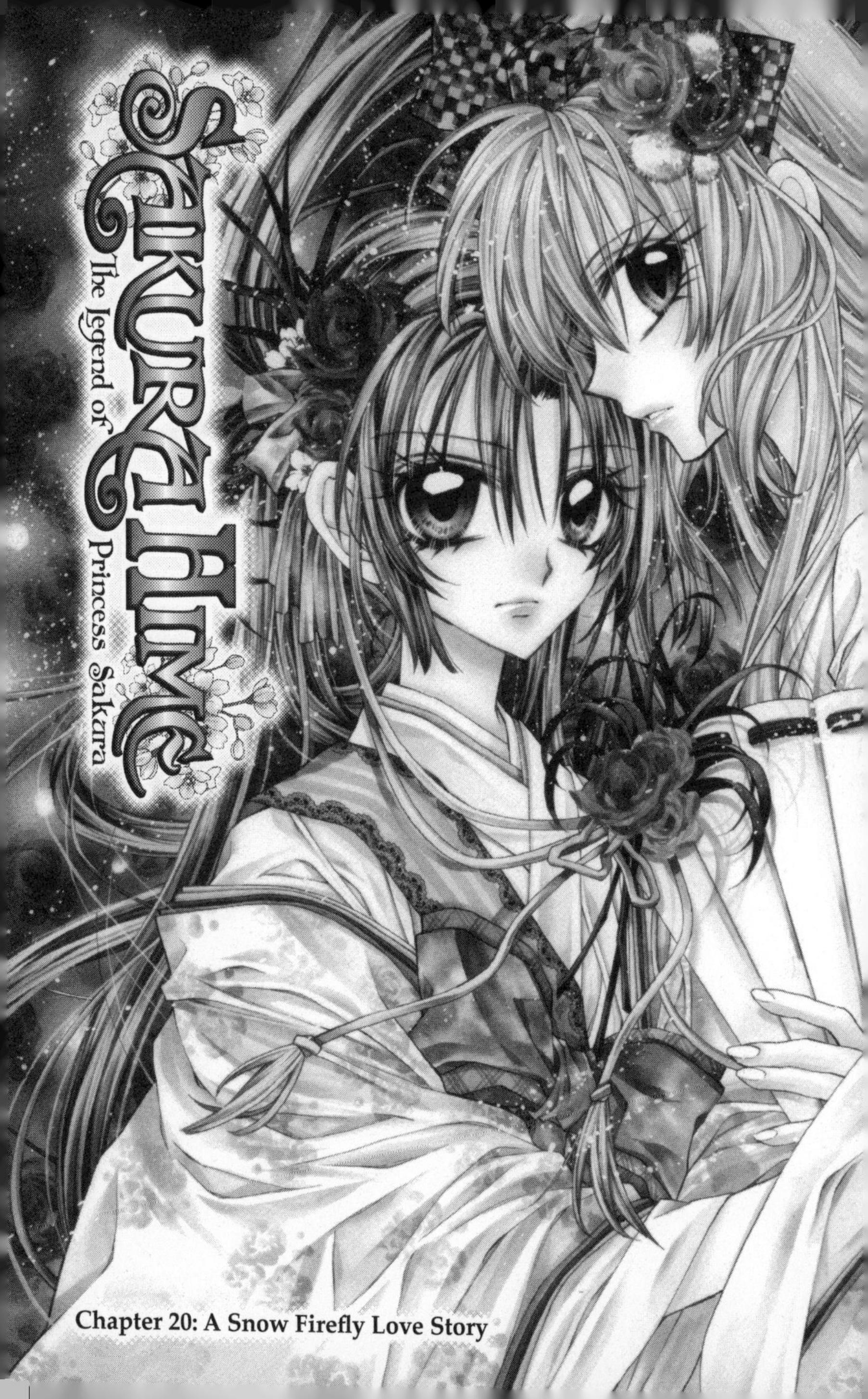
Sakura Hime
The Legend of Princess Sakura

Chapter 20: A Snow Firefly Love Story

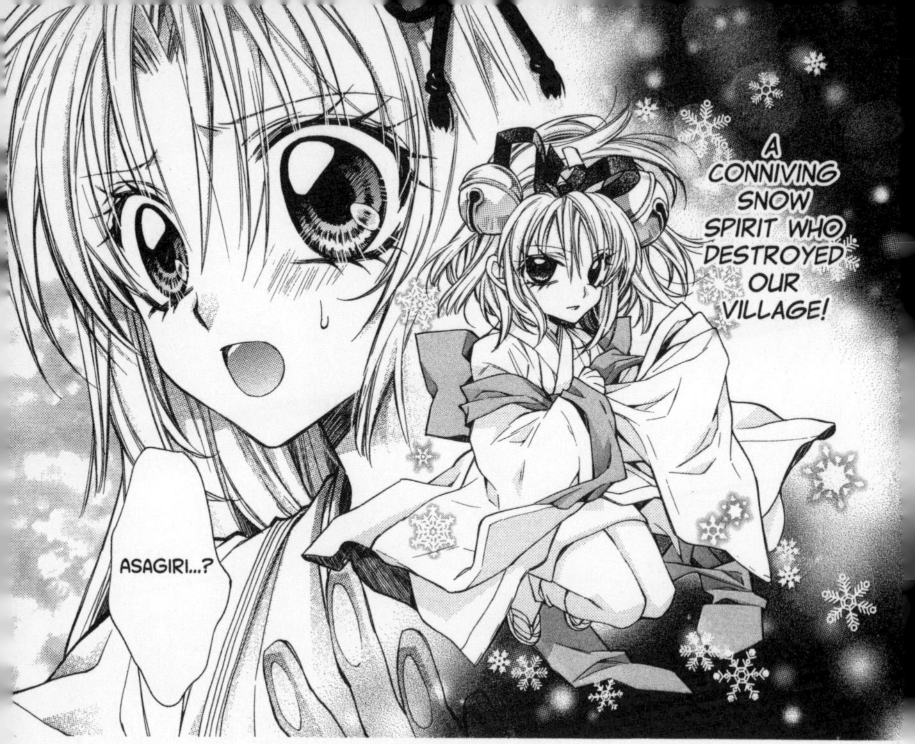
A CONNIVING SNOW SPIRIT WHO DESTROYED OUR VILLAGE!
ASAGIRI...?

Chapter 20: A Snow Firefly Love Story

※ I'm giving away the story.

Sorry to keep you all waiting (?). I bring you Asagiri's story. Asagiri received second place in the popularity vote. Personally I find her very easy to draw both physically and mentally, so it's thanks to you that I managed to complete 80 pages! (This ran in the magazine with chapter 19.)
I created Ukyo with the thought that he must be a very serious guy because Asagiri chose him. He really has no interest in anyone except Asagiri. (laugh)
I unintentionally made him look a bit like Aoba, so I gave him slightly slanted eyes, and I always felt nervous when I drew them.
I thought the Ghost Hags looked rather scary, and my assistants were scared of them too. They were worried that kids would cry when they saw them. But my motto is "things are best when they are slightly overdone," so I put my heart into drawing them. You need special skills to draw scary illustrations, and manga artists who create horror manga are extremely skilled! I still have a lot to work on...

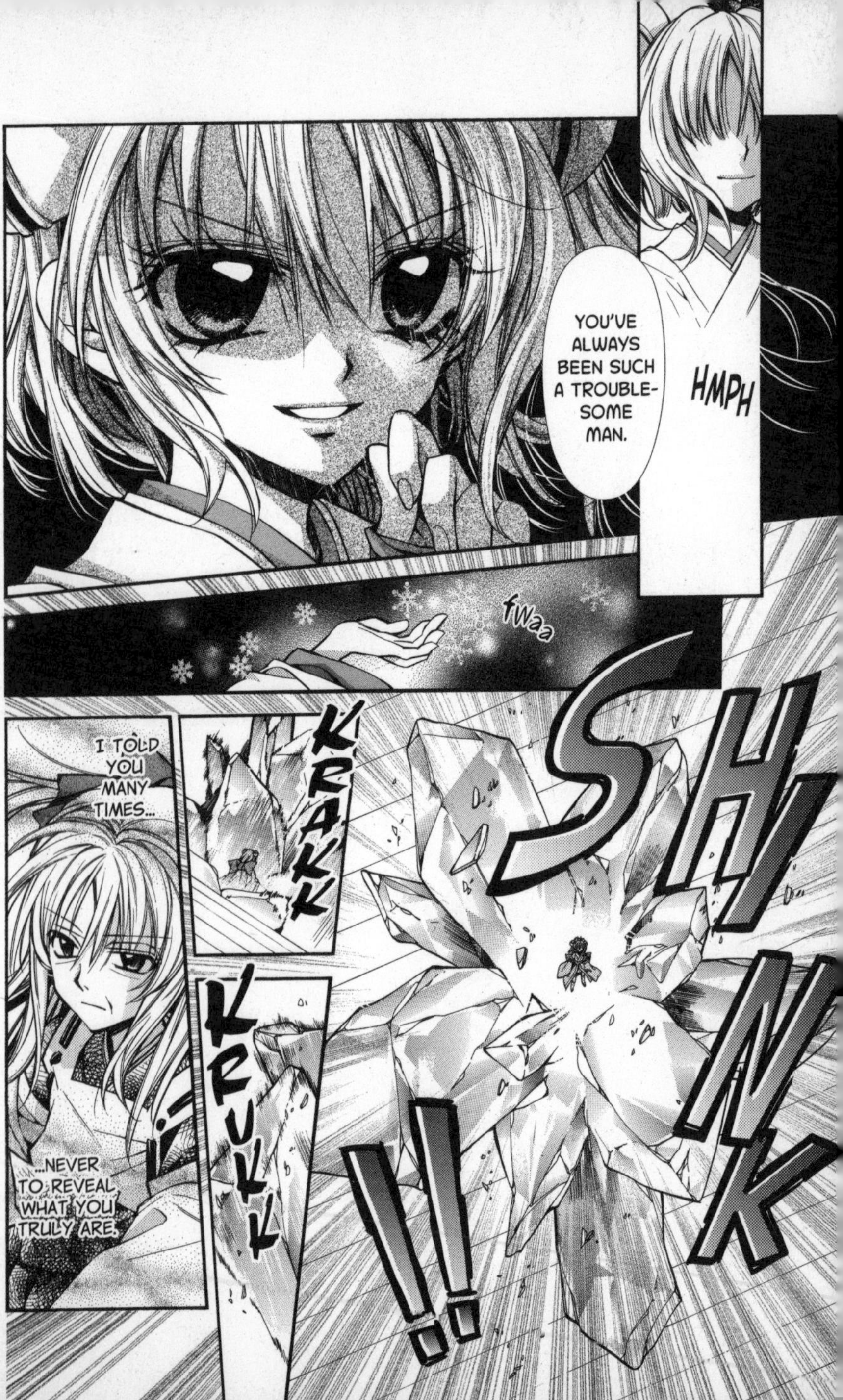
YOU'VE ALWAYS BEEN SUCH A TROUBLE-SOME MAN.
HMPH
fwaa
SHNK!!
KRAKK
KRUKK
I TOLD YOU MANY TIMES...
...NEVER TO REVEAL WHAT YOU TRULY ARE.

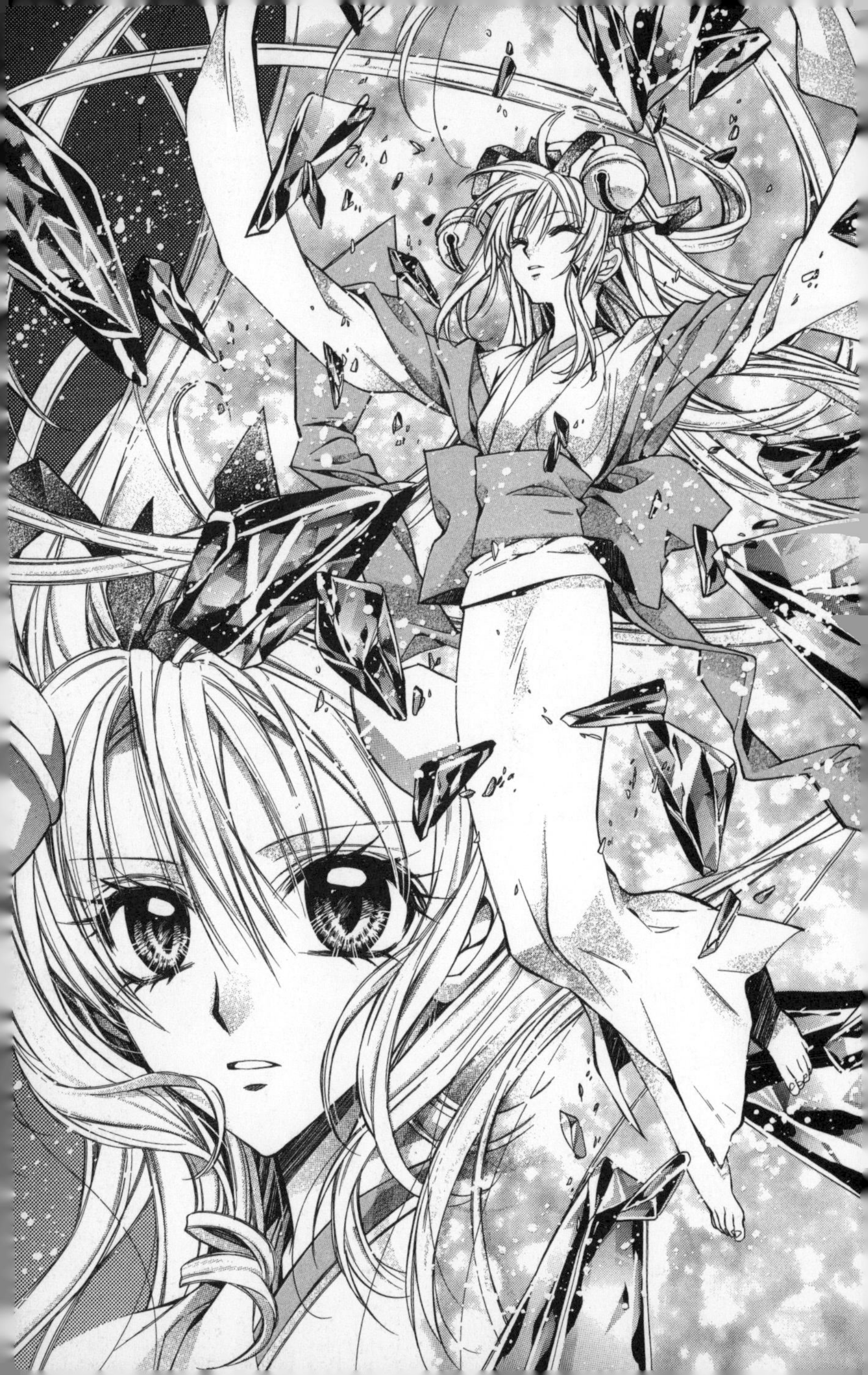

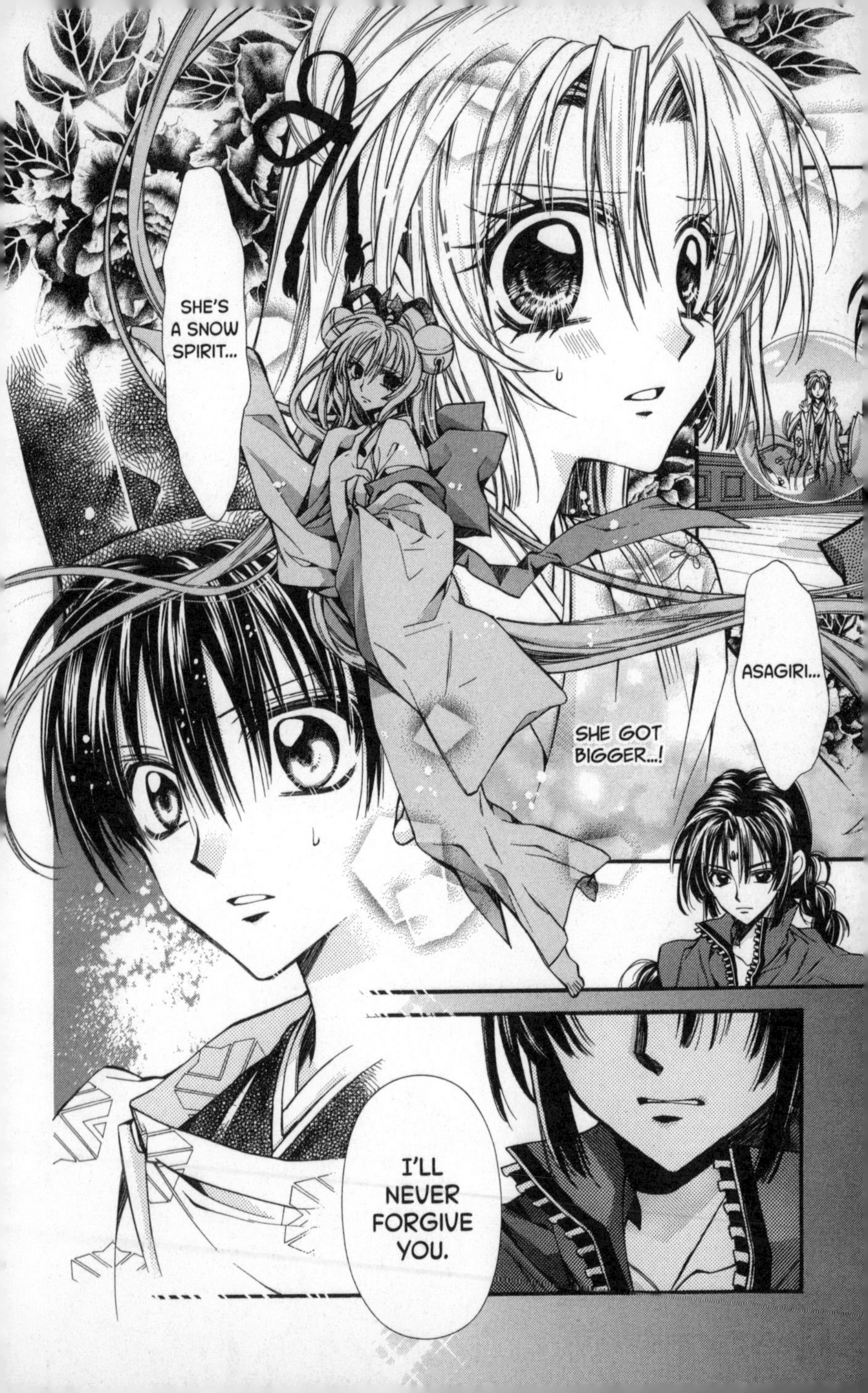
SHE'S A SNOW SPIRIT...
ASAGIRI...
SHE GOT BIGGER...!
I'LL NEVER FORGIVE YOU.

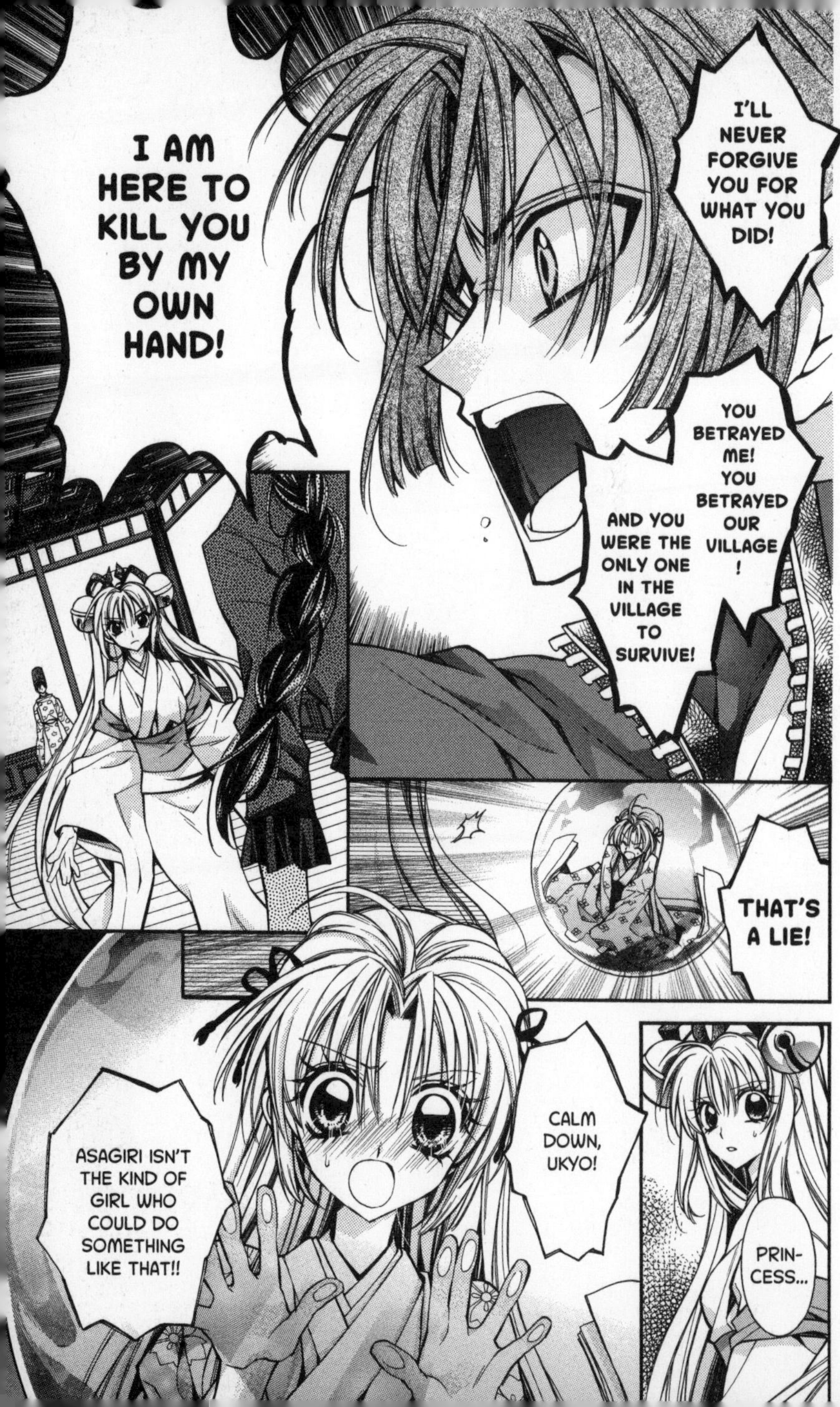

I'LL NEVER FORGIVE YOU FOR WHAT YOU DID!
I AM HERE TO KILL YOU BY MY OWN HAND!
YOU BETRAYED ME! YOU BETRAYED OUR VILLAGE!
AND YOU WERE THE ONLY ONE IN THE VILLAGE TO SURVIVE!
THAT'S A LIE!
PRIN-CESS...
CALM DOWN, UKYO!
ASAGIRI ISN'T THE KIND OF GIRL WHO COULD DO SOMETHING LIKE THAT!!

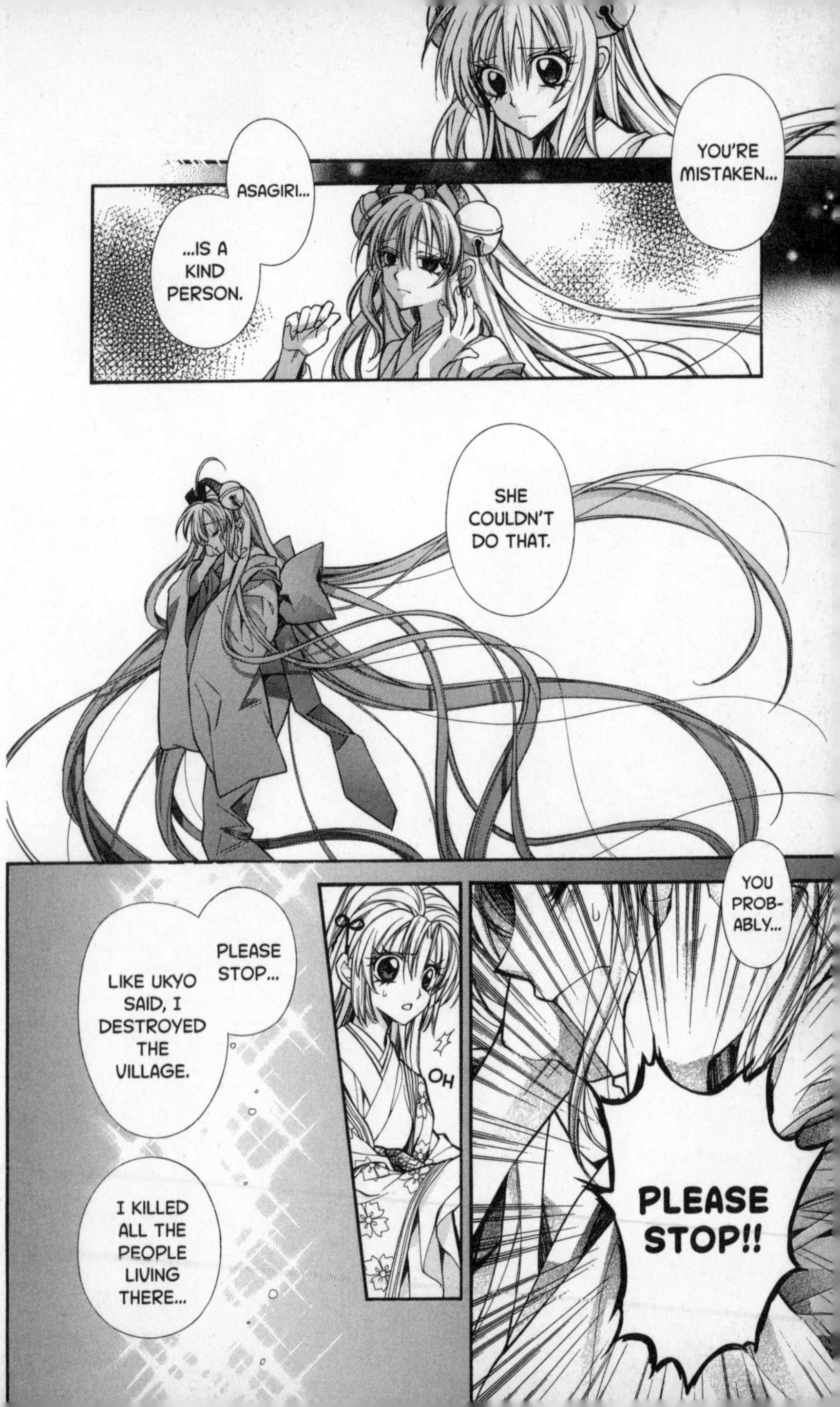
YOU'RE MISTAKEN...
ASAGIRI...
...IS A KIND PERSON.
SHE COULDN'T DO THAT.
YOU PROB-ABLY...
PLEASE STOP!!
OH
PLEASE STOP...
LIKE UKYO SAID, I DESTROYED THE VILLAGE.
I KILLED ALL THE PEOPLE LIVING THERE...

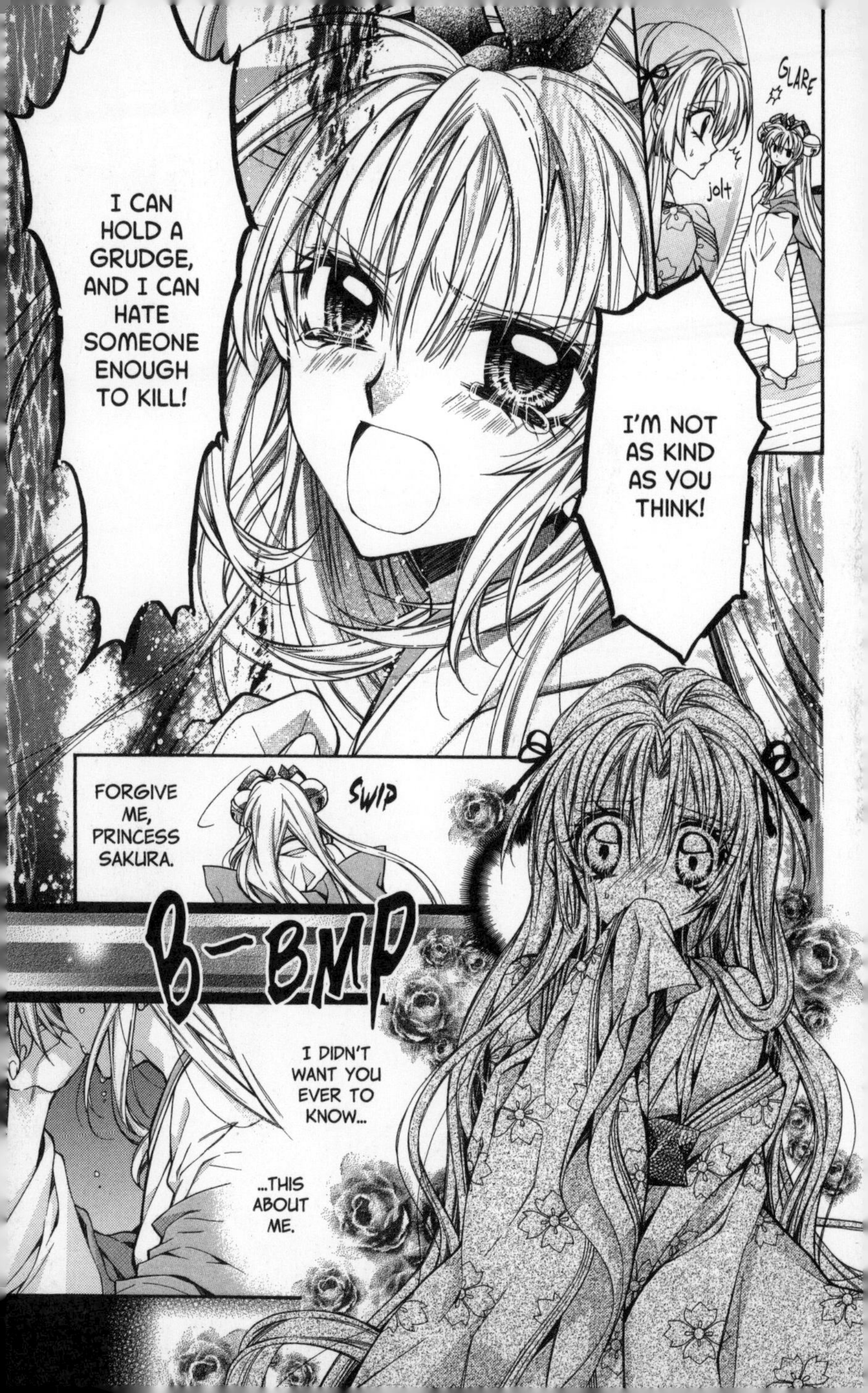
GLARE
jolt
I'M NOT AS KIND AS YOU THINK!
I CAN HOLD A GRUDGE, AND I CAN HATE SOMEONE ENOUGH TO KILL!
SWIP
FORGIVE ME, PRINCESS SAKURA.
B-BMP
I DIDN'T WANT YOU EVER TO KNOW...
...THIS ABOUT ME.

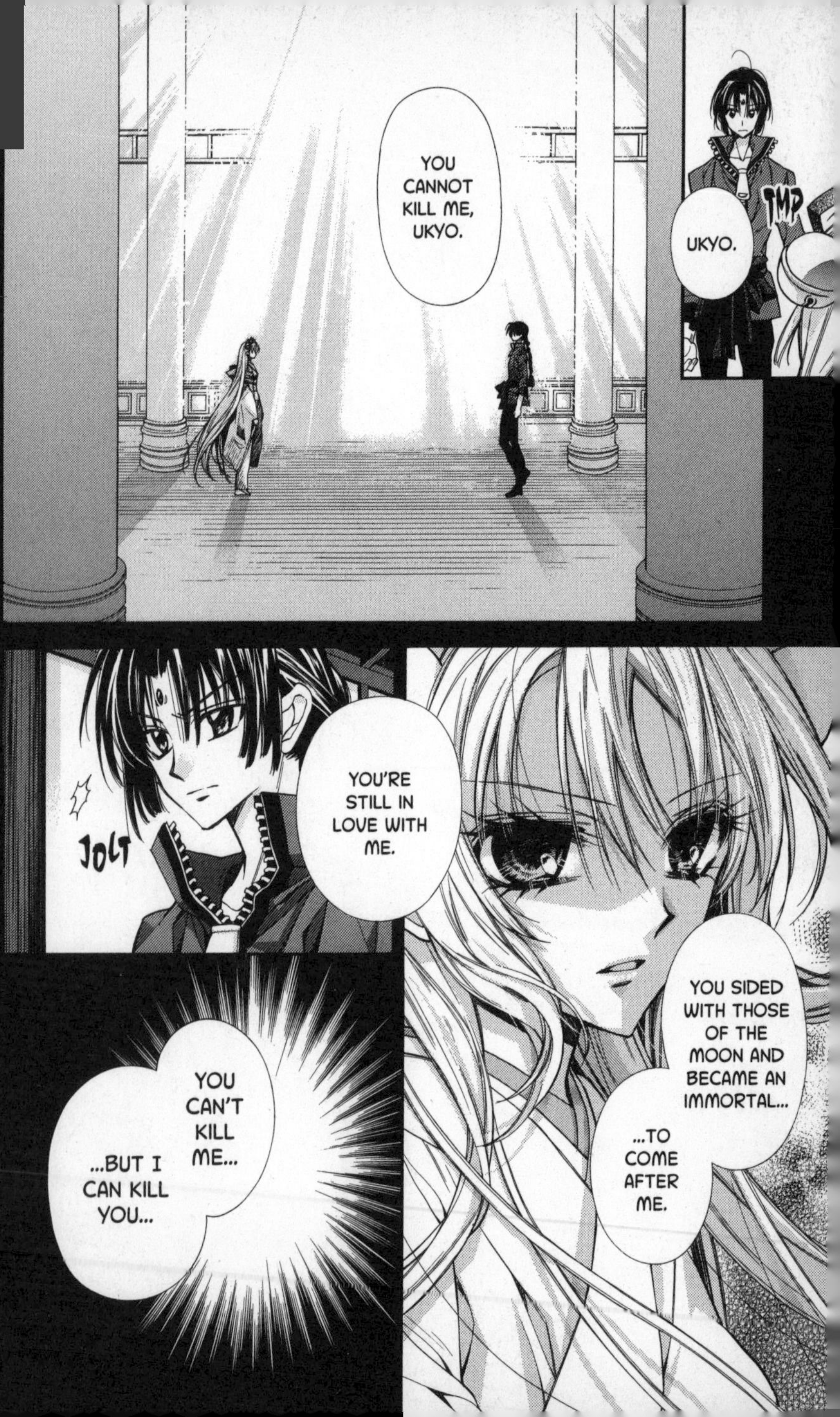

TMP
UKYO.
YOU CANNOT KILL ME, UKYO.
YOU SIDED WITH THOSE OF THE MOON AND BECAME AN IMMORTAL...
...TO COME AFTER ME.
JOLT
YOU'RE STILL IN LOVE WITH ME.
YOU CAN'T KILL ME...
...BUT I CAN KILL YOU...

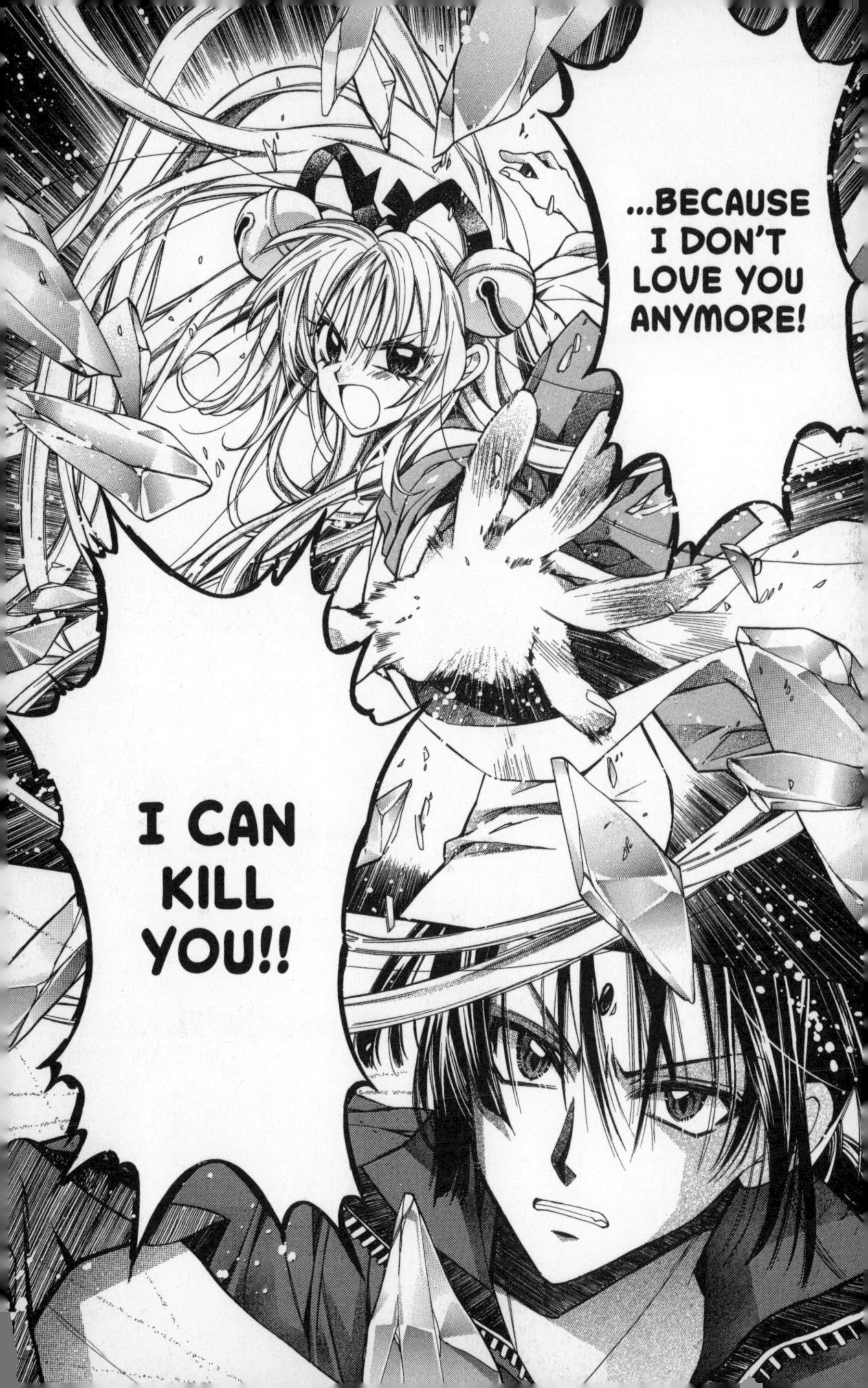
...BECAUSE I DON'T LOVE YOU ANYMORE!
I CAN KILL YOU!!

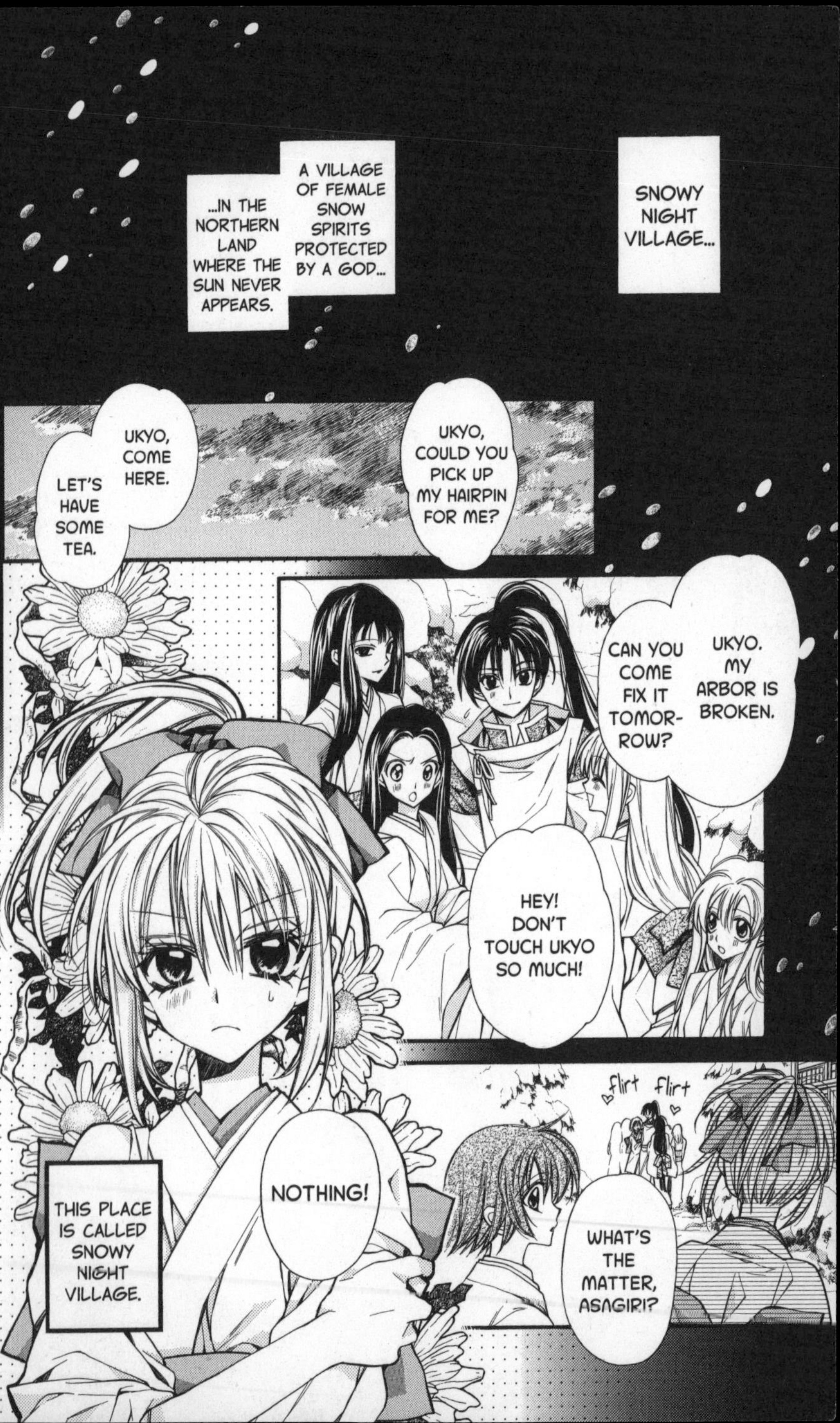
SNOWY NIGHT VILLAGE...
A VILLAGE OF FEMALE SNOW SPIRITS PROTECTED BY A GOD...
...IN THE NORTHERN LAND WHERE THE SUN NEVER APPEARS.
UKYO, COULD YOU PICK UP MY HAIRPIN FOR ME?
UKYO, COME HERE.
LET'S HAVE SOME TEA.
UKYO. MY ARBOR IS BROKEN.
CAN YOU COME FIX IT TOMORROW?
HEY! DON'T TOUCH UKYO SO MUCH!
flirt flirt
WHAT'S THE MATTER, ASAGIRI?
NOTHING!
THIS PLACE IS CALLED SNOWY NIGHT VILLAGE.

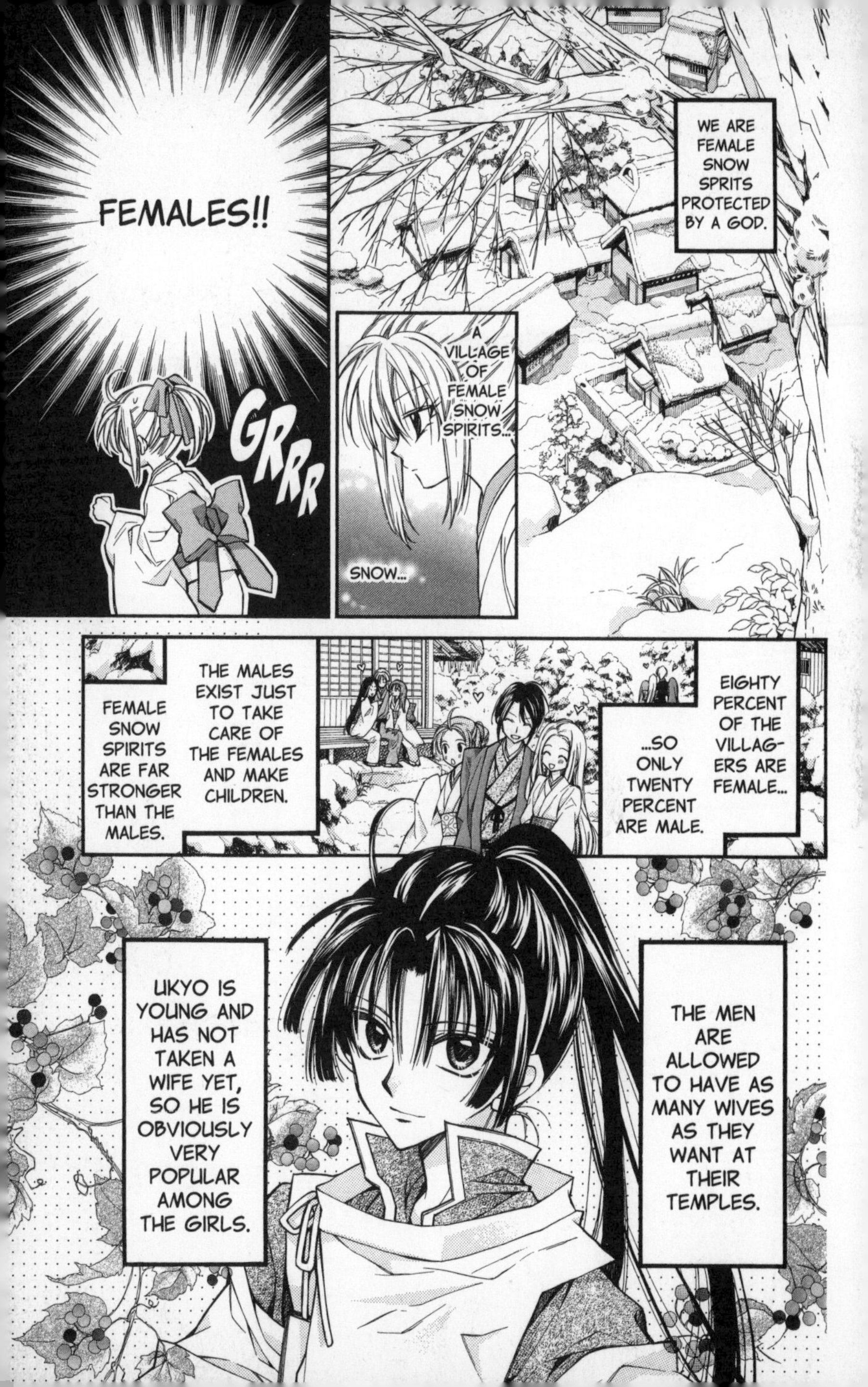
WE ARE FEMALE SNOW SPRITS PROTECTED BY A GOD.
A VILLAGE OF FEMALE SNOW SPIRITS...
SNOW...
FEMALES!!
GRRRR
EIGHTY PERCENT OF THE VILLAG-ERS ARE FEMALE...
...SO ONLY TWENTY PERCENT ARE MALE.
THE MALES EXIST JUST TO TAKE CARE OF THE FEMALES AND MAKE CHILDREN.
FEMALE SNOW SPIRITS ARE FAR STRONGER THAN THE MALES.
THE MEN ARE ALLOWED TO HAVE AS MANY WIVES AS THEY WANT AT THEIR TEMPLES.
UKYO IS YOUNG AND HAS NOT TAKEN A WIFE YET, SO HE IS OBVIOUSLY VERY POPULAR AMONG THE GIRLS.

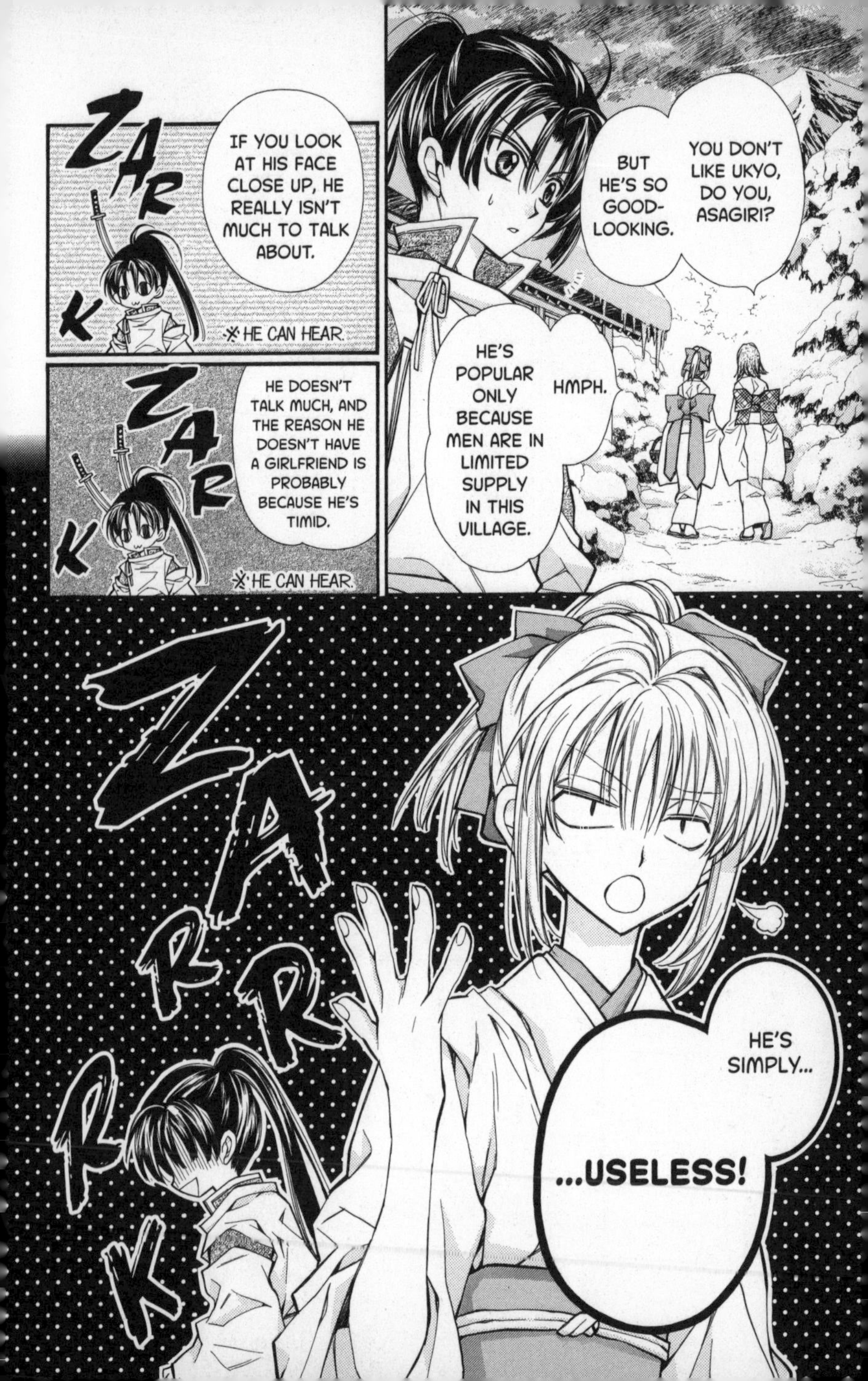
YOU DON'T LIKE UKYO, DO YOU, ASAGIRI?
BUT HE'S SO GOOD-LOOKING.
HMPH.
HE'S POPULAR ONLY BECAUSE MEN ARE IN LIMITED SUPPLY IN THIS VILLAGE.
ZARK
IF YOU LOOK AT HIS FACE CLOSE UP, HE REALLY ISN'T MUCH TO TALK ABOUT.
※HE CAN HEAR.
ZARK
HE DOESN'T TALK MUCH, AND THE REASON HE DOESN'T HAVE A GIRLFRIEND IS PROBABLY BECAUSE HE'S TIMID.
※HE CAN HEAR.
HE'S SIMPLY...
...USELESS!
ZARRRRK

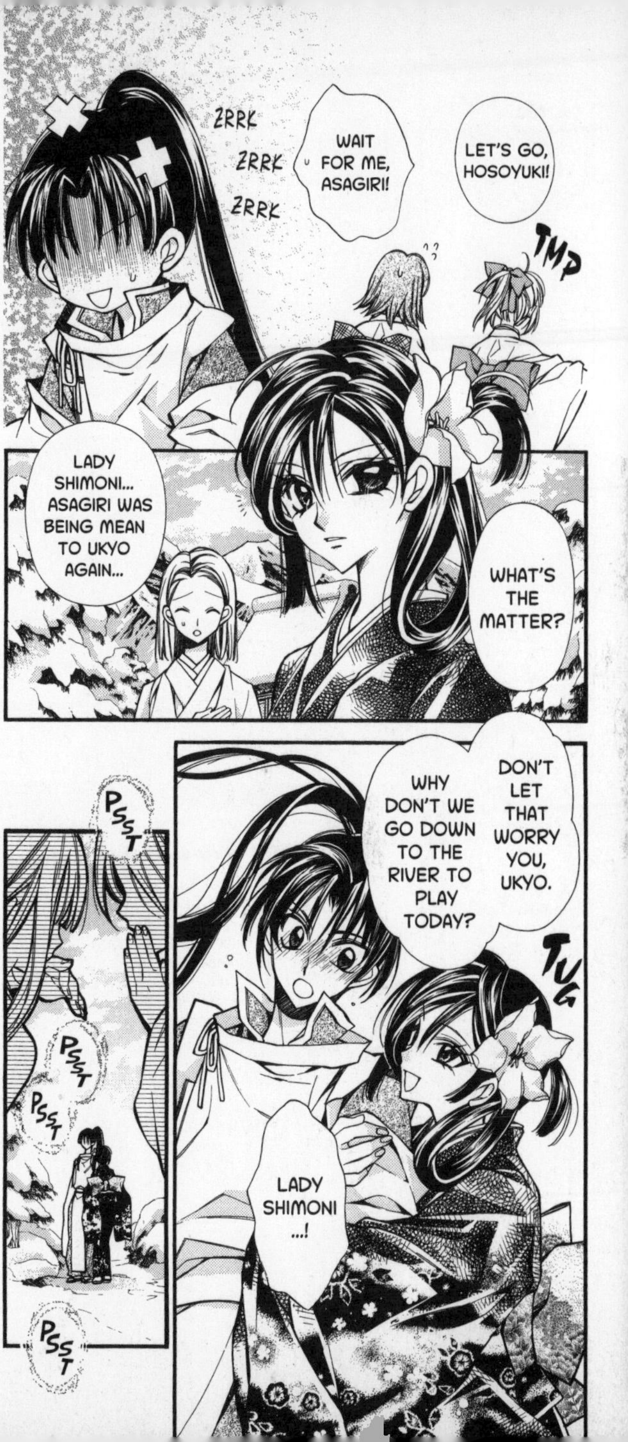
LET'S GO, HOSOYUKI!
TMP
WAIT FOR ME, ASAGIRI!
ZRRK
ZRRK
ZRRK
WHAT'S THE MATTER?
LADY SHIMONI... ASAGIRI WAS BEING MEAN TO UKYO AGAIN...
DON'T LET THAT WORRY YOU, UKYO.
WHY DON'T WE GO DOWN TO THE RIVER TO PLAY TODAY?
TUG
LADY SHIMONI ...!
PSST
PSST
PSST
PSST

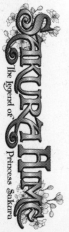

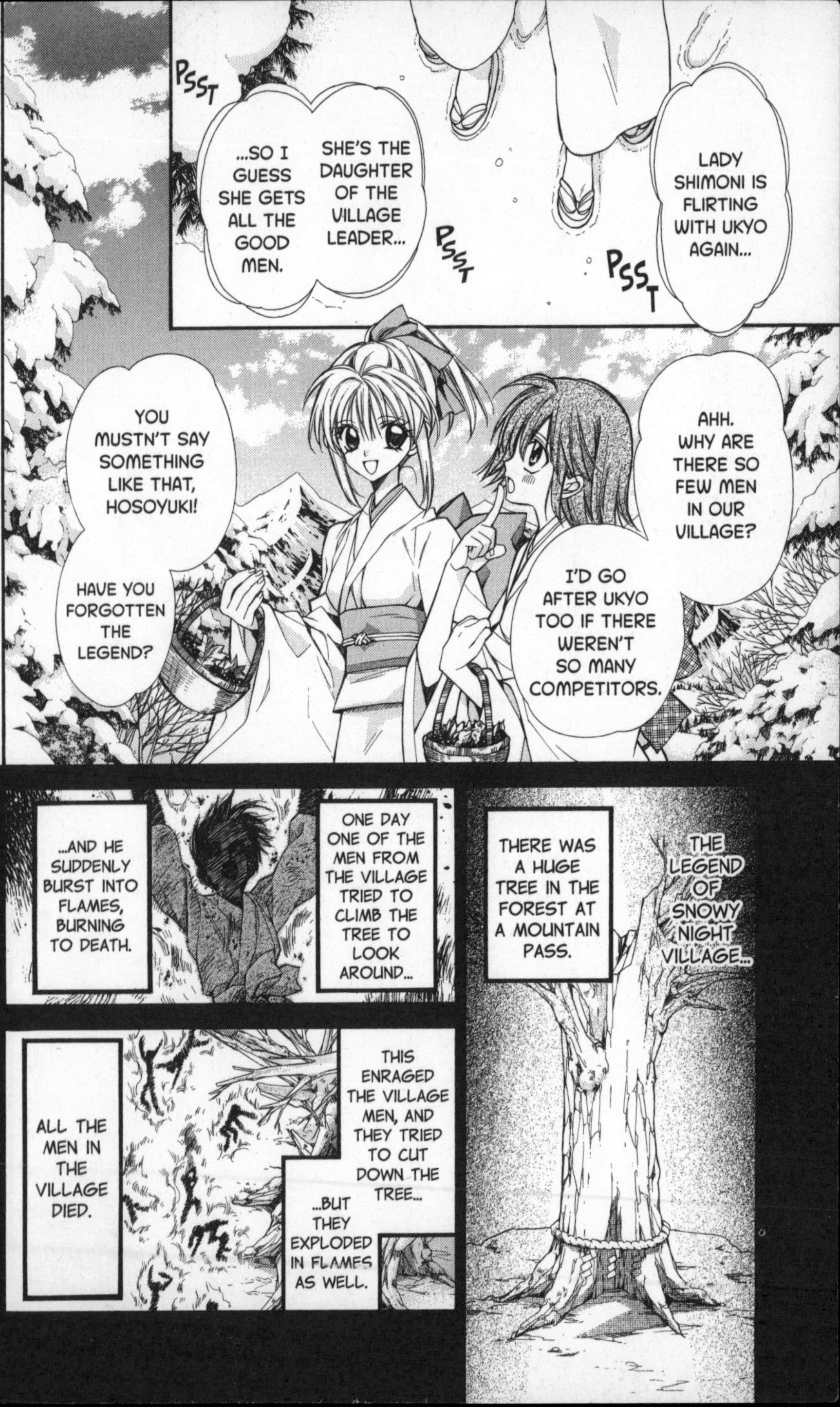
PSST
LADY SHIMONI IS FLIRTING WITH UKYO AGAIN...
PSST
SHE'S THE DAUGHTER OF THE VILLAGE LEADER...
PSST
...SO I GUESS SHE GETS ALL THE GOOD MEN.
AHH. WHY ARE THERE SO FEW MEN IN OUR VILLAGE?
I'D GO AFTER UKYO TOO IF THERE WEREN'T SO MANY COMPETITORS.
YOU MUSTN'T SAY SOMETHING LIKE THAT, HOSOYUKI!
HAVE YOU FORGOTTEN THE LEGEND?
THE LEGEND OF SNOWY NIGHT VILLAGE...
THERE WAS A HUGE TREE IN THE FOREST AT A MOUNTAIN PASS.
ONE DAY ONE OF THE MEN FROM THE VILLAGE TRIED TO CLIMB THE TREE TO LOOK AROUND...
...AND HE SUDDENLY BURST INTO FLAMES, BURNING TO DEATH.
THIS ENRAGED THE VILLAGE MEN, AND THEY TRIED TO CUT DOWN THE TREE...
...BUT THEY EXPLODED IN FLAMES AS WELL.
ALL THE MEN IN THE VILLAGE DIED.

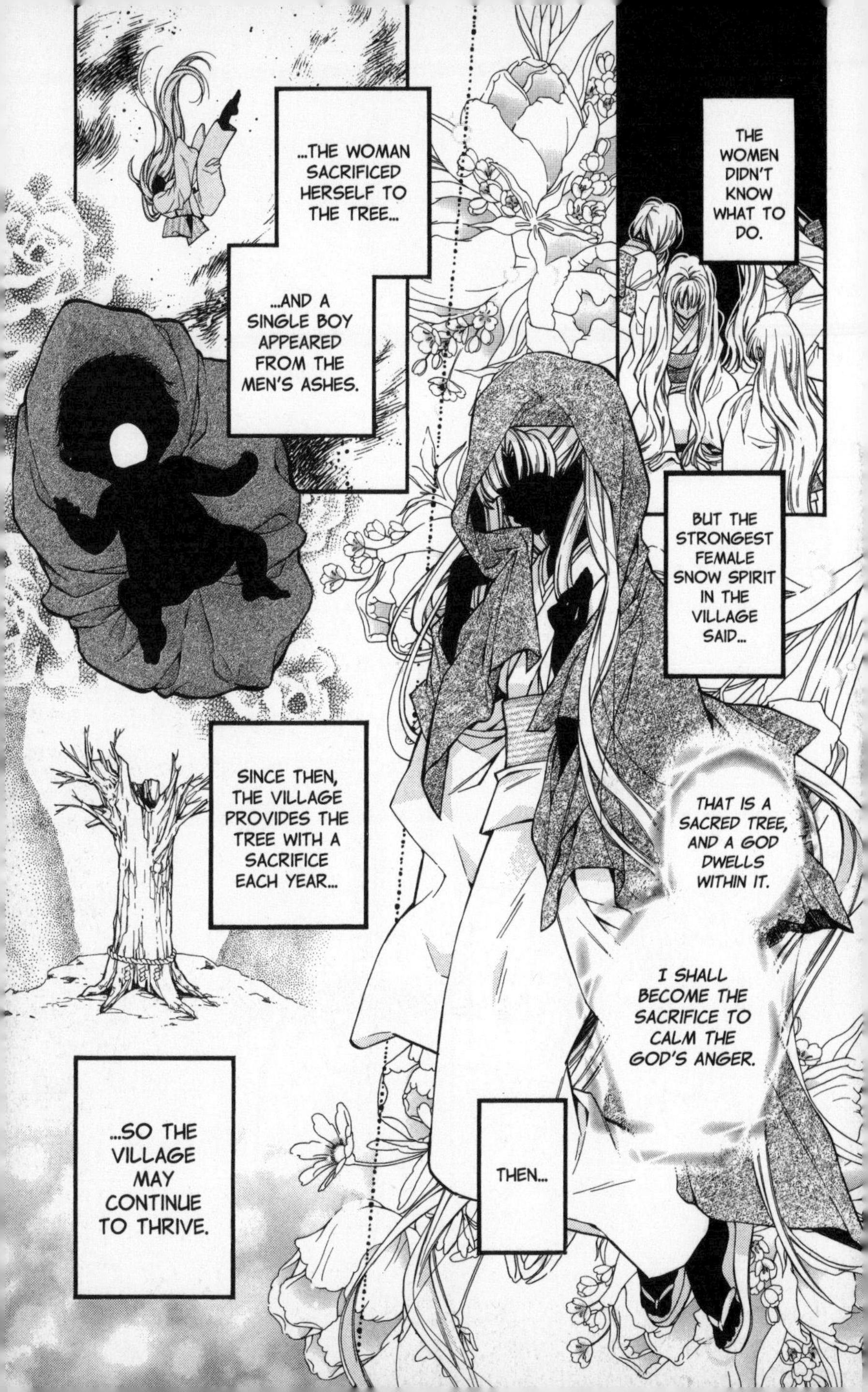
THE WOMEN DIDN'T KNOW WHAT TO DO.
BUT THE STRONGEST FEMALE SNOW SPIRIT IN THE VILLAGE SAID...
THAT IS A SACRED TREE, AND A GOD DWELLS WITHIN IT.
I SHALL BECOME THE SACRIFICE TO CALM THE GOD'S ANGER.
THEN...
...THE WOMAN SACRIFICED HERSELF TO THE TREE...
...AND A SINGLE BOY APPEARED FROM THE MEN'S ASHES.
SINCE THEN, THE VILLAGE PROVIDES THE TREE WITH A SACRIFICE EACH YEAR...
...SO THE VILLAGE MAY CONTINUE TO THRIVE.

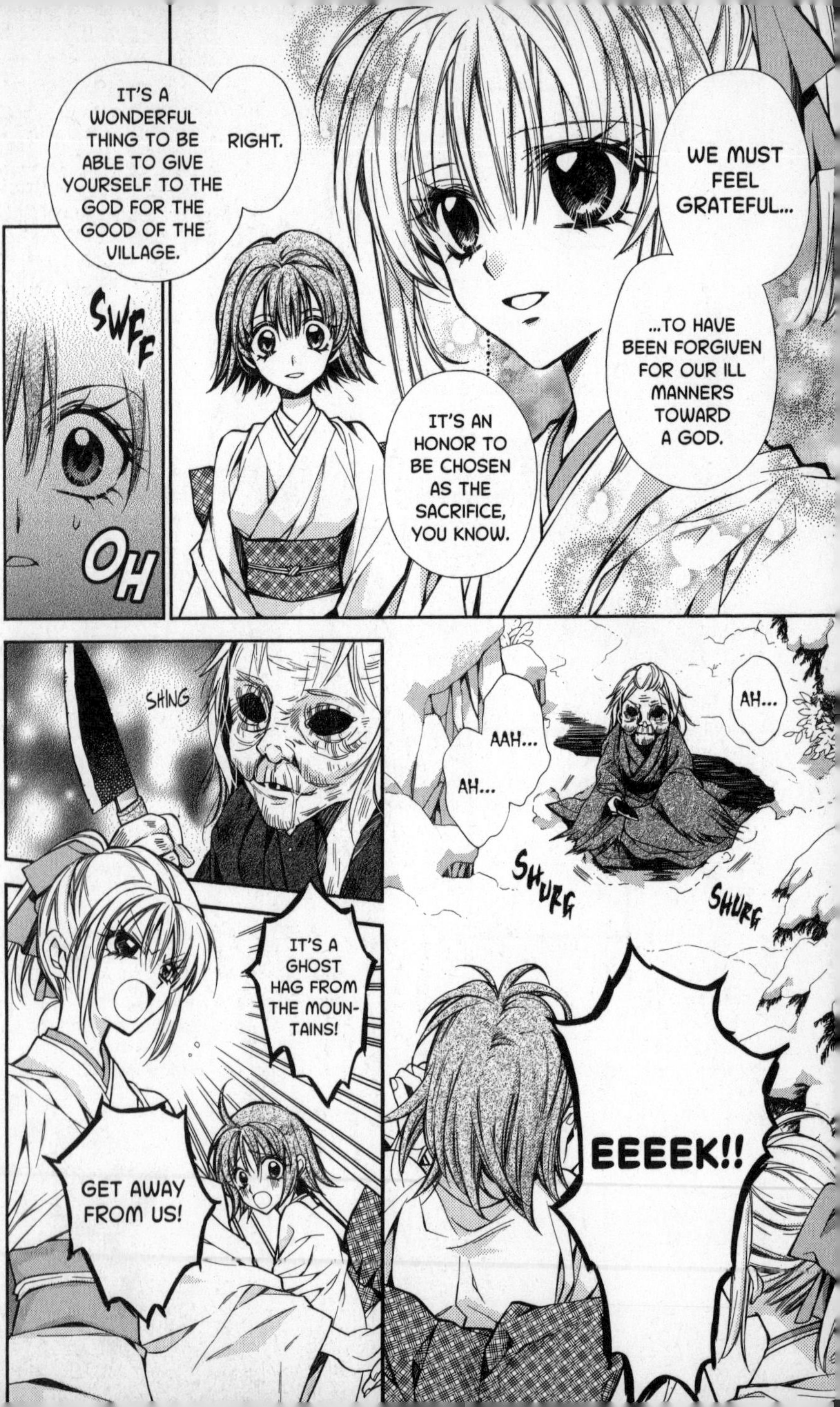
WE MUST FEEL GRATEFUL...
...TO HAVE BEEN FORGIVEN FOR OUR ILL MANNERS TOWARD A GOD.
IT'S AN HONOR TO BE CHOSEN AS THE SACRIFICE, YOU KNOW.
RIGHT.
IT'S A WONDERFUL THING TO BE ABLE TO GIVE YOURSELF TO THE GOD FOR THE GOOD OF THE VILLAGE.
SWFF
OH
AH...
AAH...
AH...
SHURG
SHURG
EEEEK!!
SHING
IT'S A GHOST HAG FROM THE MOUN-TAINS!
GET AWAY FROM US!

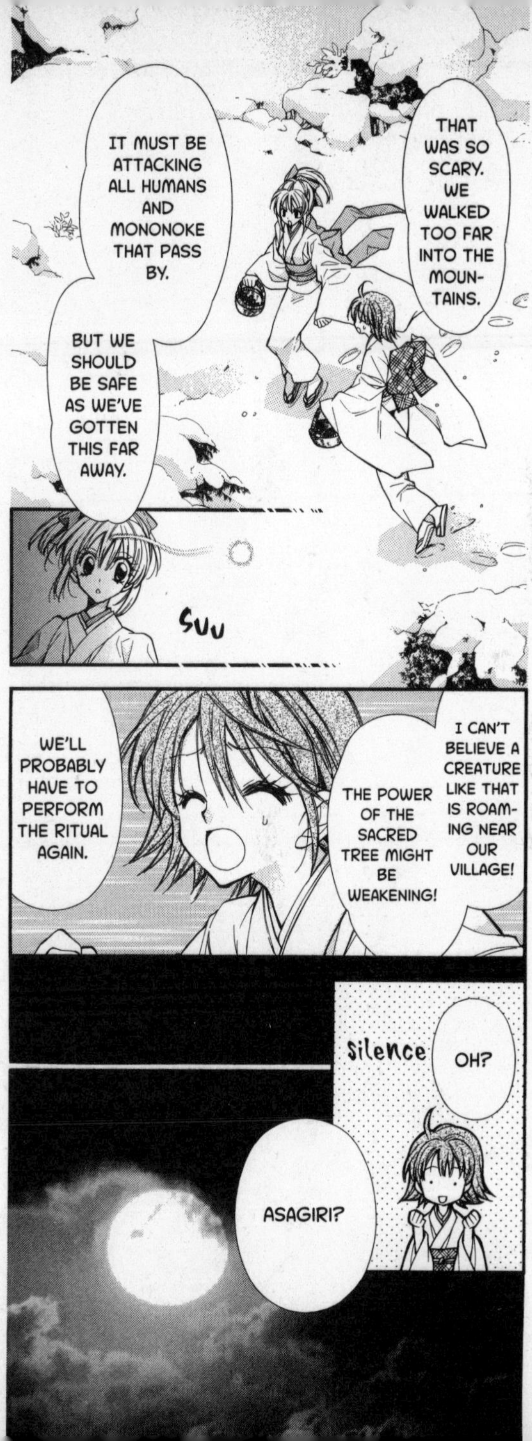
THAT WAS SO SCARY. WE WALKED TOO FAR INTO THE MOUN-TAINS.
IT MUST BE ATTACKING ALL HUMANS AND MONONOKE THAT PASS BY.
BUT WE SHOULD BE SAFE AS WE'VE GOTTEN THIS FAR AWAY.
SUU
I CAN'T BELIEVE A CREATURE LIKE THAT IS ROAM-ING NEAR OUR VILLAGE!
THE POWER OF THE SACRED TREE MIGHT BE WEAKENING!
WE'LL PROBABLY HAVE TO PERFORM THE RITUAL AGAIN.
OH?
Silence
ASAGIRI?

Toy Story 3

※ I may be giving away some of the story, so please read this after you watch the movie. ✿

It was wonderful! My favorite characters are Woody and Buzz, but I really like Andy too, although he doesn't appear that often.

My parents didn't buy me a lot of toys, but they did give me a Barbie doll and Licca-chan doll, so I'd create my own stories every time I played with them. (I may be making good use of that experience with my work now.) So I just loved the part about Barbie and Ken! And I was very happy to see the stuffed Totoro doll moving too. ♥ (After all, I'm from the country of Ghibli...) (laugh)

And my eyes were filled with tears...during the last five minutes!! The wish at the beginning of the movie was answered, and I just couldn't stop crying. ♥
It was a great movie. I love all the characters...! (Although there are exceptions.)

I want to go see it one more time... ♥

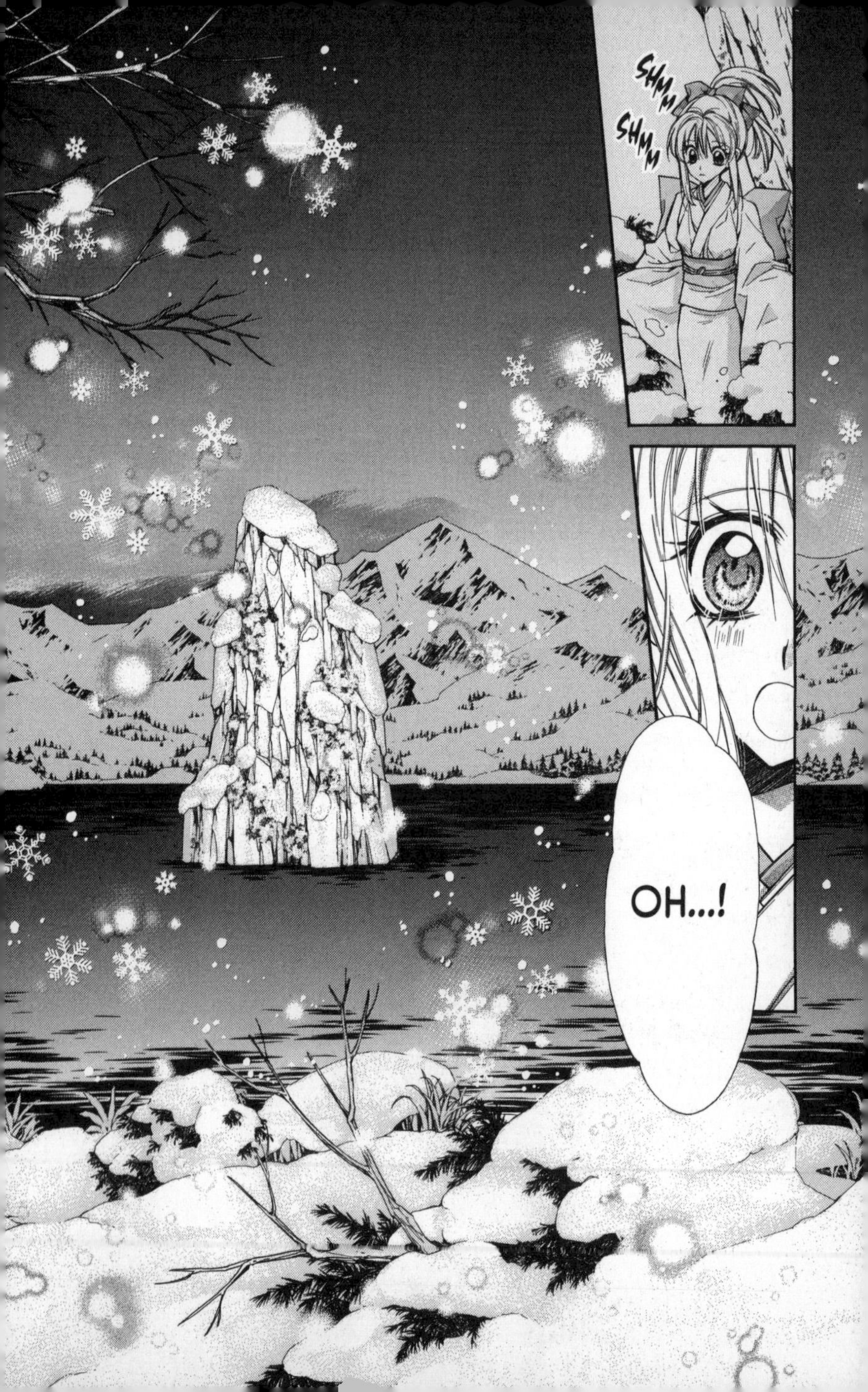
SHMM SHMM
OH...!

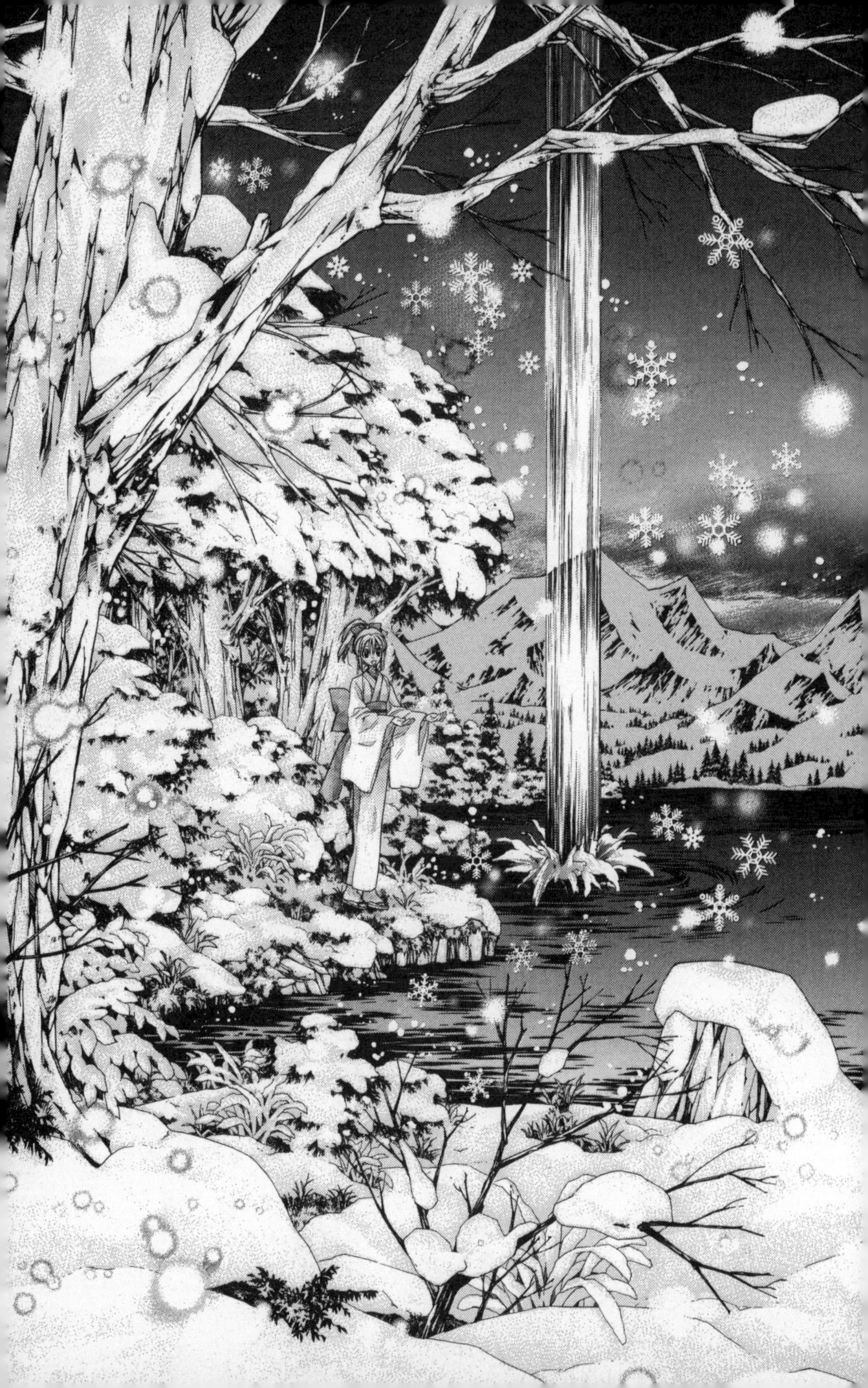

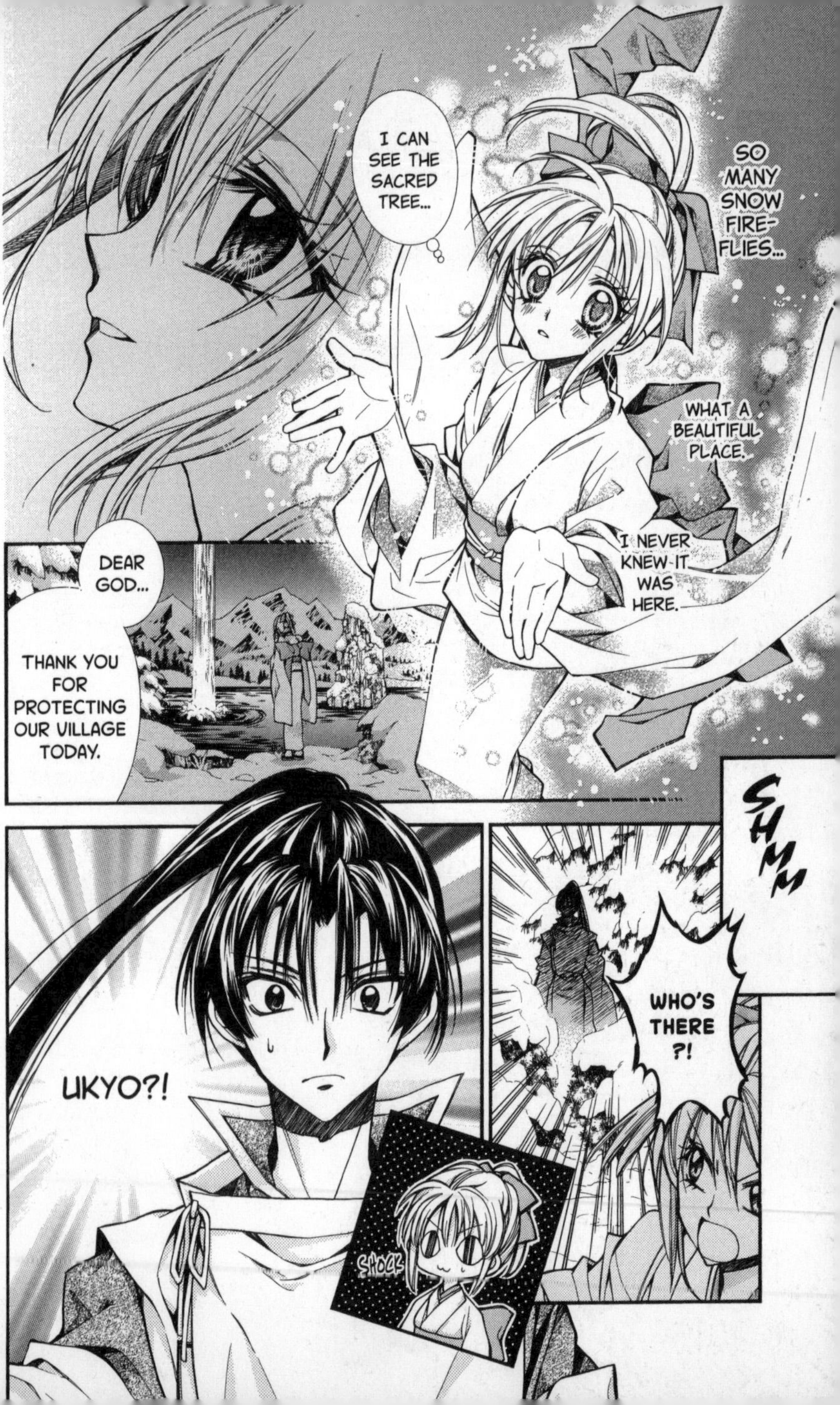
SO MANY SNOW FIRE-FLIES...
I CAN SEE THE SACRED TREE...
WHAT A BEAUTIFUL PLACE.
I NEVER KNEW IT WAS HERE.
DEAR GOD...
THANK YOU FOR PROTECTING OUR VILLAGE TODAY.
SHMM
WHO'S THERE ?!
UKYO?!
SHOCK

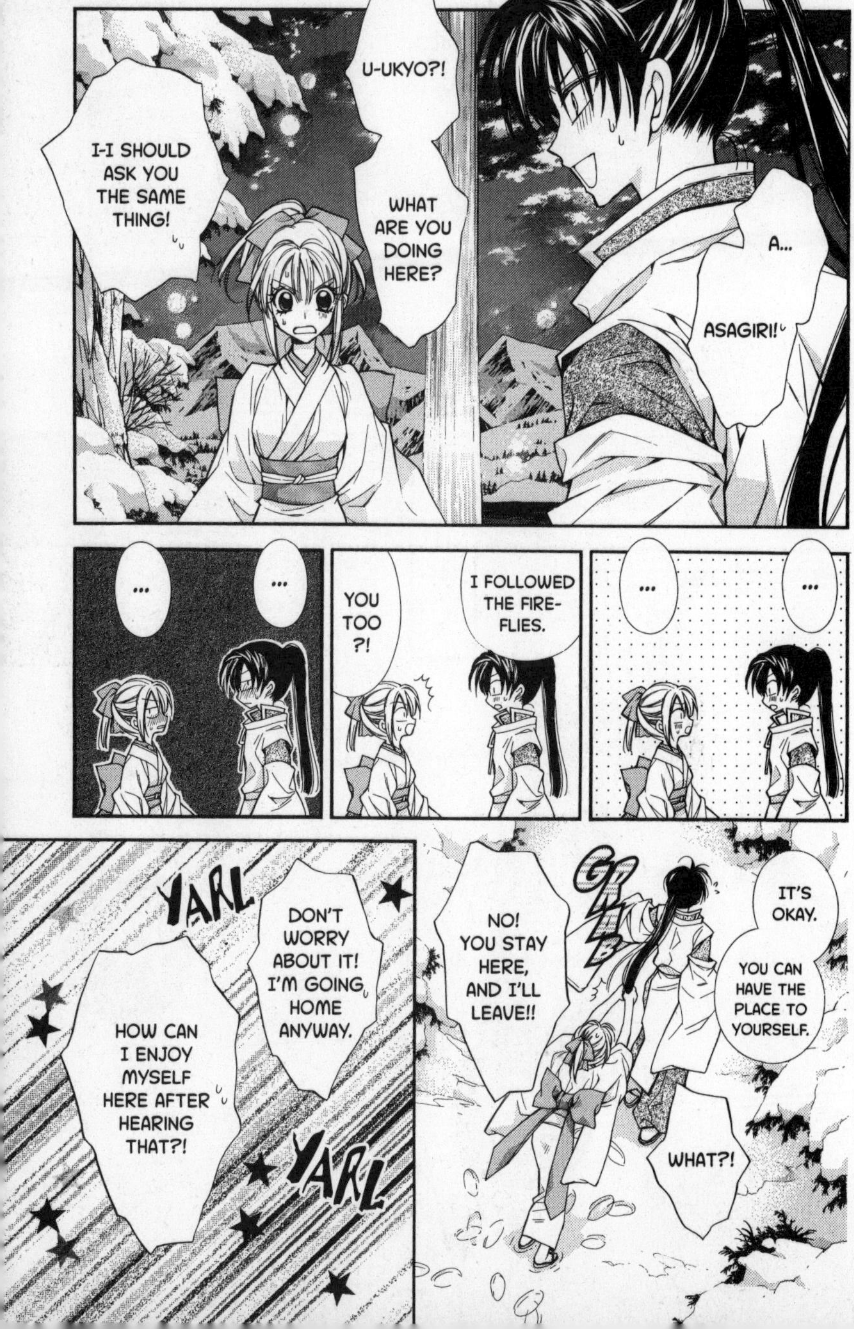
A...
ASAGIRI!
U-UKYO?!
WHAT ARE YOU DOING HERE?
I-I SHOULD ASK YOU THE SAME THING!
...
...
I FOLLOWED THE FIRE-FLIES.
YOU TOO ?!
...
...
IT'S OKAY.
YOU CAN HAVE THE PLACE TO YOURSELF.
GRAB
WHAT?!
NO! YOU STAY HERE, AND I'LL LEAVE!!
DON'T WORRY ABOUT IT! I'M GOING HOME ANYWAY.
YARL
HOW CAN I ENJOY MYSELF HERE AFTER HEARING THAT?!
YARL

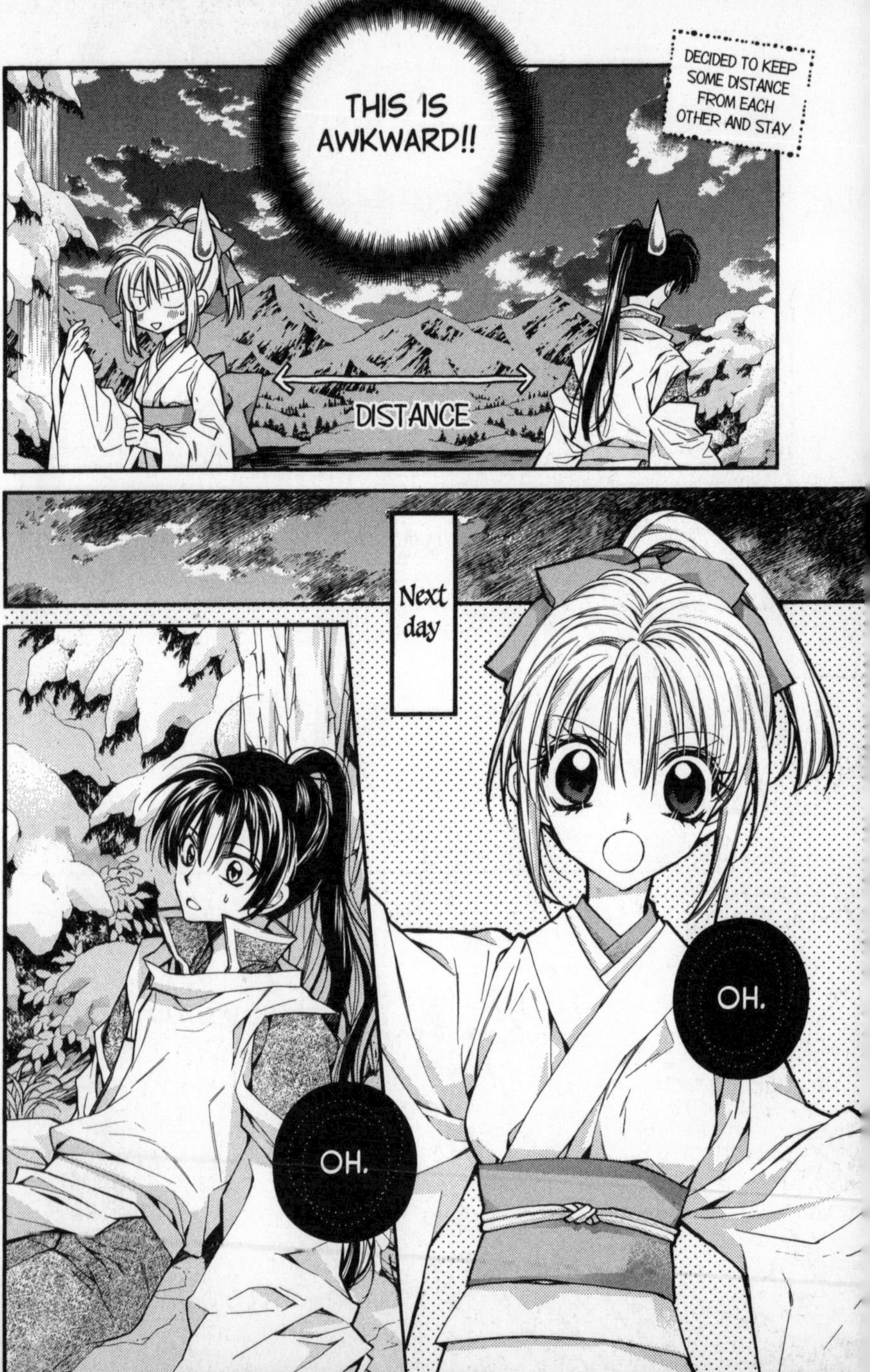
DECIDED TO KEEP SOME DISTANCE FROM EACH OTHER AND STAY
THIS IS AWKWARD!!
DISTANCE
Next day
OH.
OH.

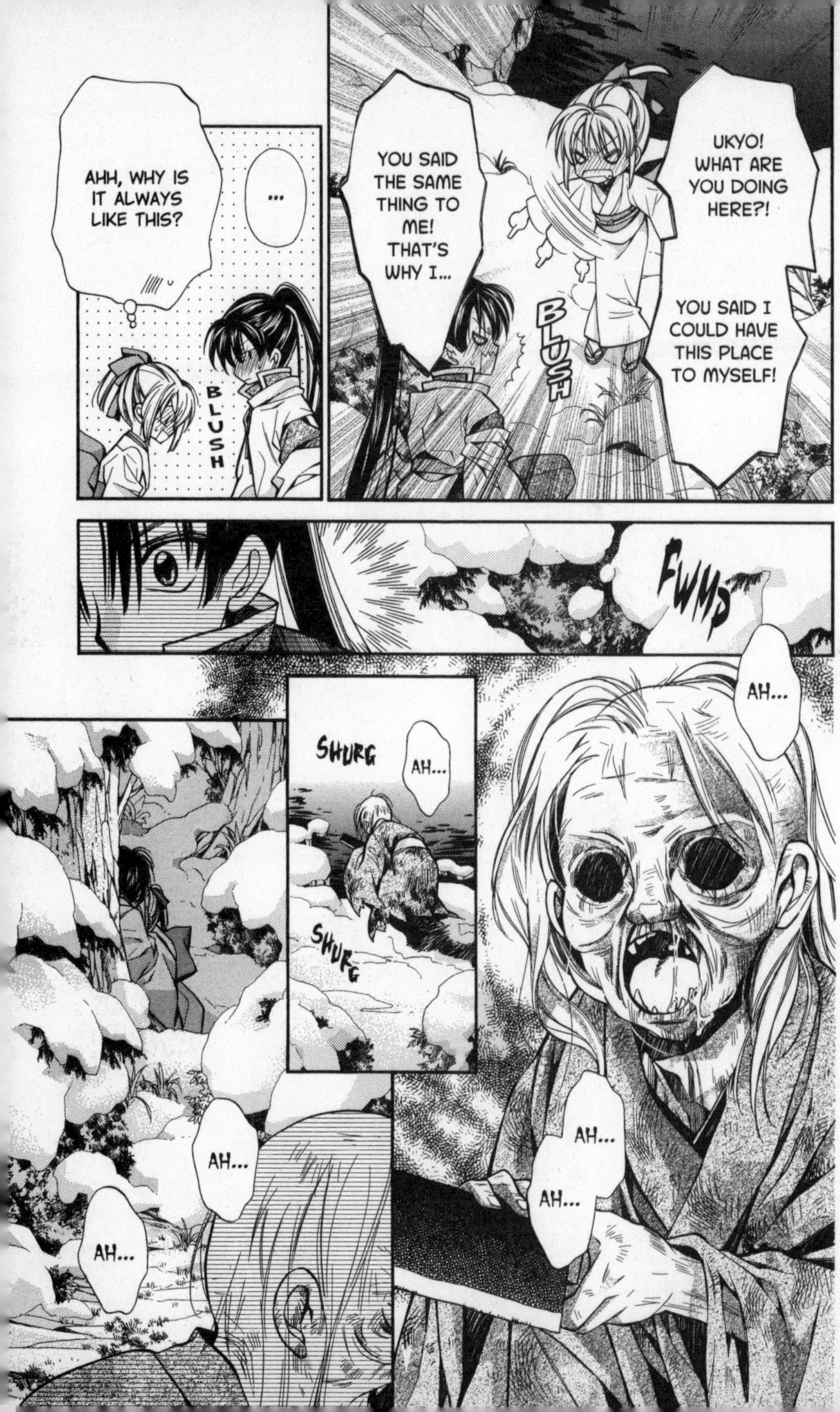
UKYO! WHAT ARE YOU DOING HERE?!
YOU SAID I COULD HAVE THIS PLACE TO MYSELF!
BLUSH
YOU SAID THE SAME THING TO ME! THAT'S WHY I...
...
AHH, WHY IS IT ALWAYS LIKE THIS?
BLUSH
FWMP
AH...
AH...
AH...
AH...
SHURG
SHURG
AH...
AH...

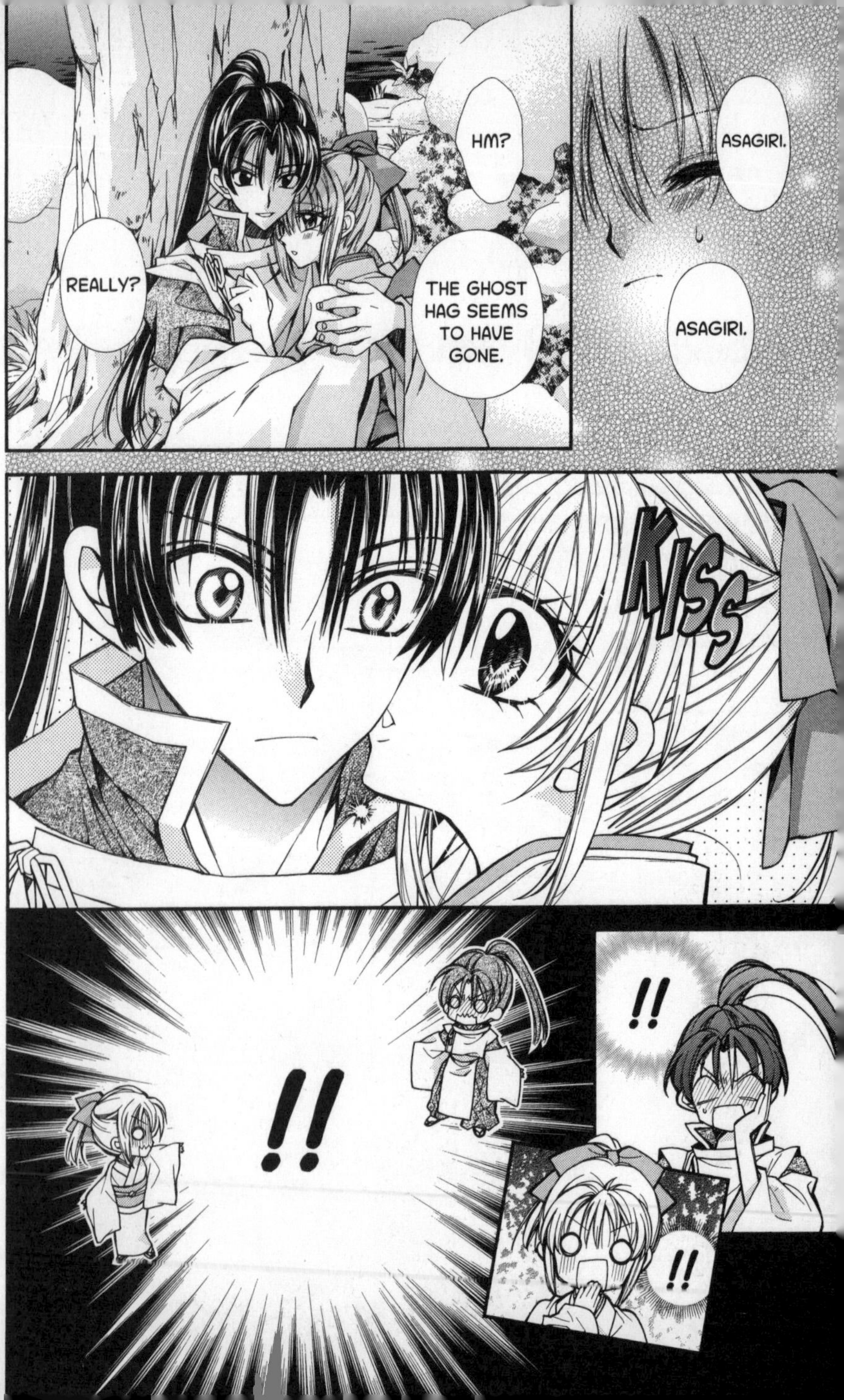
ASAGIRI.
ASAGIRI.
HM?
THE GHOST HAG SEEMS TO HAVE GONE.
REALLY?
KISS
!!
!!
!!

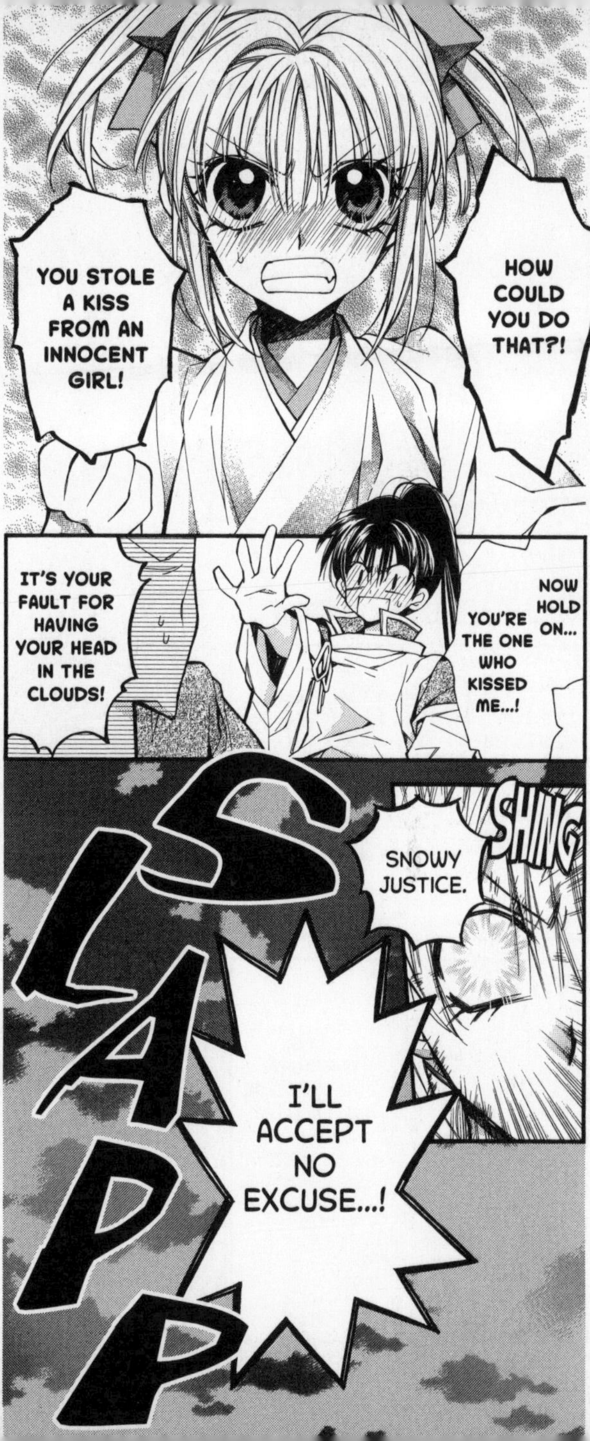
HOW COULD YOU DO THAT?!
YOU STOLE A KISS FROM AN INNOCENT GIRL!
NOW HOLD ON...
YOU'RE THE ONE WHO KISSED ME...!
IT'S YOUR FAULT FOR HAVING YOUR HEAD IN THE CLOUDS!
SHING
SNOWY JUSTICE.
I'LL ACCEPT NO EXCUSE...!
SLAPP

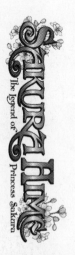

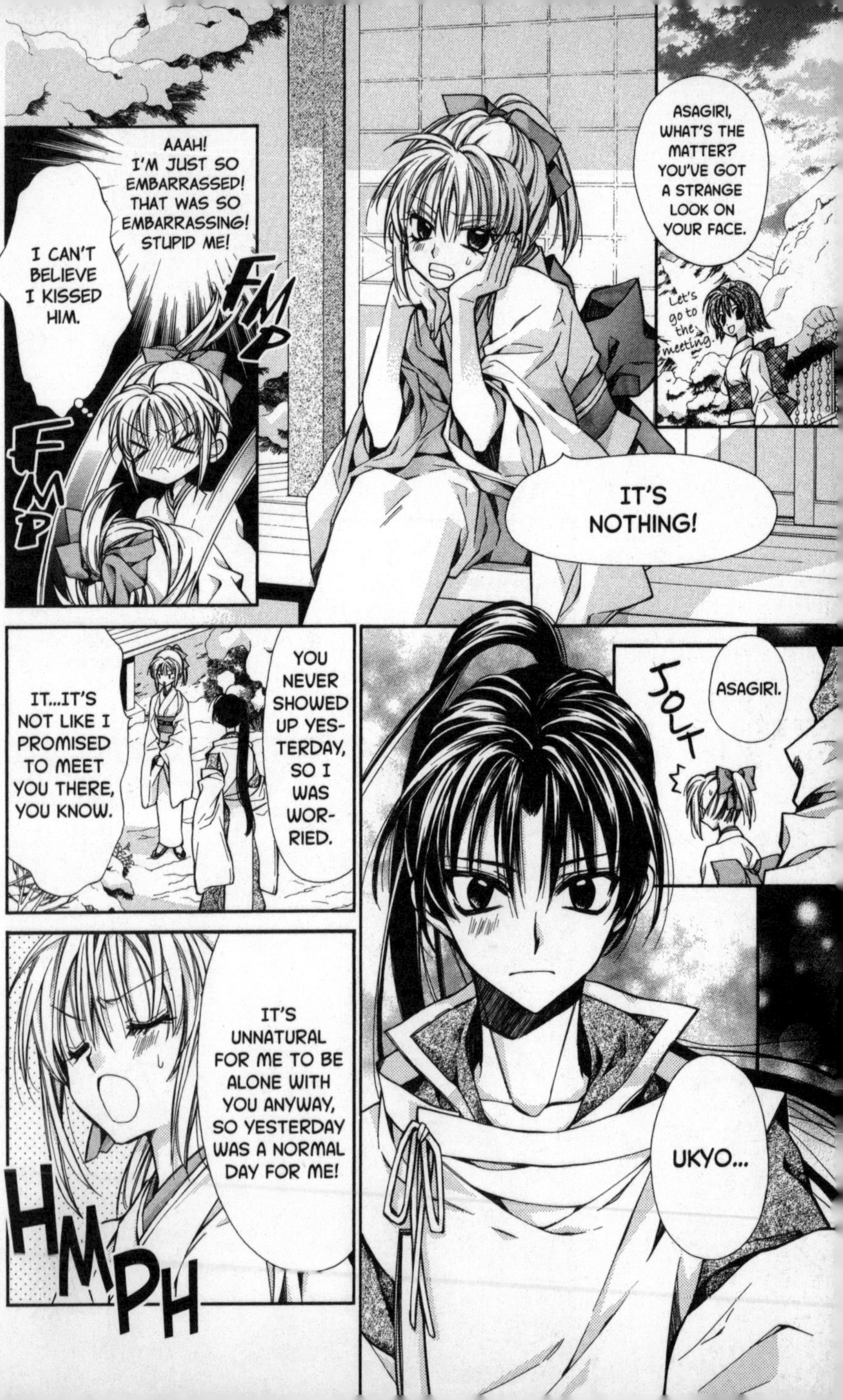
ASAGIRI, WHAT'S THE MATTER? YOU'VE GOT A STRANGE LOOK ON YOUR FACE.
Let's go to the meeting.
IT'S NOTHING!
AAAH! I'M JUST SO EMBARRASSED! THAT WAS SO EMBARRASSING! STUPID ME!
I CAN'T BELIEVE I KISSED HIM.
FMP
FMP
ASAGIRI.
JOLT
UKYO...
YOU NEVER SHOWED UP YESTERDAY, SO I WAS WORRIED.
IT...IT'S NOT LIKE I PROMISED TO MEET YOU THERE, YOU KNOW.
IT'S UNNATURAL FOR ME TO BE ALONE WITH YOU ANYWAY, SO YESTERDAY WAS A NORMAL DAY FOR ME!
HMPH

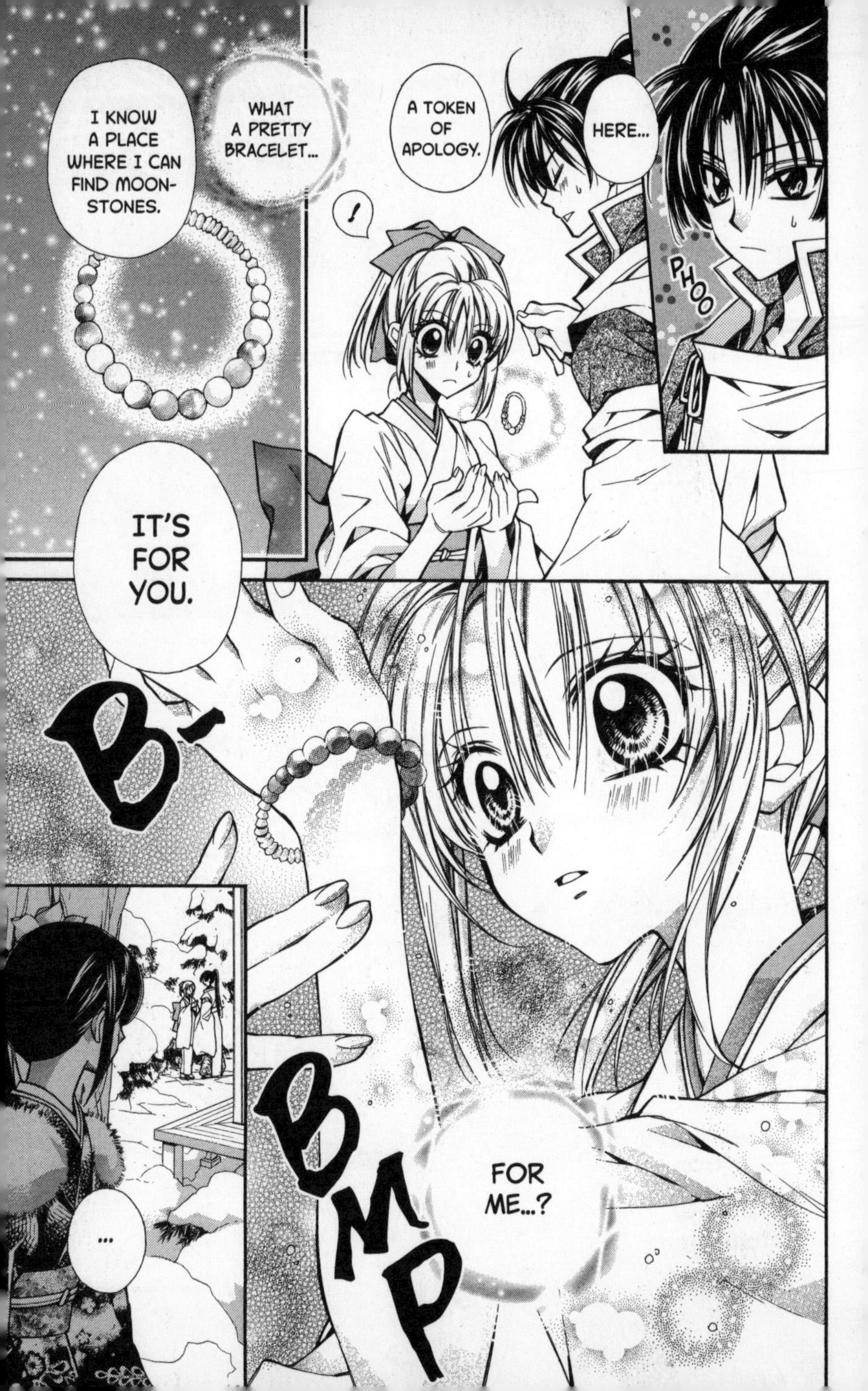
HERE...
PHOO
A TOKEN OF APOLOGY.
!
WHAT A PRETTY BRACELET...
I KNOW A PLACE WHERE I CAN FIND MOON-STONES.
IT'S FOR YOU.
B-BMP
FOR ME...?
...

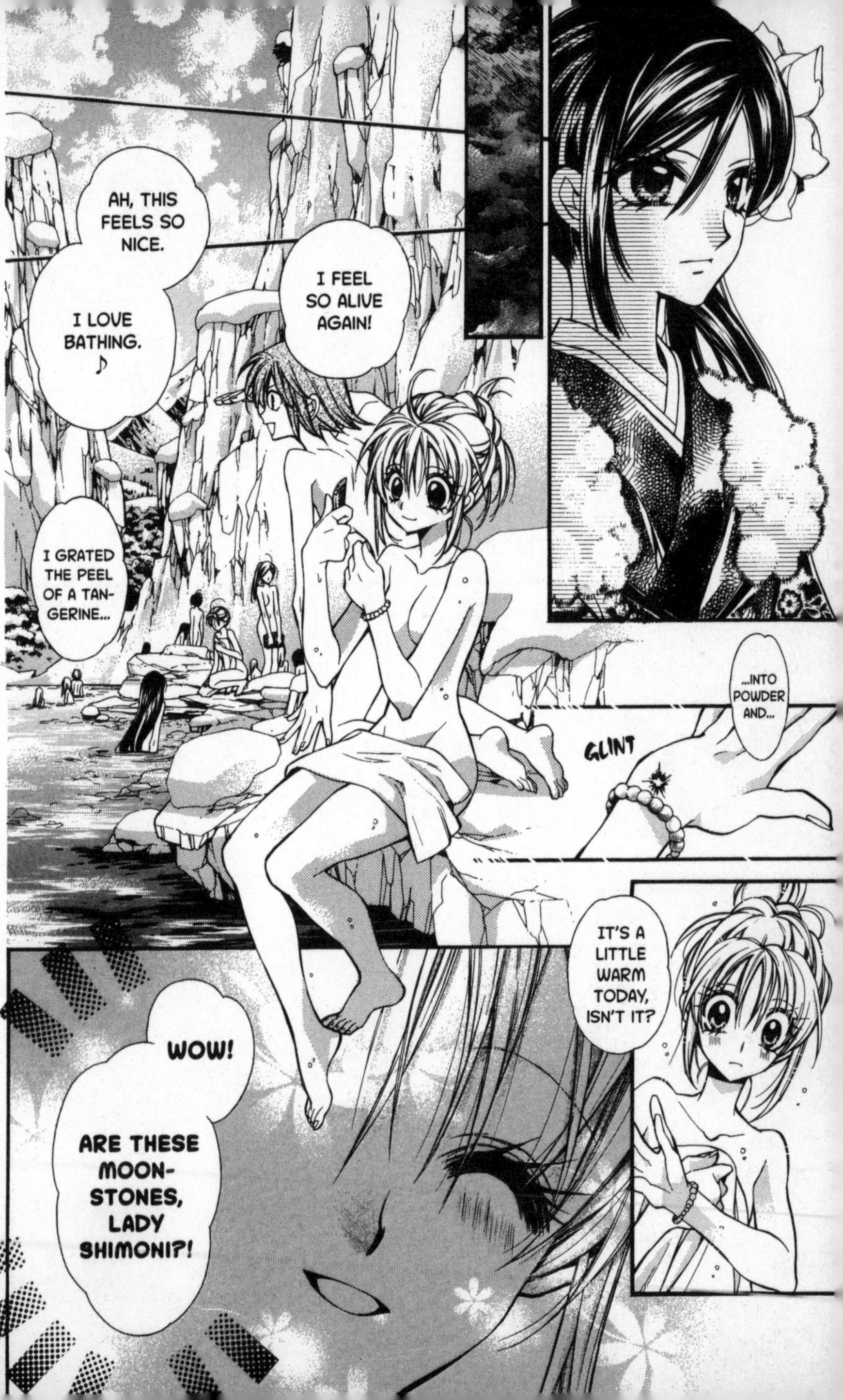
AH, THIS FEELS SO NICE.
I LOVE BATHING. ♪
I FEEL SO ALIVE AGAIN!
I GRATED THE PEEL OF A TANGERINE...
...INTO POWDER AND...
GLINT
IT'S A LITTLE WARM TODAY, ISN'T IT?
WOW!
ARE THESE MOONSTONES, LADY SHIMONI?!

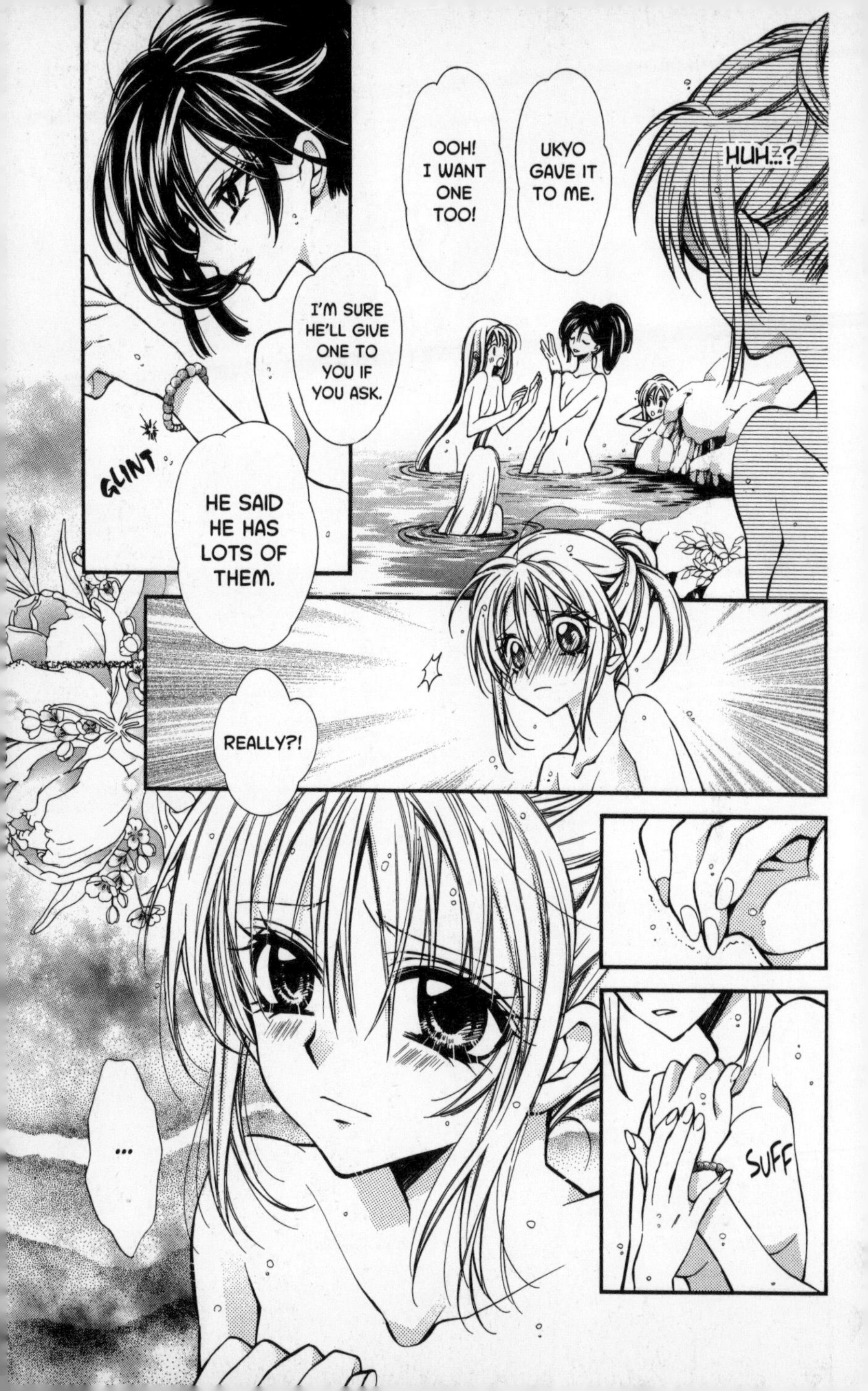
HUH...?
UKYO GAVE IT TO ME.
OOH! I WANT ONE TOO!
I'M SURE HE'LL GIVE ONE TO YOU IF YOU ASK.
GLINT
HE SAID HE HAS LOTS OF THEM.
REALLY?!
SUFF
...

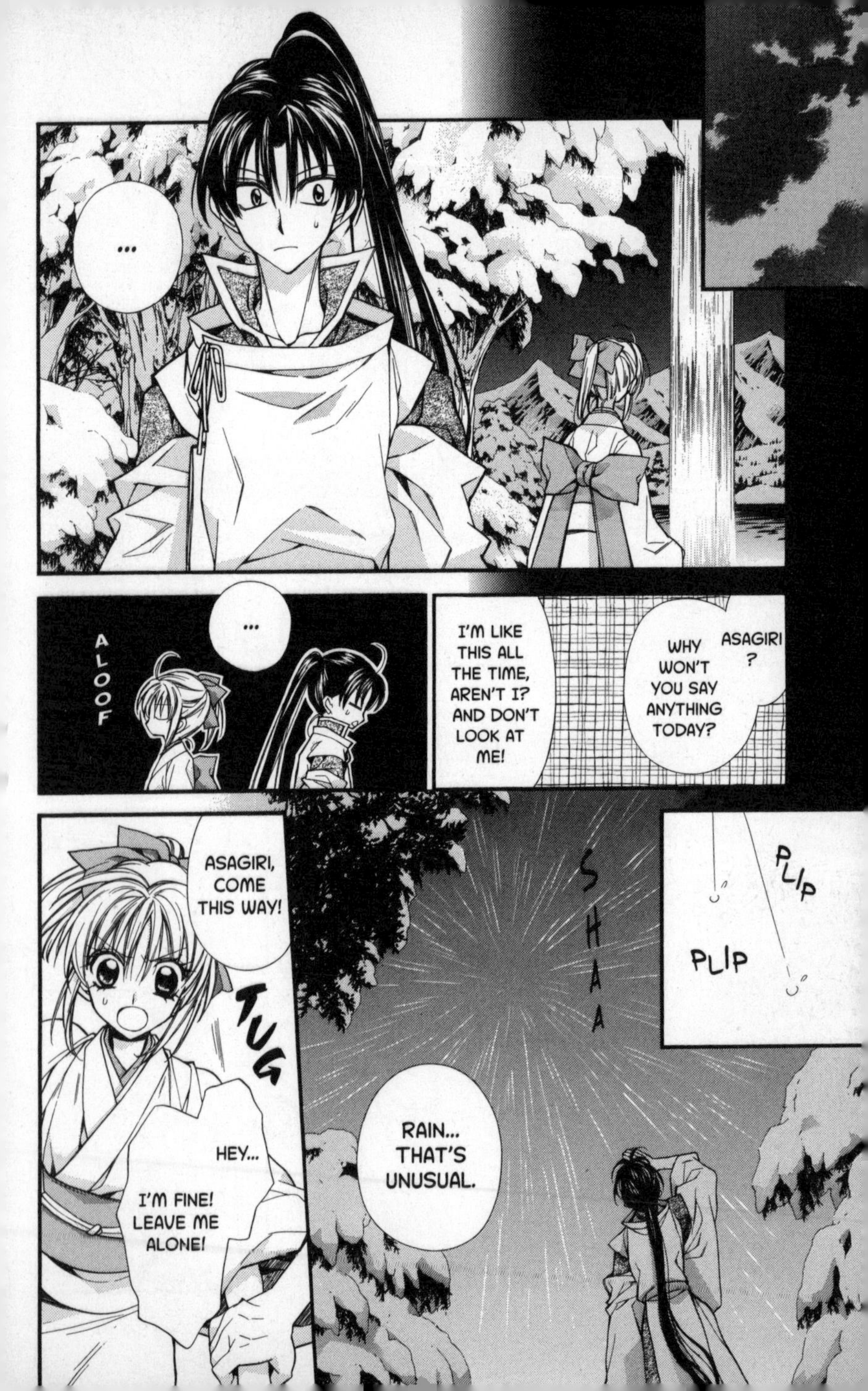
...
ASAGIRI?
WHY WON'T YOU SAY ANYTHING TODAY?
I'M LIKE THIS ALL THE TIME, AREN'T I? AND DON'T LOOK AT ME!
...
ALOOF
PLIP
PLIP
SHAA
RAIN... THAT'S UNUSUAL.
ASAGIRI, COME THIS WAY!
TUG
HEY...
I'M FINE! LEAVE ME ALONE!

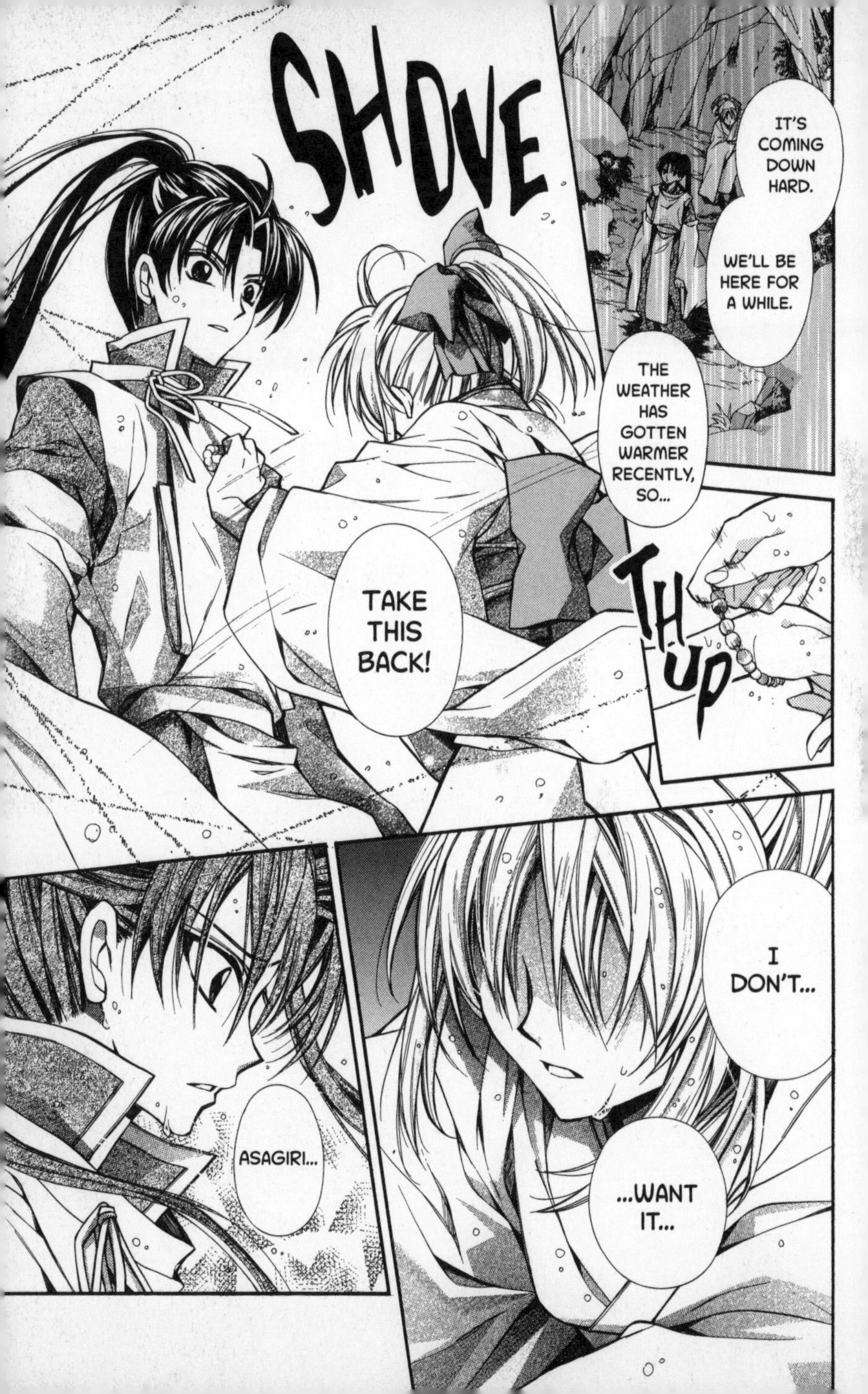
IT'S COMING DOWN HARD.
WE'LL BE HERE FOR A WHILE.
THE WEATHER HAS GOTTEN WARMER RECENTLY, SO...
THUP
SHOVE
TAKE THIS BACK!
I DON'T...
...WANT IT...
ASAGIRI...

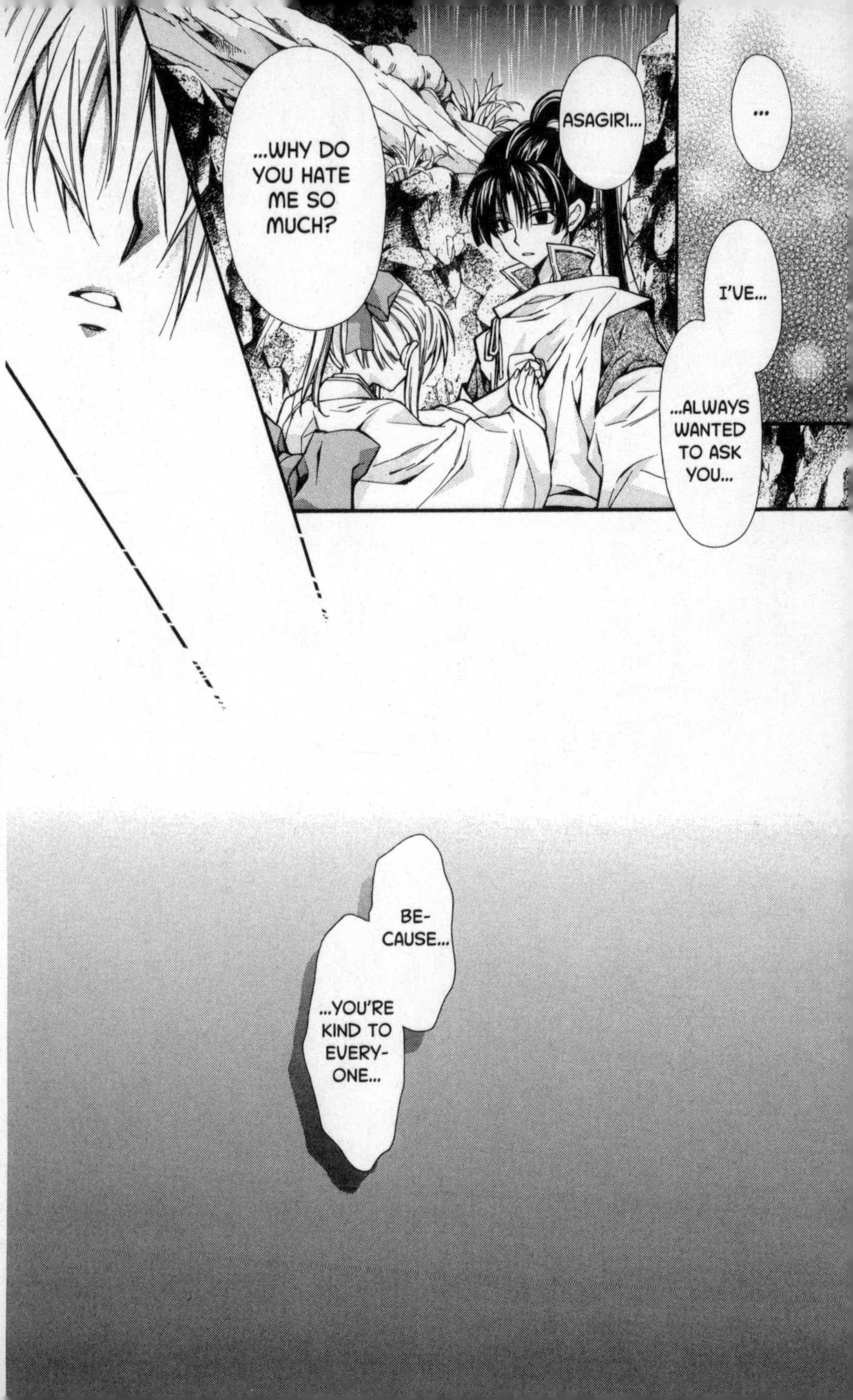
...
I'VE...
...ALWAYS WANTED TO ASK YOU...
ASAGIRI...
...WHY DO YOU HATE ME SO MUCH?
BE-CAUSE...
...YOU'RE KIND TO EVERY-ONE...

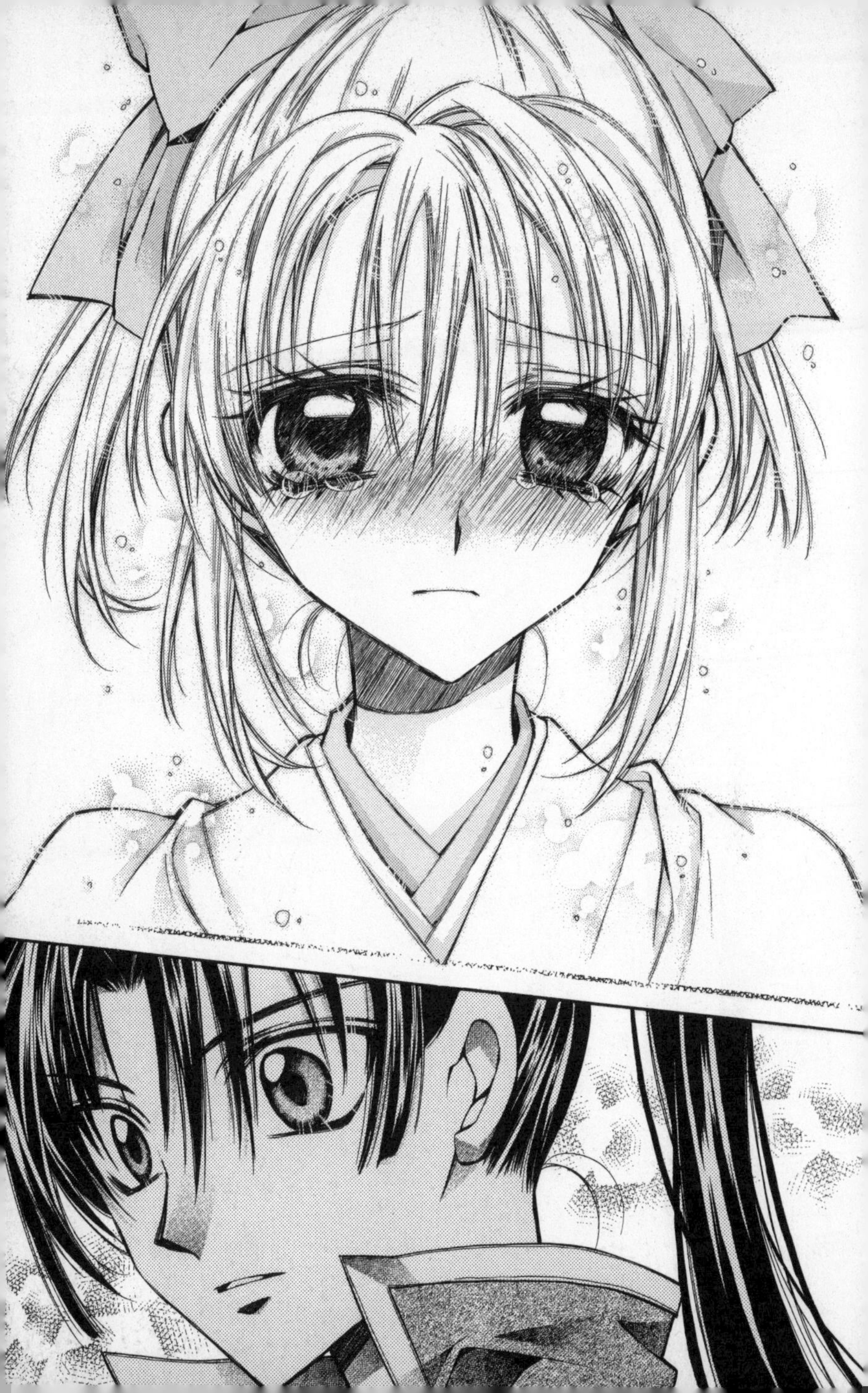

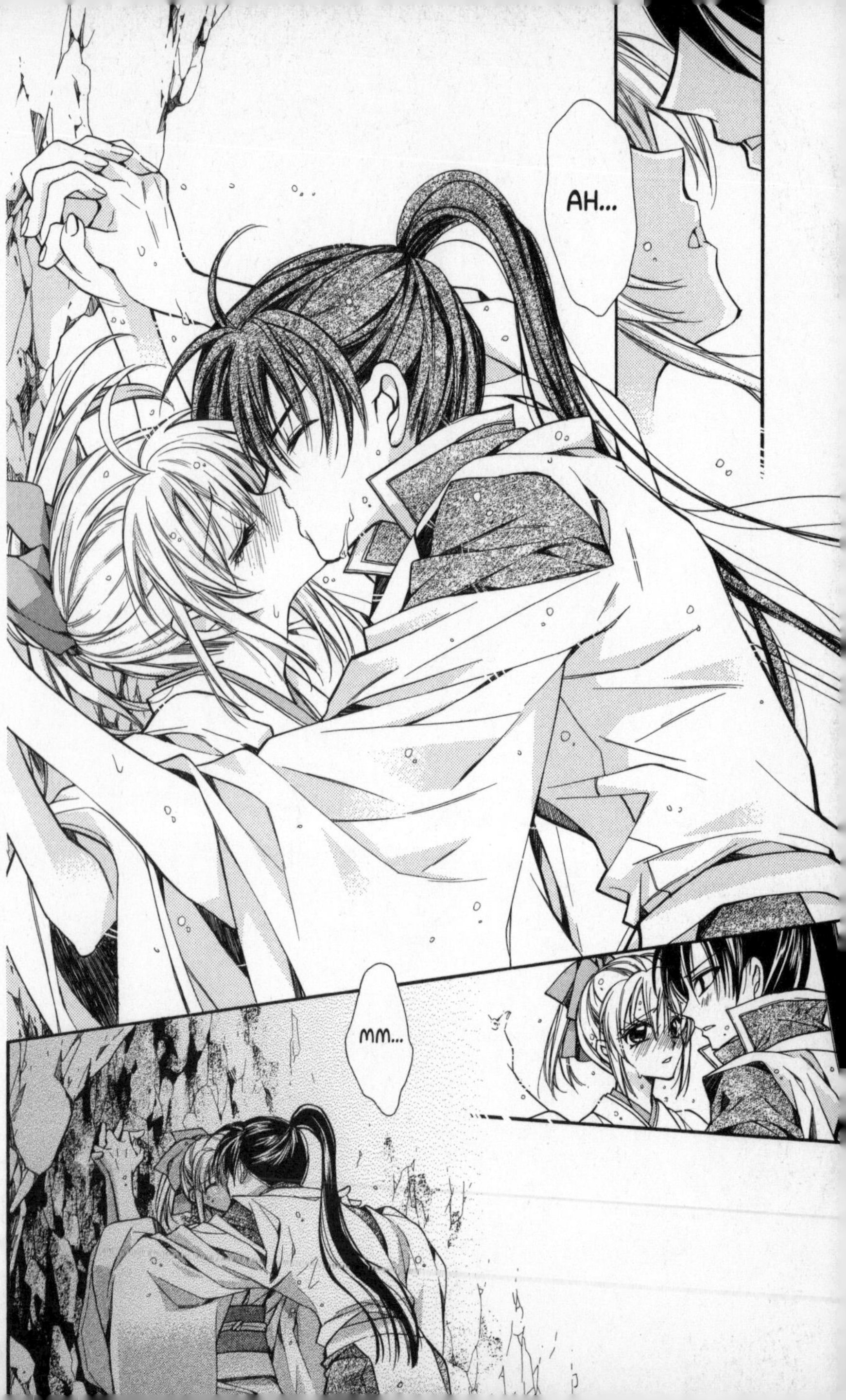
AH...
MM...

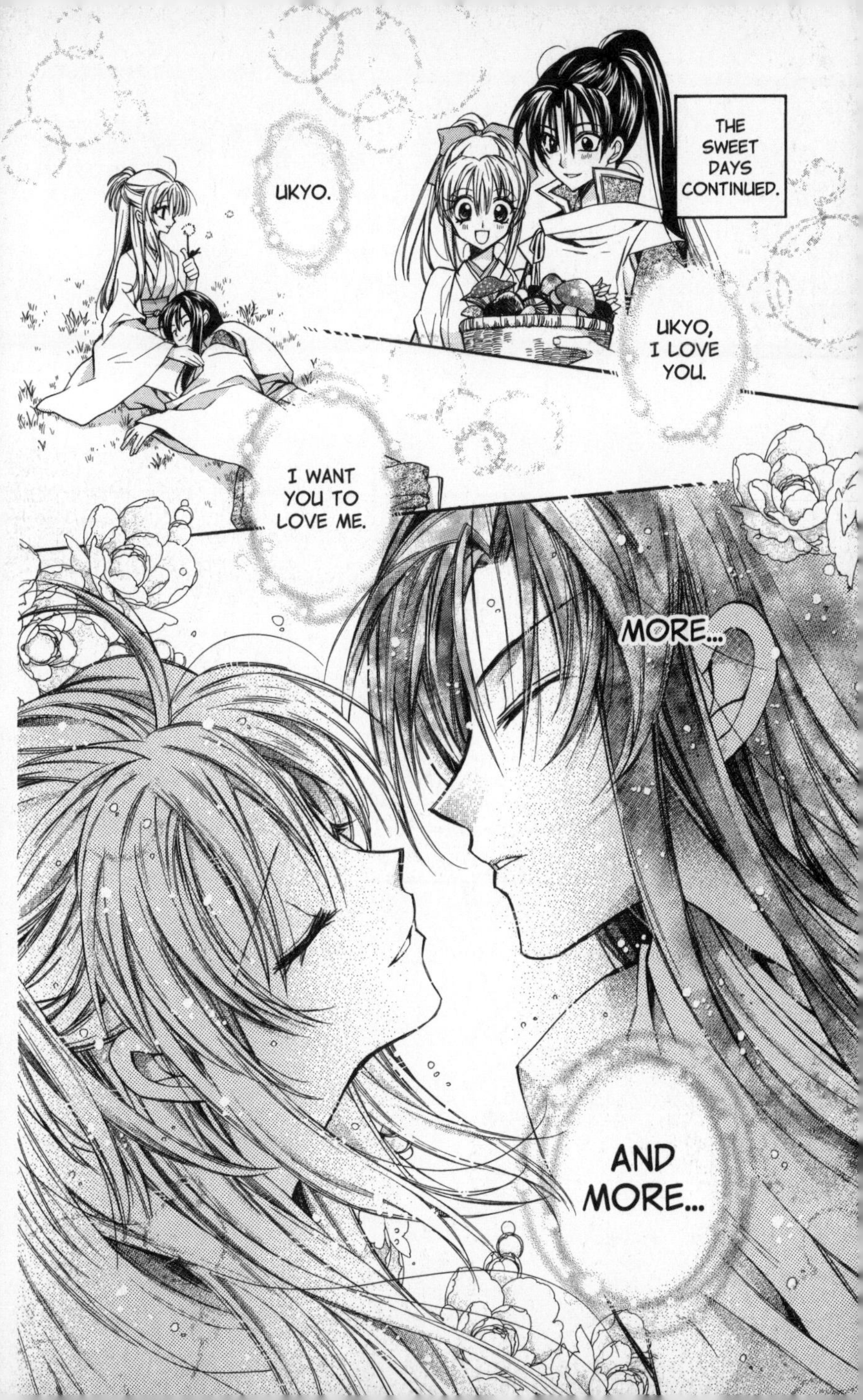
THE SWEET DAYS CONTINUED.
UKYO, I LOVE YOU.
UKYO.
I WANT YOU TO LOVE ME.
MORE...
AND MORE...

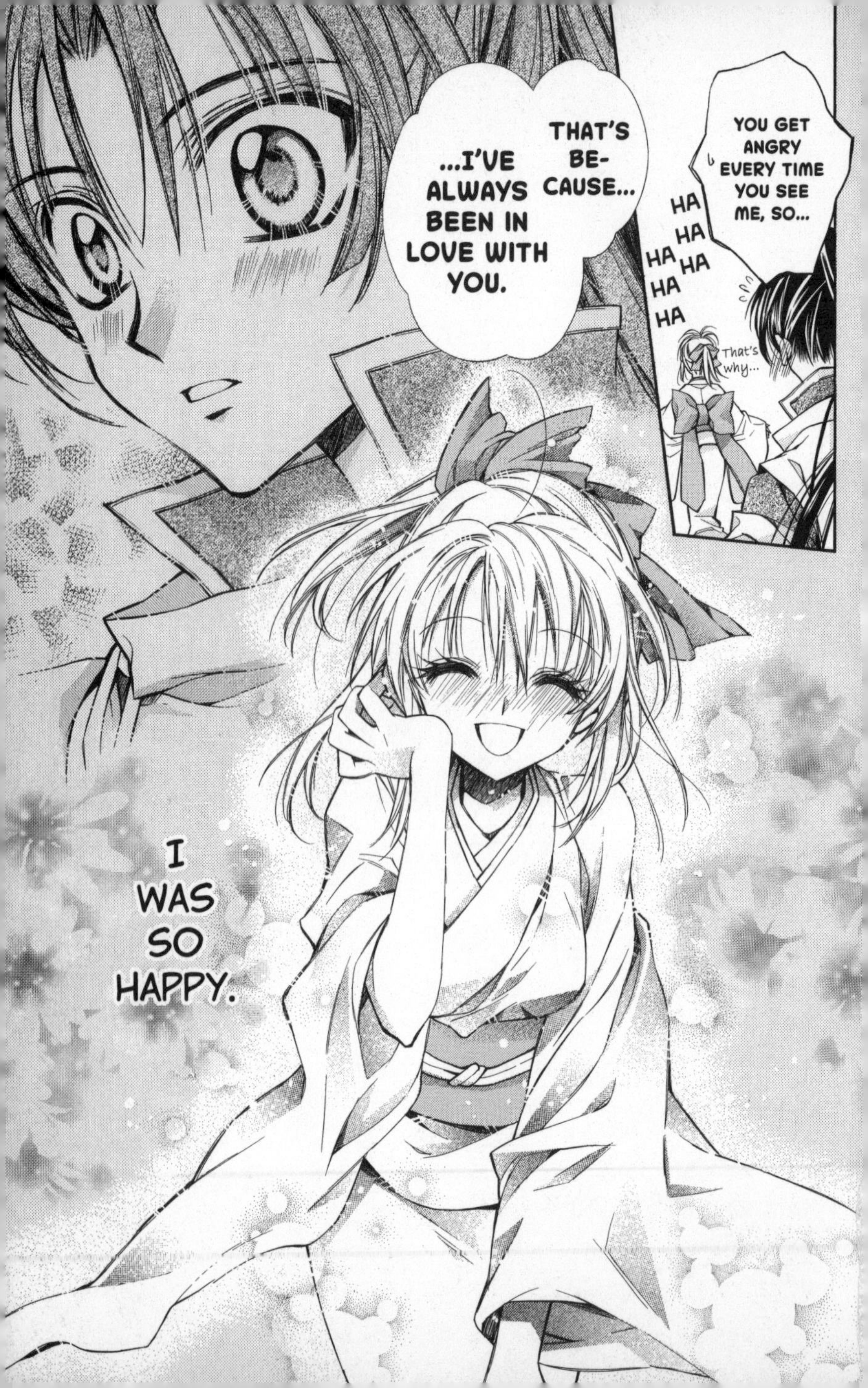
YOU GET ANGRY EVERY TIME YOU SEE ME, SO...
HA HA HA HA HA HA
That's why...
THAT'S BE-CAUSE...
...I'VE ALWAYS BEEN IN LOVE WITH YOU.
I WAS SO HAPPY.

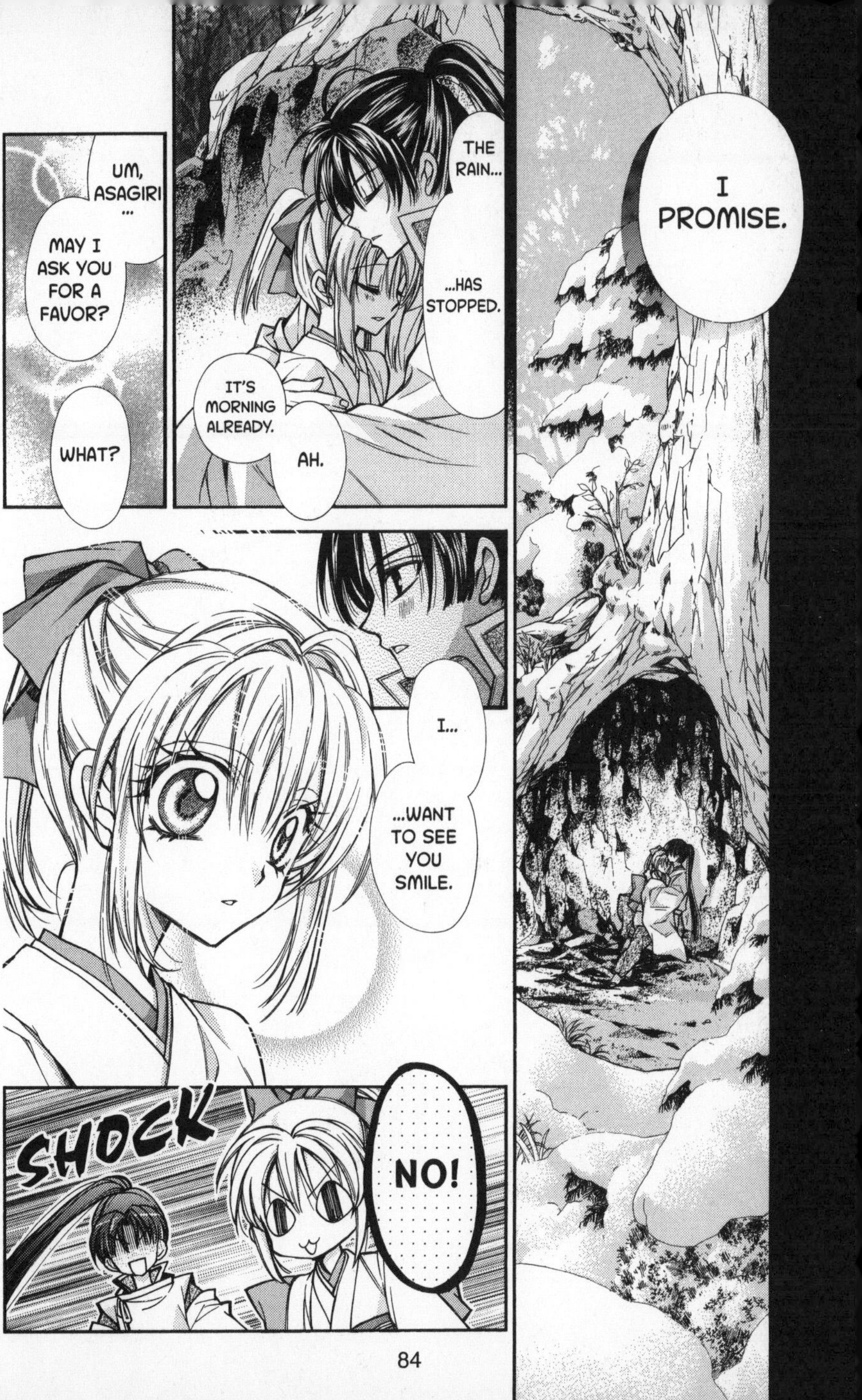
I PROMISE.
THE RAIN...
...HAS STOPPED.
IT'S MORNING ALREADY.
AH.
UM, ASAGIRI...
MAY I ASK YOU FOR A FAVOR?
WHAT?
I...
...WANT TO SEE YOU SMILE.
NO!
SHOCK

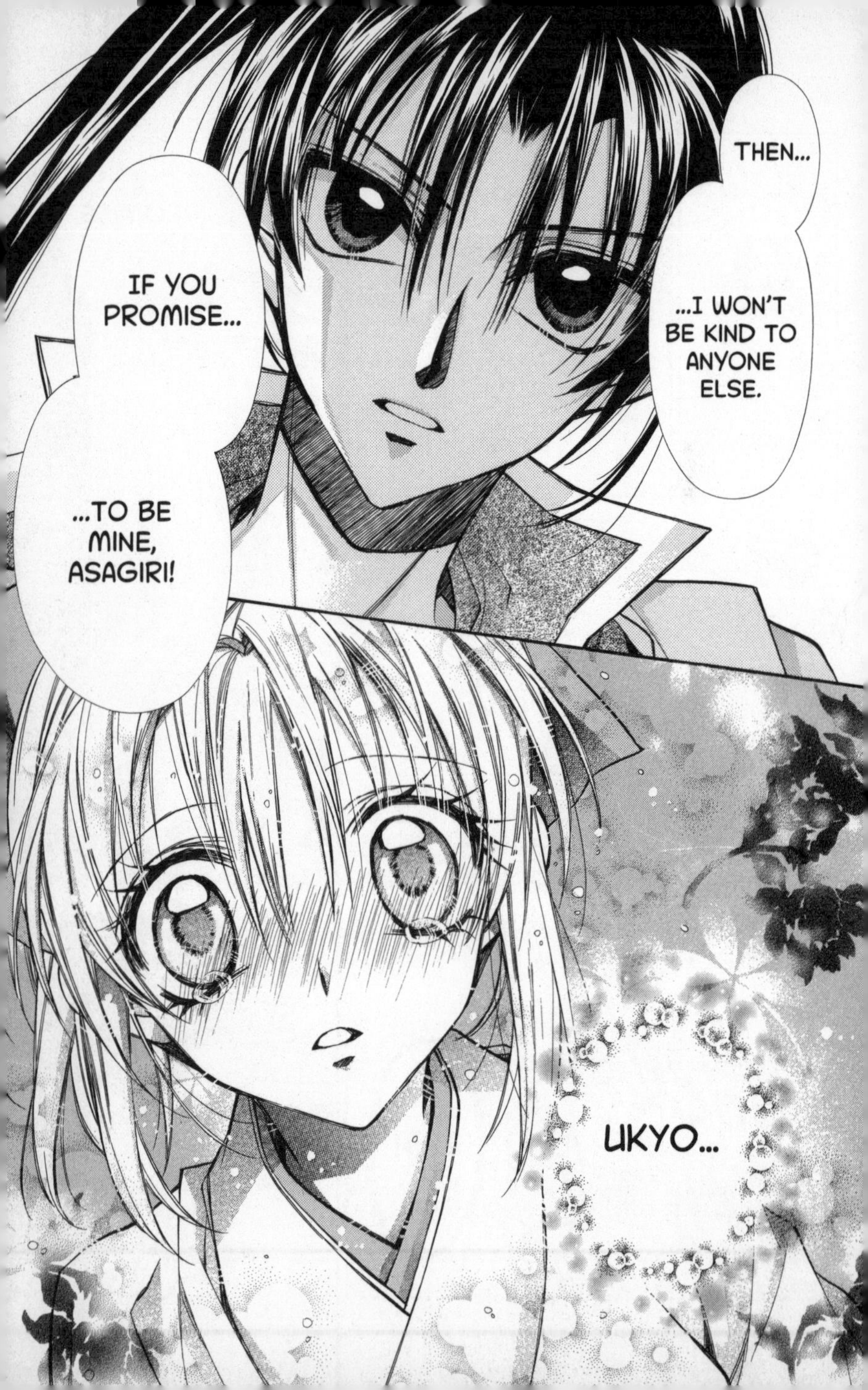
THEN...
...I WON'T BE KIND TO ANYONE ELSE.
IF YOU PROMISE...
...TO BE MINE, ASAGIRI!
UKYO...

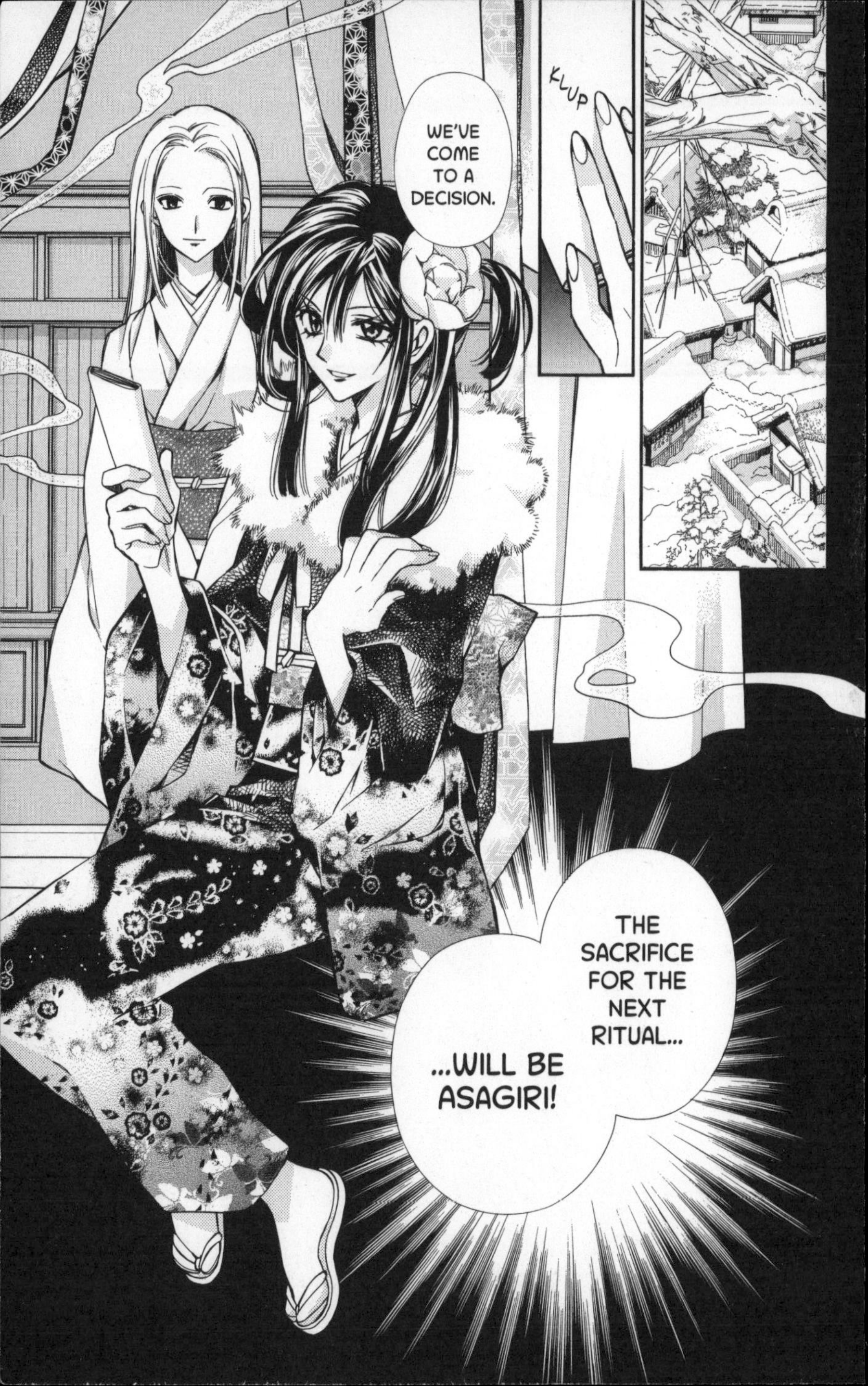
KLUP
WE'VE COME TO A DECISION.
THE SACRIFICE FOR THE NEXT RITUAL...
...WILL BE ASAGIRI!

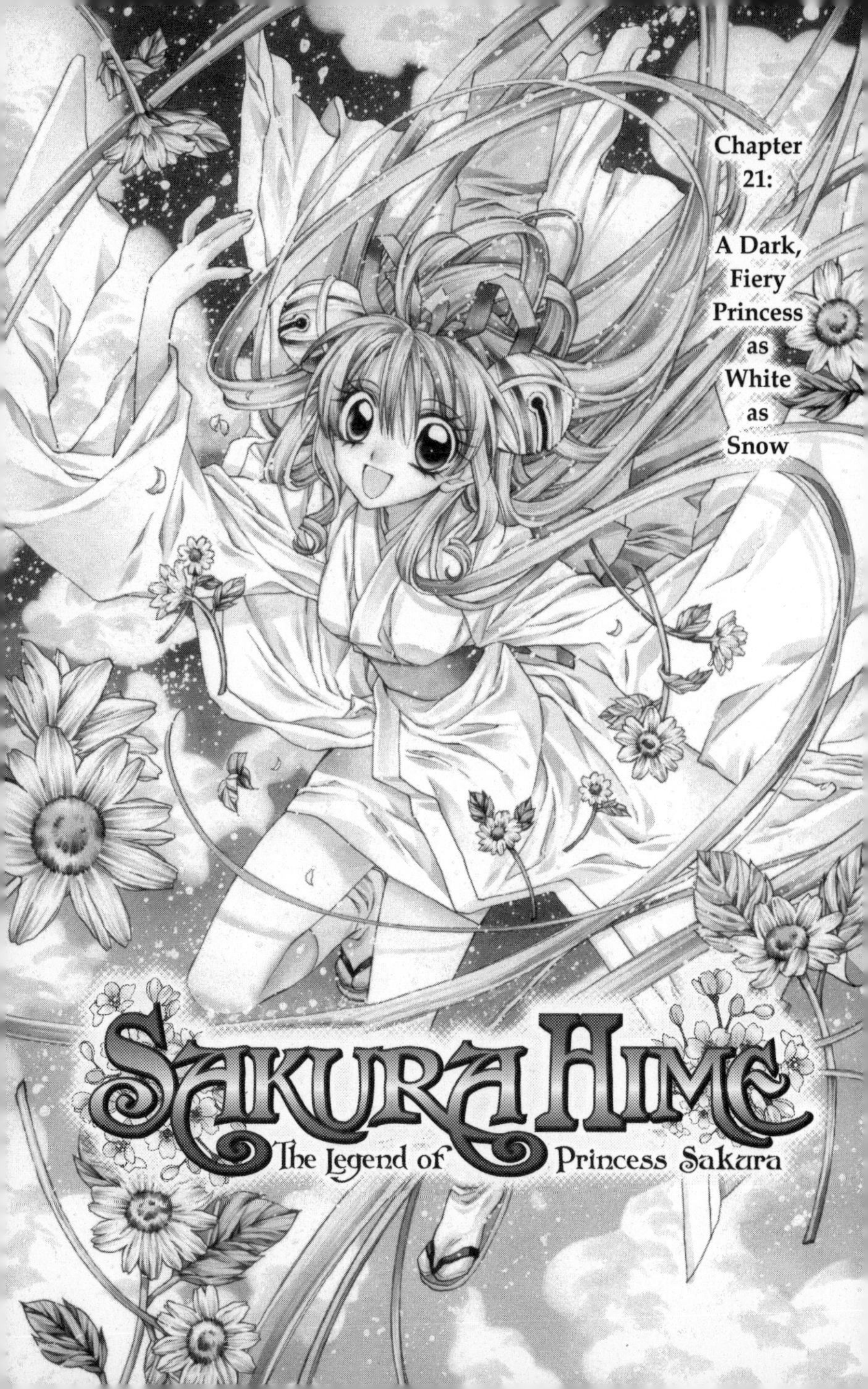
Chapter 21:
A Dark, Fiery Princess as White as Snow
SAKURA HIME
The Legend of Princess Sakura

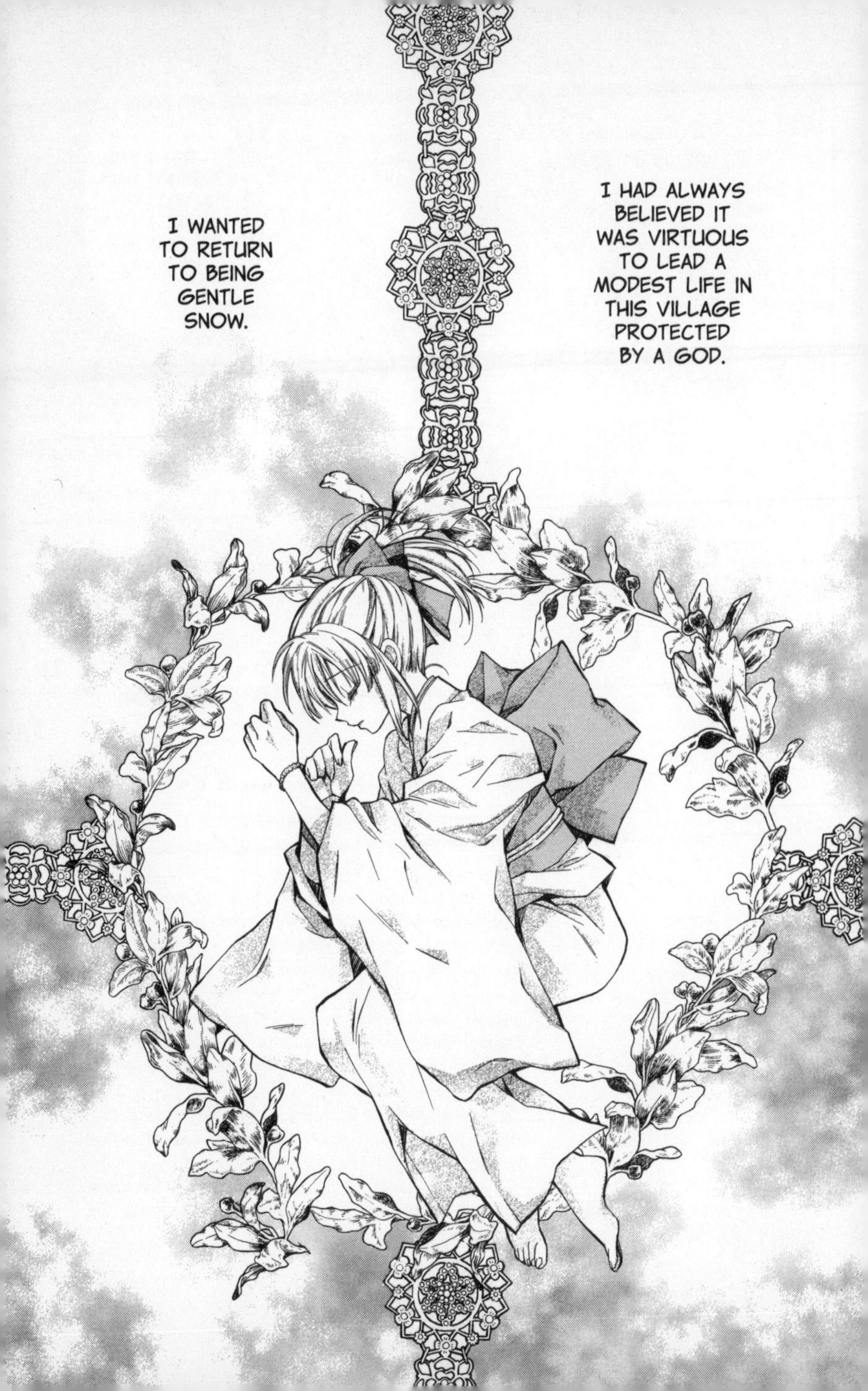
I HAD ALWAYS BELIEVED IT WAS VIRTUOUS TO LEAD A MODEST LIFE IN THIS VILLAGE PROTECTED BY A GOD.
I WANTED TO RETURN TO BEING GENTLE SNOW.

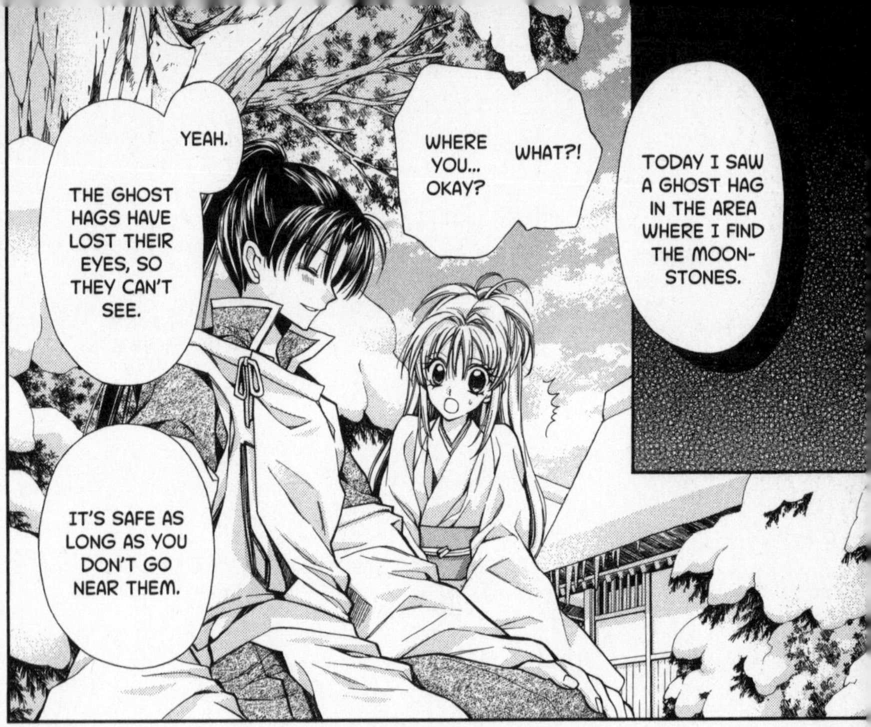
TODAY I SAW A GHOST HAG IN THE AREA WHERE I FIND THE MOON-STONES.
WHAT?!
WHERE YOU... OKAY?
YEAH.
THE GHOST HAGS HAVE LOST THEIR EYES, SO THEY CAN'T SEE.
IT'S SAFE AS LONG AS YOU DON'T GO NEAR THEM.

Chapter 21
You Are a Dark, Fiery Princess as White as Snow

※ I'm giving away the story. Please read this after you read the chapter.

I'm sorry for Ukyo, but since this is a matriarchal village, I wanted to write about the women. I think Asagiri is the kind of girl whose mere existence irritates other women. She's pretty, smart, kind, and a good friend to all. (And to think that Ukyo was disliked by someone like her...). Hosoyuki never had the skills to correct herself—she could only hold grudges against people—so it was a sad twist of fate... Shimoni will become the next leader of the village, so she must have given up and decided to protect the two after finding out they were in love.

I'm very satisfied how the two-page spread turned out. It represents the image inside Asagiri's heart exactly the way I imagined it.

The term "sly snow spirit" became somewhat of a fad among my assistants and we'd talk about the "sly manga artist" and "sly assistants" during our work. (laugh)

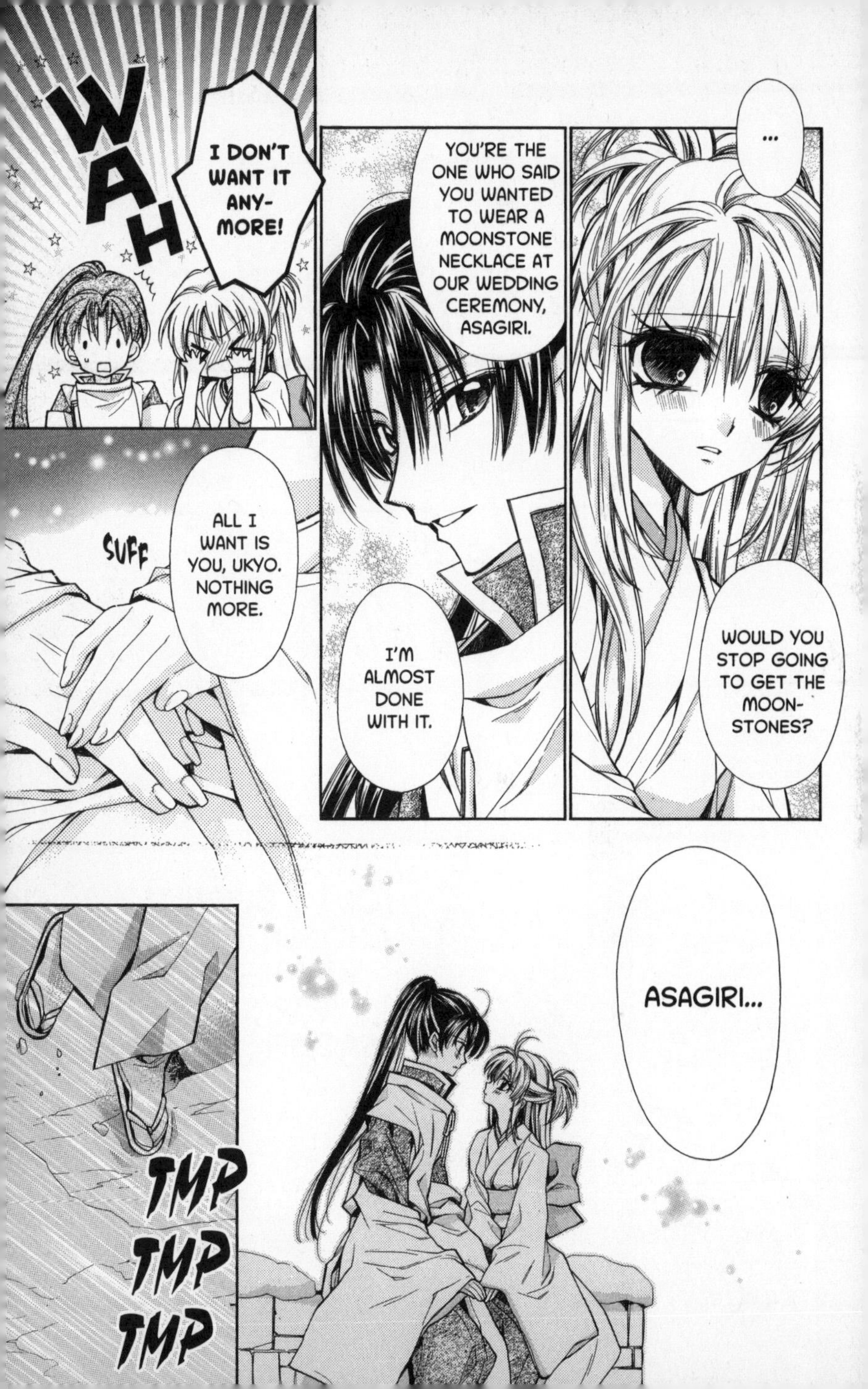
...
WOULD YOU STOP GOING TO GET THE MOON-STONES?
YOU'RE THE ONE WHO SAID YOU WANTED TO WEAR A MOONSTONE NECKLACE AT OUR WEDDING CEREMONY, ASAGIRI.
I'M ALMOST DONE WITH IT.
I DON'T WANT IT ANY-MORE!
WAH
ALL I WANT IS YOU, UKYO. NOTHING MORE.
SUFF
ASAGIRI...
TMP TMP TMP

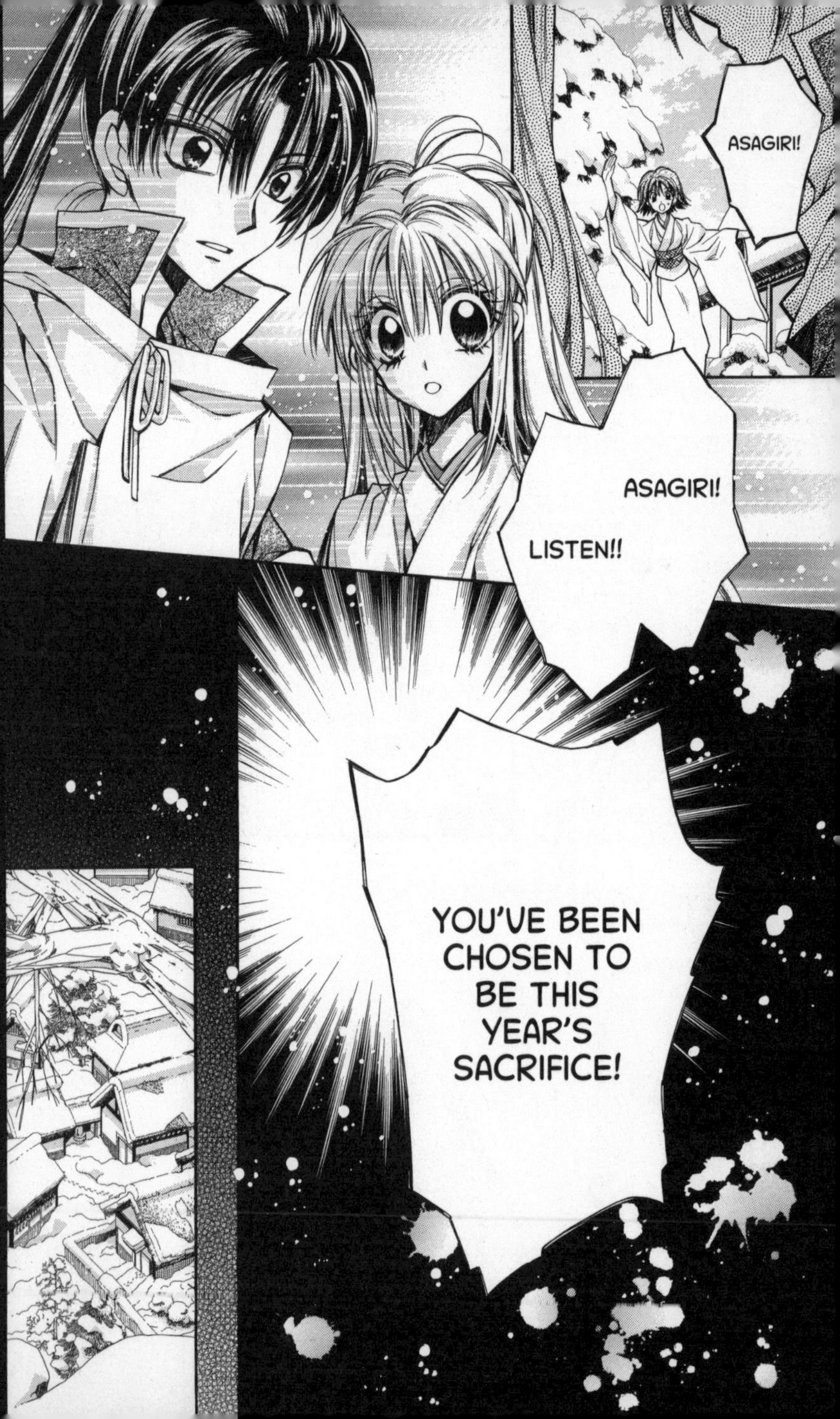
ASAGIRI!
ASAGIRI!
LISTEN!!
YOU'VE BEEN CHOSEN TO BE THIS YEAR'S SACRIFICE!

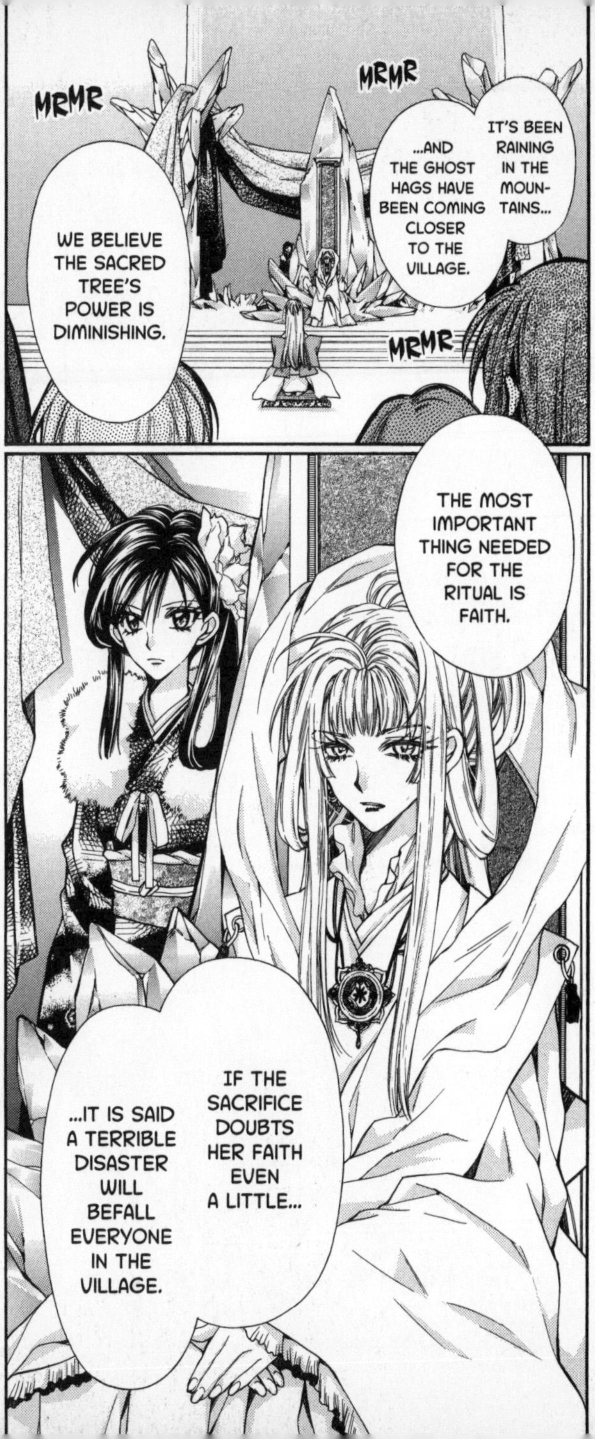
MRMR
IT'S BEEN RAINING IN THE MOUNTAINS...
...AND THE GHOST HAGS HAVE BEEN COMING CLOSER TO THE VILLAGE.
MRMR
WE BELIEVE THE SACRED TREE'S POWER IS DIMINISHING.
MRMR
THE MOST IMPORTANT THING NEEDED FOR THE RITUAL IS FAITH.
IF THE SACRIFICE DOUBTS HER FAITH EVEN A LITTLE...
...IT IS SAID A TERRIBLE DISASTER WILL BEFALL EVERYONE IN THE VILLAGE.

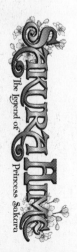

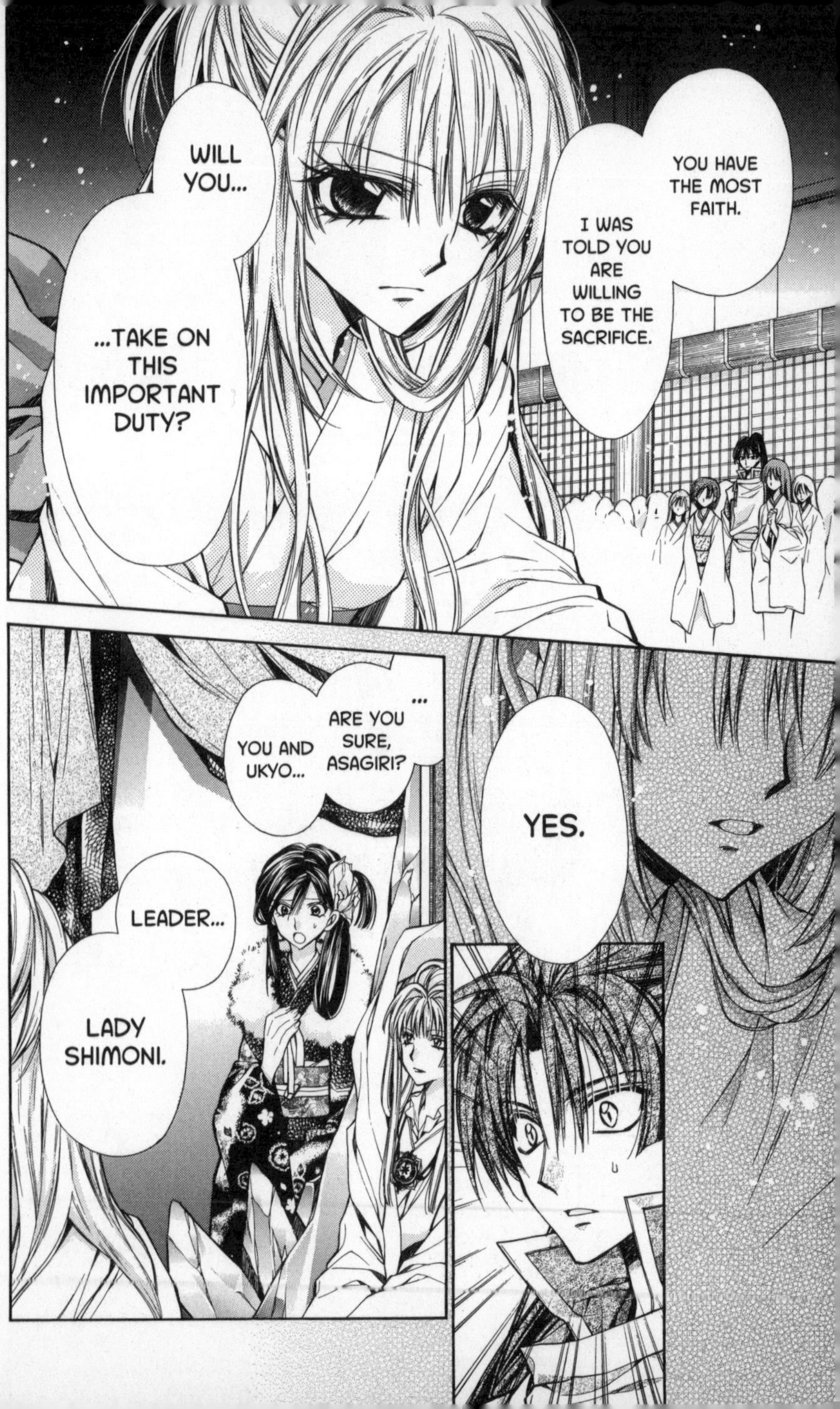
YOU HAVE THE MOST FAITH.
I WAS TOLD YOU ARE WILLING TO BE THE SACRIFICE.
WILL YOU...
...TAKE ON THIS IMPORTANT DUTY?
YES.
...
ARE YOU SURE, ASAGIRI?
YOU AND UKYO...
LEADER...
LADY SHIMONI.

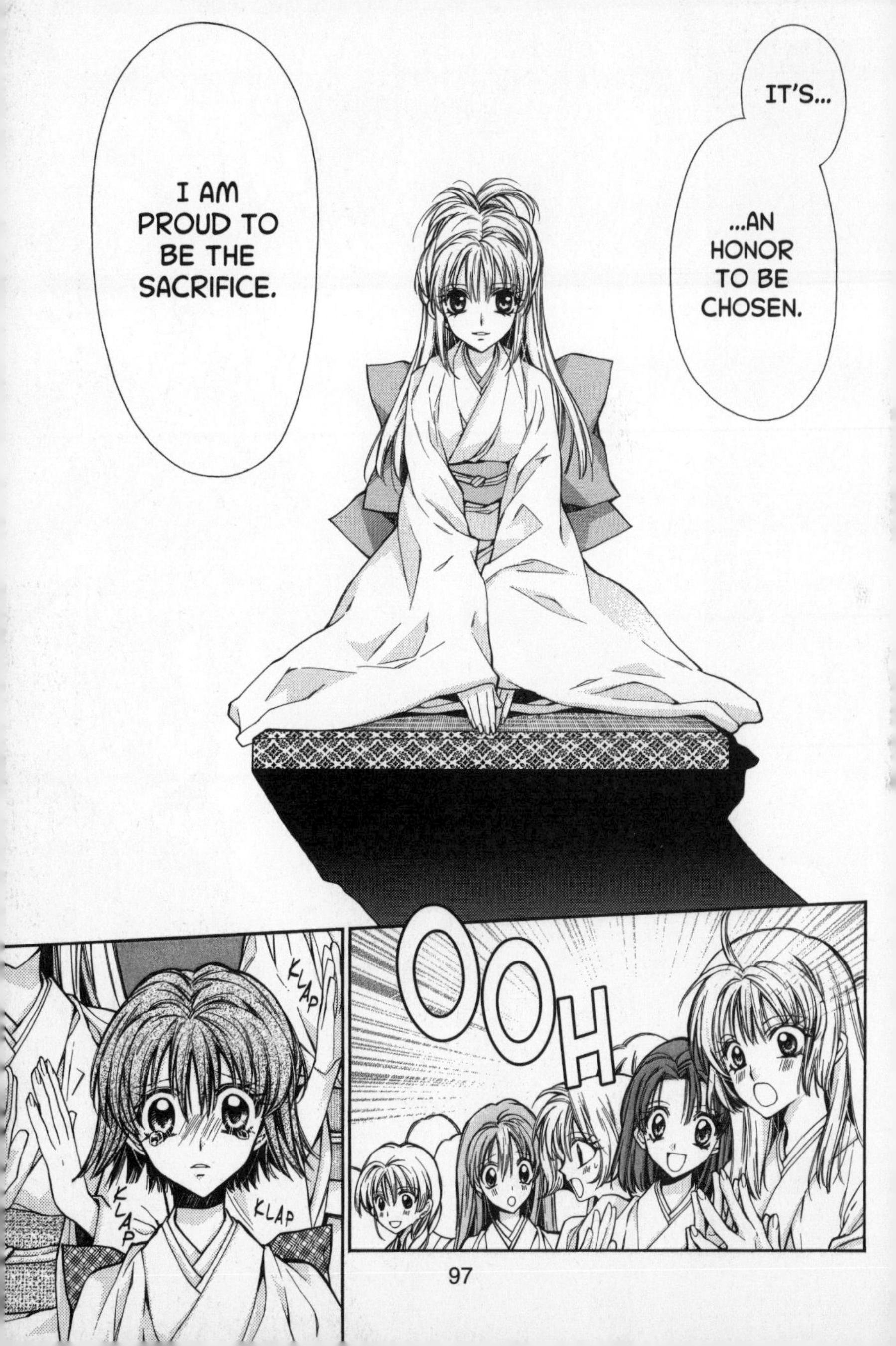
IT'S...
...AN HONOR TO BE CHOSEN.
I AM PROUD TO BE THE SACRIFICE.
OOH
KLAP
KLAP
KLAP
KLAP

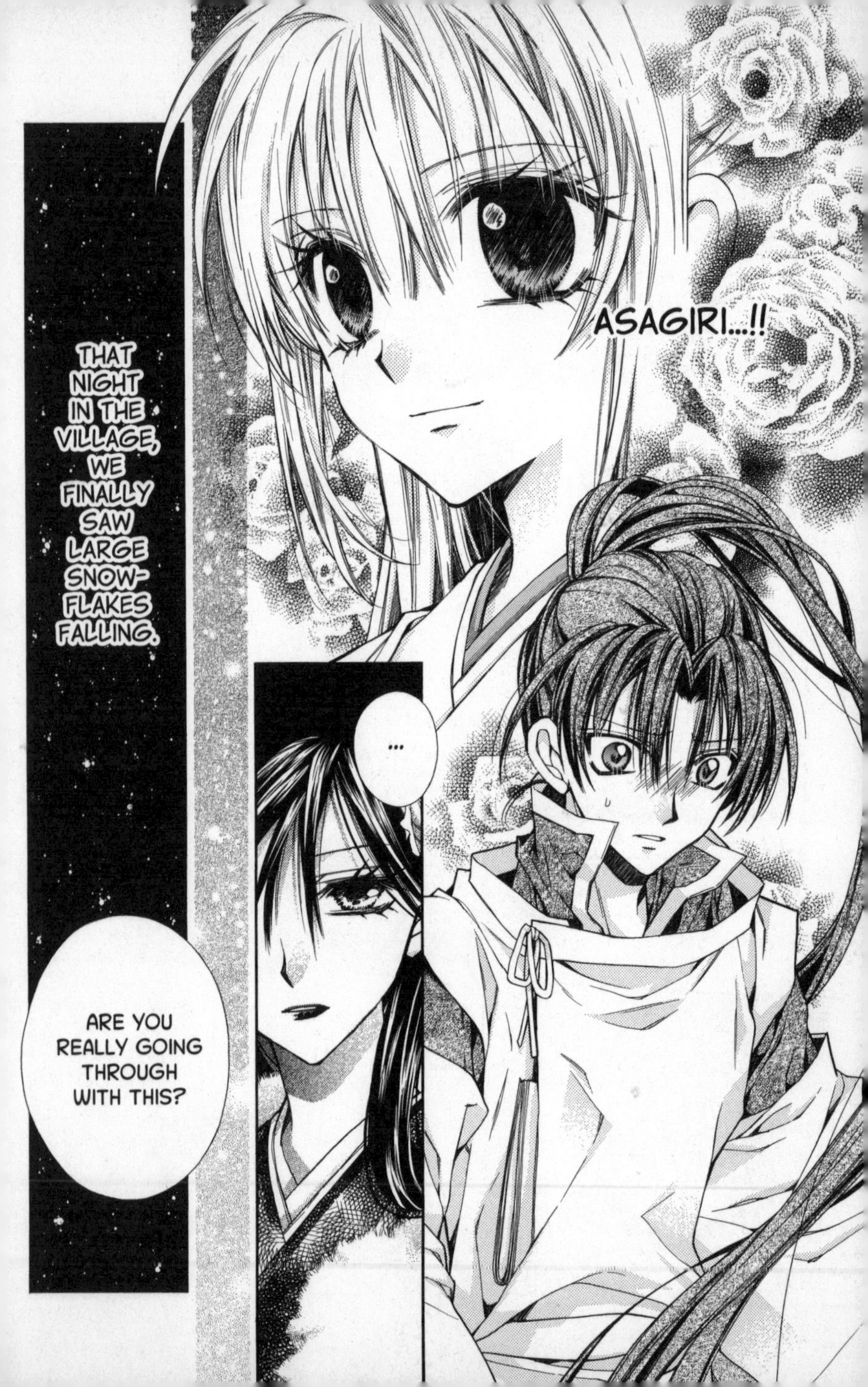
ASAGIRI...!!
THAT NIGHT IN THE VILLAGE, WE FINALLY SAW LARGE SNOW-FLAKES FALLING.
...
ARE YOU REALLY GOING THROUGH WITH THIS?

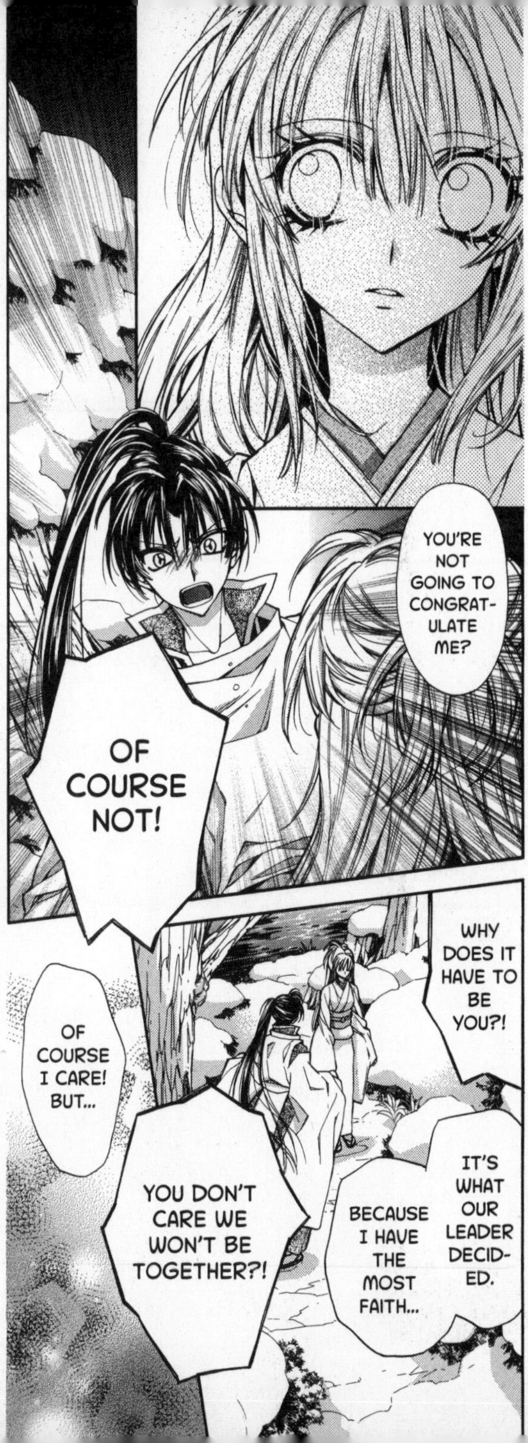
YOU'RE NOT GOING TO CONGRAT-ULATE ME?
OF COURSE NOT!
WHY DOES IT HAVE TO BE YOU?!
IT'S WHAT OUR LEADER DECID-ED.
BECAUSE I HAVE THE MOST FAITH...
YOU DON'T CARE WE WON'T BE TOGETHER?!
OF COURSE I CARE! BUT...

ARINA TANEMURA'S PENCHI DE SHAKIN☆

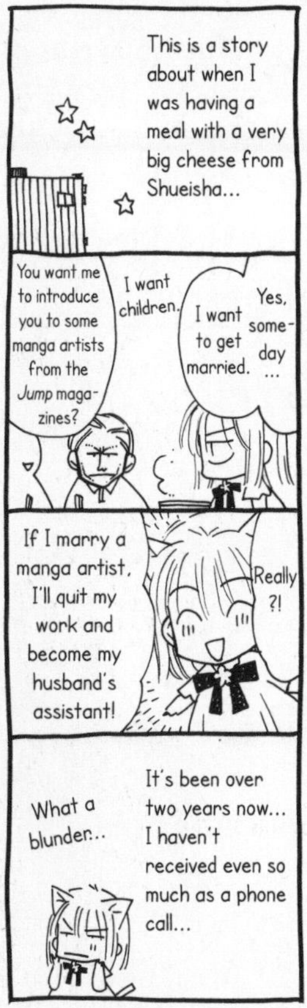
This is a story about when I was having a meal with a very big cheese from Shueisha...
Yes, some-day...
I want to get married.
I want children.
You want me to introduce you to some manga artists from the *Jump* maga-zines?
If I marry a manga artist, I'll quit my work and become my husband's assistant!
Really?!
It's been over two years now... I haven't received even so much as a phone call...
What a blunder...

I shouldn't have told him I'd quit my work... (laugh)

I'll probably never quit anyway. (laugh)

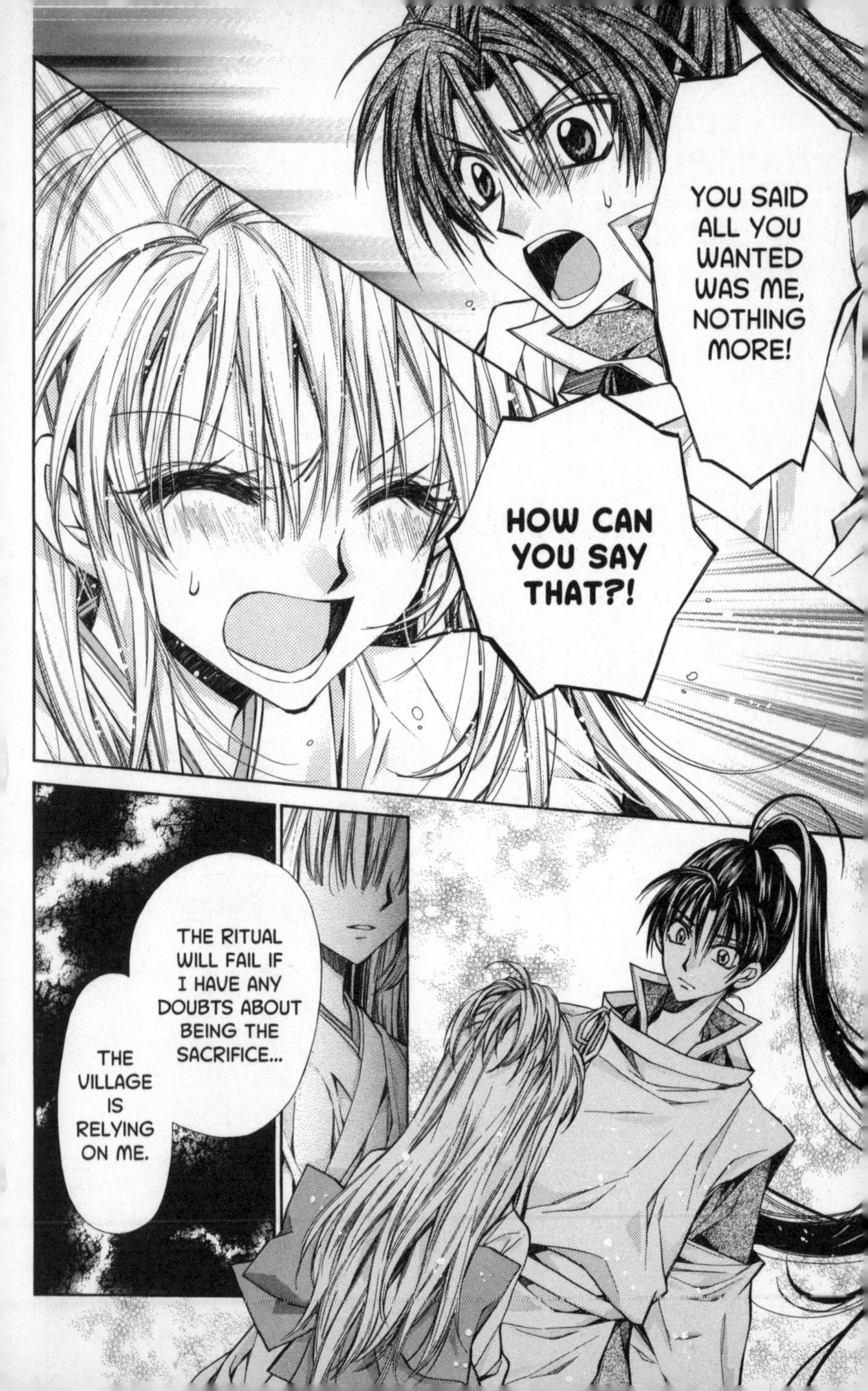
YOU SAID ALL YOU WANTED WAS ME, NOTHING MORE!
HOW CAN YOU SAY THAT?!
THE RITUAL WILL FAIL IF I HAVE ANY DOUBTS ABOUT BEING THE SACRIFICE...
THE VILLAGE IS RELYING ON ME.

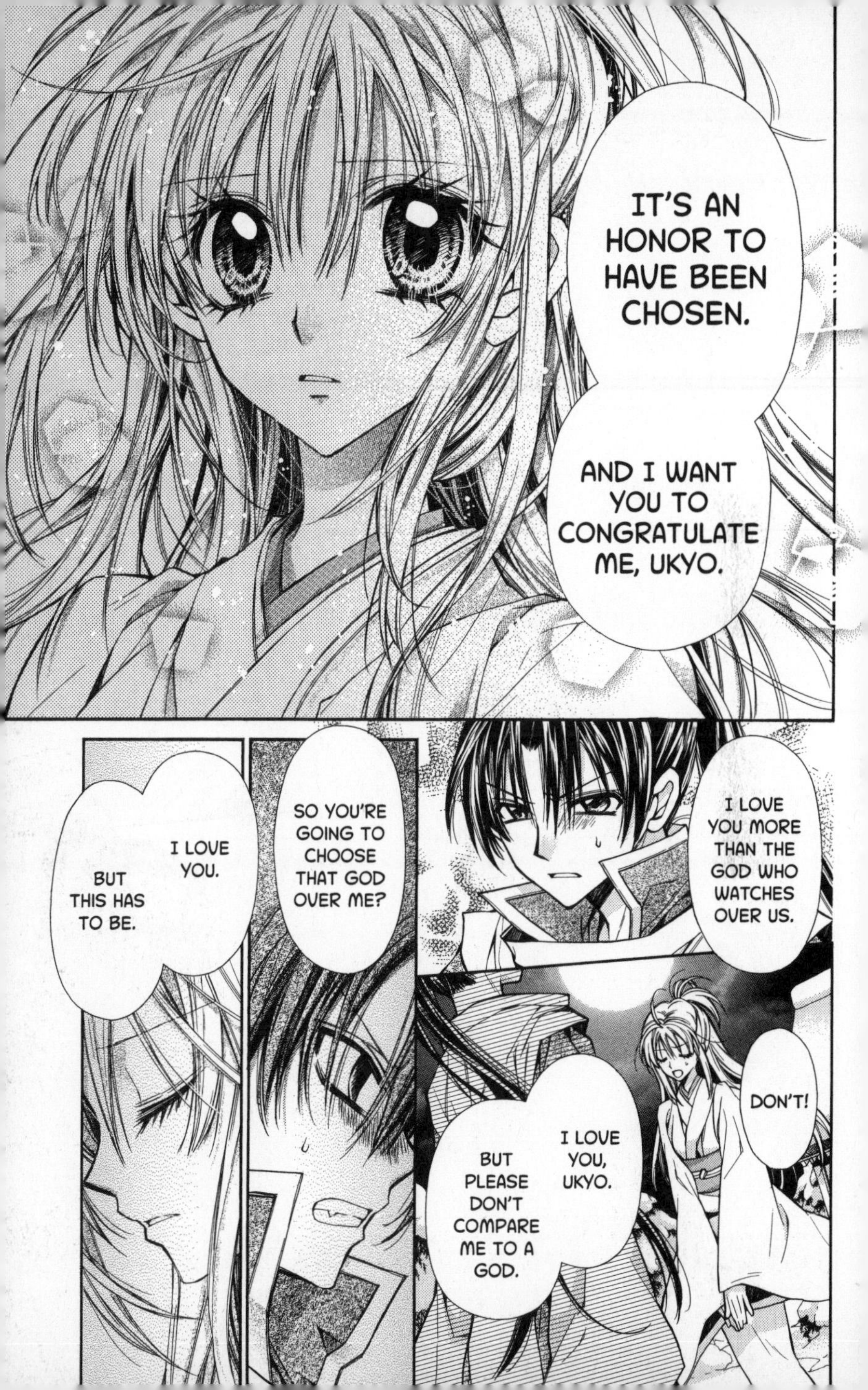
IT'S AN HONOR TO HAVE BEEN CHOSEN.
AND I WANT YOU TO CONGRATULATE ME, UKYO.
I LOVE YOU MORE THAN THE GOD WHO WATCHES OVER US.
DON'T!
I LOVE YOU, UKYO.
BUT PLEASE DON'T COMPARE ME TO A GOD.
SO YOU'RE GOING TO CHOOSE THAT GOD OVER ME?
I LOVE YOU.
BUT THIS HAS TO BE.

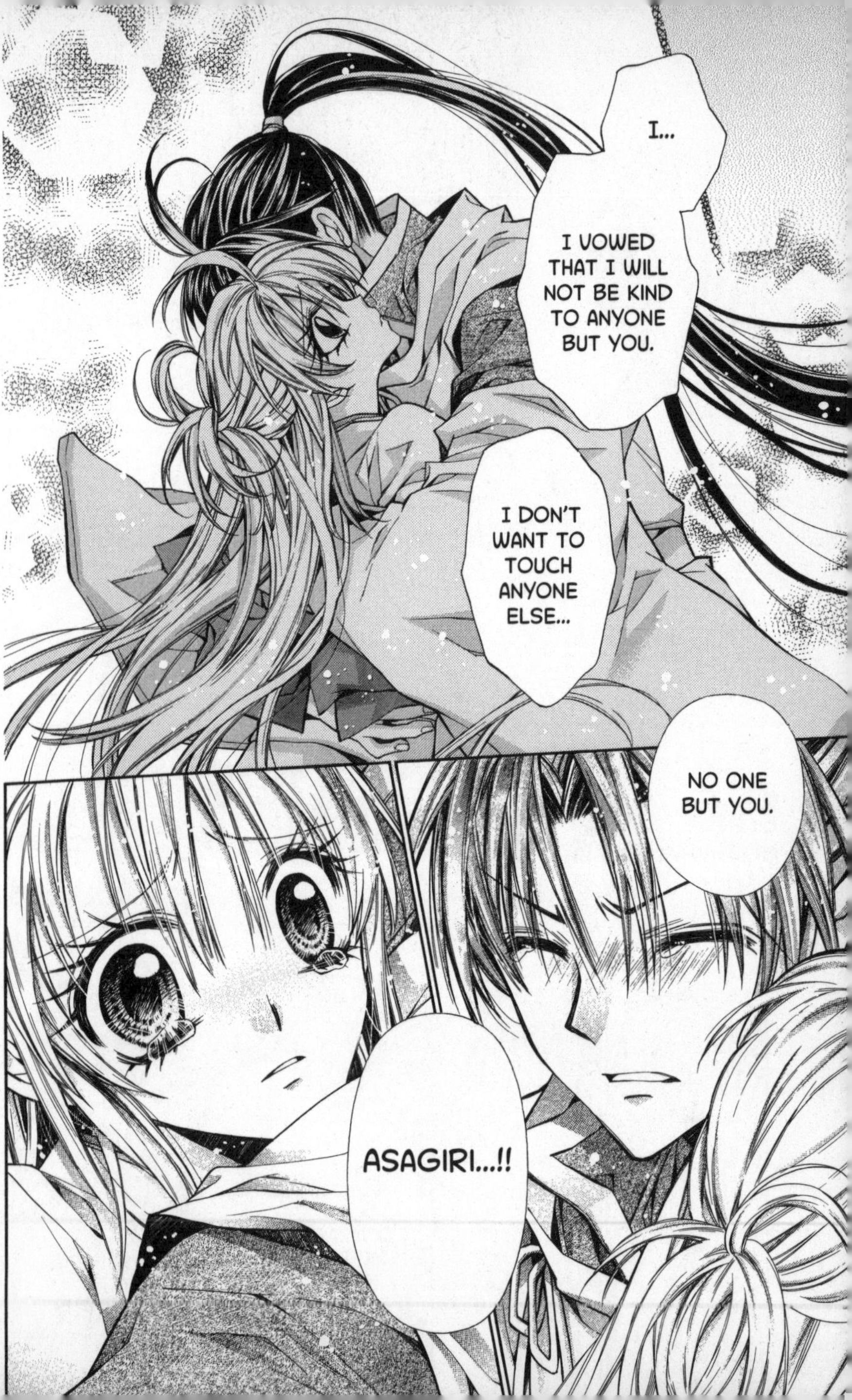
I...
I VOWED THAT I WILL NOT BE KIND TO ANYONE BUT YOU.
I DON'T WANT TO TOUCH ANYONE ELSE...
NO ONE BUT YOU.
ASAGIRI...!!

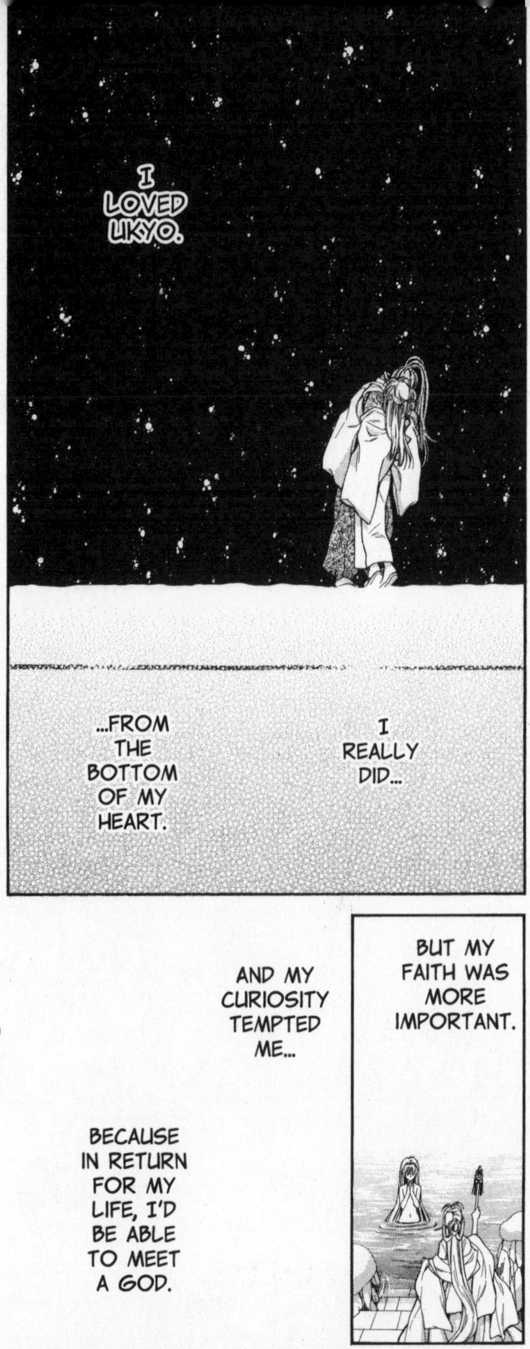
I LOVED UKYO.
I REALLY DID...
...FROM THE BOTTOM OF MY HEART.
BUT MY FAITH WAS MORE IMPORTANT.
AND MY CURIOSITY TEMPTED ME...
BECAUSE IN RETURN FOR MY LIFE, I'D BE ABLE TO MEET A GOD.

GOODBYE

I'm challenging myself to work on various kinds of new stuff.
I'll announce it on my blog or on twitter when the time is right.

Blog ↓
http://rikukai.arina.lolipop.jp/

Twitter ↓
@arinacchi

✿ Special Thanks ✿

✿ Nakame
✿ Miichi
✿ Kawanishi-san
✿ Yamada-san
✿ Kyomoto-san
✿ Mari
✿ Nami-san
✿ Momoko-chan
✿ Sakakura-san
✿ Ikurun
✿ Hina-chan
✿ Kato-san
✿ Konako
✿ Yukimura-san
✿ Momo-san
✿ Kawamura-san

Ribon Editorial Department, Shueisha
Ammonite, Inc.

Previous Editor T-san
Current Editor F-san

Kunta-san

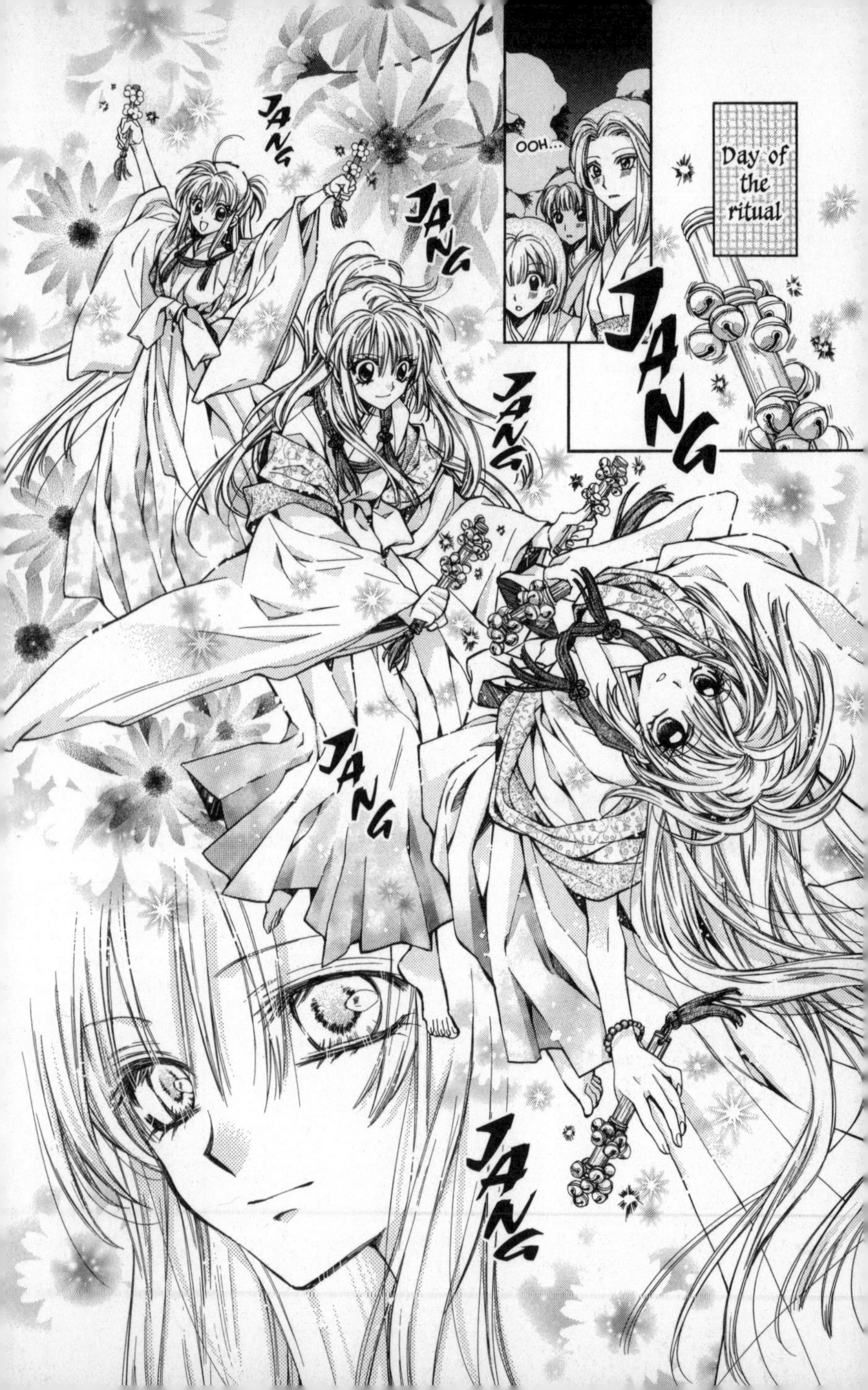
Day of the ritual
JANG
OOH...
JANG
JANG
JANG
JANG
JANG
JANG

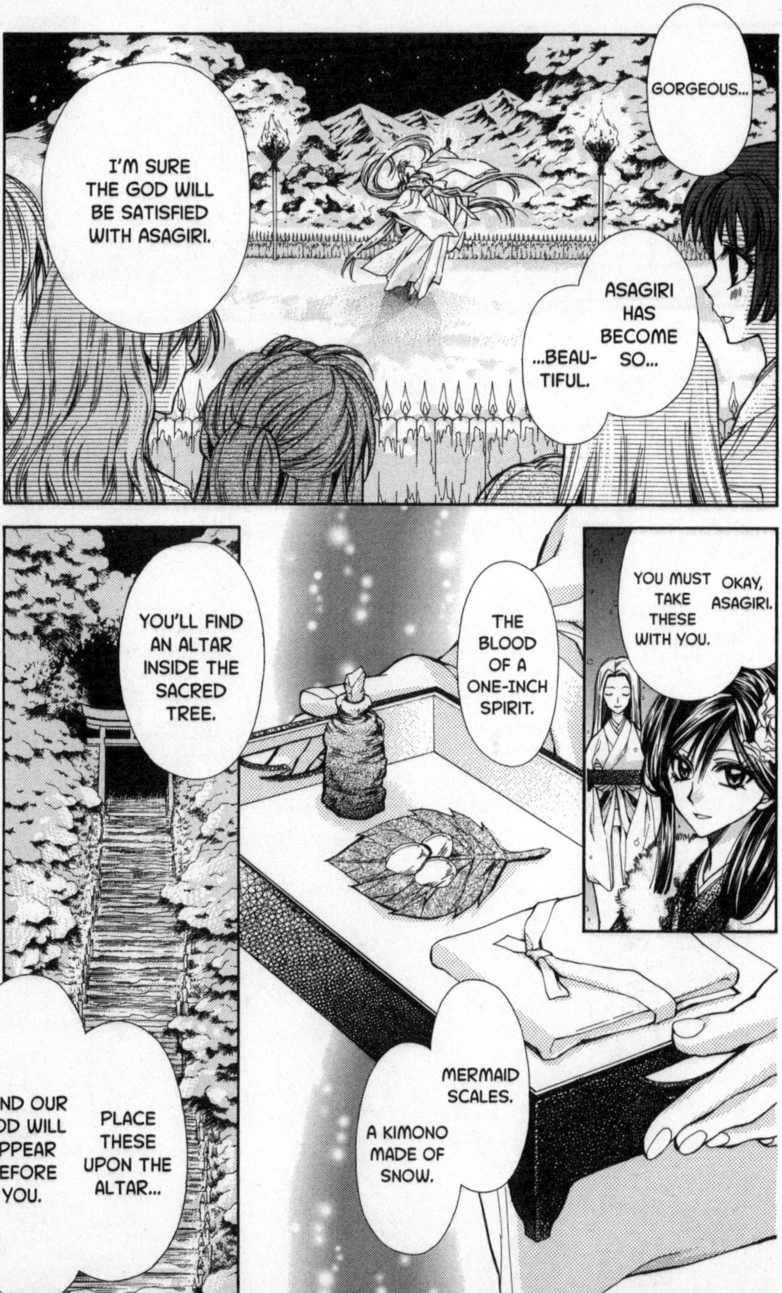
GORGEOUS...
ASAGIRI HAS BECOME SO... ...BEAU-TIFUL.
I'M SURE THE GOD WILL BE SATISFIED WITH ASAGIRI.
OKAY, ASAGIRI.
YOU MUST TAKE THESE WITH YOU.
THE BLOOD OF A ONE-INCH SPIRIT.
MERMAID SCALES.
A KIMONO MADE OF SNOW.
YOU'LL FIND AN ALTAR INSIDE THE SACRED TREE.
PLACE THESE UPON THE ALTAR...
...AND OUR GOD WILL APPEAR BEFORE YOU.

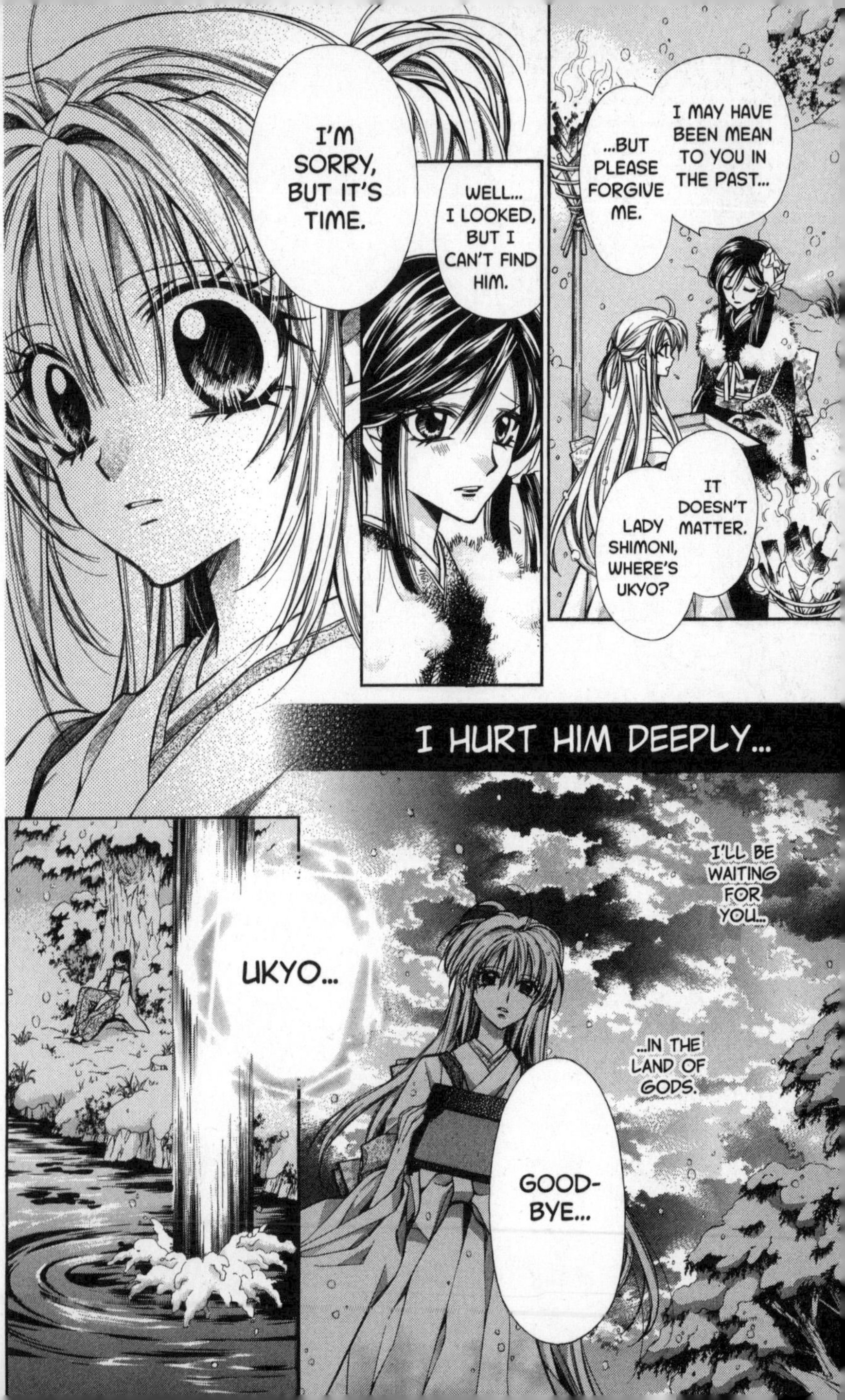

I MAY HAVE BEEN MEAN TO YOU IN THE PAST...
...BUT PLEASE FORGIVE ME.
IT DOESN'T MATTER.
LADY SHIMONI, WHERE'S UKYO?
WELL... I LOOKED, BUT I CAN'T FIND HIM.
I'M SORRY, BUT IT'S TIME.
I HURT HIM DEEPLY...
I'LL BE WAITING FOR YOU...
...IN THE LAND OF GODS.
GOOD-BYE...
UKYO...

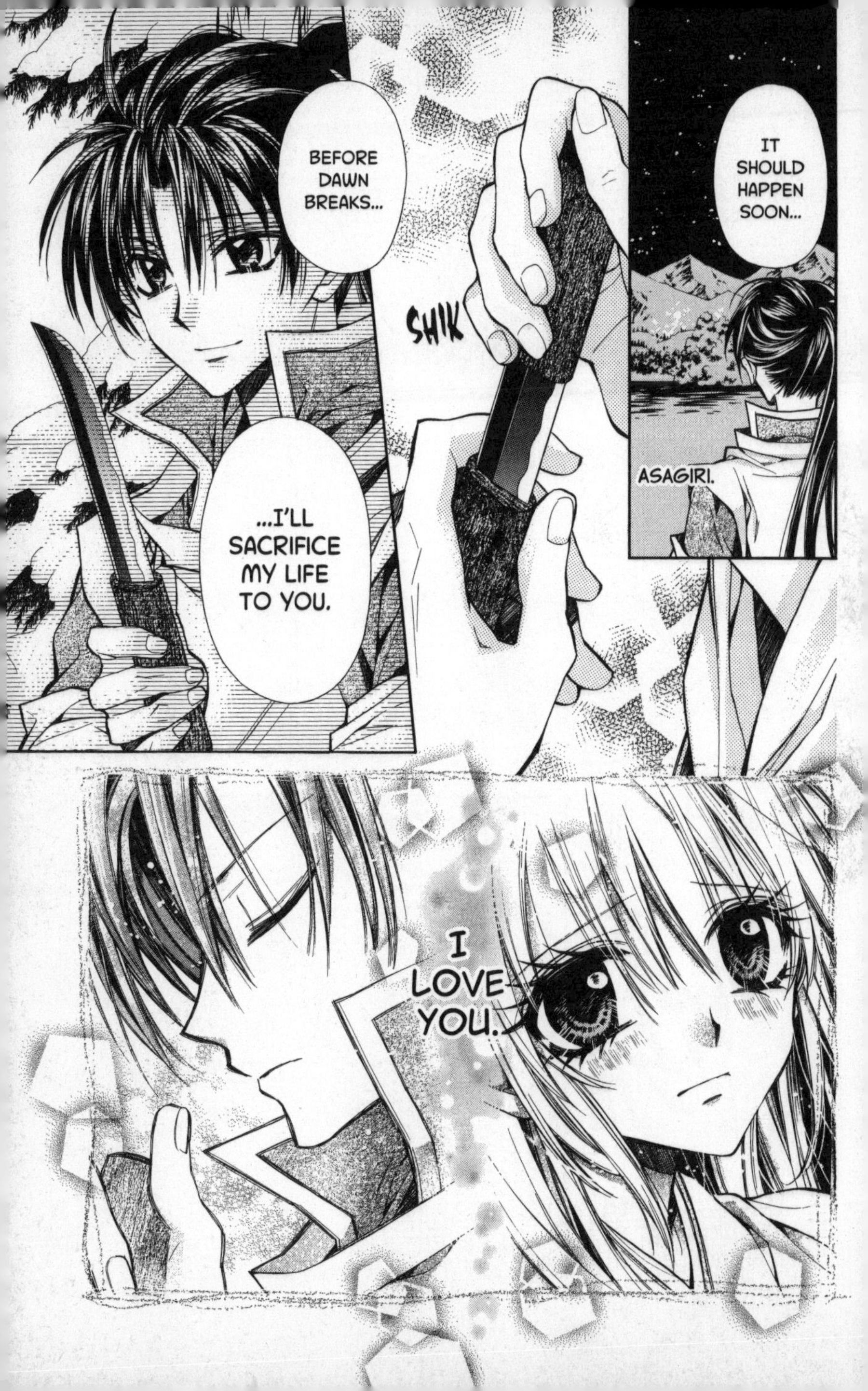
IT SHOULD HAPPEN SOON...
ASAGIRI.
SHIK
BEFORE DAWN BREAKS...
...I'LL SACRIFICE MY LIFE TO YOU.
I LOVE YOU.

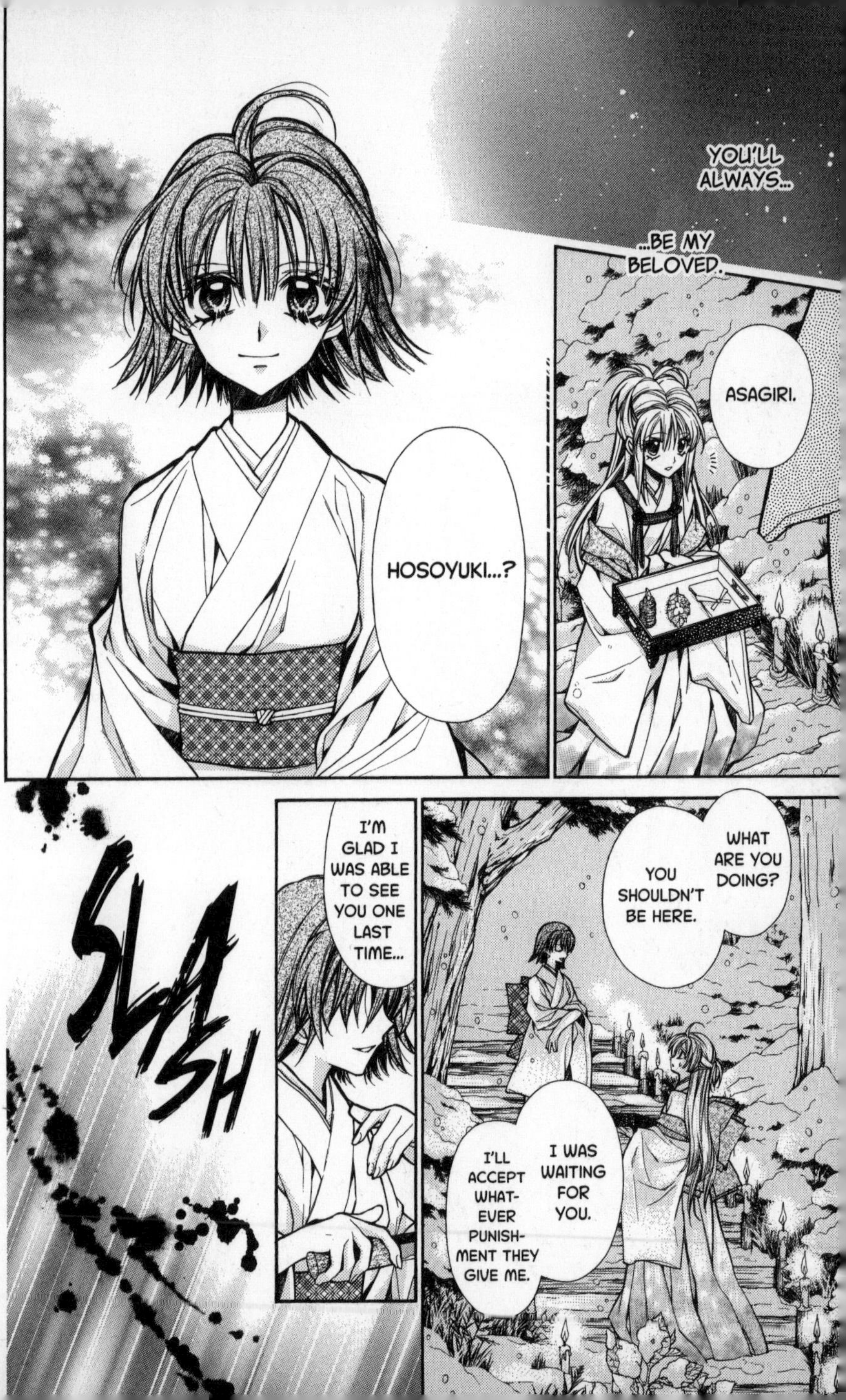
YOU'LL ALWAYS...
...BE MY BELOVED.
ASAGIRI.
HOSOYUKI...?
WHAT ARE YOU DOING?
YOU SHOULDN'T BE HERE.
I WAS WAITING FOR YOU.
I'LL ACCEPT WHAT-EVER PUNISH-MENT THEY GIVE ME.
I'M GLAD I WAS ABLE TO SEE YOU ONE LAST TIME...
SLASH

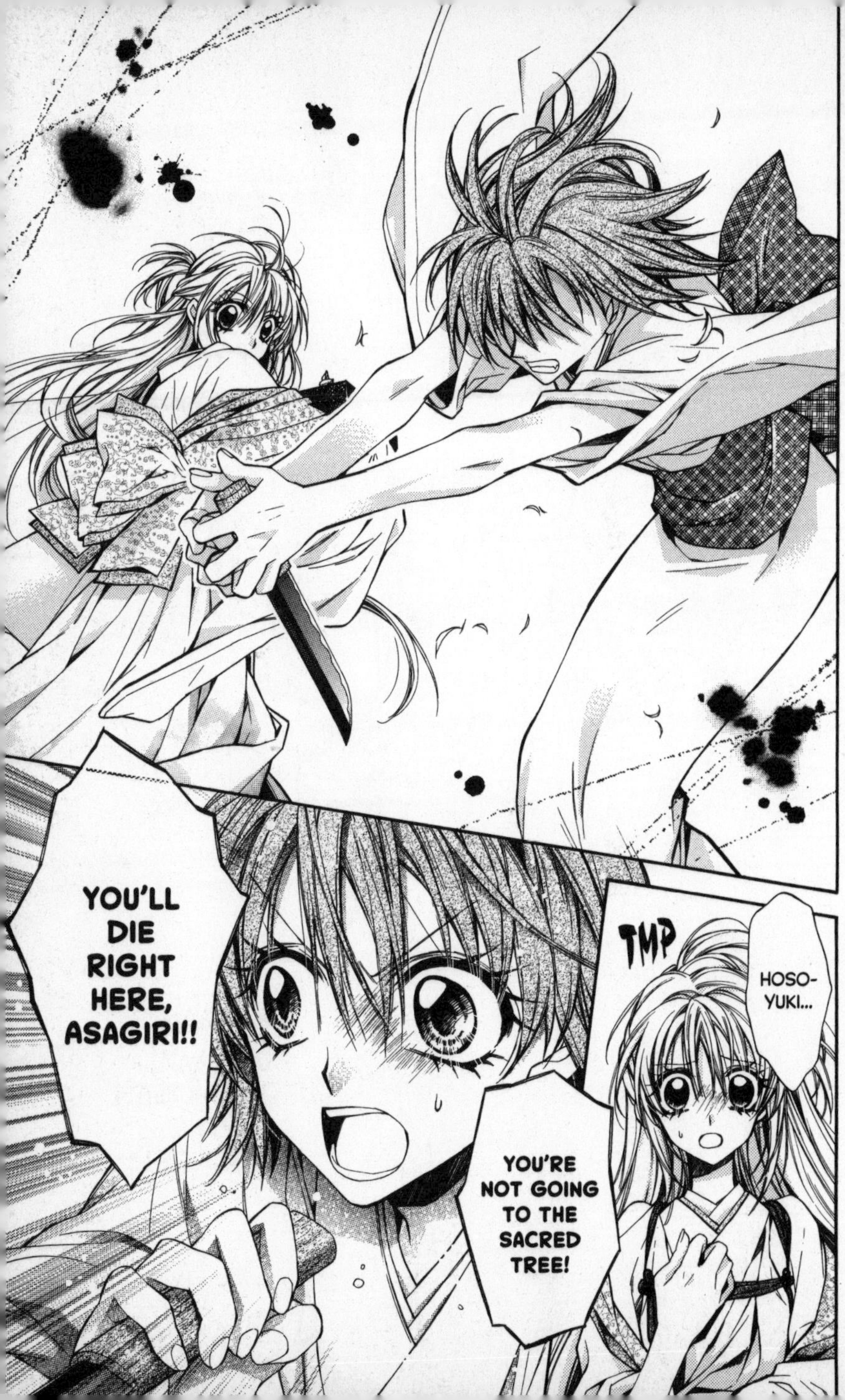
TMP
HOSO-YUKI...
YOU'RE NOT GOING TO THE SACRED TREE!
YOU'LL DIE RIGHT HERE, ASAGIRI!!

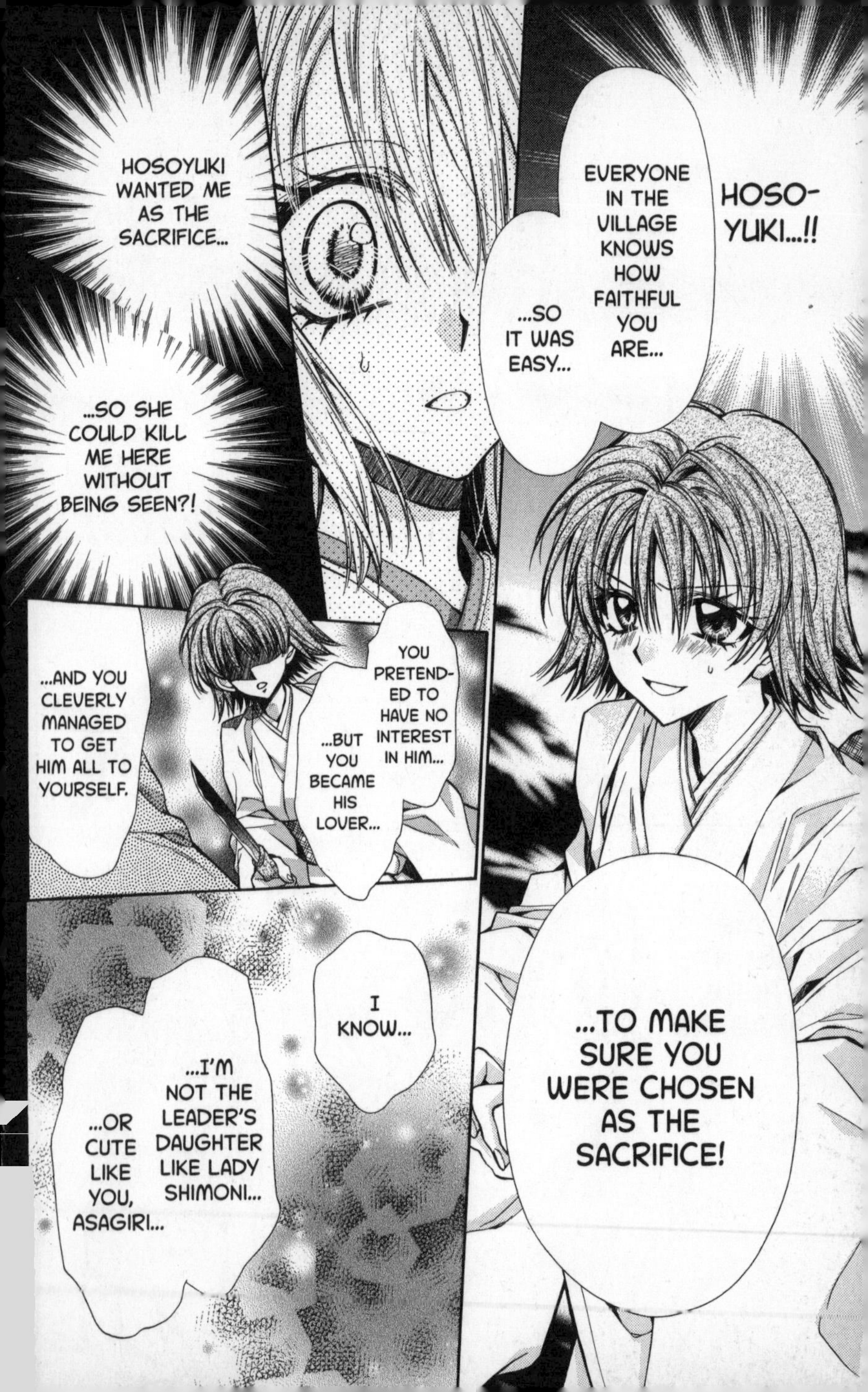
HOSO-YUKI...!!
EVERYONE IN THE VILLAGE KNOWS HOW FAITHFUL YOU ARE...
...SO IT WAS EASY...
...TO MAKE SURE YOU WERE CHOSEN AS THE SACRIFICE!
HOSOYUKI WANTED ME AS THE SACRIFICE...
...SO SHE COULD KILL ME HERE WITHOUT BEING SEEN?!
YOU PRETENDED TO HAVE NO INTEREST IN HIM...
...BUT YOU BECAME HIS LOVER...
...AND YOU CLEVERLY MANAGED TO GET HIM ALL TO YOURSELF.
I KNOW...
...I'M NOT THE LEADER'S DAUGHTER LIKE LADY SHIMONI...
...OR CUTE LIKE YOU, ASAGIRI...

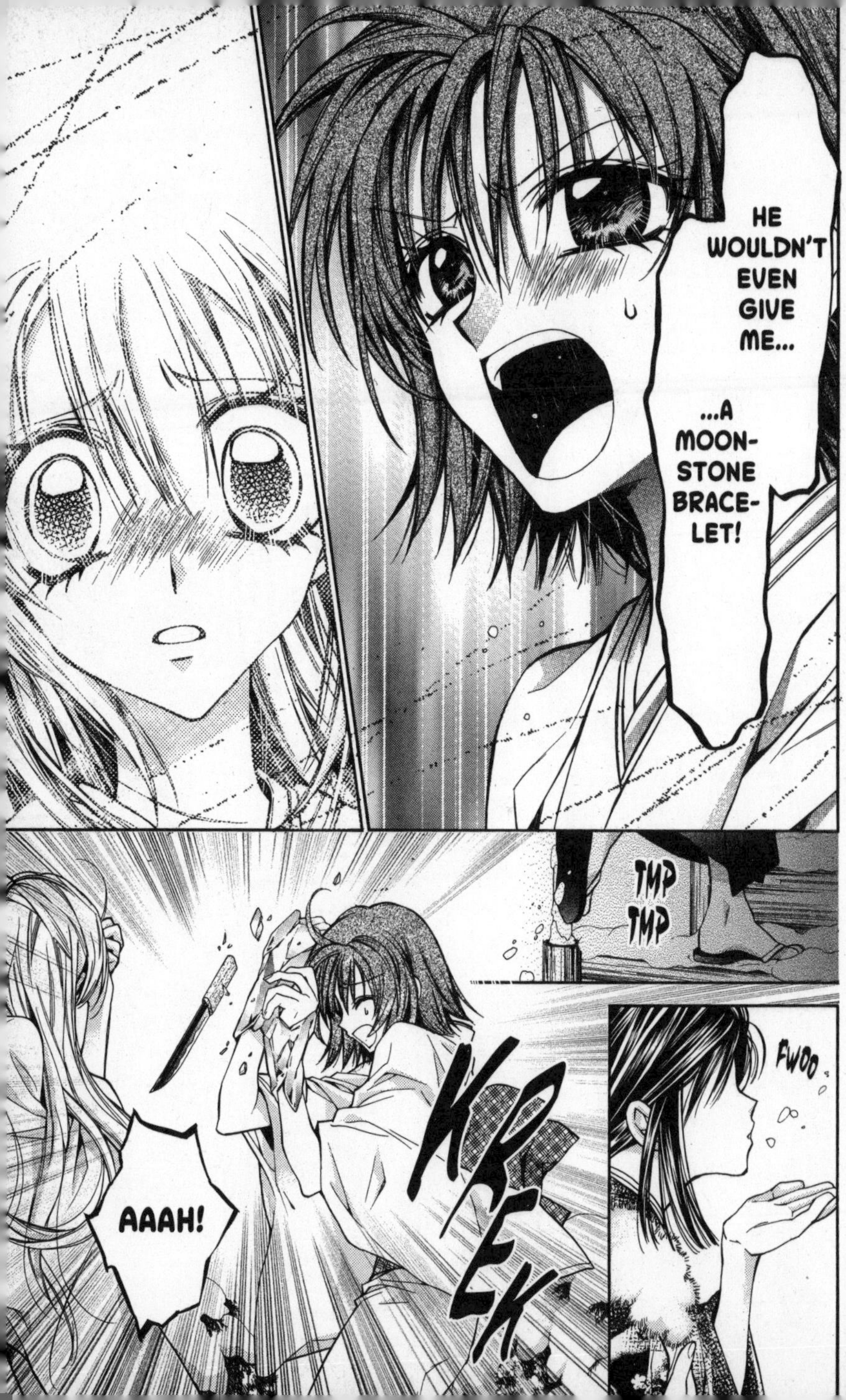
HE WOULDN'T EVEN GIVE ME...
...A MOON-STONE BRACE-LET!
TMP TMP
FWOO
KRREK
AAAH!

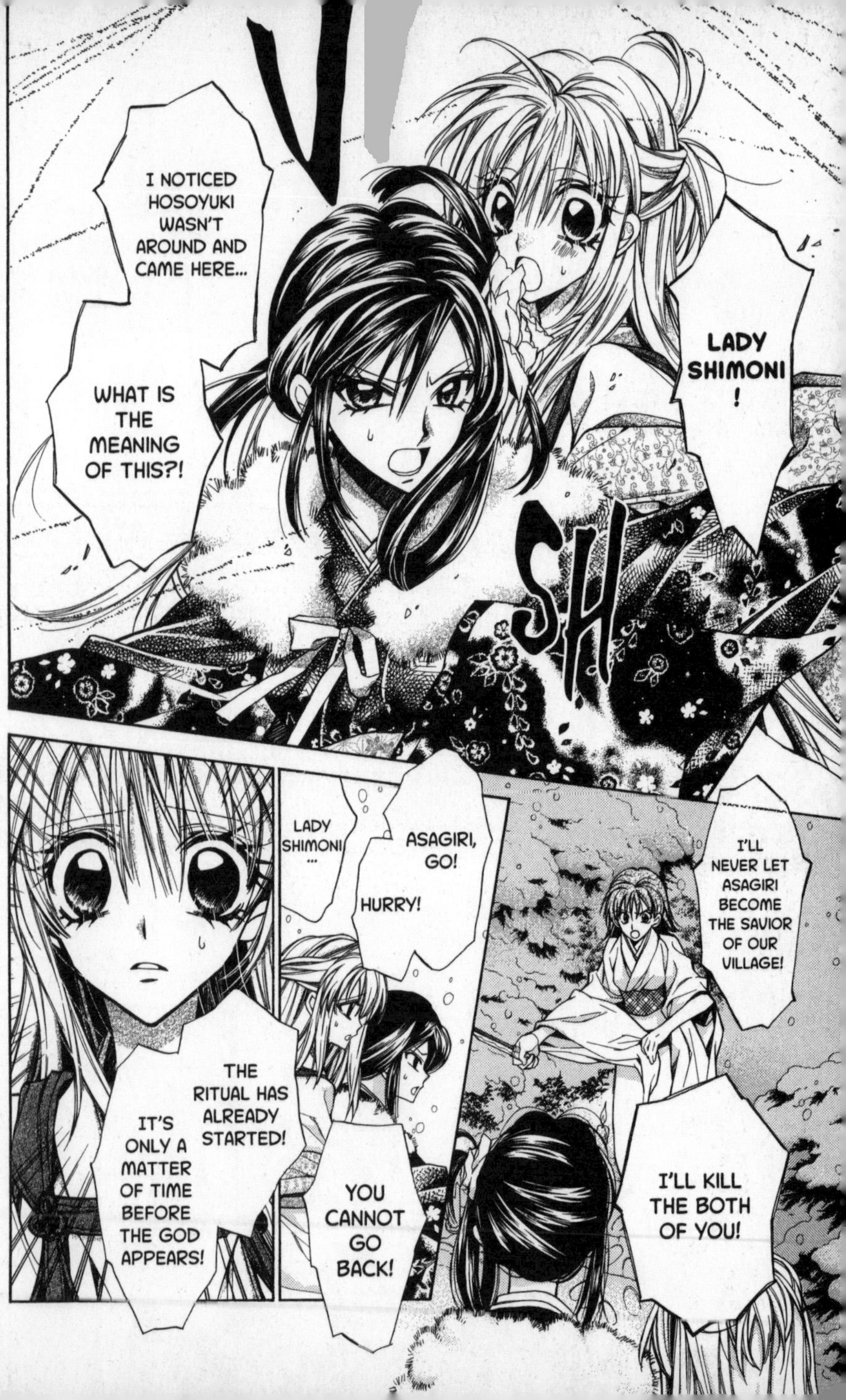
V
LADY SHIMONI !
SH
I NOTICED HOSOYUKI WASN'T AROUND AND CAME HERE...
WHAT IS THE MEANING OF THIS?!
I'LL NEVER LET ASAGIRI BECOME THE SAVIOR OF OUR VILLAGE!
I'LL KILL THE BOTH OF YOU!
ASAGIRI, GO!
HURRY!
LADY SHIMONI ...
YOU CANNOT GO BACK!
THE RITUAL HAS ALREADY STARTED!
IT'S ONLY A MATTER OF TIME BEFORE THE GOD APPEARS!

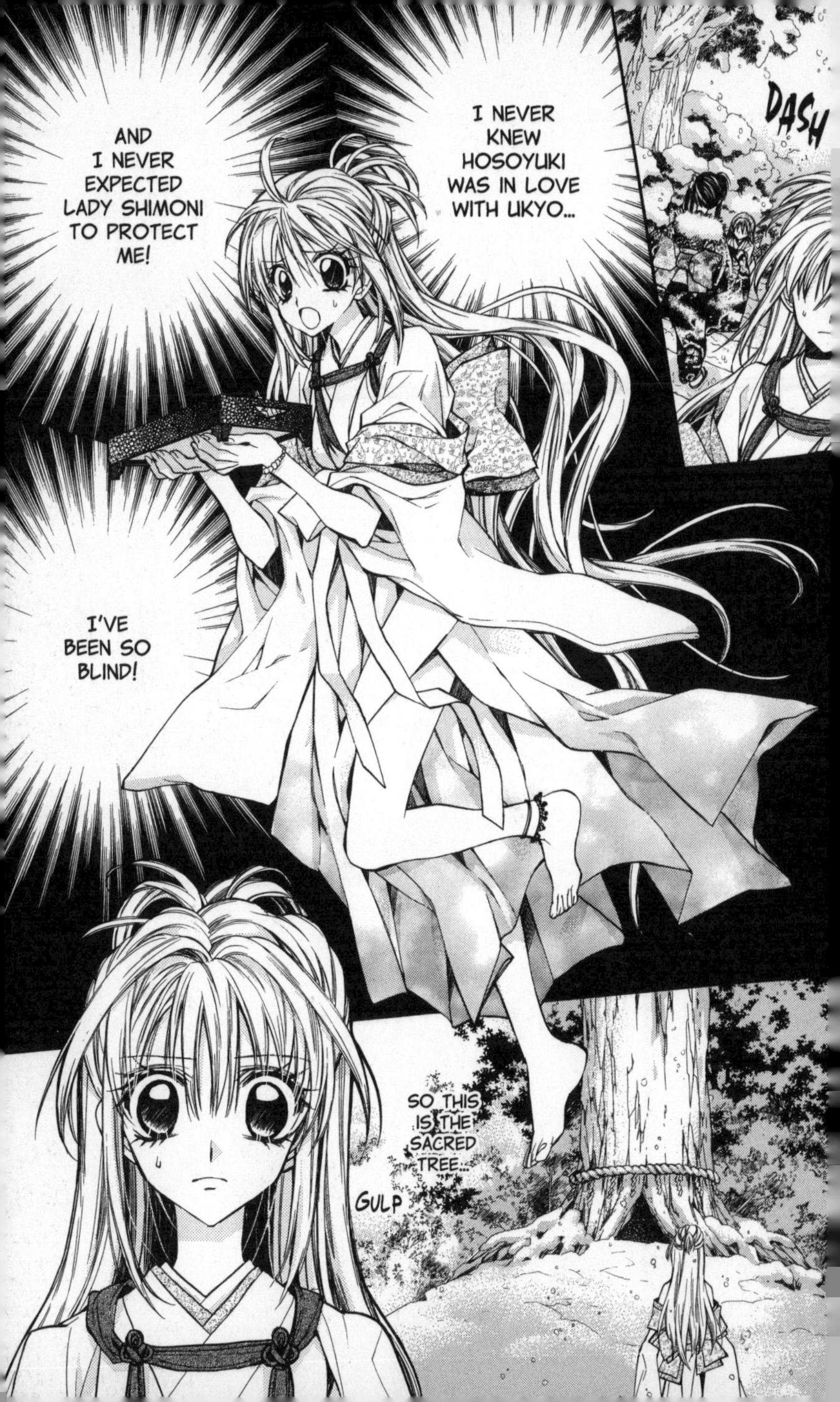
DASH
I NEVER KNEW HOSOYUKI WAS IN LOVE WITH UKYO...
AND I NEVER EXPECTED LADY SHIMONI TO PROTECT ME!
I'VE BEEN SO BLIND!
SO THIS IS THE SACRED TREE...
GULP

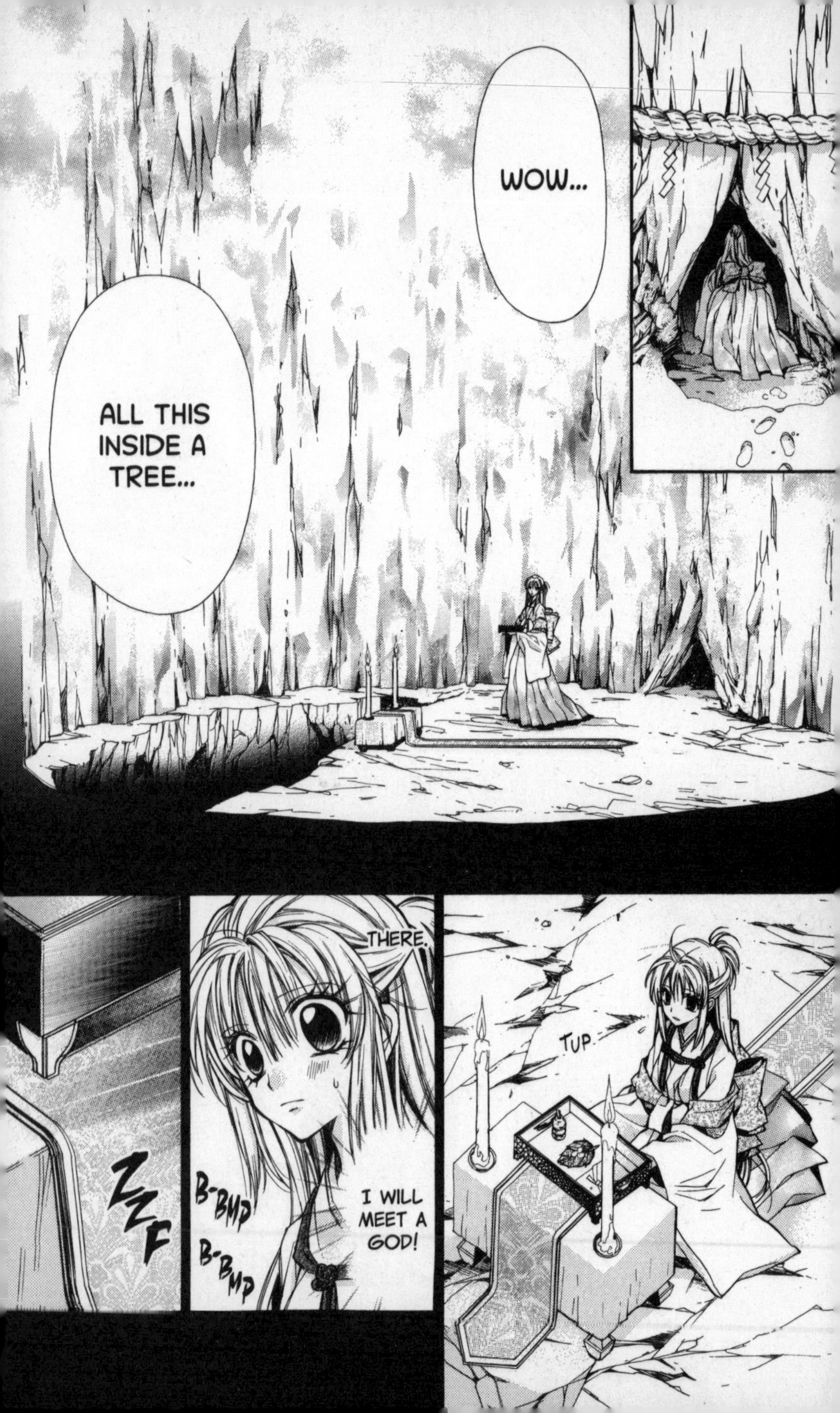
WOW...
ALL THIS INSIDE A TREE...
TUP
THERE.
I WILL MEET A GOD!
B-BMP
B-BMP
ZZF

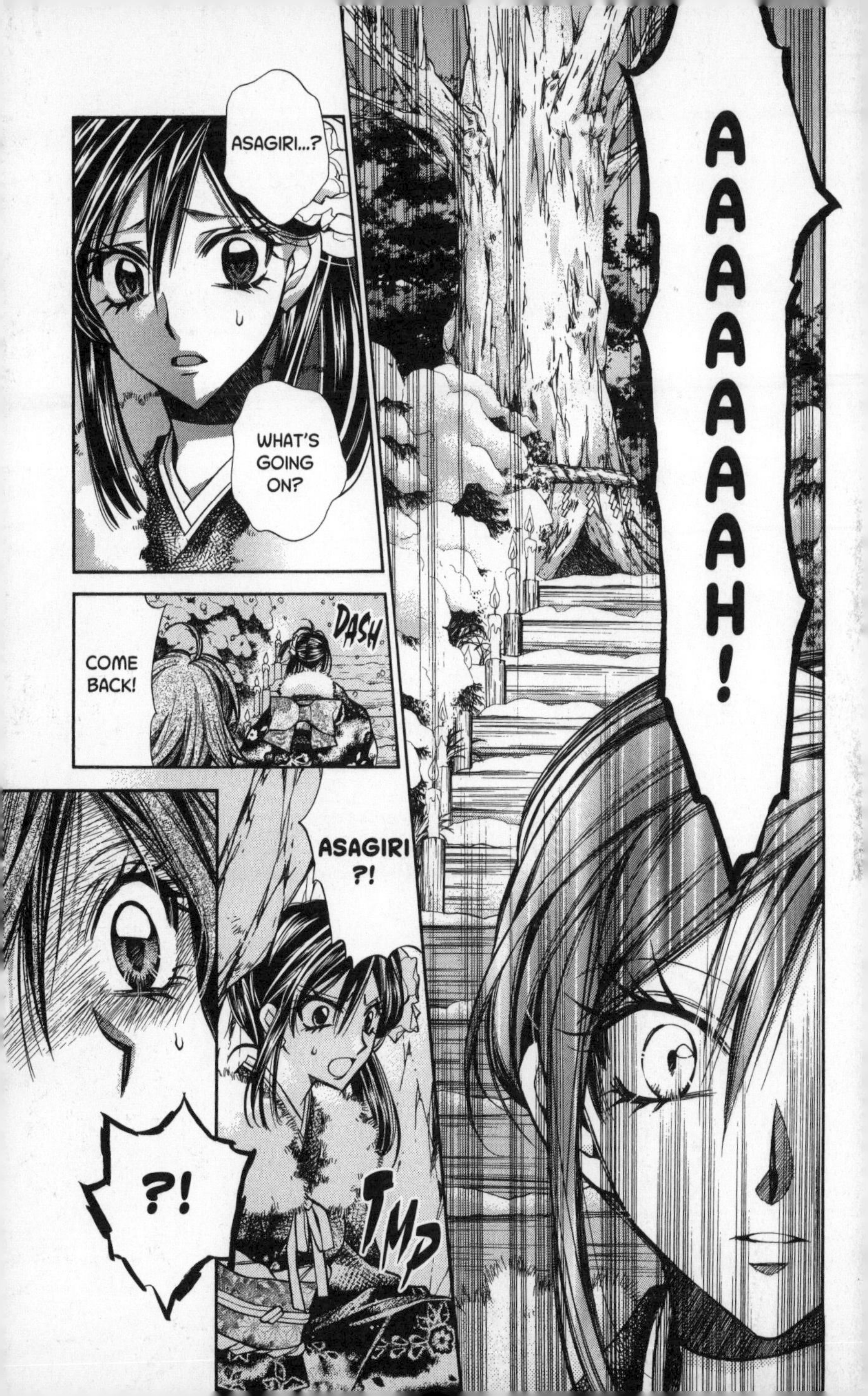
AAAAAAAH!
ASAGIRI...?
WHAT'S GOING ON?
DASH
COME BACK!
ASAGIRI ?!
TMP
?!

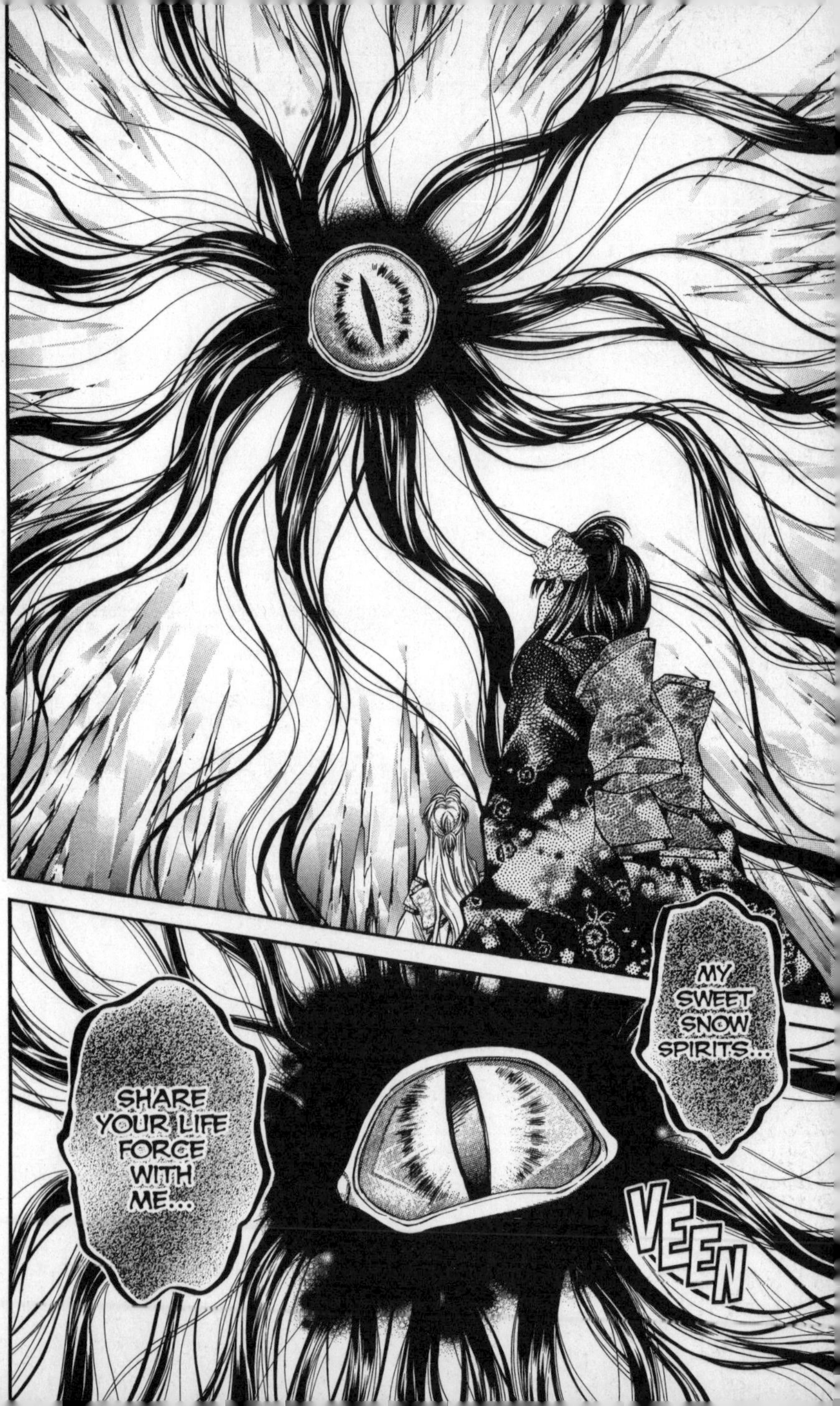
MY SWEET SNOW SPIRITS...
SHARE YOUR LIFE FORCE WITH ME...
VEEN

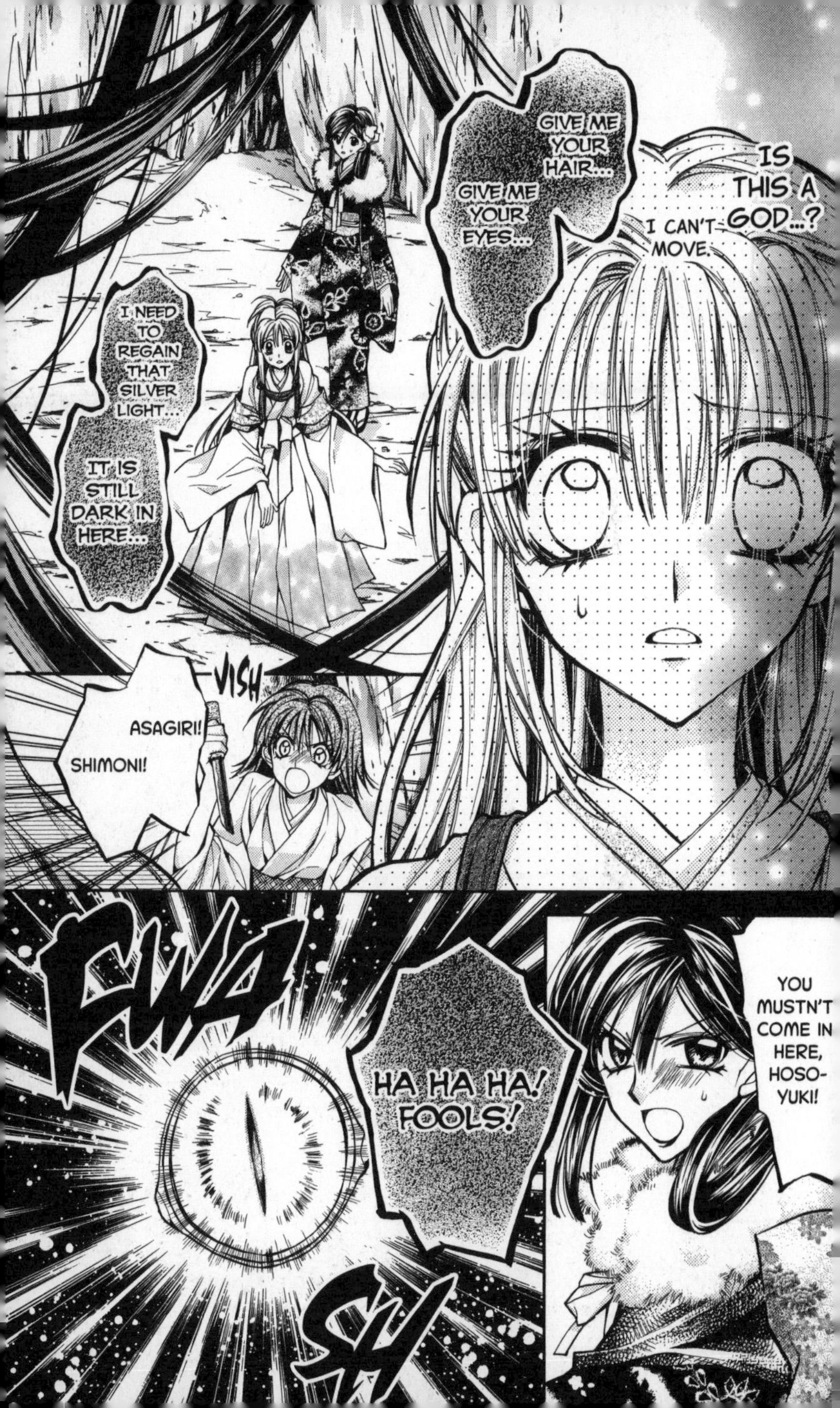
IS THIS A GOD...?
I CAN'T MOVE.
GIVE ME YOUR HAIR...
GIVE ME YOUR EYES...
I NEED TO REGAIN THAT SILVER LIGHT...
IT IS STILL DARK IN HERE...
VISH
ASAGIRI!
SHIMONI!
YOU MUSTN'T COME IN HERE, HOSO-YUKI!
HA HA HA! FOOLS!

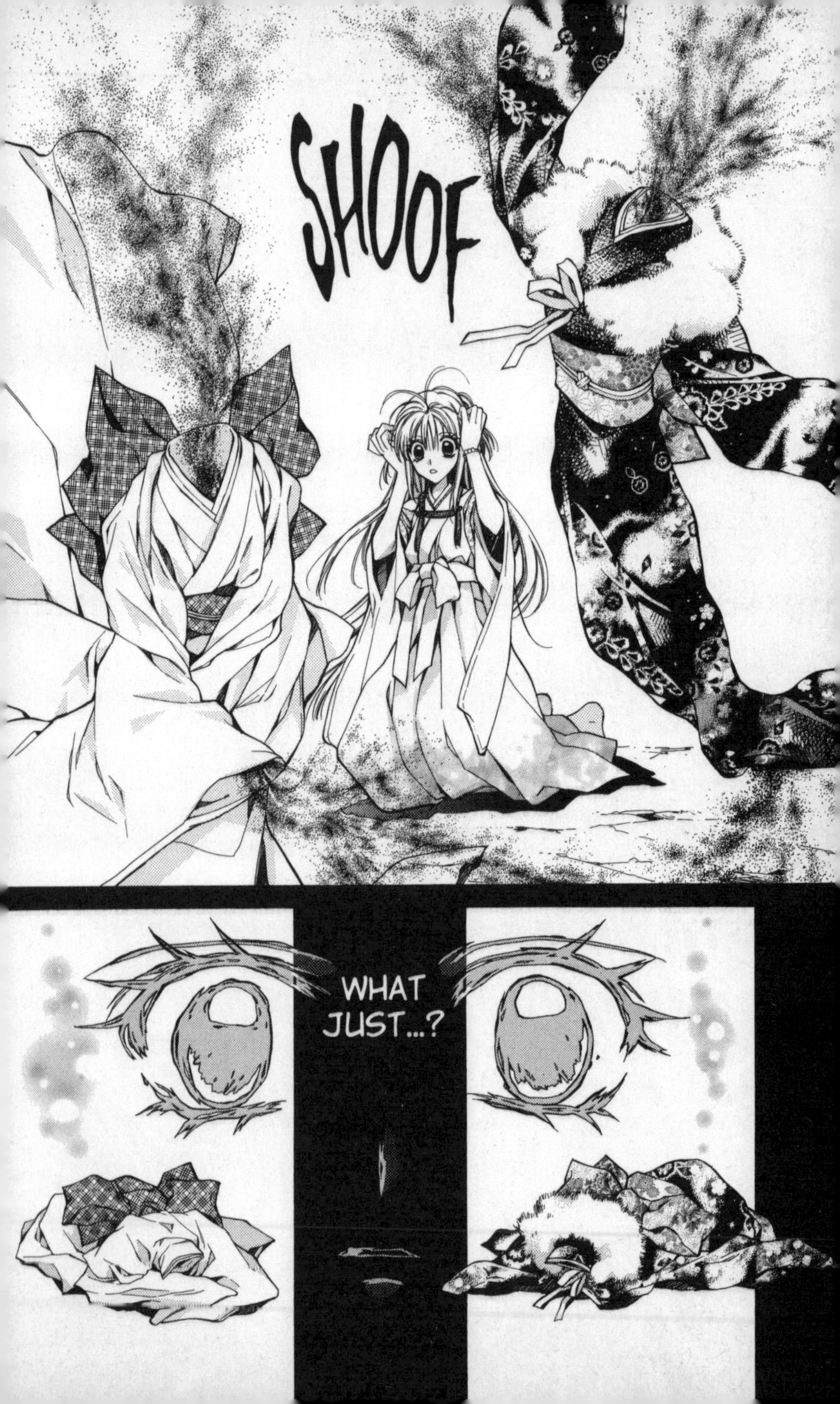
SHOOF
WHAT JUST...?

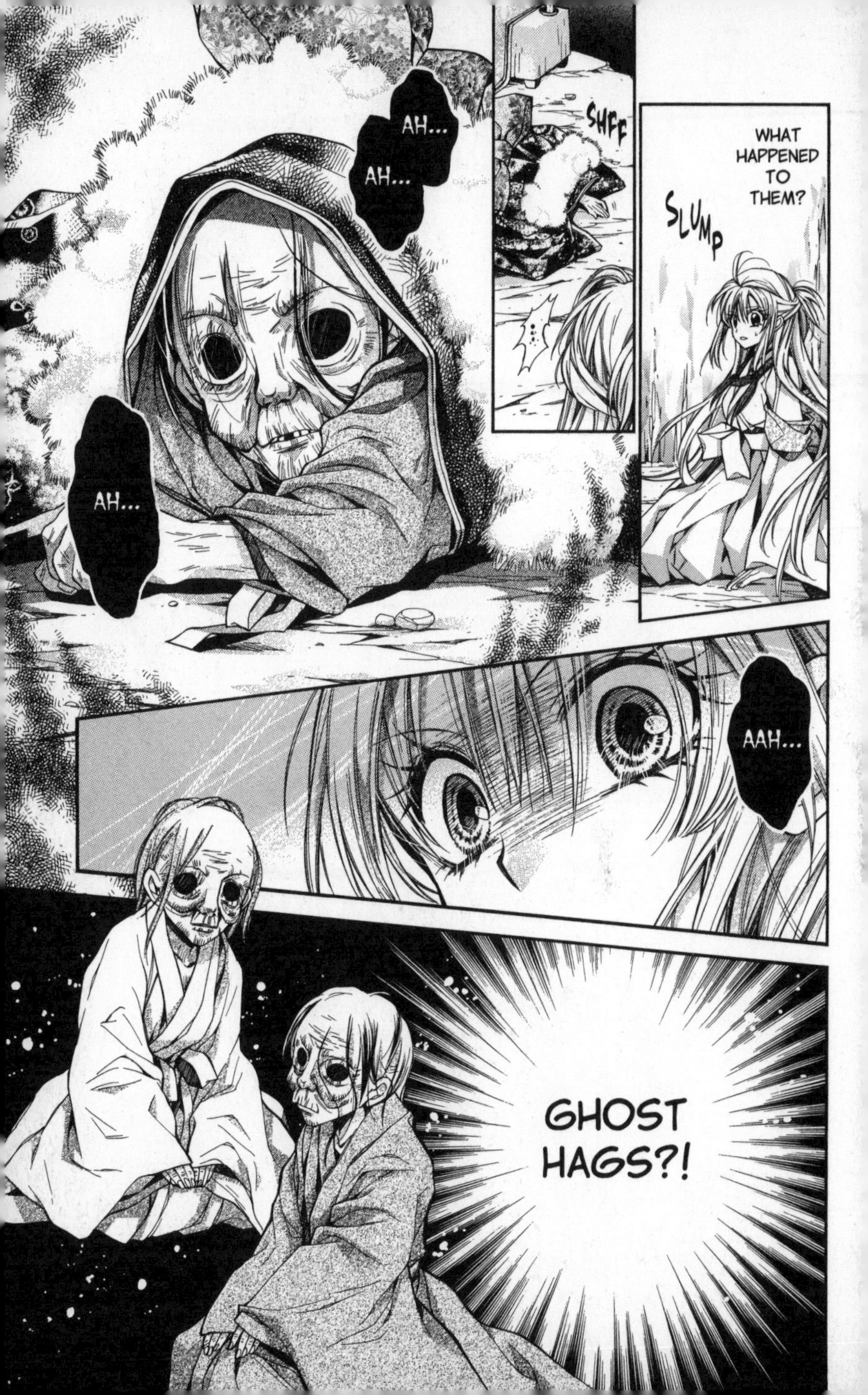
WHAT HAPPENED TO THEM?
SLUMP
SHFF
AH...
AH...
AH...
AAH...
GHOST HAGS?!

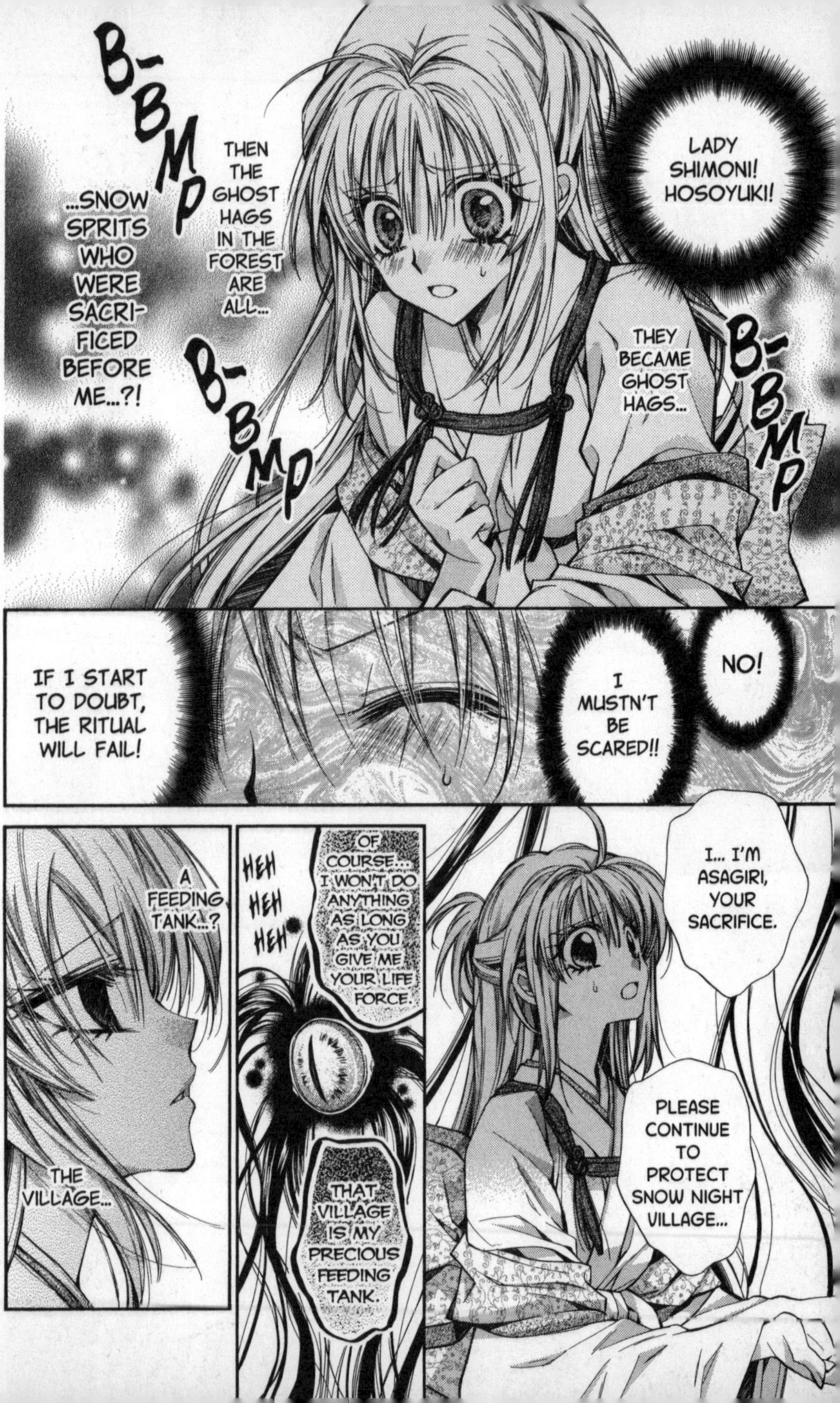
LADY SHIMONI! HOSOYUKI!
B-BMP
THEY BECAME GHOST HAGS...
B-BMP
THEN THE GHOST HAGS IN THE FOREST ARE ALL...
B-BMP
...SNOW SPRITS WHO WERE SACRI-FICED BEFORE ME...?!
NO!
I MUSTN'T BE SCARED!!
IF I START TO DOUBT, THE RITUAL WILL FAIL!
I... I'M ASAGIRI, YOUR SACRIFICE.
PLEASE CONTINUE TO PROTECT SNOW NIGHT VILLAGE...
OF COURSE... I WON'T DO ANYTHING AS LONG AS YOU GIVE ME YOUR LIFE FORCE.
HEH HEH HEH
THAT VILLAGE IS MY PRECIOUS FEEDING TANK.
A FEEDING TANK...?
THE VILLAGE...

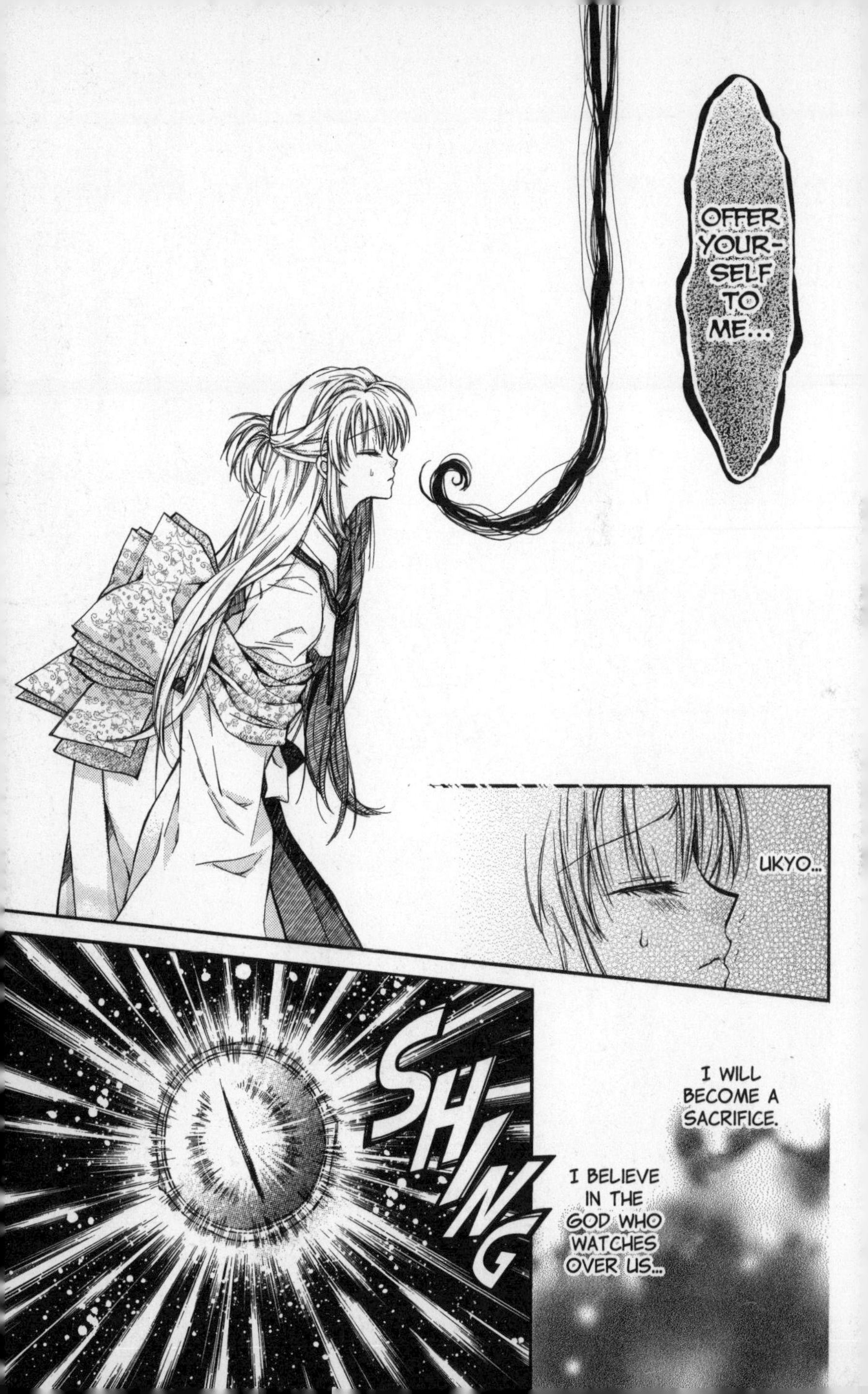
OFFER YOUR-SELF TO ME...
UKYO...
I WILL BECOME A SACRIFICE.
I BELIEVE IN THE GOD WHO WATCHES OVER US...
SHING

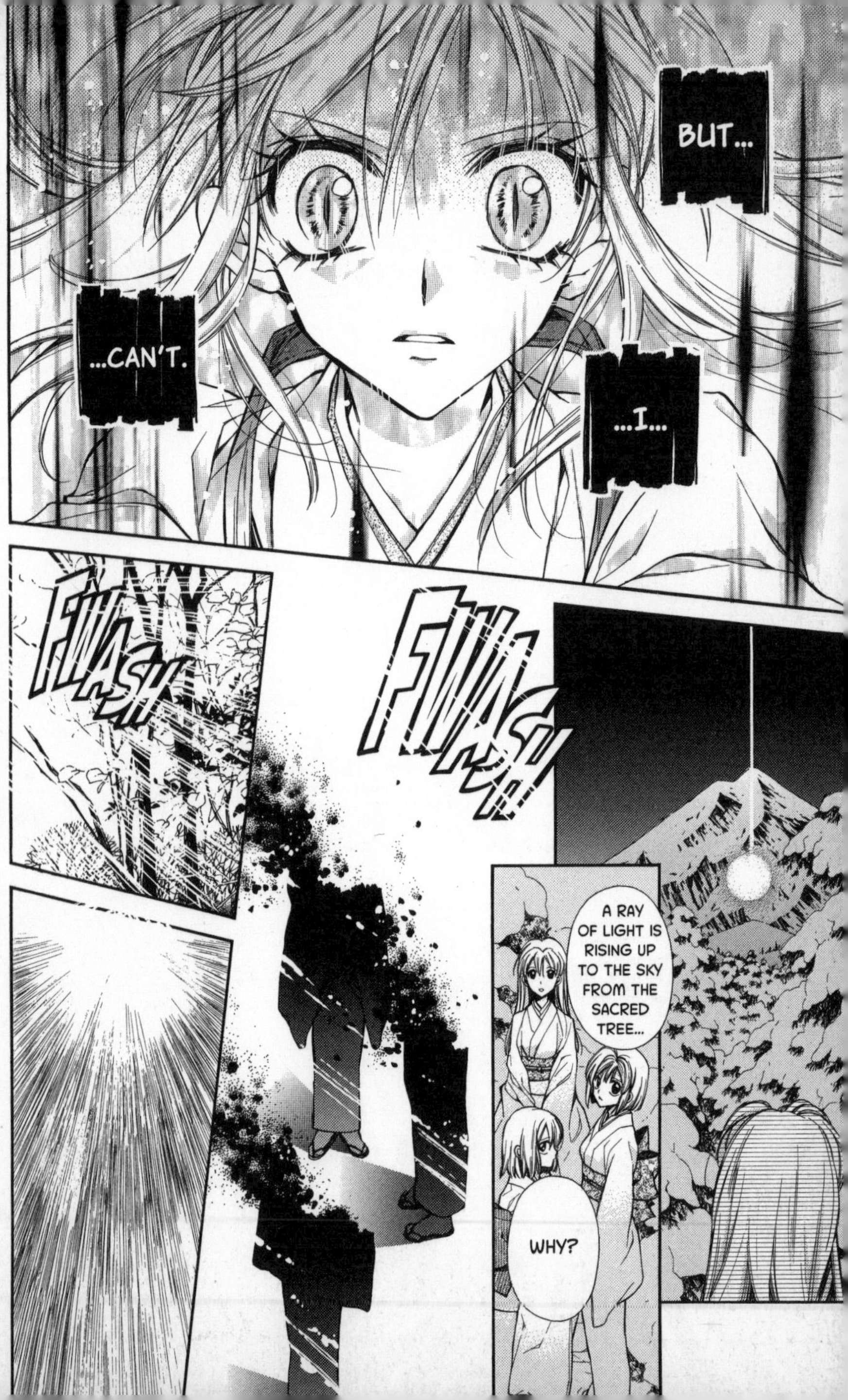
BUT...
...I...
...CAN'T.
A RAY OF LIGHT IS RISING UP TO THE SKY FROM THE SACRED TREE...
WHY?
FWASH
FWASH

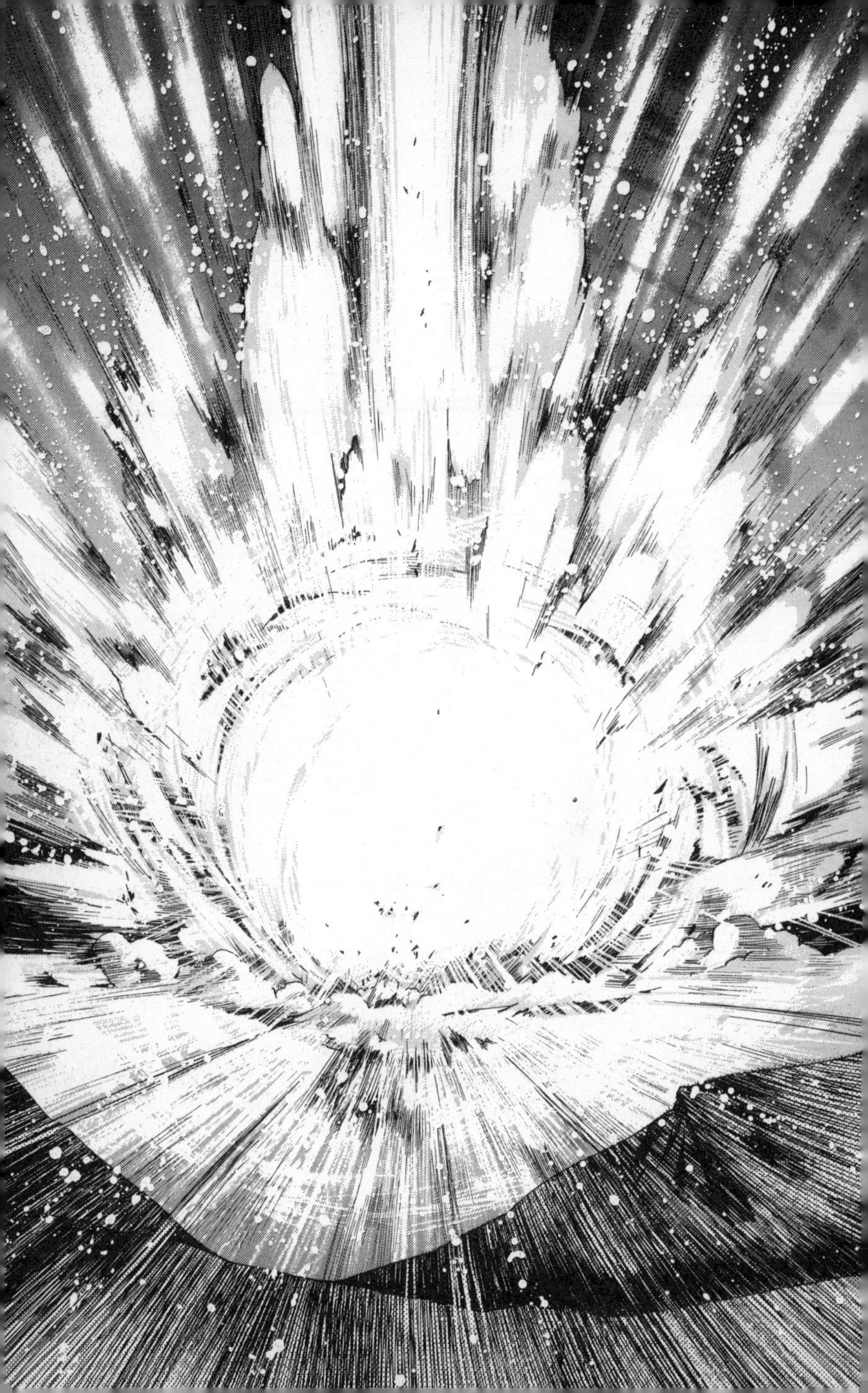

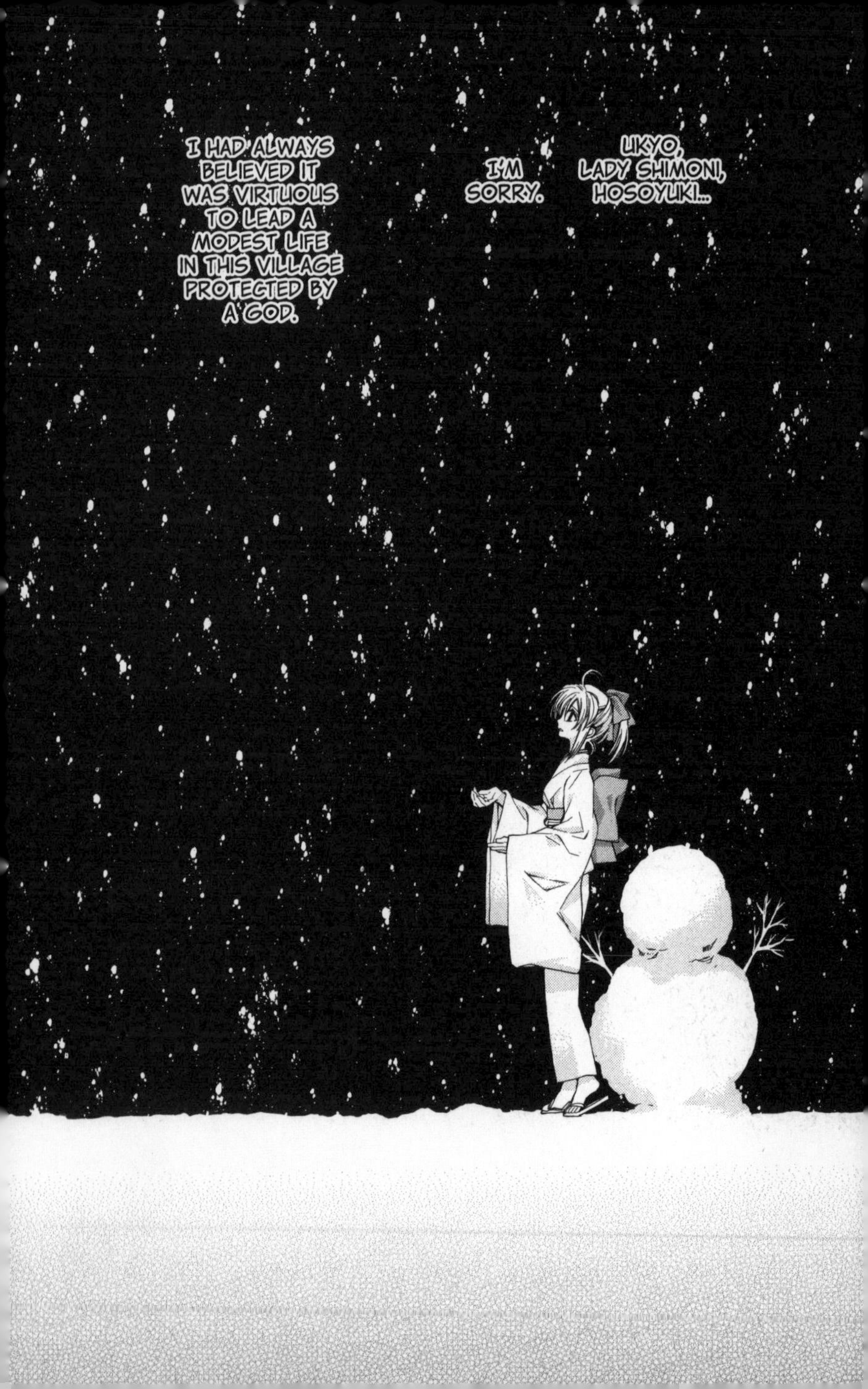
UKYO, LADY SHIMONI, HOSOYUKI...
I'M SORRY.
I HAD ALWAYS BELIEVED IT WAS VIRTUOUS TO LEAD A MODEST LIFE IN THIS VILLAGE PROTECTED BY A GOD.

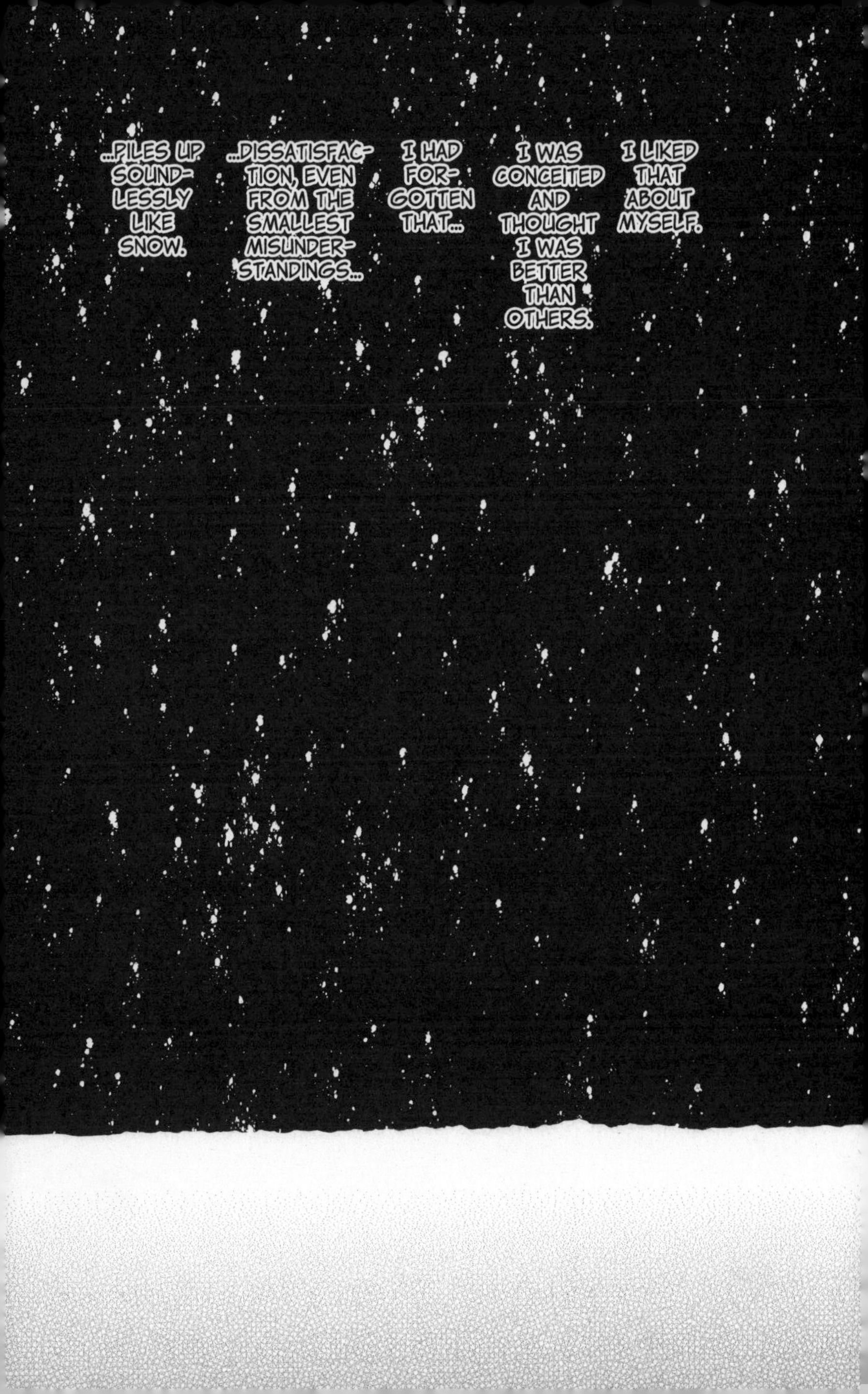
I LIKED THAT ABOUT MYSELF.
I WAS CONCEITED AND THOUGHT I WAS BETTER THAN OTHERS.
I HAD FORGOTTEN THAT...
...DISSATISFACTION, EVEN FROM THE SMALLEST MISUNDERSTANDINGS...
...PILES UP SOUNDLESSLY LIKE SNOW.

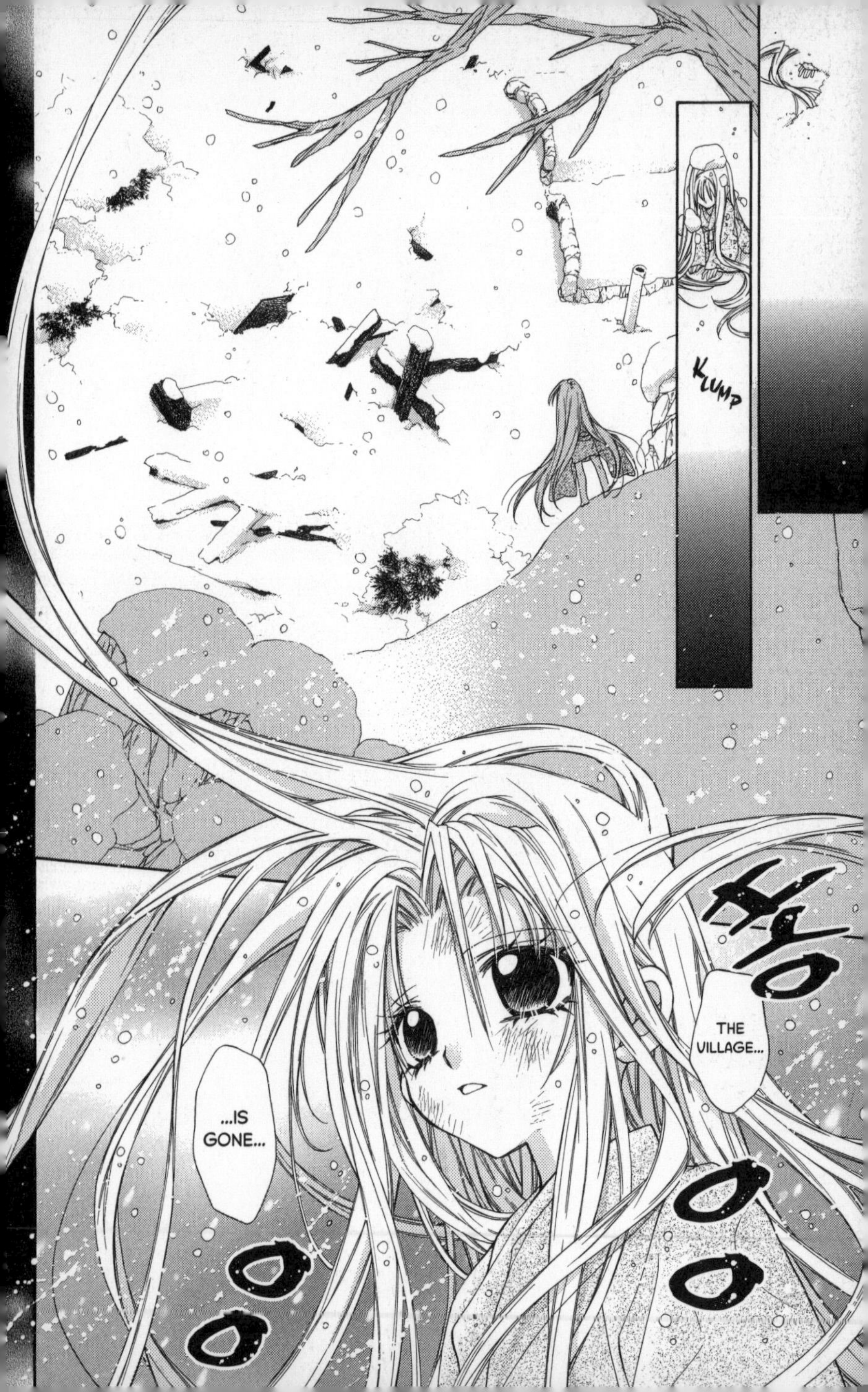
KLUMP
HYOOOOOO
THE VILLAGE...
...IS GONE...

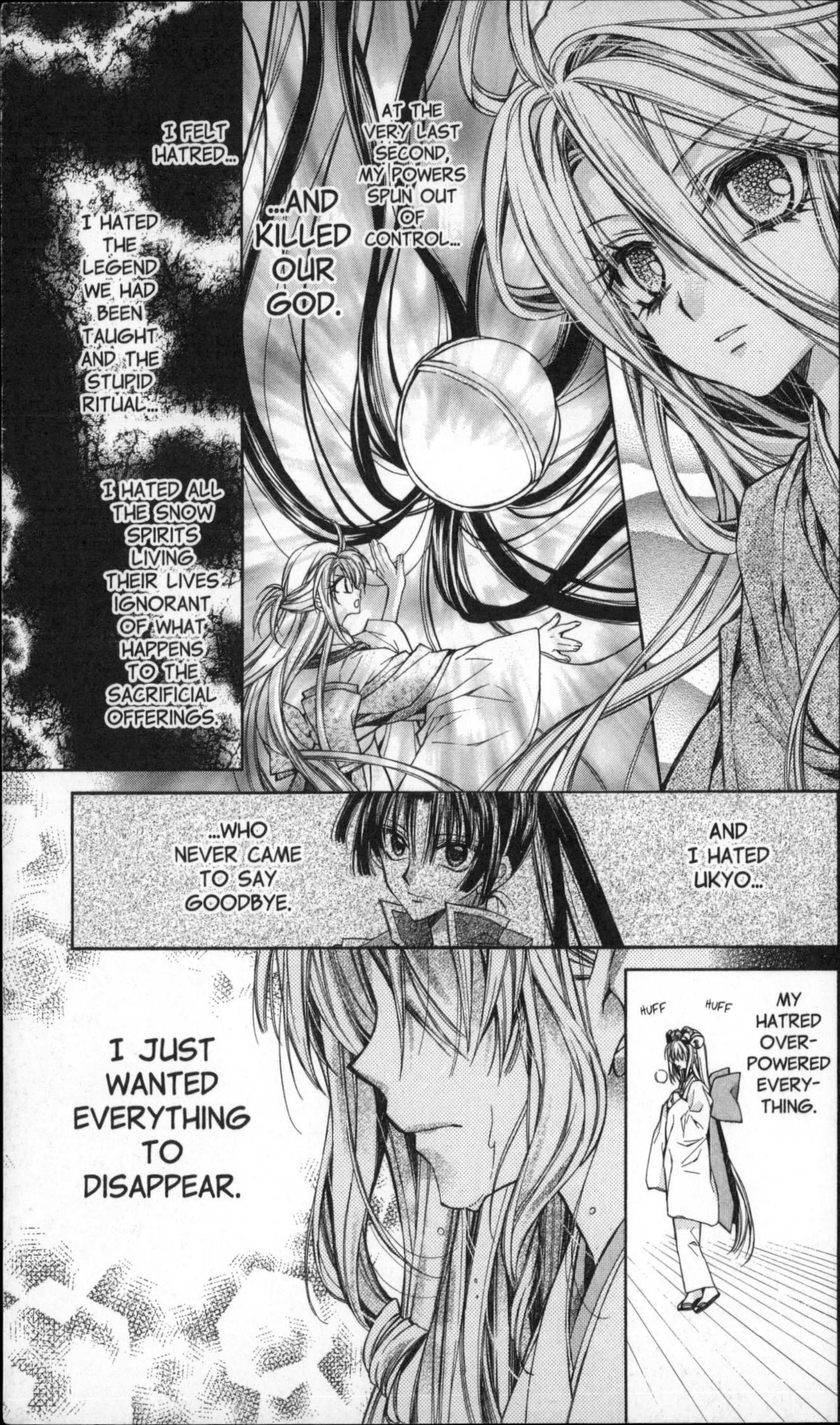
AT THE VERY LAST SECOND, MY POWERS SPUN OUT OF CONTROL...
...AND KILLED OUR GOD.
I FELT HATRED...
I HATED THE LEGEND WE HAD BEEN TAUGHT AND THE STUPID RITUAL...
I HATED ALL THE SNOW SPIRITS LIVING THEIR LIVES IGNORANT OF WHAT HAPPENS TO THE SACRIFICIAL OFFERINGS.
AND I HATED UKYO...
...WHO NEVER CAME TO SAY GOODBYE.
HUFF
HUFF
MY HATRED OVER-POWERED EVERY-THING.
I JUST WANTED EVERYTHING TO DISAPPEAR.

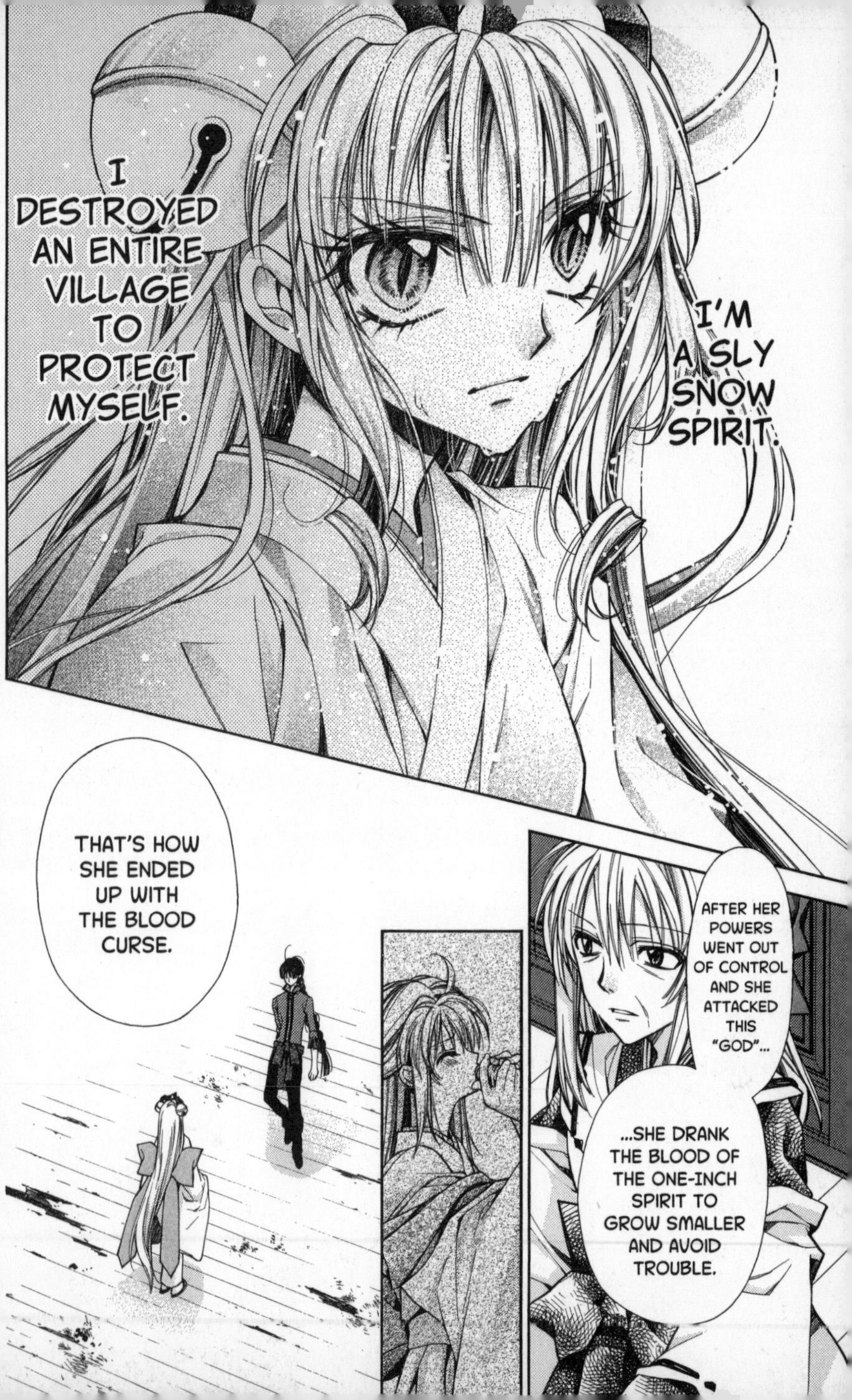
I'M A SLY SNOW SPIRIT.
I DESTROYED AN ENTIRE VILLAGE TO PROTECT MYSELF.
AFTER HER POWERS WENT OUT OF CONTROL AND SHE ATTACKED THIS "GOD"...
...SHE DRANK THE BLOOD OF THE ONE-INCH SPIRIT TO GROW SMALLER AND AVOID TROUBLE.
THAT'S HOW SHE ENDED UP WITH THE BLOOD CURSE.

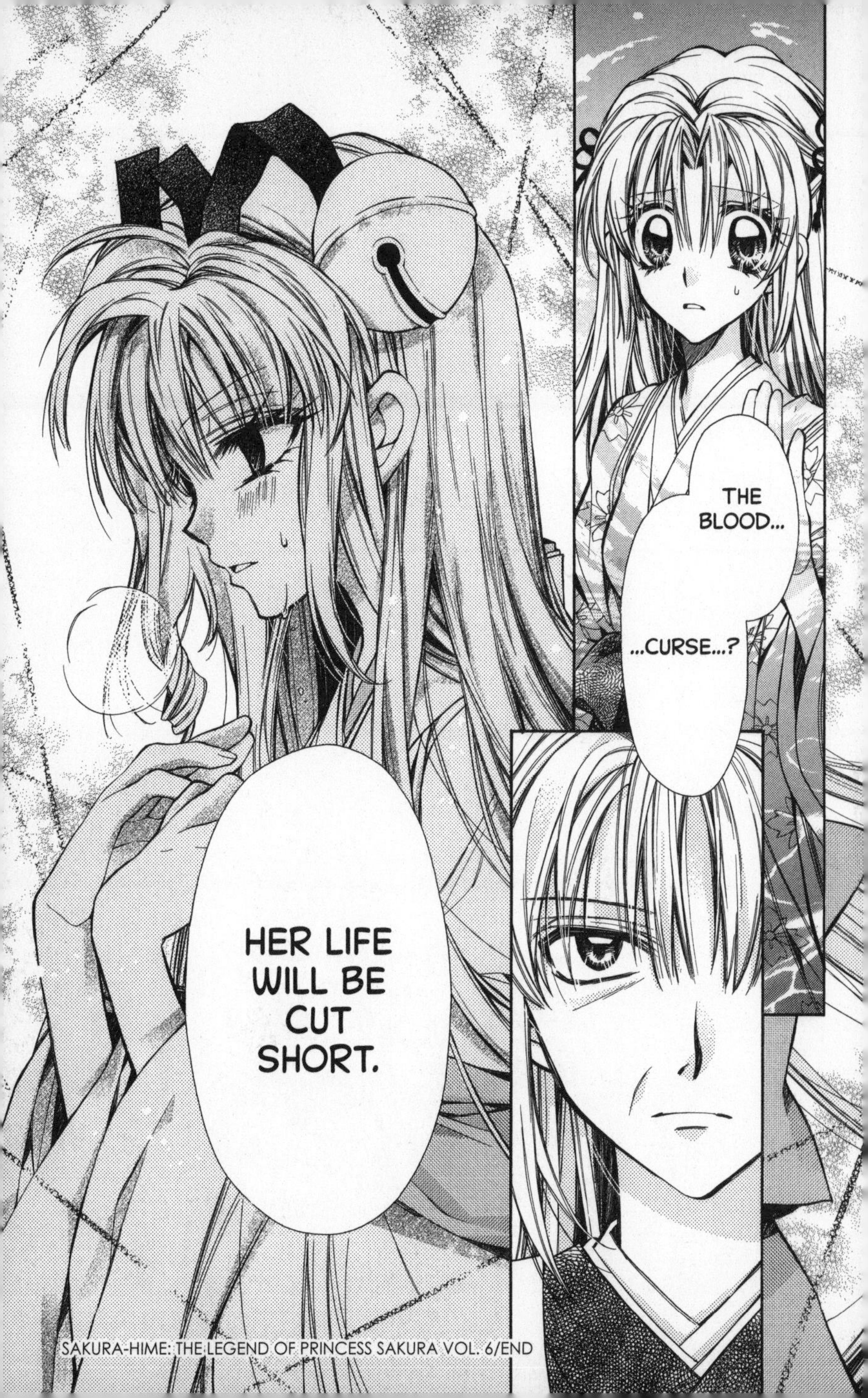
THE BLOOD...
...CURSE...?
HER LIFE WILL BE CUT SHORT.
SAKURA-HIME: THE LEGEND OF PRINCESS SAKURA VOL. 6/END

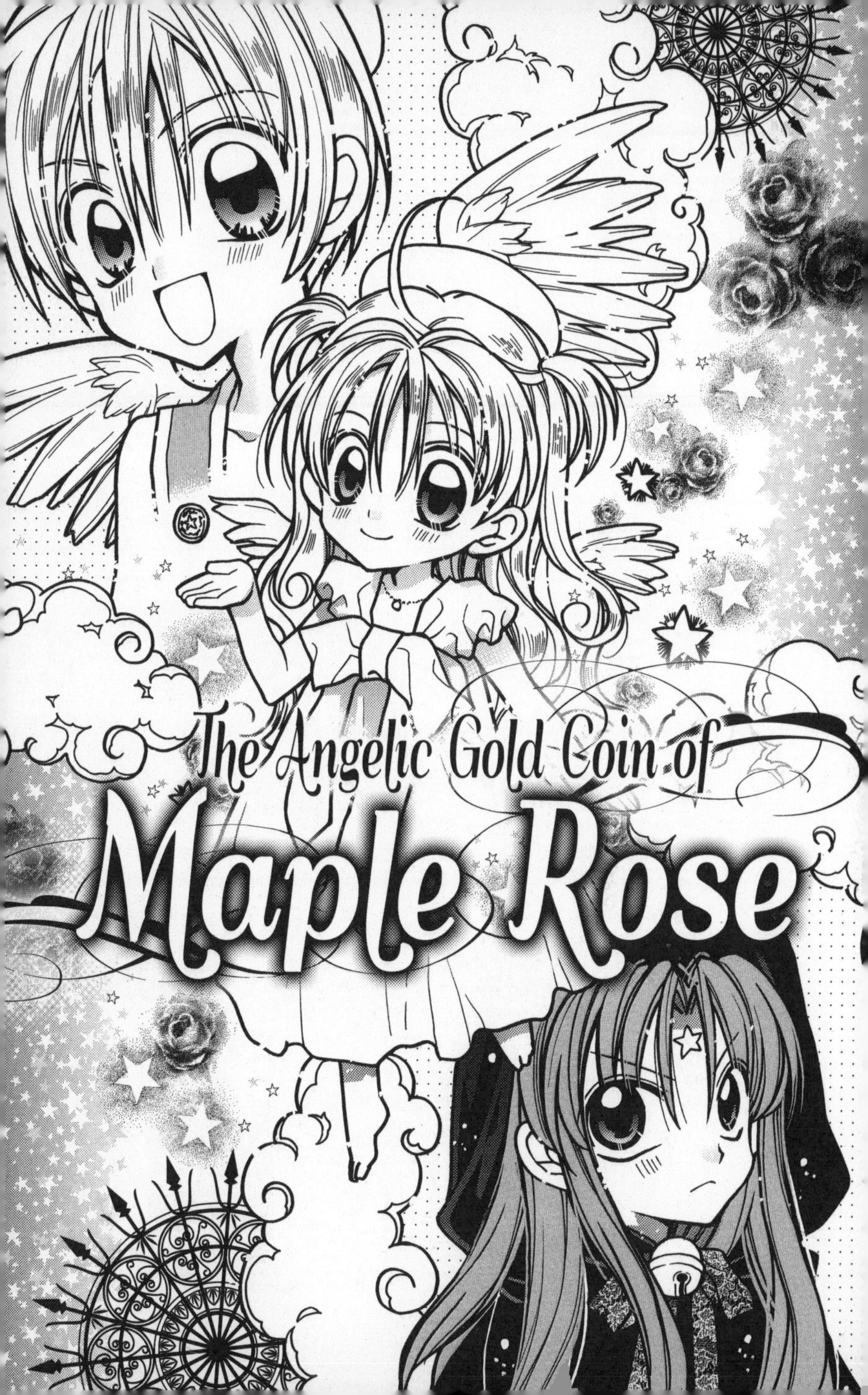
The Angelic Gold Coin of
Maple Rose

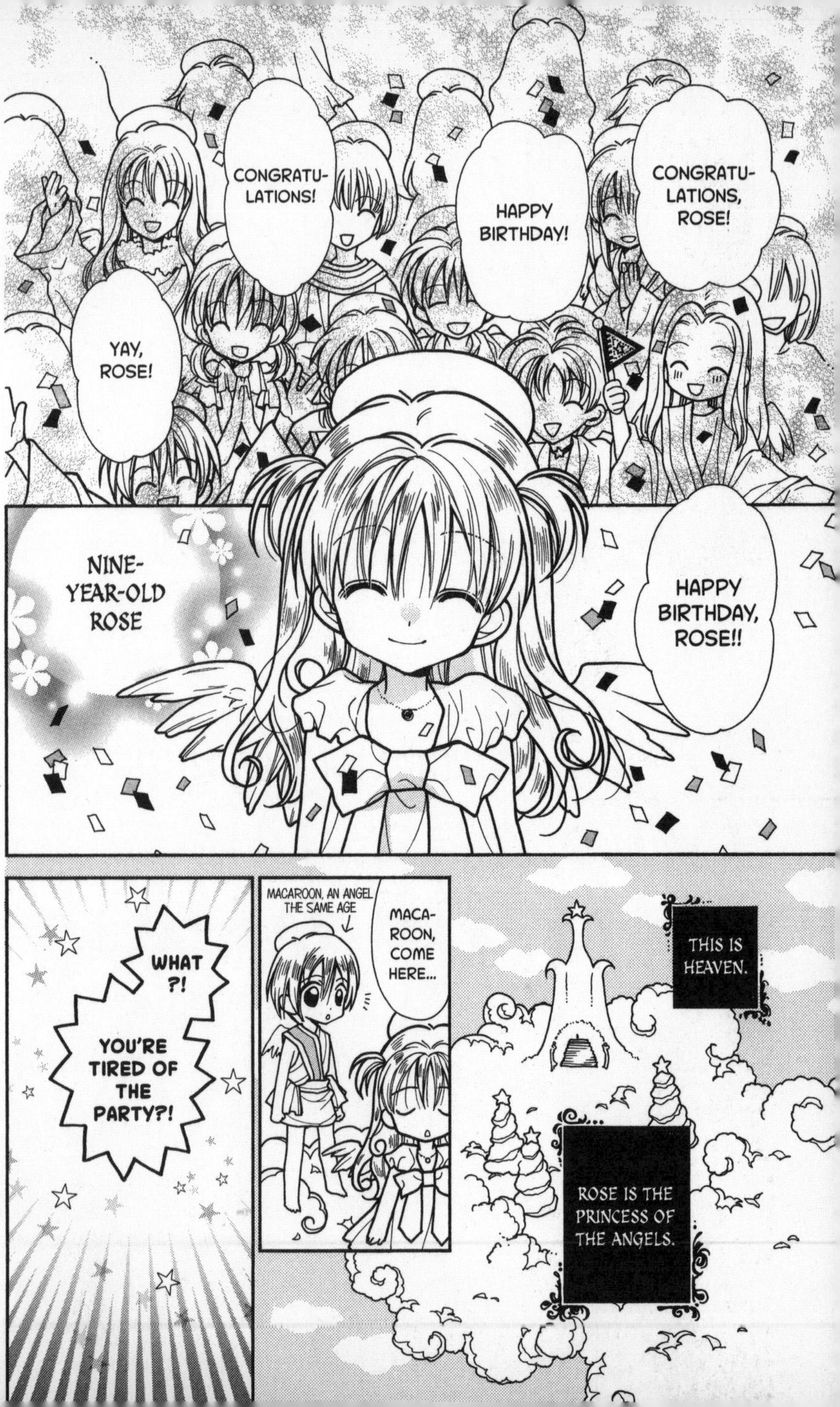
CONGRATU-LATIONS, ROSE!
HAPPY BIRTHDAY!
CONGRATU-LATIONS!
YAY, ROSE!
HAPPY BIRTHDAY, ROSE!!
NINE-YEAR-OLD ROSE
THIS IS HEAVEN.
ROSE IS THE PRINCESS OF THE ANGELS.
MACA-ROON, COME HERE...
MACAROON, AN ANGEL THE SAME AGE
WHAT?!
YOU'RE TIRED OF THE PARTY?!

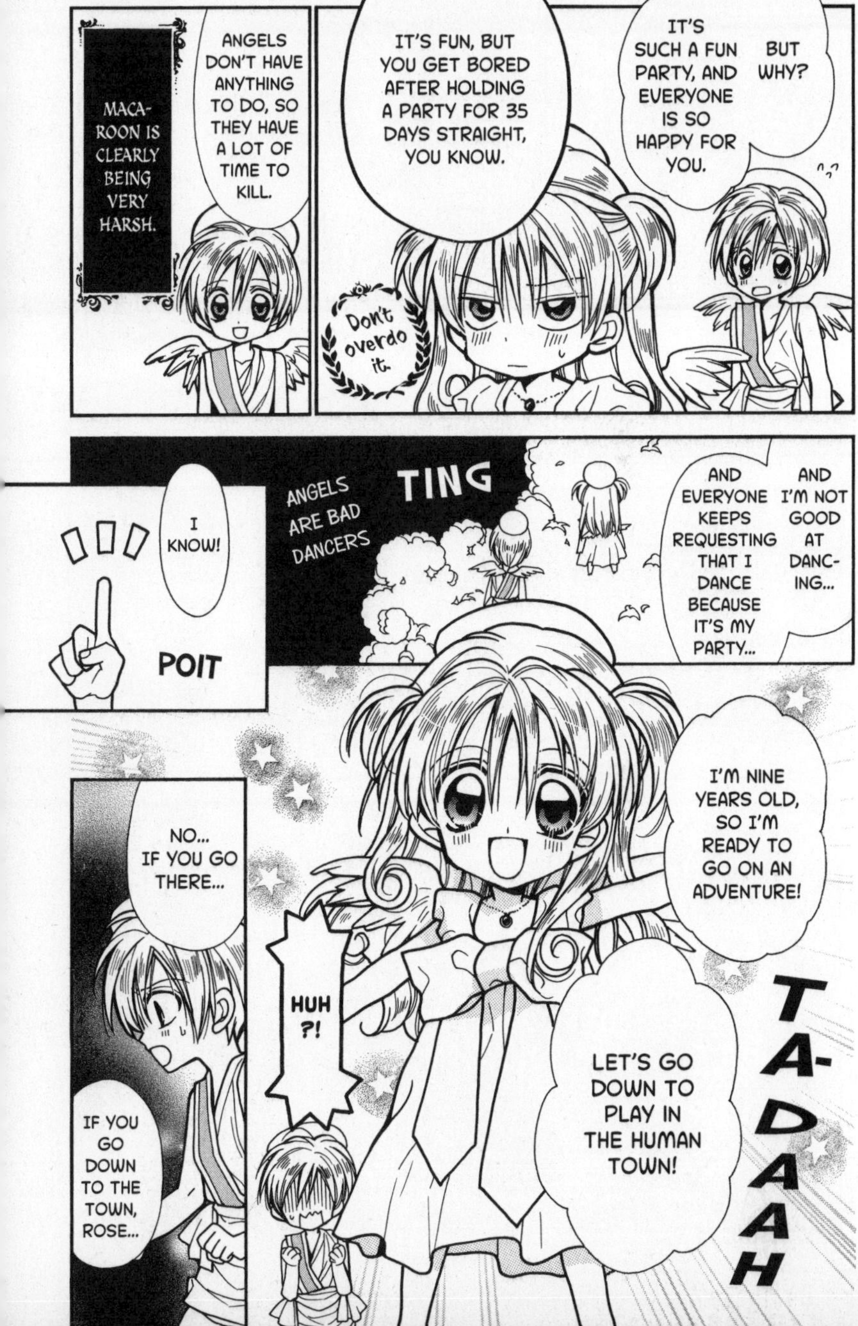
BUT WHY?
IT'S SUCH A FUN PARTY, AND EVERYONE IS SO HAPPY FOR YOU.
IT'S FUN, BUT YOU GET BORED AFTER HOLDING A PARTY FOR 35 DAYS STRAIGHT, YOU KNOW.
Don't overdo it.
ANGELS DON'T HAVE ANYTHING TO DO, SO THEY HAVE A LOT OF TIME TO KILL.
MACA-ROON IS CLEARLY BEING VERY HARSH.
AND I'M NOT GOOD AT DANC-ING...
AND EVERYONE KEEPS REQUESTING THAT I DANCE BECAUSE IT'S MY PARTY...
TING
ANGELS ARE BAD DANCERS
I KNOW!
POIT
I'M NINE YEARS OLD, SO I'M READY TO GO ON AN ADVENTURE!
TA-DAAH
LET'S GO DOWN TO PLAY IN THE HUMAN TOWN!
HUH?!
NO... IF YOU GO THERE...
IF YOU GO DOWN TO THE TOWN, ROSE...

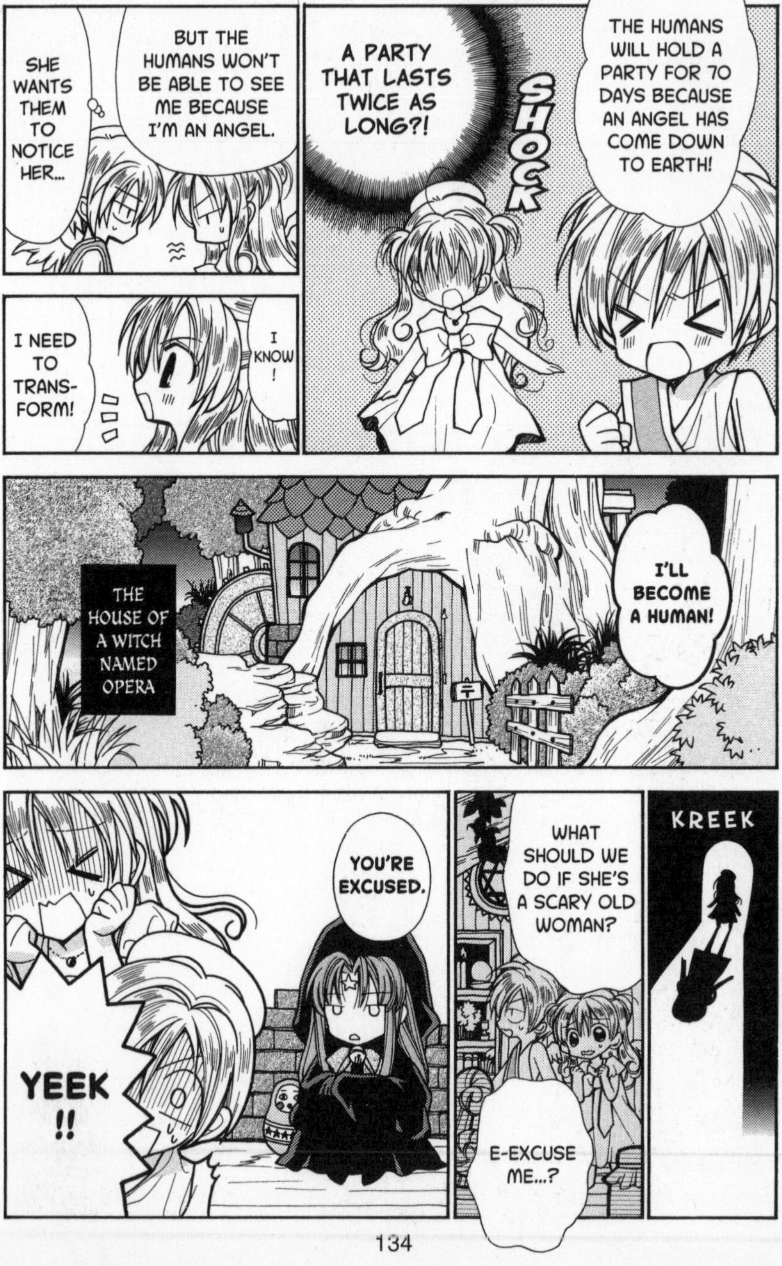
THE HUMANS WILL HOLD A PARTY FOR 70 DAYS BECAUSE AN ANGEL HAS COME DOWN TO EARTH!
SHOCK
A PARTY THAT LASTS TWICE AS LONG?!
BUT THE HUMANS WON'T BE ABLE TO SEE ME BECAUSE I'M AN ANGEL.
SHE WANTS THEM TO NOTICE HER...
I KNOW!
I NEED TO TRANSFORM!
I'LL BECOME A HUMAN!
THE HOUSE OF A WITCH NAMED OPERA
KREEK
WHAT SHOULD WE DO IF SHE'S A SCARY OLD WOMAN?
E-EXCUSE ME...?
YOU'RE EXCUSED.
YEEK!!

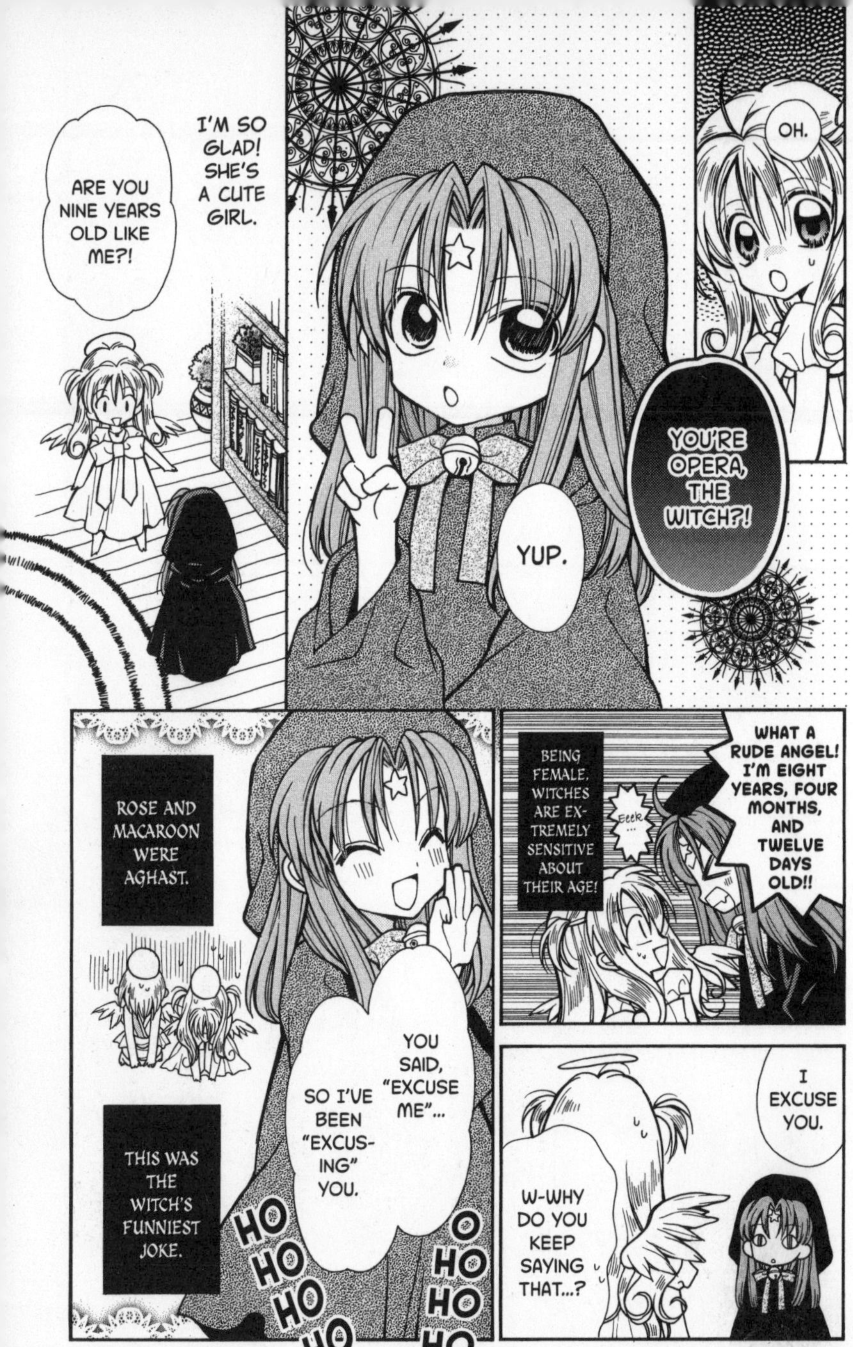
OH.
YOU'RE OPERA, THE WITCH?!
YUP.
I'M SO GLAD! SHE'S A CUTE GIRL.
ARE YOU NINE YEARS OLD LIKE ME?!
WHAT A RUDE ANGEL! I'M EIGHT YEARS, FOUR MONTHS, AND TWELVE DAYS OLD!!
Eeek...
BEING FEMALE, WITCHES ARE EXTREMELY SENSITIVE ABOUT THEIR AGE!
I EXCUSE YOU.
W-WHY DO YOU KEEP SAYING THAT...?
YOU SAID, "EXCUSE ME"...
SO I'VE BEEN "EXCUSING" YOU.
HO HO HO HO
HO HO HO HO
ROSE AND MACAROON WERE AGHAST.
THIS WAS THE WITCH'S FUNNIEST JOKE.

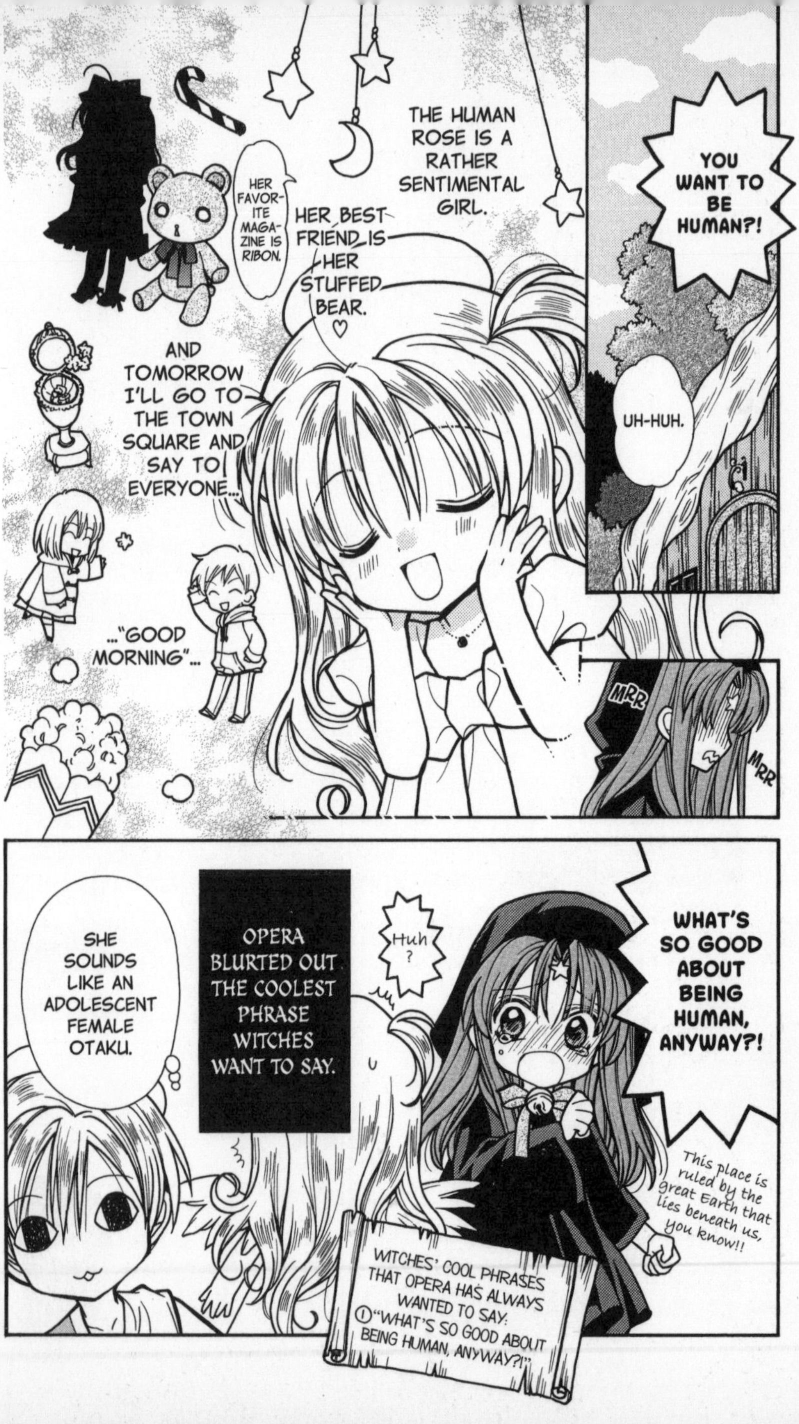
YOU WANT TO BE HUMAN?!
UH-HUH.
MRR
MRR
THE HUMAN ROSE IS A RATHER SENTIMENTAL GIRL.
HER BEST FRIEND IS HER STUFFED BEAR. ♡
HER FAVORITE MAGAZINE IS RIBON.
AND TOMORROW I'LL GO TO THE TOWN SQUARE AND SAY TO EVERYONE...
..."GOOD MORNING"...
WHAT'S SO GOOD ABOUT BEING HUMAN, ANYWAY?!
This place is ruled by the great Earth that lies beneath us, you know!!
Huh?
WITCHES' COOL PHRASES THAT OPERA HAS ALWAYS WANTED TO SAY: ① "WHAT'S SO GOOD ABOUT BEING HUMAN, ANYWAY?!"
OPERA BLURTED OUT THE COOLEST PHRASE WITCHES WANT TO SAY.
SHE SOUNDS LIKE AN ADOLESCENT FEMALE OTAKU.

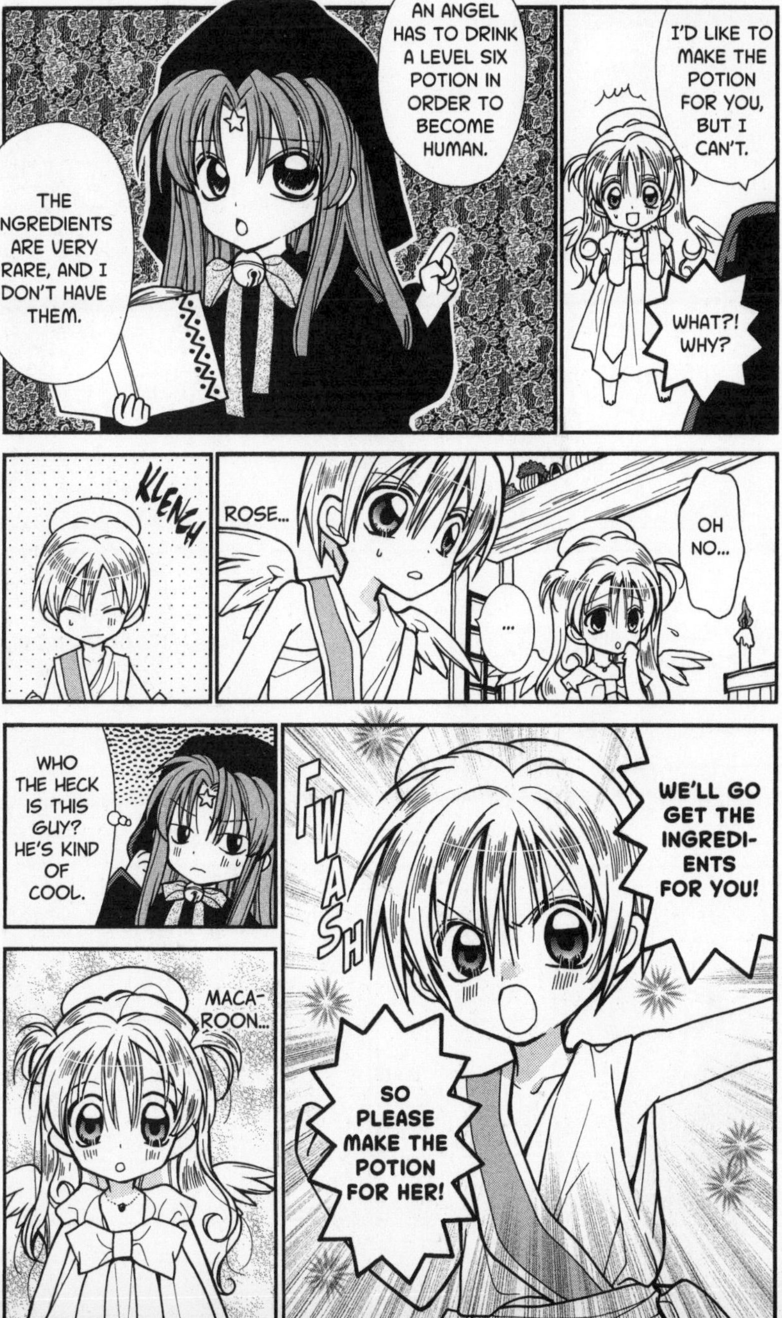
I'D LIKE TO MAKE THE POTION FOR YOU, BUT I CAN'T.
WHAT?! WHY?
AN ANGEL HAS TO DRINK A LEVEL SIX POTION IN ORDER TO BECOME HUMAN.
THE INGREDIENTS ARE VERY RARE, AND I DON'T HAVE THEM.
OH NO...
...
ROSE...
KLENCH
WE'LL GO GET THE INGREDI- ENTS FOR YOU!
FWASH
SO PLEASE MAKE THE POTION FOR HER!
WHO THE HECK IS THIS GUY? HE'S KIND OF COOL.
MACA- ROON...

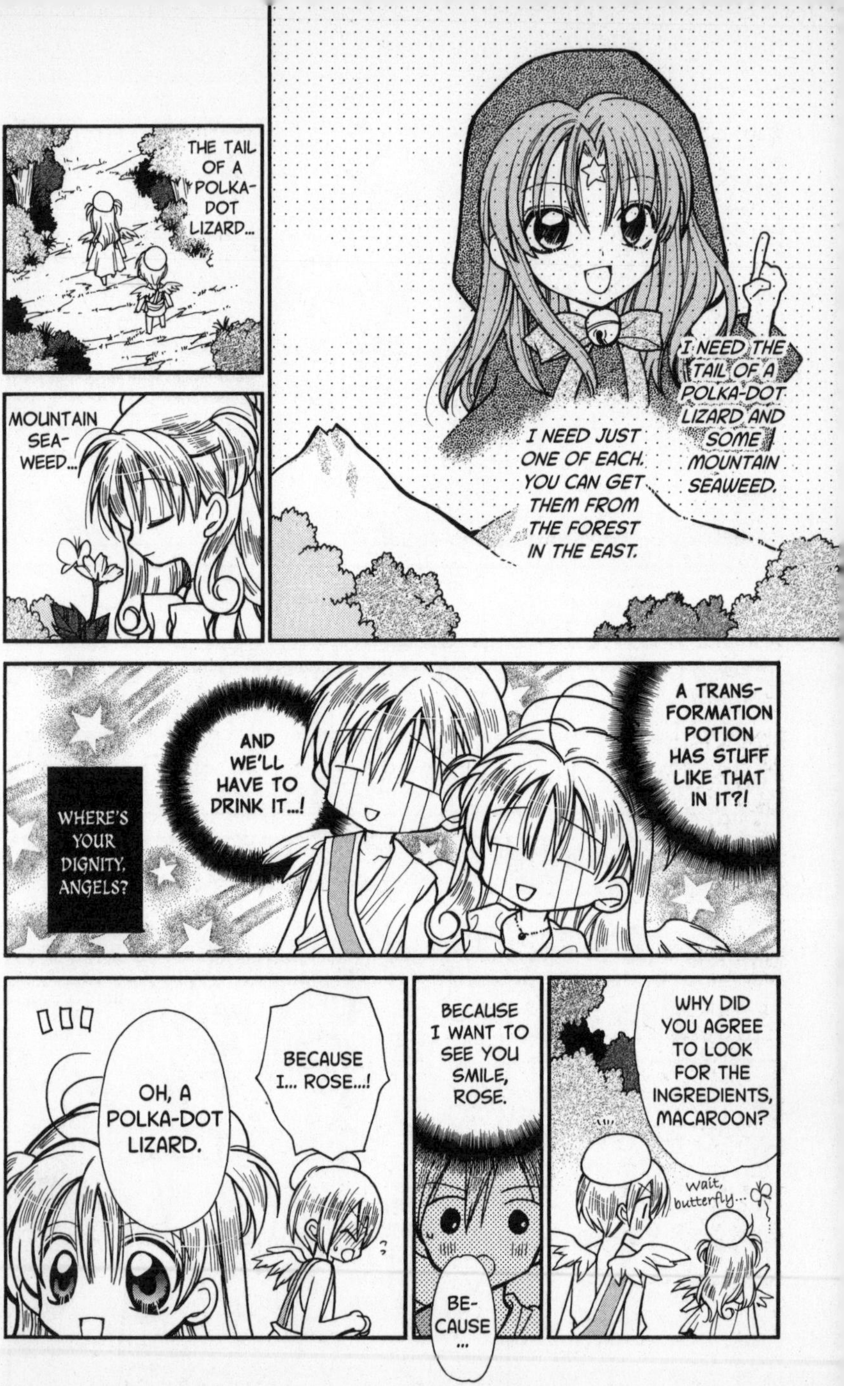
I NEED THE TAIL OF A POLKA-DOT LIZARD AND SOME MOUNTAIN SEAWEED.
I NEED JUST ONE OF EACH. YOU CAN GET THEM FROM THE FOREST IN THE EAST.
THE TAIL OF A POLKA-DOT LIZARD...
MOUNTAIN SEA-WEED...
A TRANS-FORMATION POTION HAS STUFF LIKE THAT IN IT?!
AND WE'LL HAVE TO DRINK IT...!
WHERE'S YOUR DIGNITY, ANGELS?
WHY DID YOU AGREE TO LOOK FOR THE INGREDIENTS, MACAROON?
wait, butterfly...
BECAUSE I WANT TO SEE YOU SMILE, ROSE.
BE-CAUSE ...
BECAUSE I... ROSE...!
OH, A POLKA-DOT LIZARD.

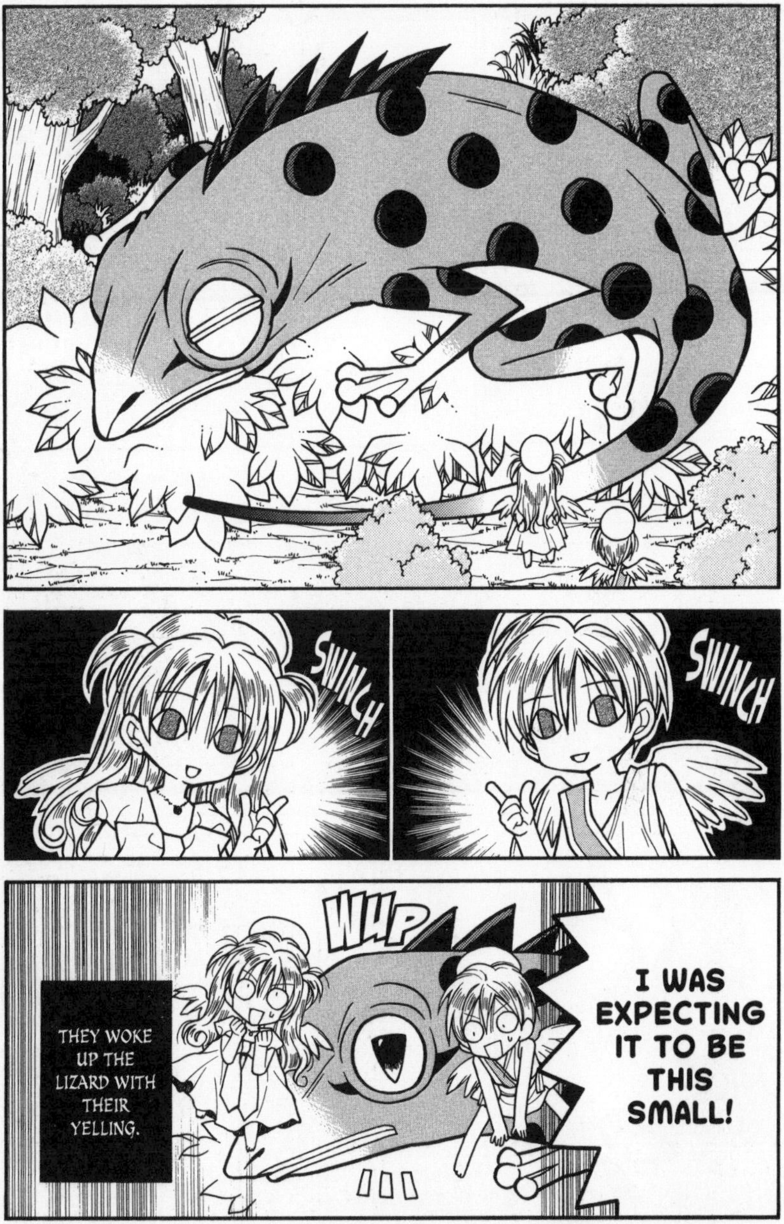
SWINCH
SWINCH
I WAS EXPECTING IT TO BE THIS SMALL!
WUP
THEY WOKE UP THE LIZARD WITH THEIR YELLING.

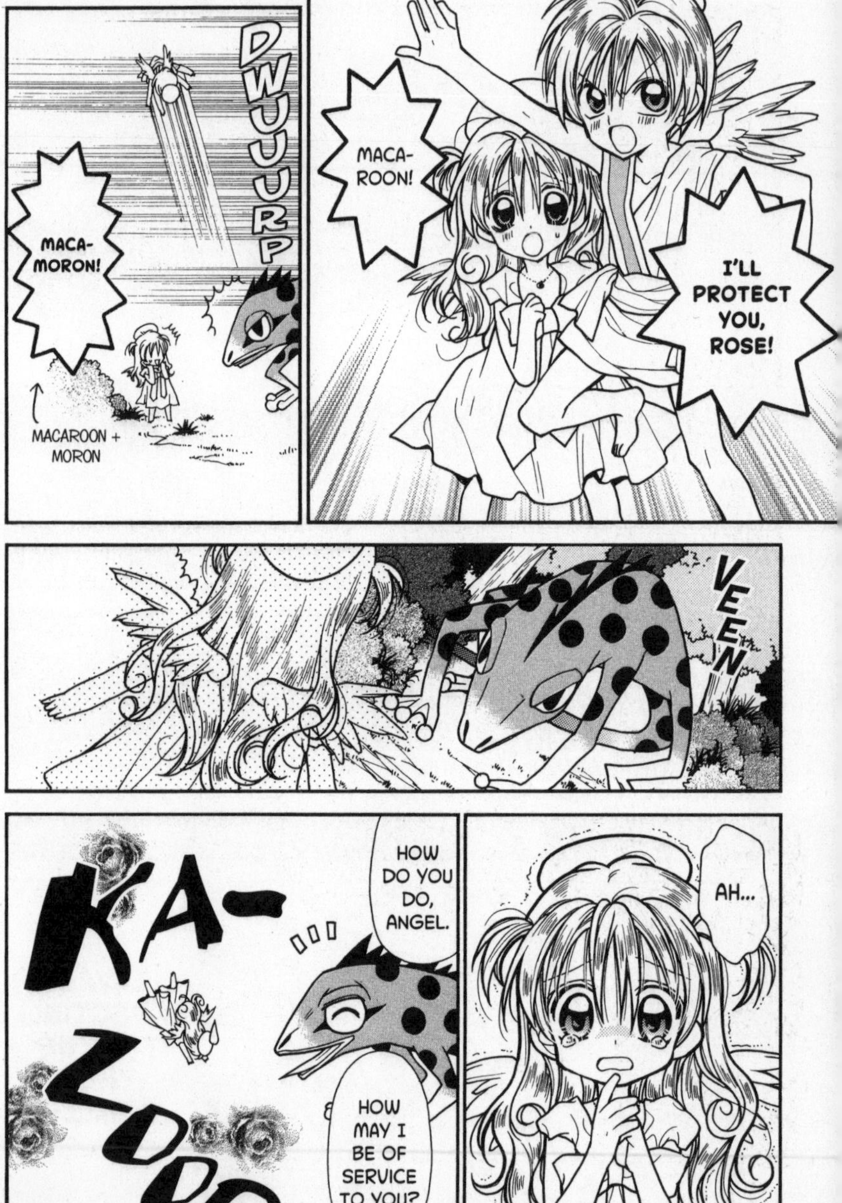
MACA-ROON!
I'LL PROTECT YOU, ROSE!
DWJUURP
MACA-MORON!
MACAROON + MORON
VEEN
AH...
HOW DO YOU DO, ANGEL.
HOW MAY I BE OF SERVICE TO YOU?
KA-ZDDB

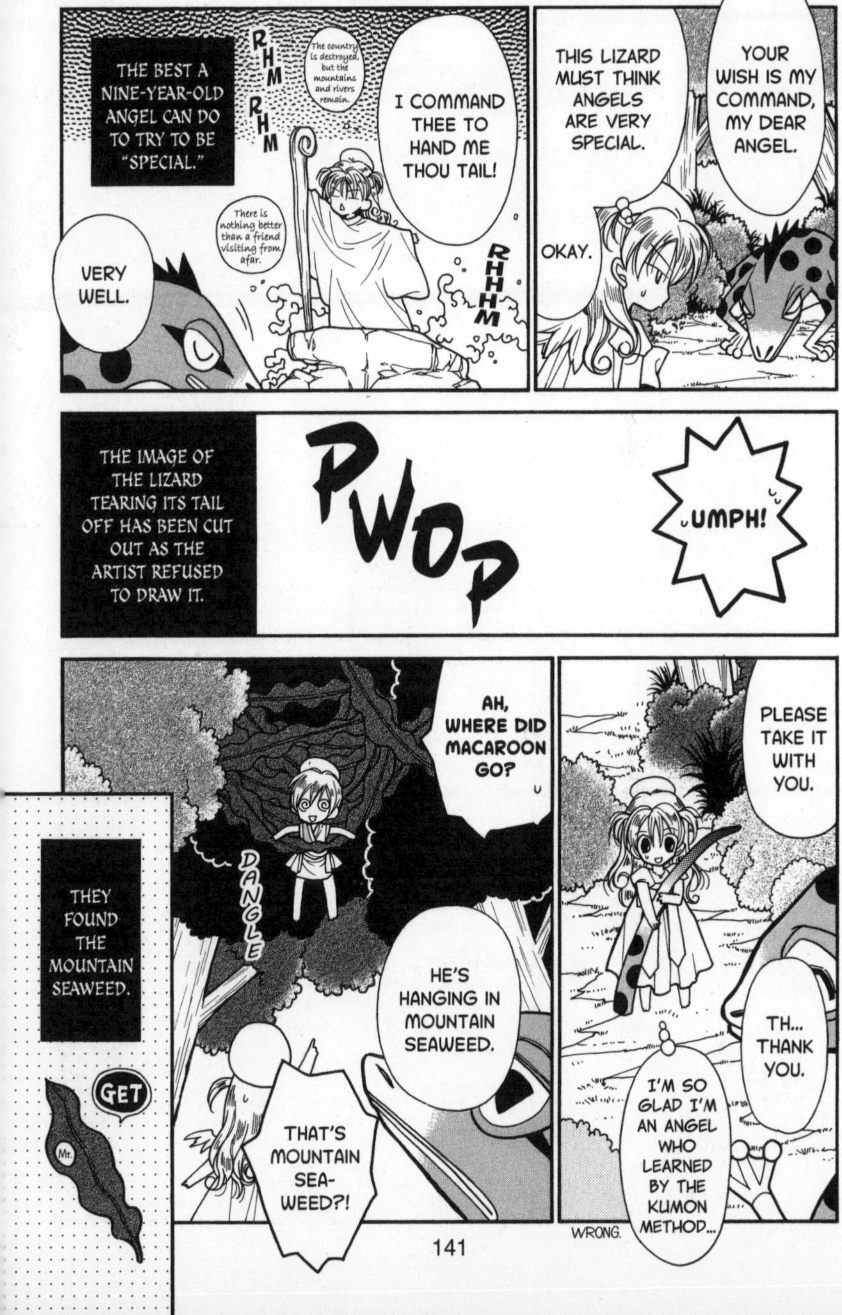
YOUR WISH IS MY COMMAND, MY DEAR ANGEL.
THIS LIZARD MUST THINK ANGELS ARE VERY SPECIAL.
OKAY.
I COMMAND THEE TO HAND ME THOU TAIL!
The country is destroyed, but the mountains and rivers remain.
RHM RHM
RHHHM
THE BEST A NINE-YEAR-OLD ANGEL CAN DO TO TRY TO BE "SPECIAL."
There is nothing better than a friend visiting from afar.
VERY WELL.
UMPH!
PWOP
THE IMAGE OF THE LIZARD TEARING ITS TAIL OFF HAS BEEN CUT OUT AS THE ARTIST REFUSED TO DRAW IT.
PLEASE TAKE IT WITH YOU.
TH... THANK YOU.
I'M SO GLAD I'M AN ANGEL WHO LEARNED BY THE KUMON METHOD...
WRONG.
AH, WHERE DID MACAROON GO?
DANGLE
HE'S HANGING IN MOUNTAIN SEAWEED.
THAT'S MOUNTAIN SEA-WEED?!
THEY FOUND THE MOUNTAIN SEAWEED.
GET
Mt.

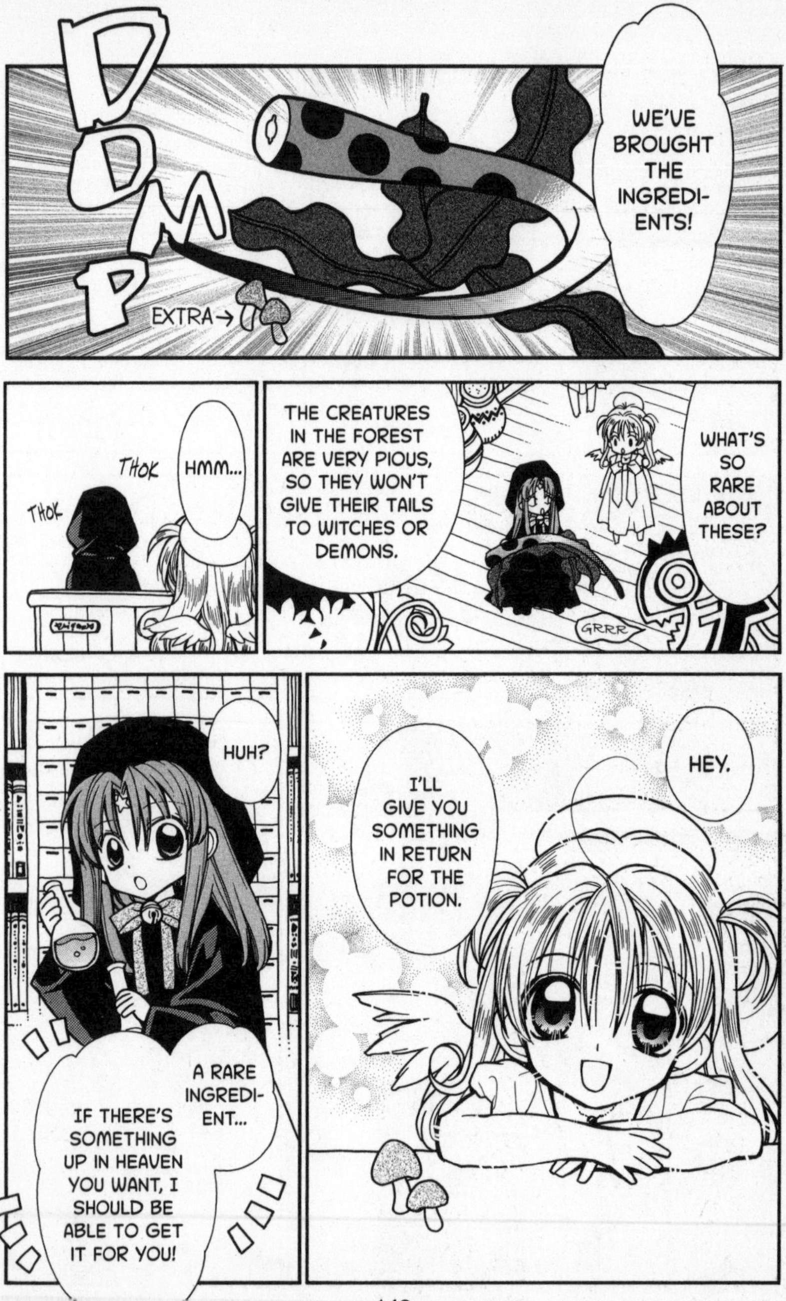
WE'VE BROUGHT THE INGREDI- ENTS!
DMP
EXTRA→
WHAT'S SO RARE ABOUT THESE?
GRRR
THE CREATURES IN THE FOREST ARE VERY PIOUS, SO THEY WON'T GIVE THEIR TAILS TO WITCHES OR DEMONS.
HMM...
THOK
THOK
HEY.
I'LL GIVE YOU SOMETHING IN RETURN FOR THE POTION.
HUH?
A RARE INGREDI- ENT...
IF THERE'S SOMETHING UP IN HEAVEN YOU WANT, I SHOULD BE ABLE TO GET IT FOR YOU!

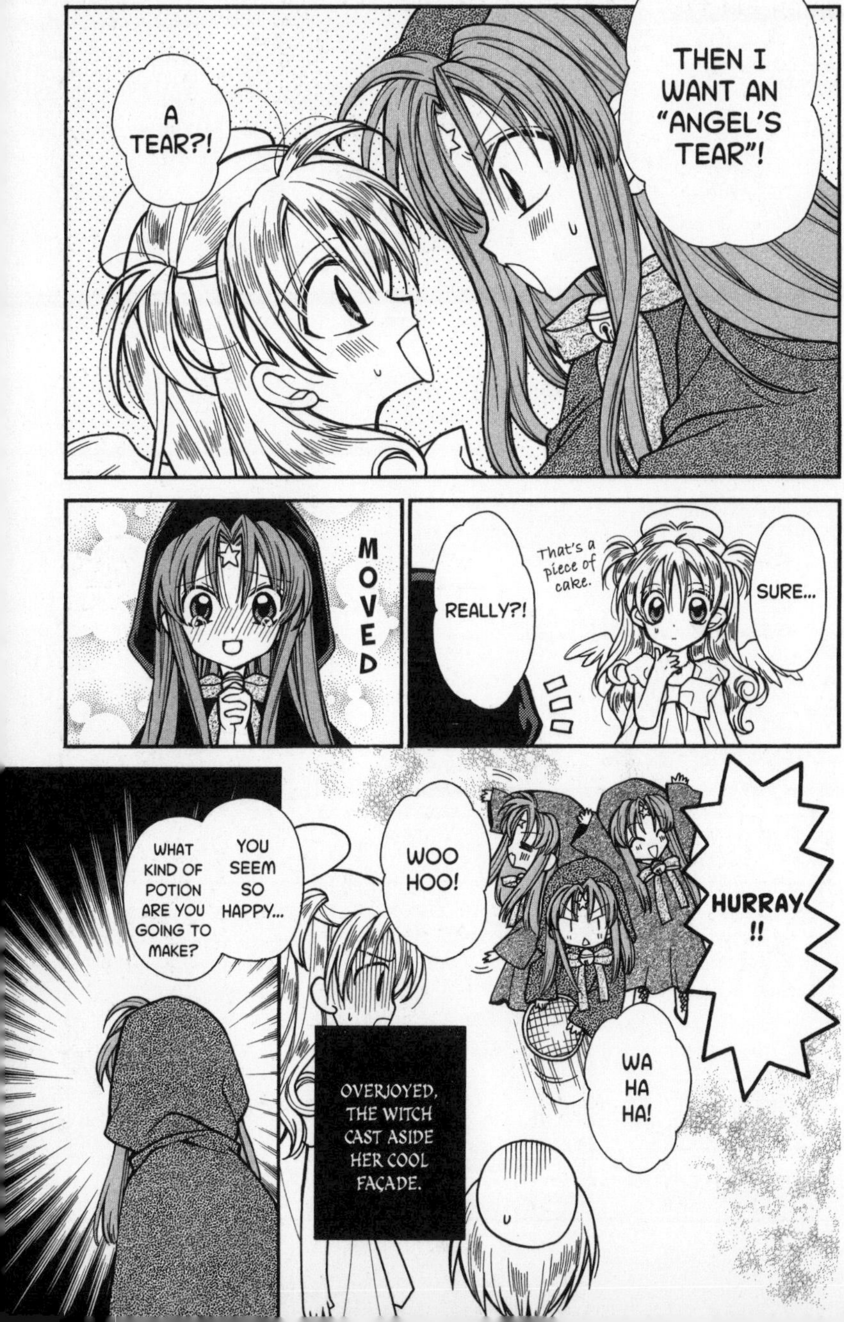
THEN I WANT AN "ANGEL'S TEAR"!
A TEAR?!
SURE...
That's a piece of cake.
REALLY?!
MOVED
HURRAY!!
WA HA HA!
WOO HOO!
YOU SEEM SO HAPPY...
WHAT KIND OF POTION ARE YOU GOING TO MAKE?
OVERJOYED, THE WITCH CAST ASIDE HER COOL FAÇADE.

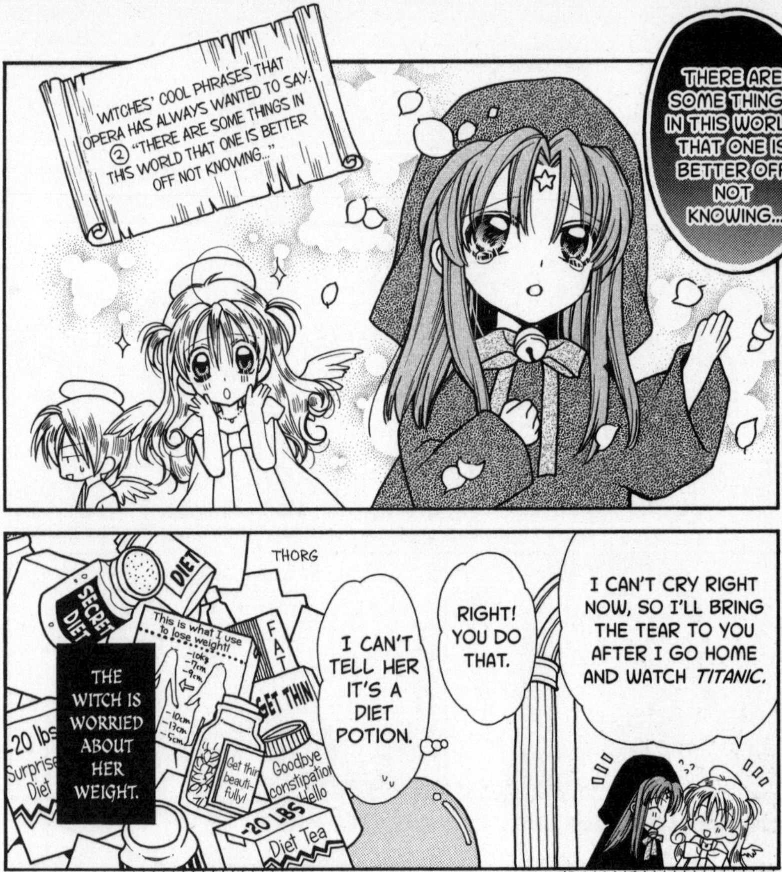
THERE ARE SOME THINGS IN THIS WORLD THAT ONE IS BETTER OFF NOT KNOWING...
WITCHES' COOL PHRASES THAT OPERA HAS ALWAYS WANTED TO SAY: ② "THERE ARE SOME THINGS IN THIS WORLD THAT ONE IS BETTER OFF NOT KNOWING..."
I CAN'T CRY RIGHT NOW, SO I'LL BRING THE TEAR TO YOU AFTER I GO HOME AND WATCH *TITANIC.*
RIGHT! YOU DO THAT.
I CAN'T TELL HER IT'S A DIET POTION.
THORG
THE WITCH IS WORRIED ABOUT HER WEIGHT.
DIET
SECRET DIET
This is what I use to lose weight!
FAT
GET THIN
-20 lbs Surprise Diet
Get thin beautifully!
Goodbye constipation Hello
-20 LBS Diet Tea

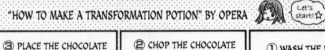

"HOW TO MAKE A TRANSFORMATION POTION" BY OPERA

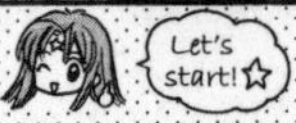
Let's start!☆

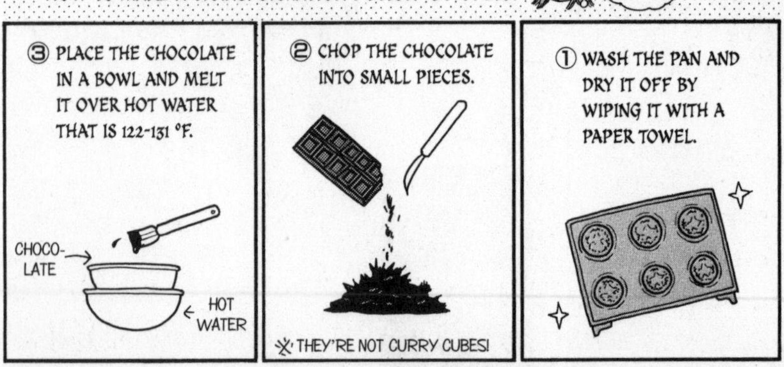
① WASH THE PAN AND DRY IT OFF BY WIPING IT WITH A PAPER TOWEL.
② CHOP THE CHOCOLATE INTO SMALL PIECES.
※ THEY'RE NOT CURRY CUBES!
③ PLACE THE CHOCOLATE IN A BOWL AND MELT IT OVER HOT WATER THAT IS 122-131 °F.
CHOCO-LATE
HOT WATER

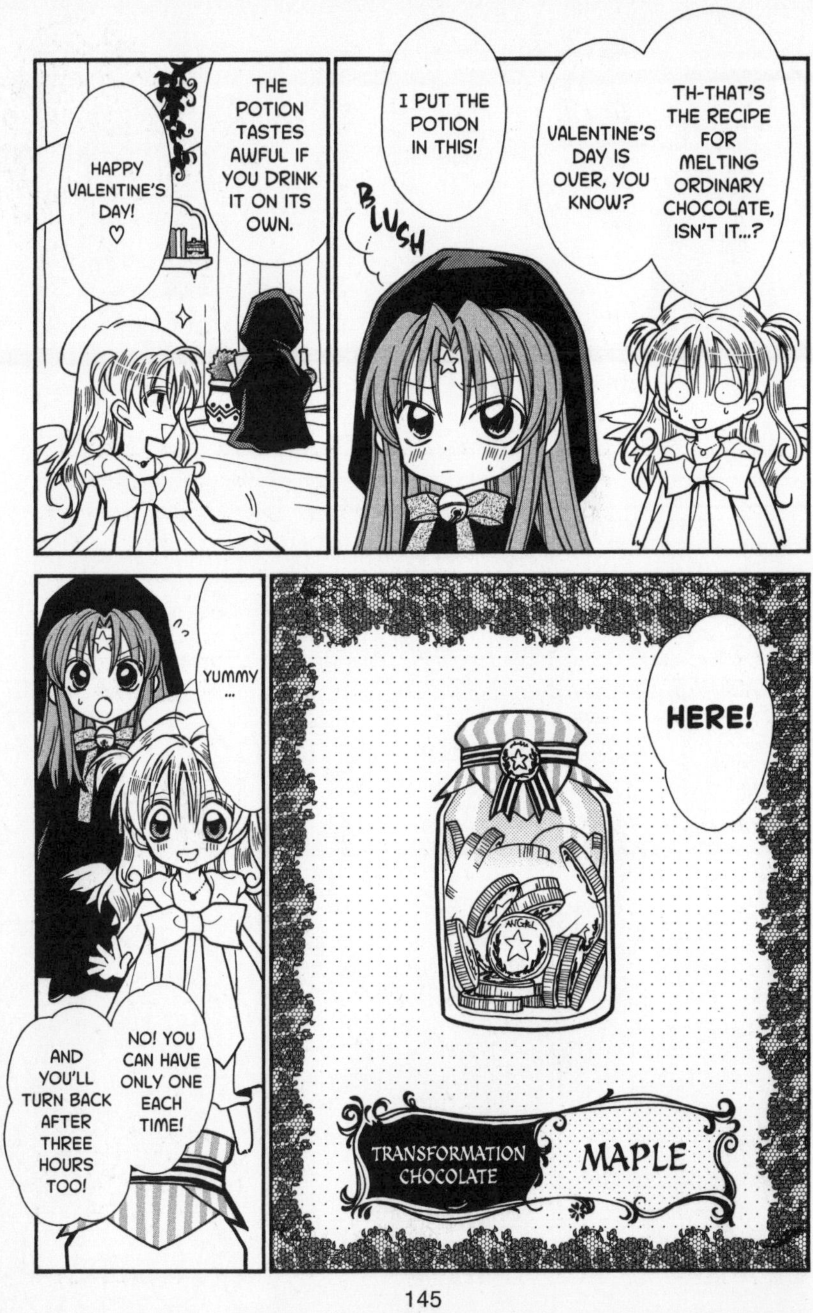
TH-THAT'S THE RECIPE FOR MELTING ORDINARY CHOCOLATE, ISN'T IT...?
VALENTINE'S DAY IS OVER, YOU KNOW?
I PUT THE POTION IN THIS!
BLUSH
THE POTION TASTES AWFUL IF YOU DRINK IT ON ITS OWN.
HAPPY VALENTINE'S DAY! ♡
HERE!
TRANSFORMATION CHOCOLATE
MAPLE
YUMMY...
NO! YOU CAN HAVE ONLY ONE EACH TIME!
AND YOU'LL TURN BACK AFTER THREE HOURS TOO!

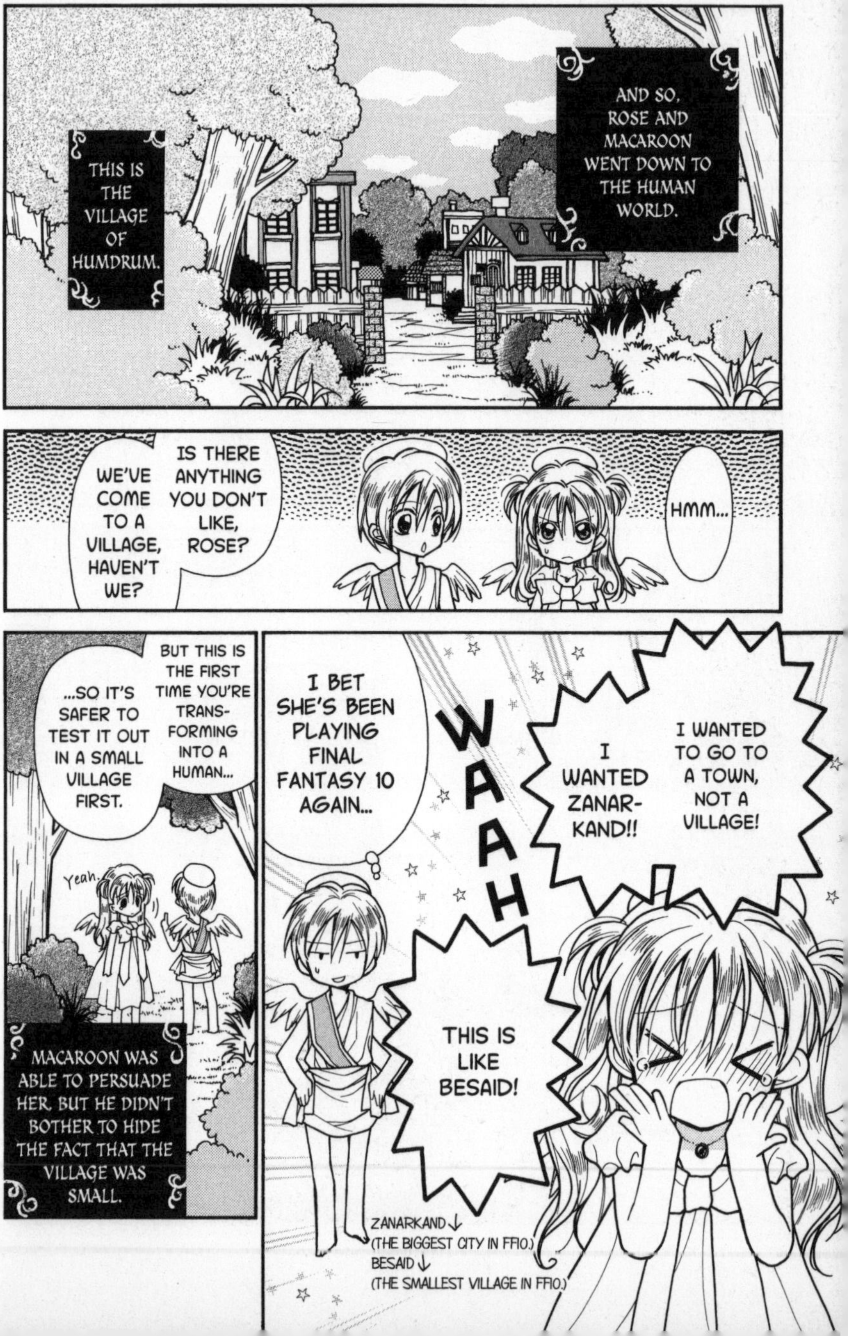
AND SO, ROSE AND MACAROON WENT DOWN TO THE HUMAN WORLD.
THIS IS THE VILLAGE OF HUMDRUM.
HMM...
IS THERE ANYTHING YOU DON'T LIKE, ROSE?
WE'VE COME TO A VILLAGE, HAVEN'T WE?
I WANTED TO GO TO A TOWN, NOT A VILLAGE!
I WANTED ZANARKAND!!
WAAH
I BET SHE'S BEEN PLAYING FINAL FANTASY 10 AGAIN...
THIS IS LIKE BESAID!
ZANARKAND↓
(THE BIGGEST CITY IN FF10.)
BESAID↓
(THE SMALLEST VILLAGE IN FF10.)
BUT THIS IS THE FIRST TIME YOU'RE TRANSFORMING INTO A HUMAN...
...SO IT'S SAFER TO TEST IT OUT IN A SMALL VILLAGE FIRST.
Yeah.
MACAROON WAS ABLE TO PERSUADE HER, BUT HE DIDN'T BOTHER TO HIDE THE FACT THAT THE VILLAGE WAS SMALL.

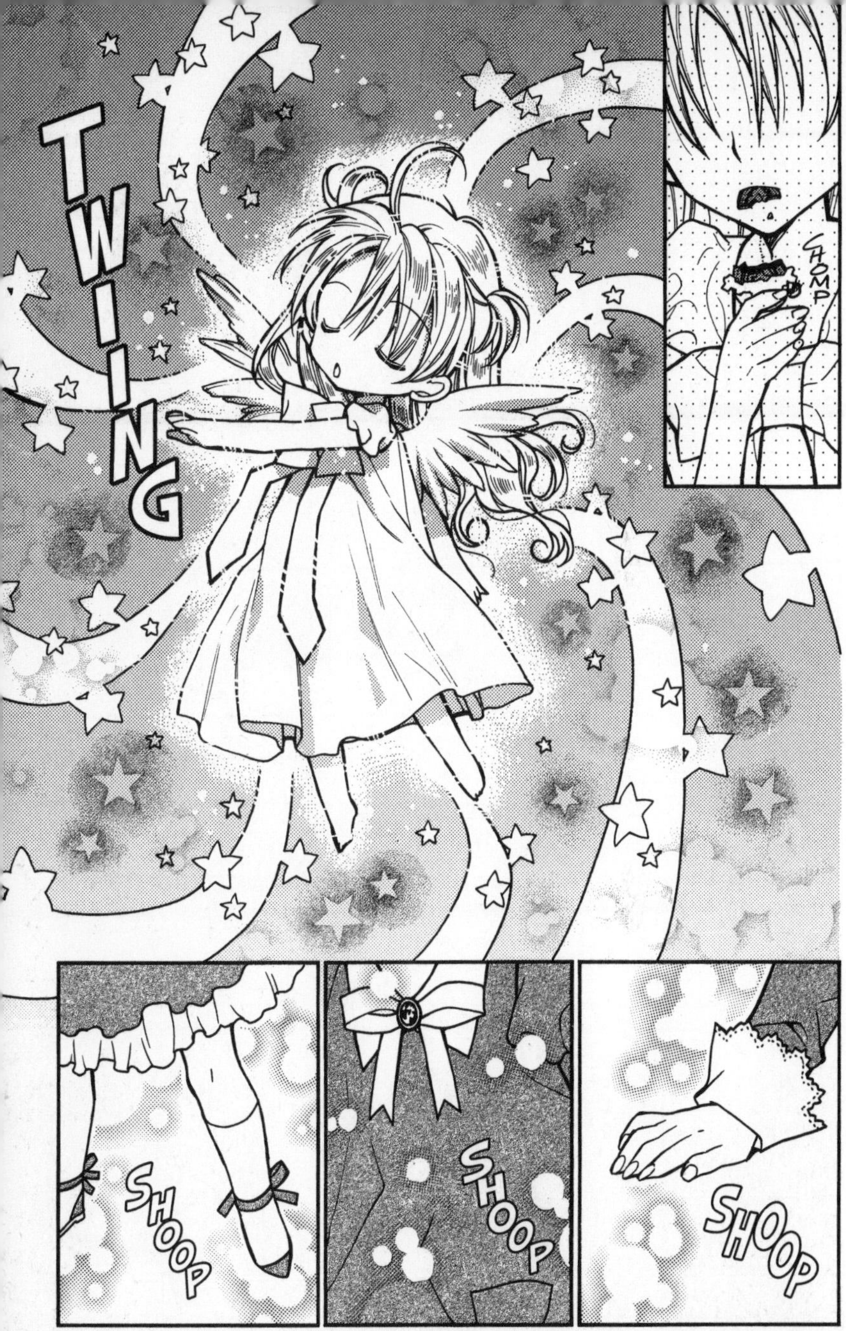
CHOMP
TWING
SHOOP
SHOOP
SHOOP

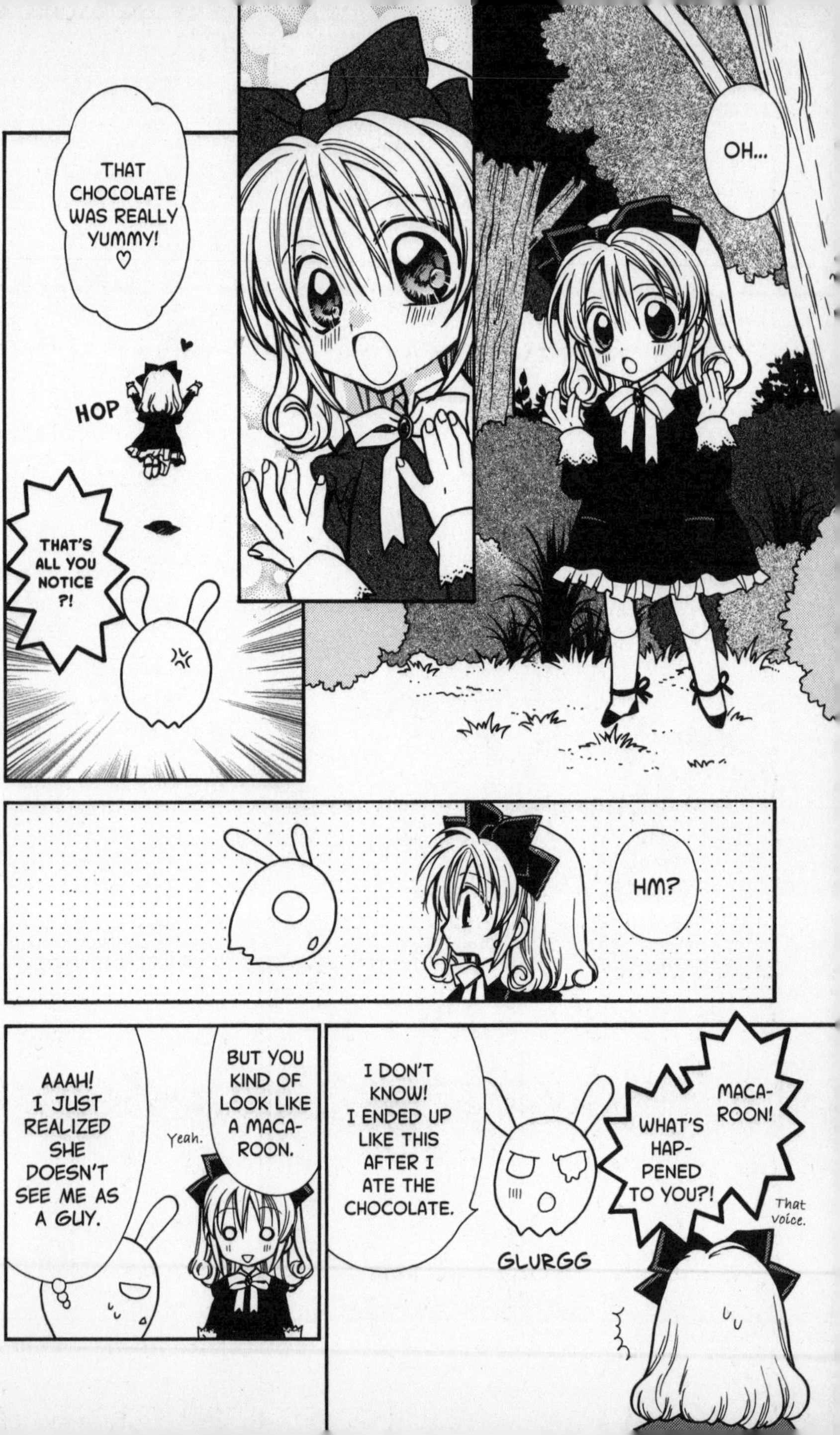
OH...
THAT CHOCOLATE WAS REALLY YUMMY! ♡
HOP
THAT'S ALL YOU NOTICE?!
HM?
That voice.
MACAROON!
WHAT'S HAPPENED TO YOU?!
GLURGG
I DON'T KNOW! I ENDED UP LIKE THIS AFTER I ATE THE CHOCOLATE.
BUT YOU KIND OF LOOK LIKE A MACAROON.
Yeah.
AAAH! I JUST REALIZED SHE DOESN'T SEE ME AS A GUY.

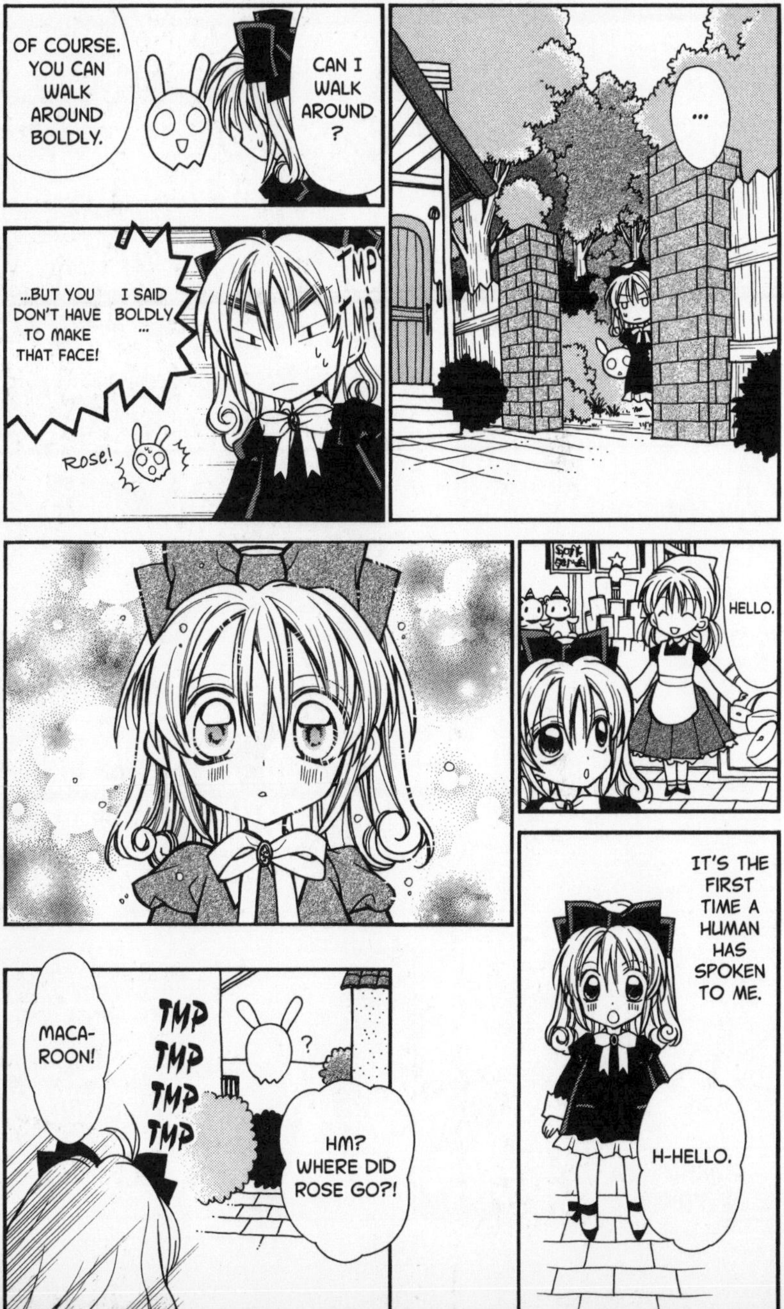
...
CAN I WALK AROUND?
OF COURSE. YOU CAN WALK AROUND BOLDLY.
TMP TMP
I SAID BOLDLY...
...BUT YOU DON'T HAVE TO MAKE THAT FACE!
Rose!
HELLO.
IT'S THE FIRST TIME A HUMAN HAS SPOKEN TO ME.
H-HELLO.
HM? WHERE DID ROSE GO?!
?
TMP TMP TMP TMP
MACA-ROON!

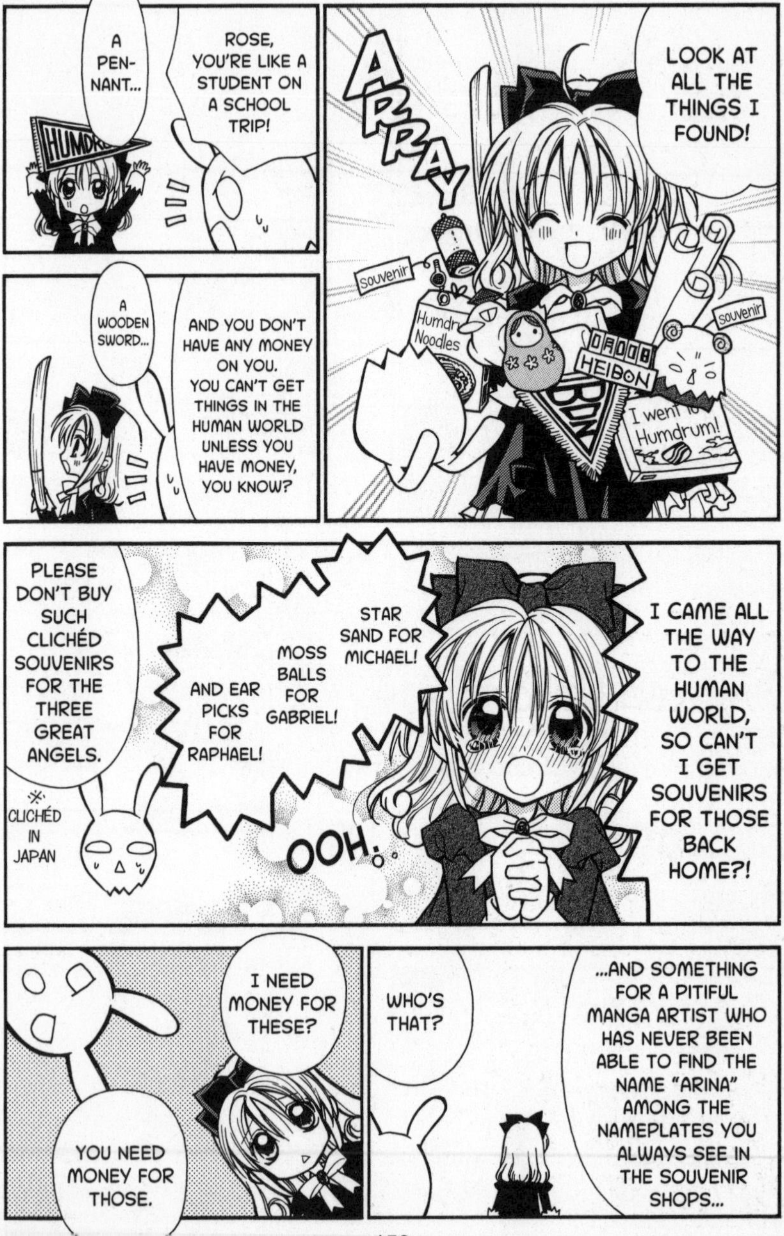
LOOK AT ALL THE THINGS I FOUND!
ARRAY
souvenir
Souvenir
HEIDON
Noodles
ROSE, YOU'RE LIKE A STUDENT ON A SCHOOL TRIP!
A PEN-NANT...
AND YOU DON'T HAVE ANY MONEY ON YOU. YOU CAN'T GET THINGS IN THE HUMAN WORLD UNLESS YOU HAVE MONEY, YOU KNOW?
A WOODEN SWORD...
I CAME ALL THE WAY TO THE HUMAN WORLD, SO CAN'T I GET SOUVENIRS FOR THOSE BACK HOME?!
STAR SAND FOR MICHAEL!
MOSS BALLS FOR GABRIEL!
AND EAR PICKS FOR RAPHAEL!
OOH.
PLEASE DON'T BUY SUCH CLICHÉD SOUVENIRS FOR THE THREE GREAT ANGELS.
※CLICHÉD IN JAPAN
...AND SOMETHING FOR A PITIFUL MANGA ARTIST WHO HAS NEVER BEEN ABLE TO FIND THE NAME "ARINA" AMONG THE NAMEPLATES YOU ALWAYS SEE IN THE SOUVENIR SHOPS...
WHO'S THAT?
I NEED MONEY FOR THESE?
YOU NEED MONEY FOR THOSE.

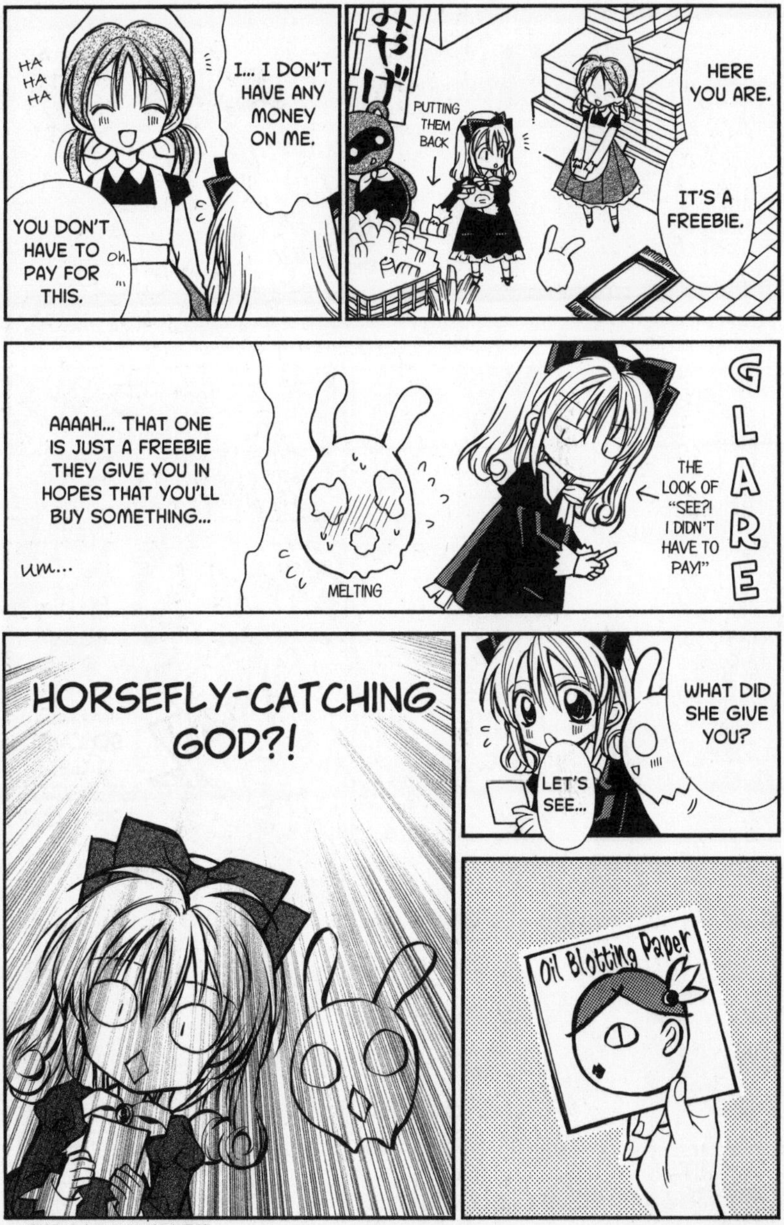
みやげ
HERE YOU ARE.
IT'S A FREEBIE.
PUTTING THEM BACK
I... I DON'T HAVE ANY MONEY ON ME.
HA HA HA
YOU DON'T HAVE TO PAY FOR THIS.
Oh.
GLARE
THE LOOK OF "SEE?! I DIDN'T HAVE TO PAY!"
MELTING
AAAAH... THAT ONE IS JUST A FREEBIE THEY GIVE YOU IN HOPES THAT YOU'LL BUY SOMETHING...
um...
WHAT DID SHE GIVE YOU?
LET'S SEE...
Oil Blotting Paper
HORSEFLY-CATCHING GOD?!

*THIS IS A PUN IN JAPANESE

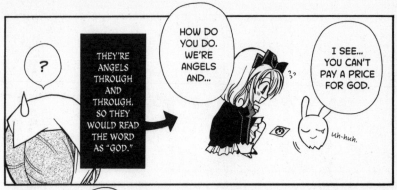

I SEE... YOU CAN'T PAY A PRICE FOR GOD.
Uh-huh.
HOW DO YOU DO. WE'RE ANGELS AND...
THEY'RE ANGELS THROUGH AND THROUGH, SO THEY WOULD READ THE WORD AS "GOD."
?
YAY
YAY
MRMR
MRMR
THEY'RE HAVING A FESTIVAL TONIGHT.
YOU RAN AWAY FROM YOUR PARTY...
...BUT IT LOOKS LIKE YOU CAN'T ESCAPE FESTIVITIES AFTER ALL.
I BET THE ANGELS ARE STILL CELEBRATING YOUR BIRTHDAY UP IN HEAVEN.
HERE, HAVE SOME CANDIES.

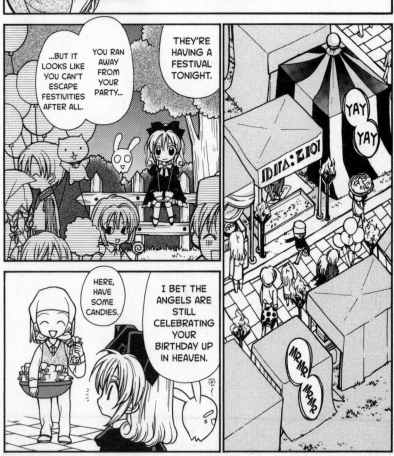

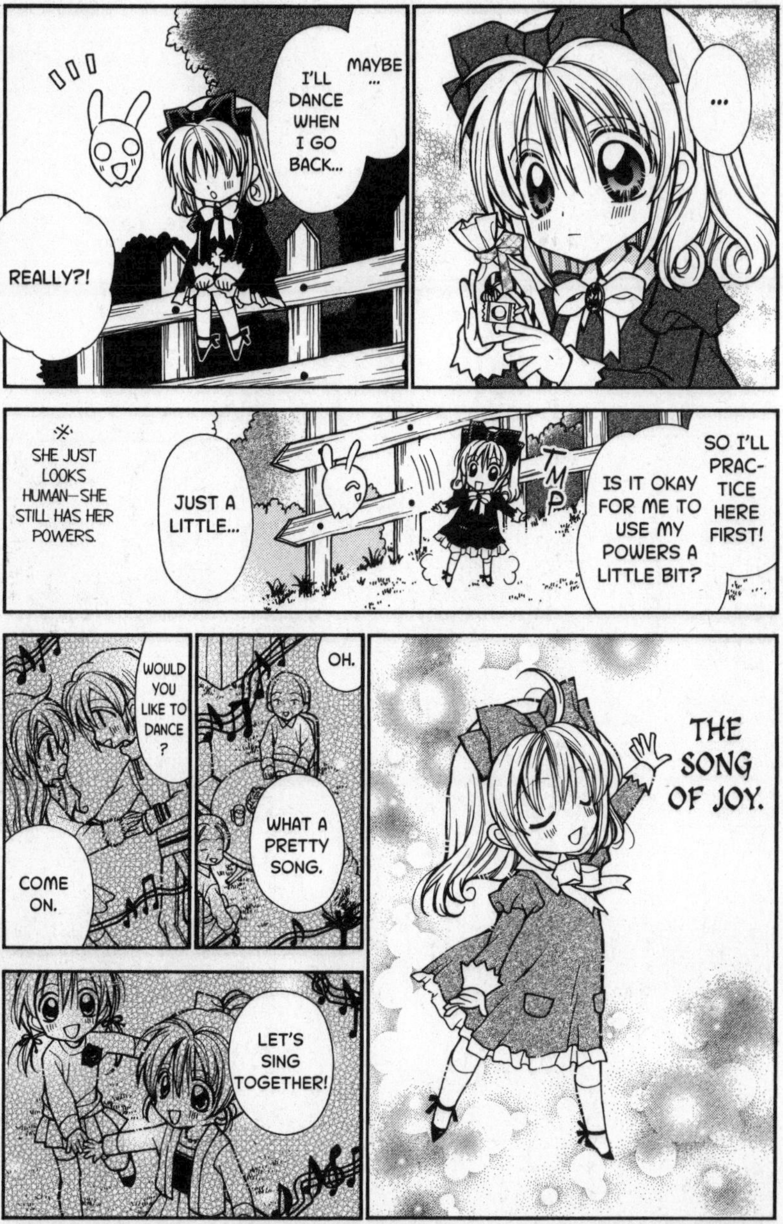
...
MAYBE ...
I'LL DANCE WHEN I GO BACK...
REALLY?!
SO I'LL PRAC-TICE HERE FIRST!
IS IT OKAY FOR ME TO USE MY POWERS A LITTLE BIT?
TMP
JUST A LITTLE...
※ SHE JUST LOOKS HUMAN—SHE STILL HAS HER POWERS.
THE SONG OF JOY.
OH.
WHAT A PRETTY SONG.
WOULD YOU LIKE TO DANCE?
COME ON.
LET'S SING TOGETHER!

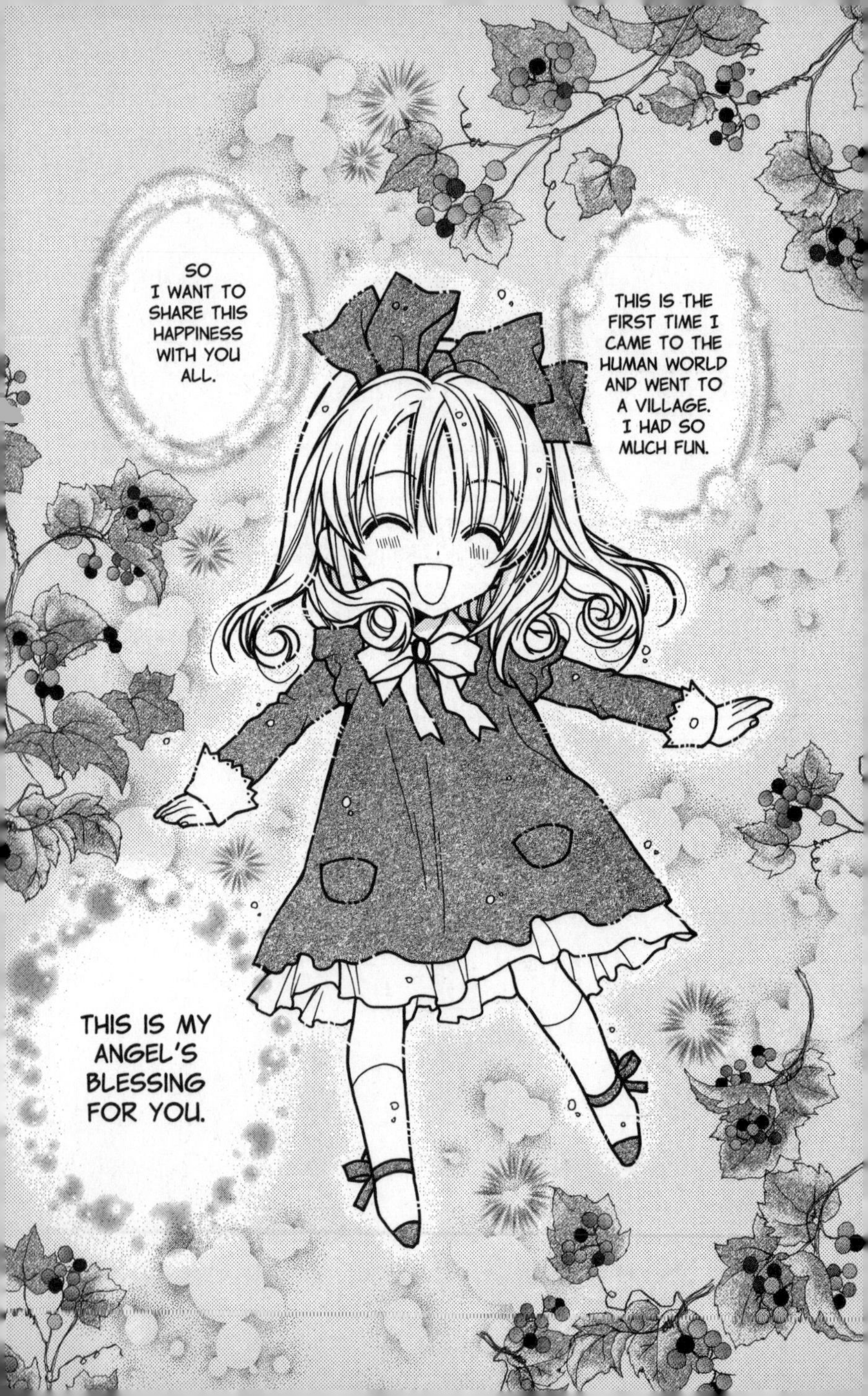
THIS IS THE FIRST TIME I CAME TO THE HUMAN WORLD AND WENT TO A VILLAGE. I HAD SO MUCH FUN.
SO I WANT TO SHARE THIS HAPPINESS WITH YOU ALL.
THIS IS MY ANGEL'S BLESSING FOR YOU.

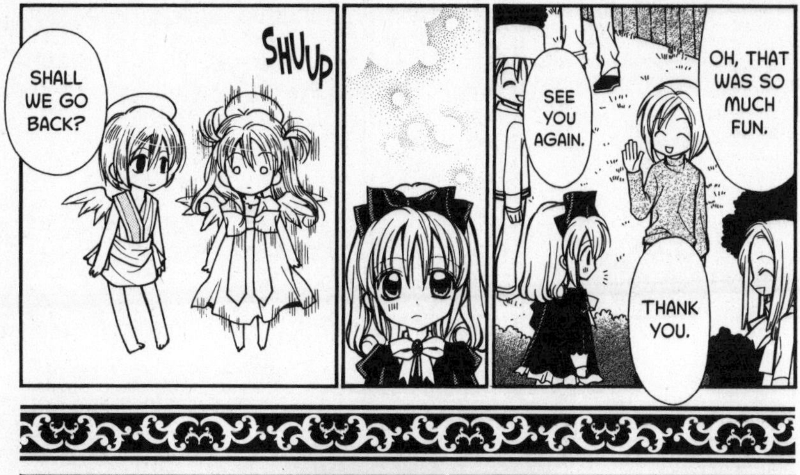
OH, THAT WAS SO MUCH FUN.
SEE YOU AGAIN.
THANK YOU.
SHUUP
SHALL WE GO BACK?

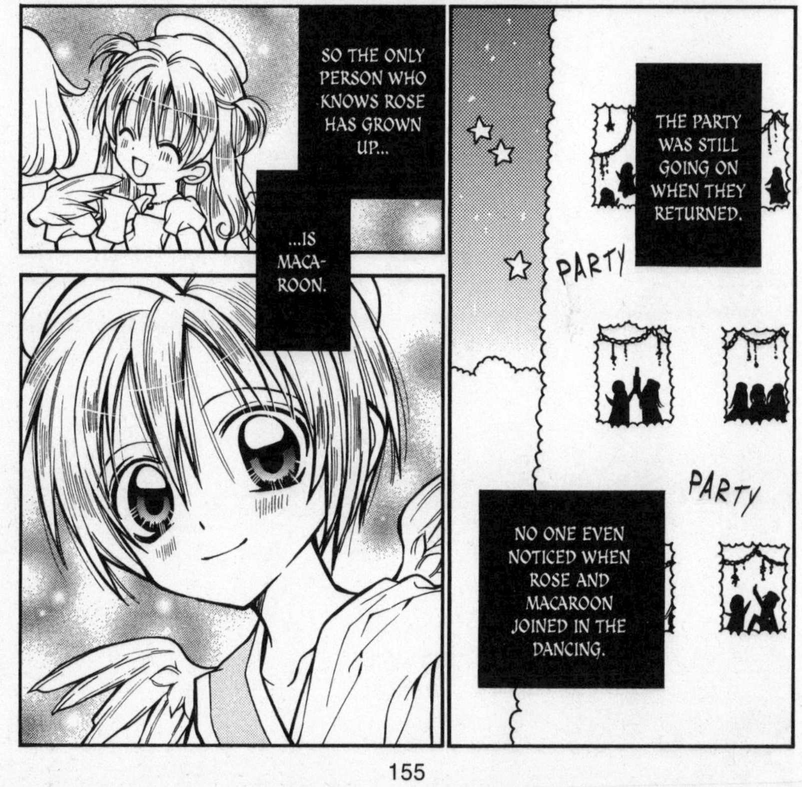
THE PARTY WAS STILL GOING ON WHEN THEY RETURNED.
PARTY
PARTY
NO ONE EVEN NOTICED WHEN ROSE AND MACAROON JOINED IN THE DANCING.
SO THE ONLY PERSON WHO KNOWS ROSE HAS GROWN UP...
...IS MACA-ROON.

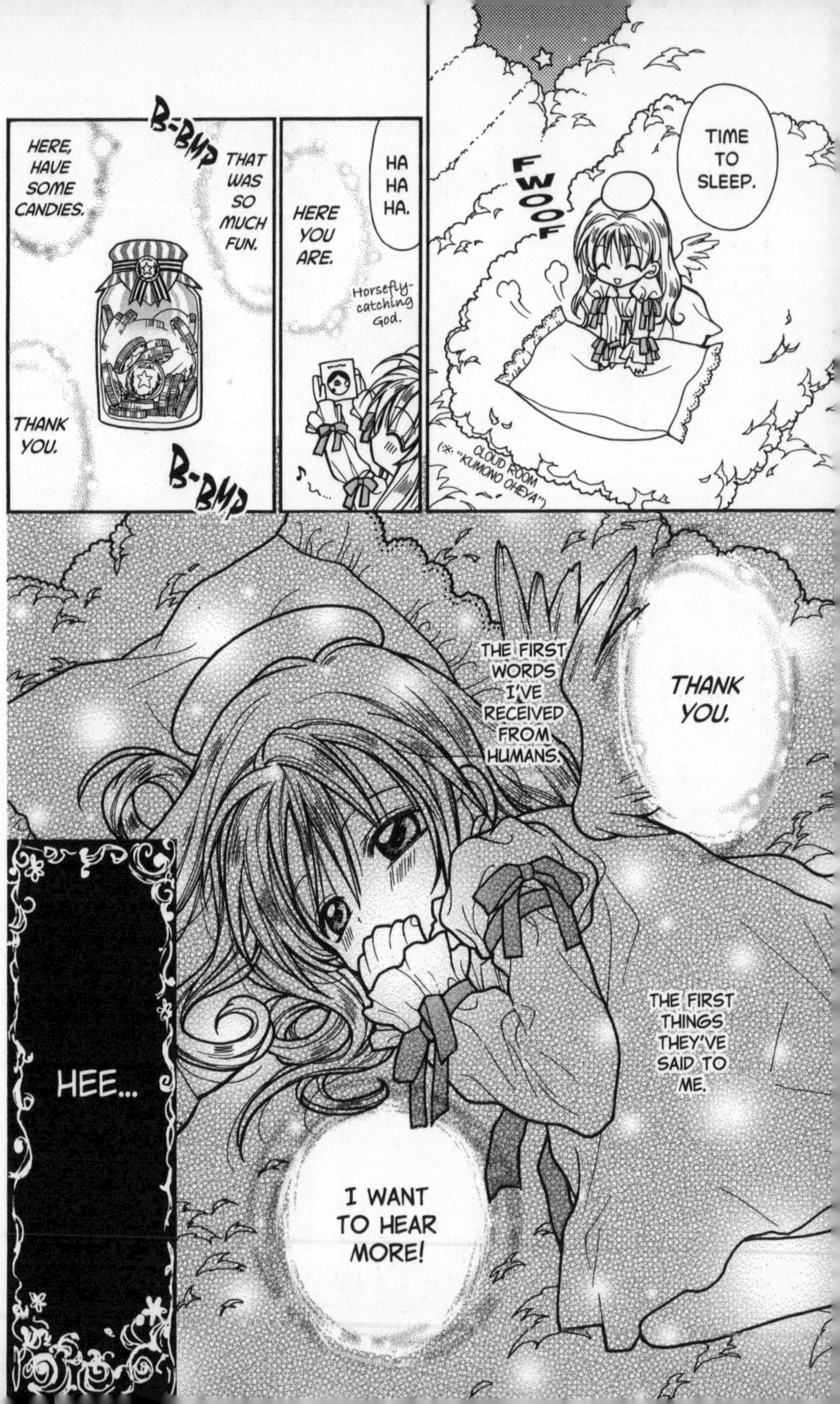
TIME TO SLEEP.
FWOOF
CLOUD ROOM (※ "KUMONO OHEYA")
HA HA HA.
HERE YOU ARE.
Horsefly-catching God.
B-BMP
THAT WAS SO MUCH FUN.
HERE, HAVE SOME CANDIES.
THANK YOU.
B-BMP
THANK YOU.
THE FIRST WORDS I'VE RECEIVED FROM HUMANS.
THE FIRST THINGS THEY'VE SAID TO ME.
I WANT TO HEAR MORE!
HEE...

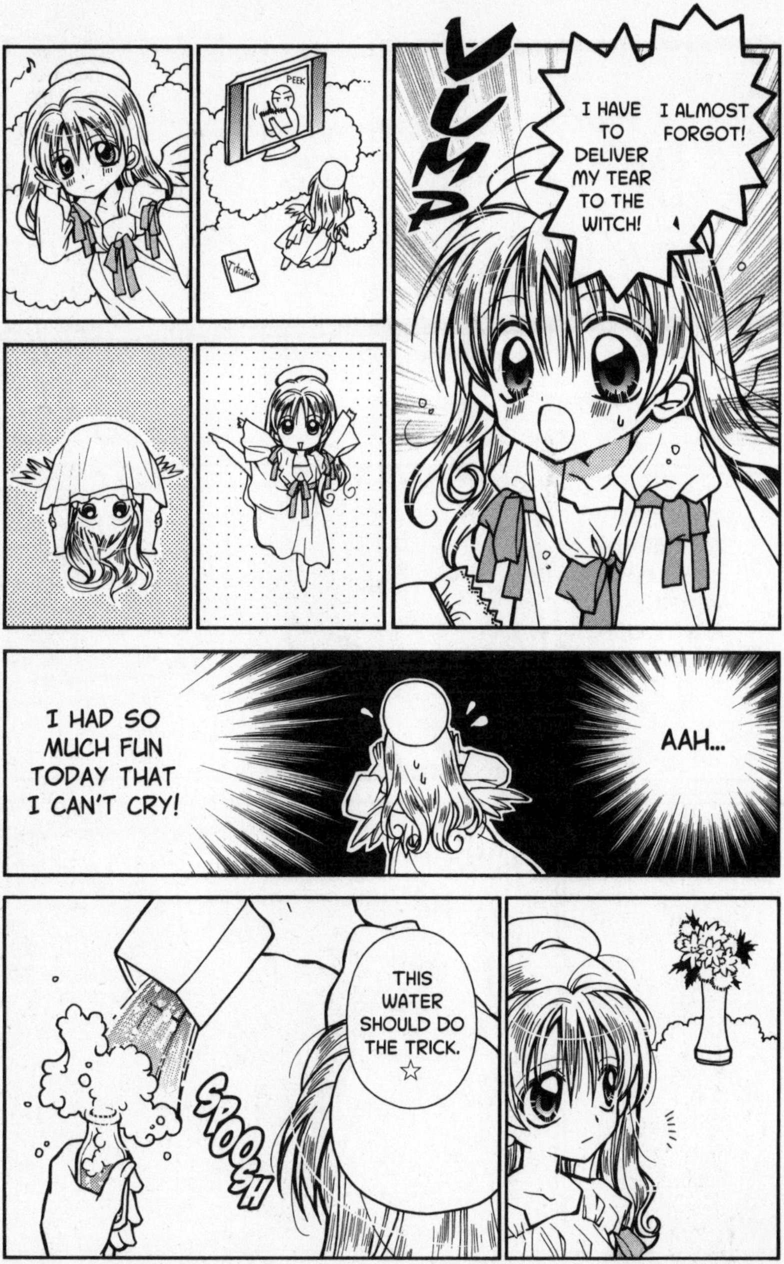
JUMP
I ALMOST FORGOT!
I HAVE TO DELIVER MY TEAR TO THE WITCH!
PEEK
Titanic
AAH...
I HAD SO MUCH FUN TODAY THAT I CAN'T CRY!
THIS WATER SHOULD DO THE TRICK. ☆
SPOOSH

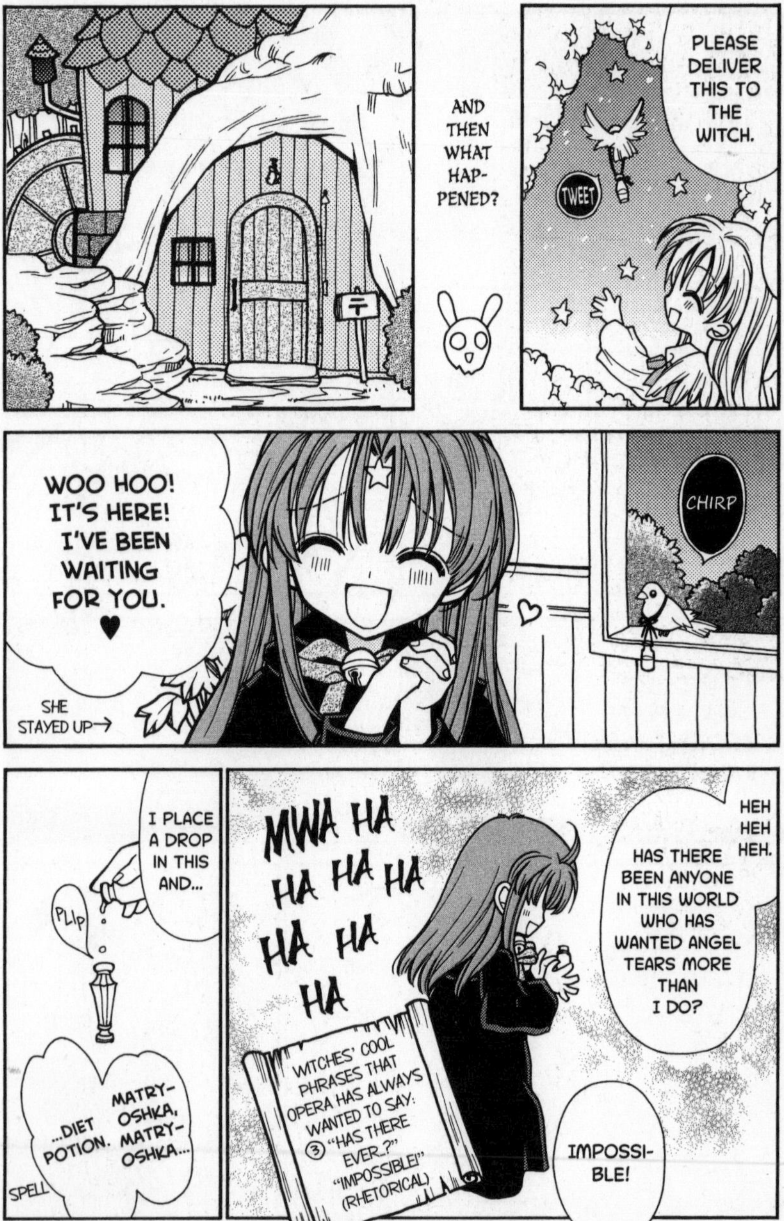
PLEASE DELIVER THIS TO THE WITCH.
TWEET
AND THEN WHAT HAP-PENED?
CHIRP
WOO HOO! IT'S HERE! I'VE BEEN WAITING FOR YOU. ♥
SHE STAYED UP→
HEH HEH HEH.
HAS THERE BEEN ANYONE IN THIS WORLD WHO HAS WANTED ANGEL TEARS MORE THAN I DO?
MWA HA HA HA HA HA HA HA
IMPOSSI-BLE!
WITCHES' COOL PHRASES THAT OPERA HAS ALWAYS WANTED TO SAY: ③ "HAS THERE EVER..?" "IMPOSSIBLE!" (RHETORICAL)
I PLACE A DROP IN THIS AND...
PLIP
MATRY-OSHKA, MATRY-OSHKA... ...DIET POTION.
SPELL

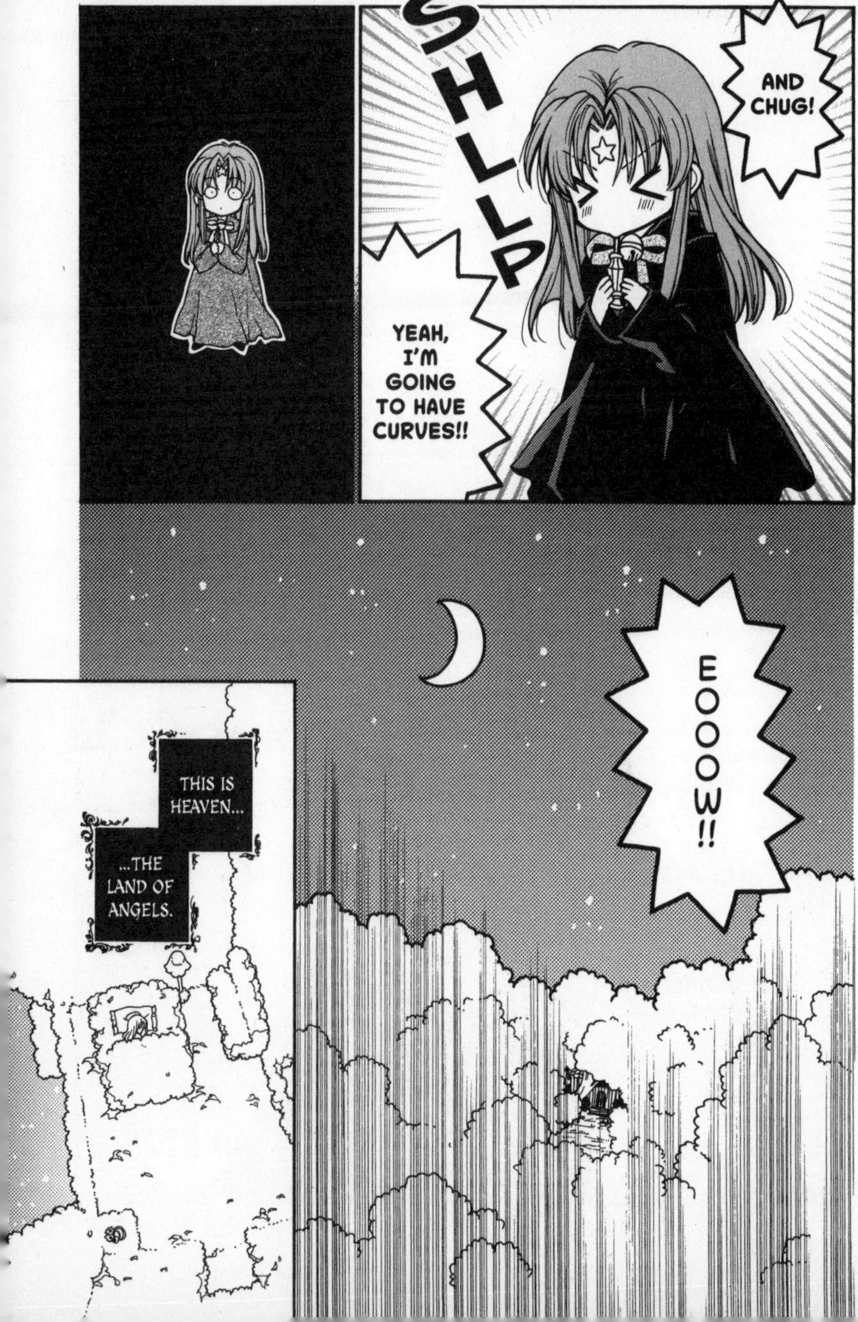
AND CHUG!
SHLLP
YEAH, I'M GOING TO HAVE CURVES!!
EOOOW!!
THIS IS HEAVEN...
...THE LAND OF ANGELS.

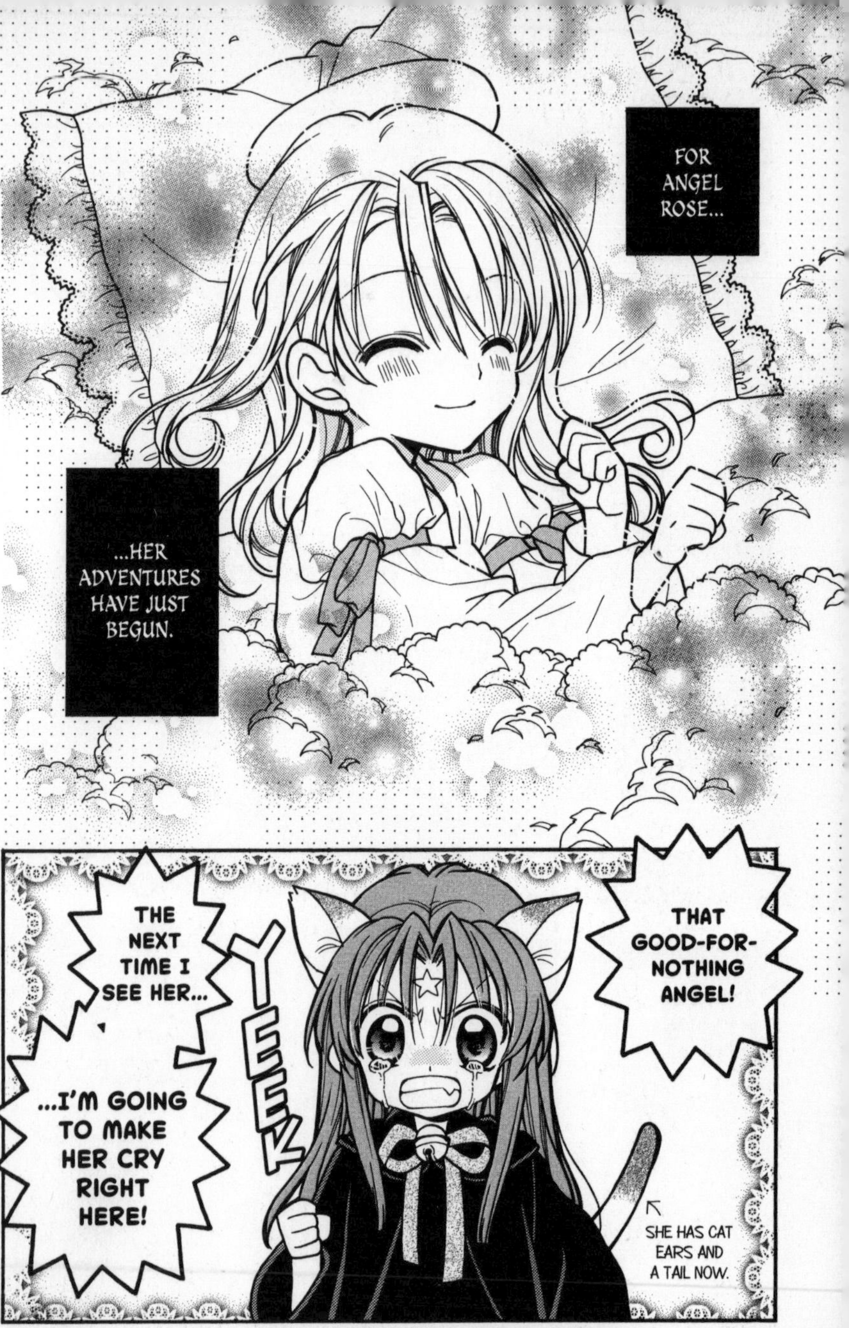
FOR ANGEL ROSE...
...HER ADVENTURES HAVE JUST BEGUN.
THAT GOOD-FOR-NOTHING ANGEL!
YEEK
THE NEXT TIME I SEE HER...
...I'M GOING TO MAKE HER CRY RIGHT HERE!
SHE HAS CAT EARS AND A TAIL NOW.

The Angelic Gold Coin of Maple Rose/End

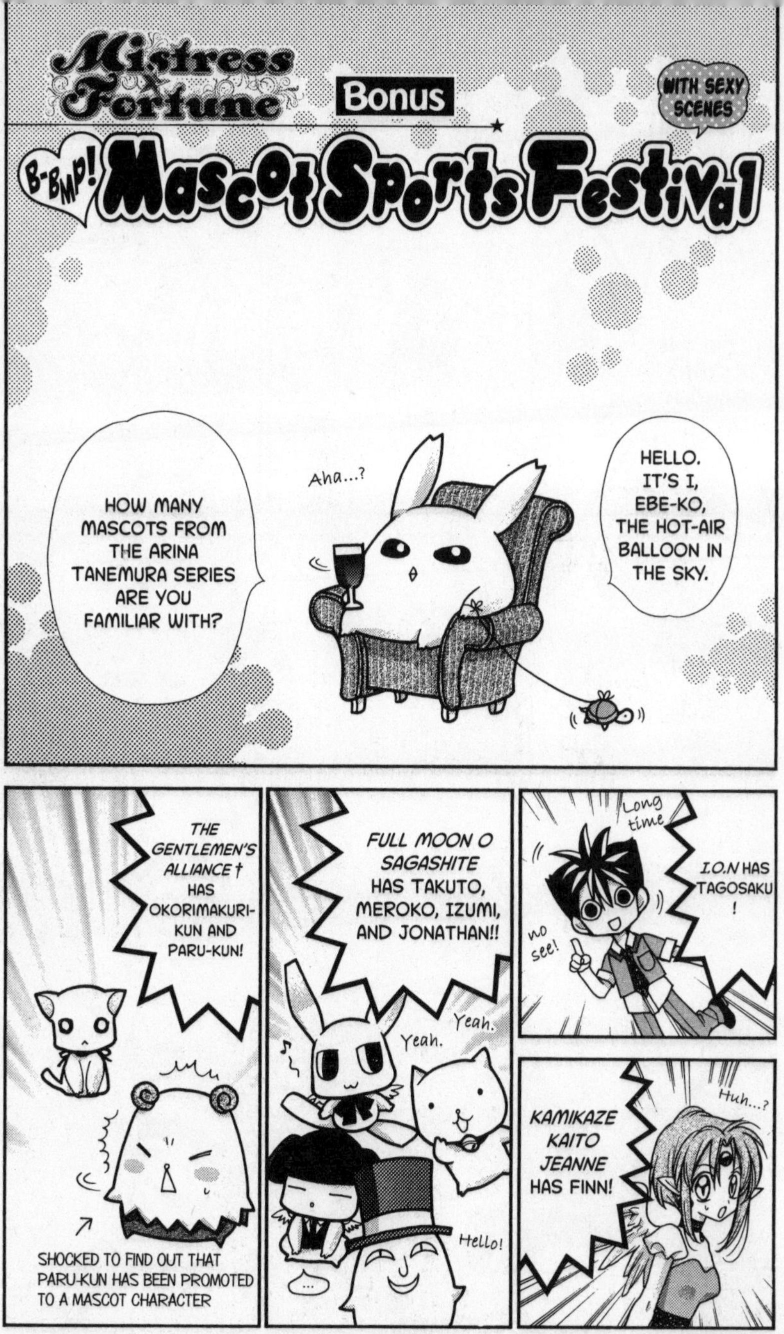
Mistress x Fortune
Bonus
WITH SEXY SCENES
B-BMP! Mascot Sports Festival
HELLO. IT'S I, EBE-KO, THE HOT-AIR BALLOON IN THE SKY.
Aha...?
HOW MANY MASCOTS FROM THE ARINA TANEMURA SERIES ARE YOU FAMILIAR WITH?
Long time no see!
I.O.N HAS TAGOSAKU!
KAMIKAZE KAITO JEANNE HAS FINN!
Huh...?
FULL MOON O SAGASHITE HAS TAKUTO, MEROKO, IZUMI, AND JONATHAN!!
Yeah.
Yeah.
Hello!
...
THE GENTLEMEN'S ALLIANCE † HAS OKORIMAKURI-KUN AND PARU-KUN!
SHOCKED TO FIND OUT THAT PARU-KUN HAS BEEN PROMOTED TO A MASCOT CHARACTER

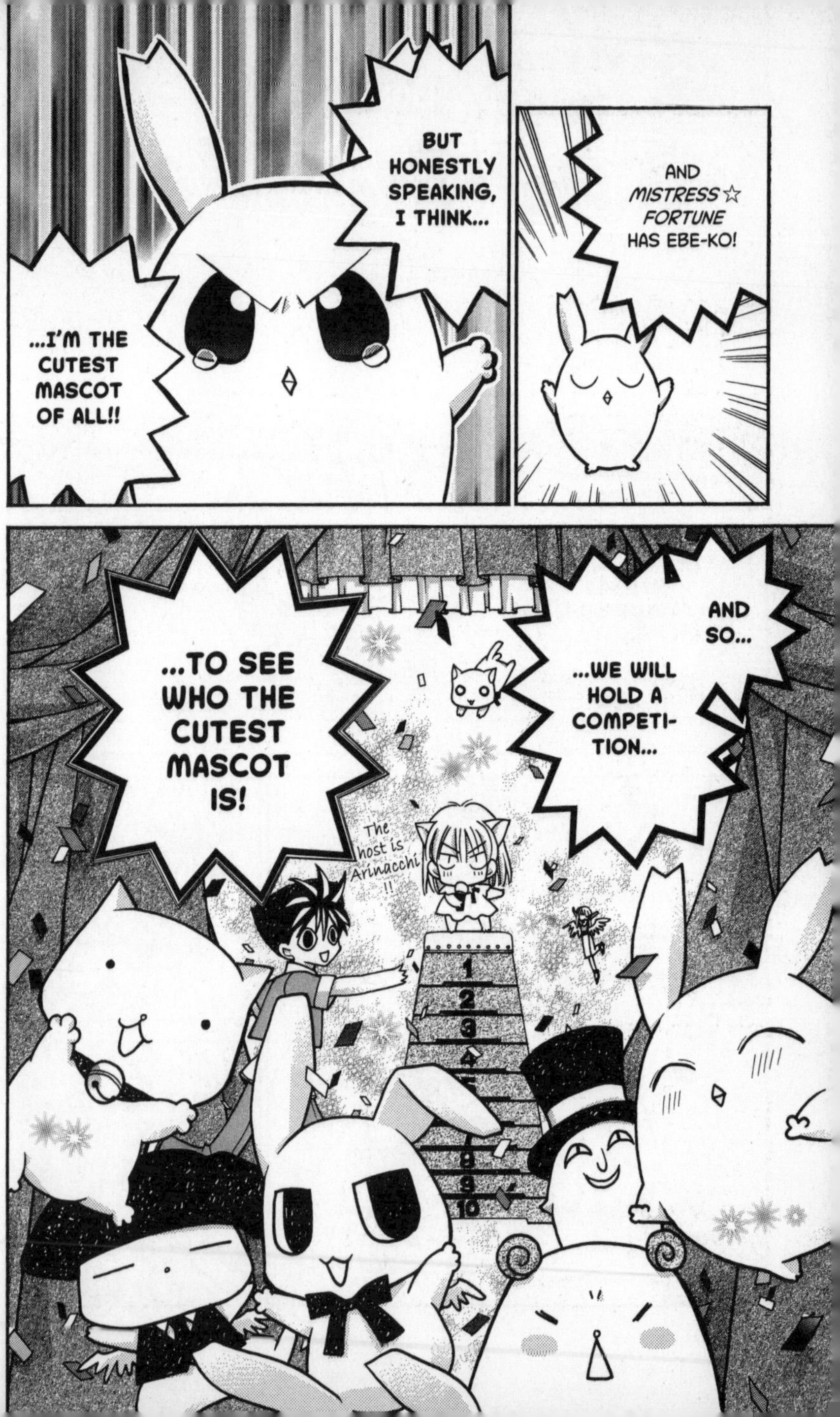
AND MISTRESS☆FORTUNE HAS EBE-KO!
BUT HONESTLY SPEAKING, I THINK...
...I'M THE CUTEST MASCOT OF ALL!!
AND SO...
...WE WILL HOLD A COMPETITION...
...TO SEE WHO THE CUTEST MASCOT IS!
The host is Arinacchi!!

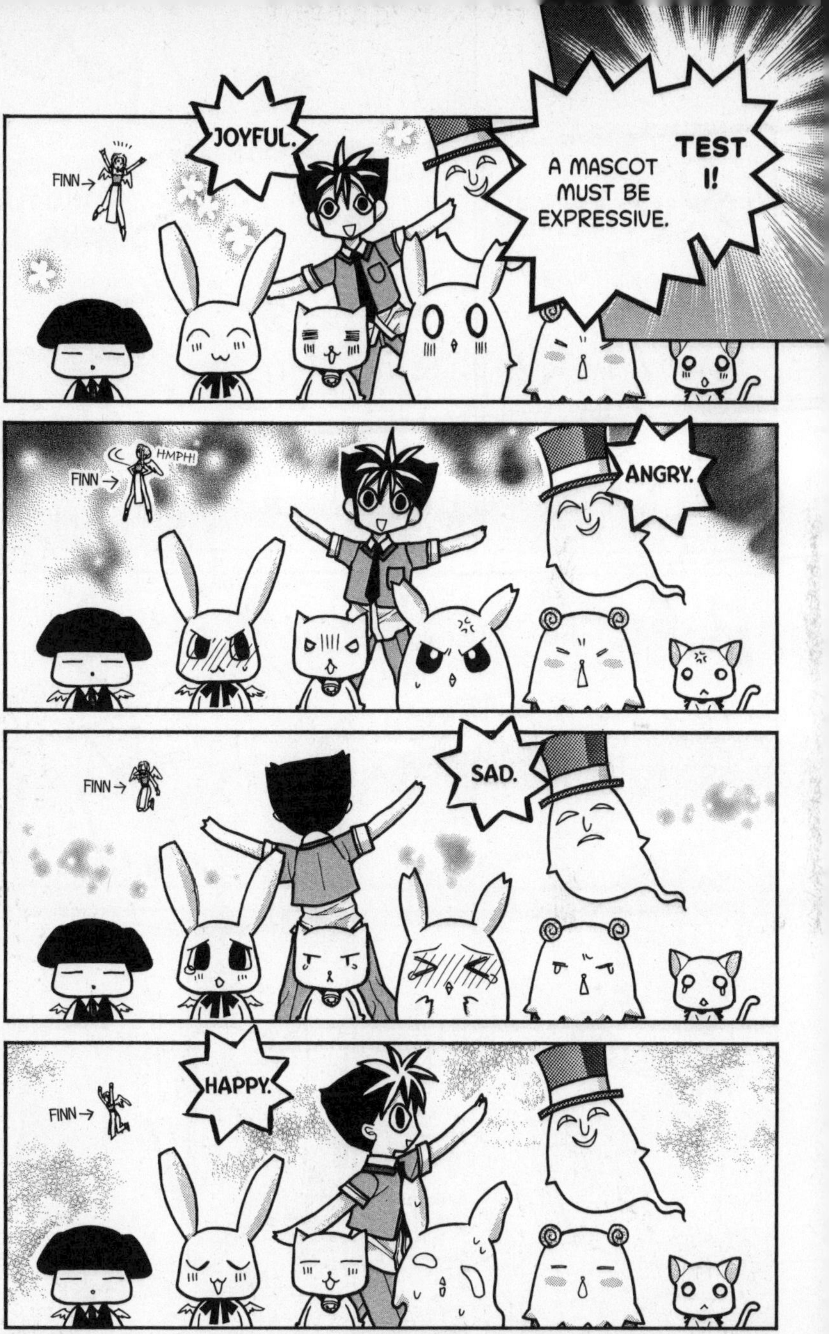
TEST I!
A MASCOT MUST BE EXPRESSIVE.
JOYFUL.
FINN →
ANGRY.
HMPH!
FINN →
SAD.
FINN →
HAPPY.
FINN →

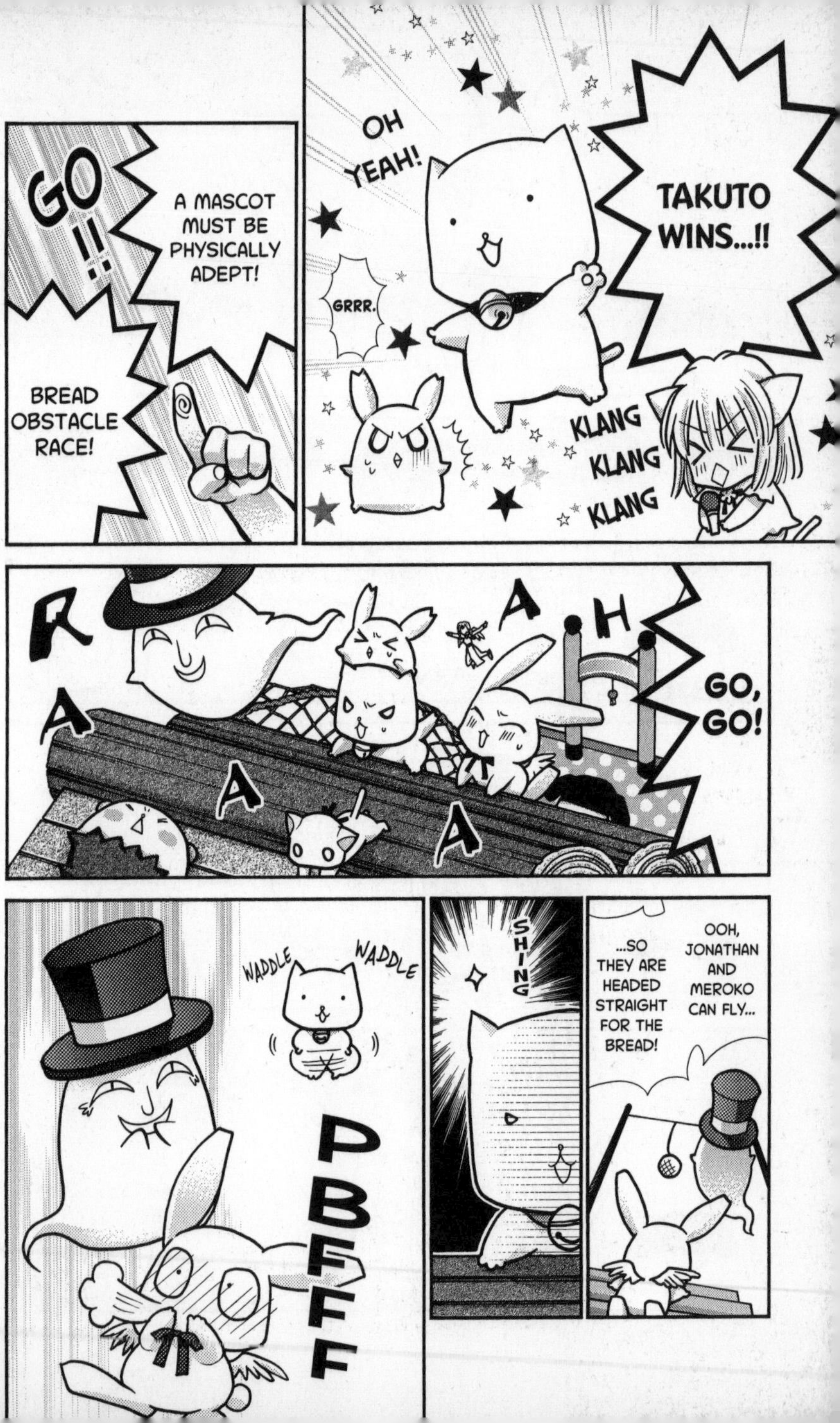
TAKUTO WINS...!!
OH YEAH!
GRRR.
KLANG
KLANG
KLANG
A MASCOT MUST BE PHYSICALLY ADEPT!
GO!!
BREAD OBSTACLE RACE!
GO, GO!
RAAAAH
OOH, JONATHAN AND MEROKO CAN FLY...
...SO THEY ARE HEADED STRAIGHT FOR THE BREAD!
SHING
WADDLE
WADDLE
PBFFF

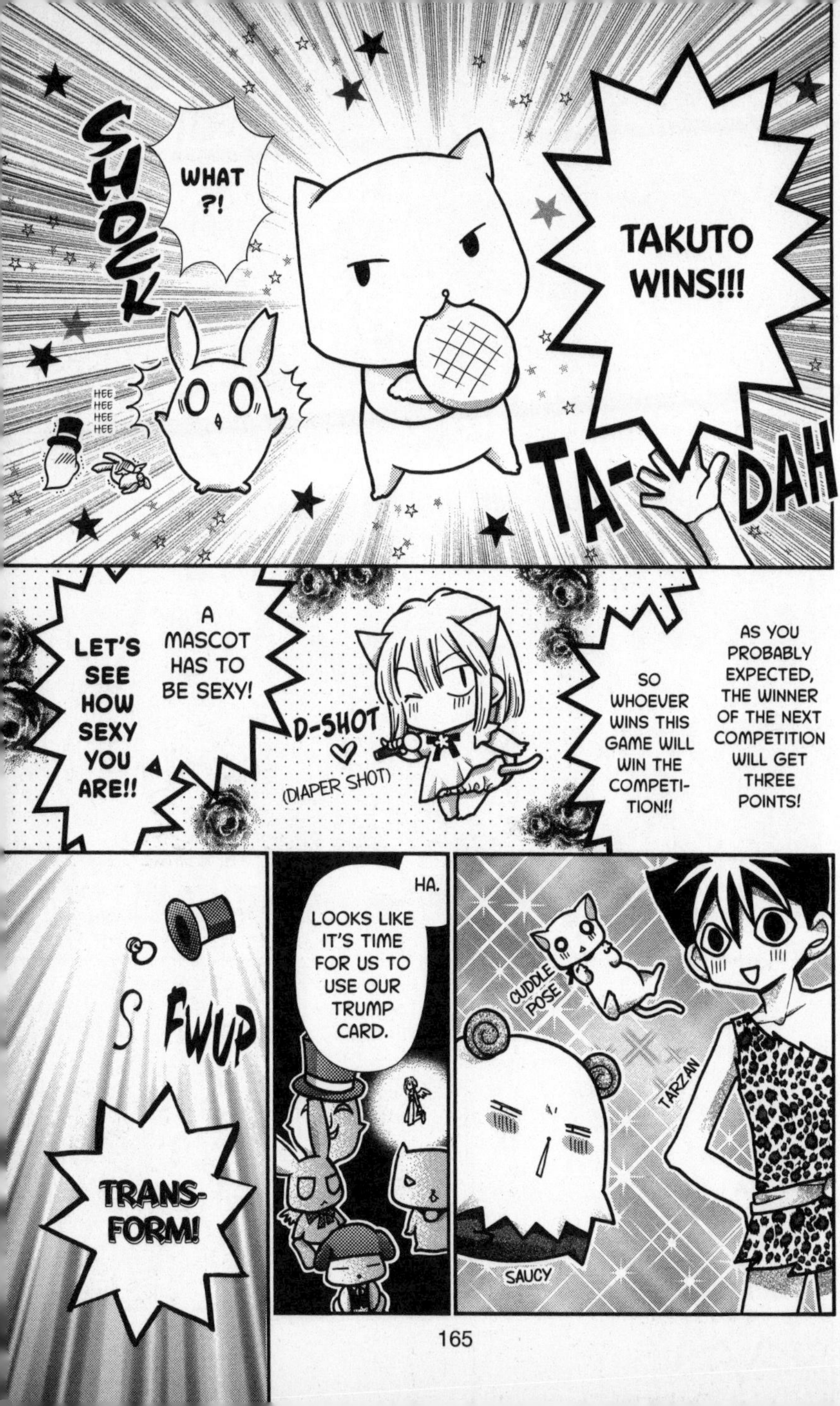
TAKUTO WINS!!!
TA-DAH
WHAT ?!
SHOCK
HEE HEE HEE HEE
AS YOU PROBABLY EXPECTED, THE WINNER OF THE NEXT COMPETITION WILL GET THREE POINTS!
SO WHOEVER WINS THIS GAME WILL WIN THE COMPETI-TION!!
D-SHOT
(DIAPER SHOT)
A MASCOT HAS TO BE SEXY!
LET'S SEE HOW SEXY YOU ARE!!
CUDDLE POSE
TARZAN
SAUCY
HA.
LOOKS LIKE IT'S TIME FOR US TO USE OUR TRUMP CARD.
FWUP
TRANS-FORM!

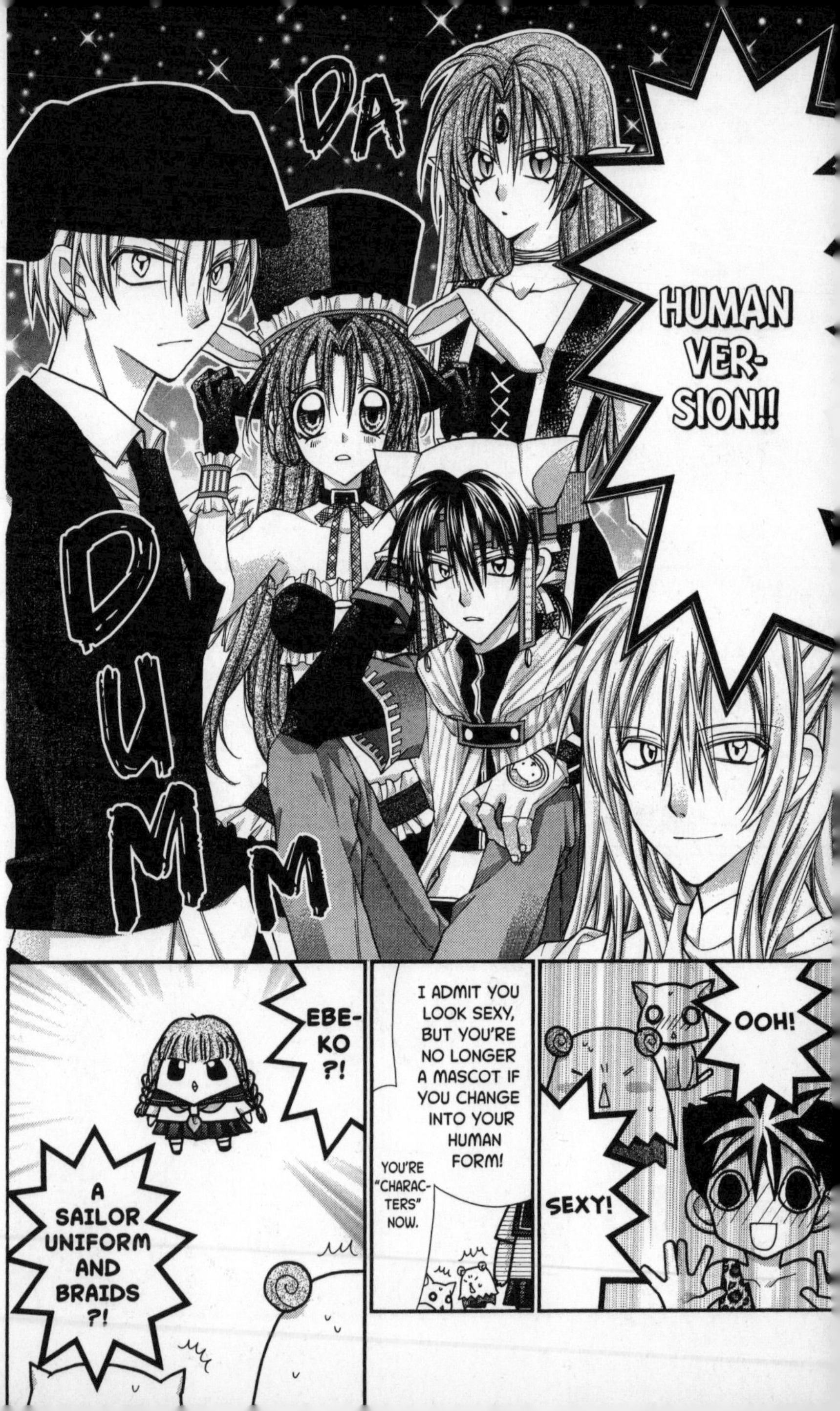
DA
DUMMM
HUMAN VERSION!!
OOH!
SEXY!
I ADMIT YOU LOOK SEXY, BUT YOU'RE NO LONGER A MASCOT IF YOU CHANGE INTO YOUR HUMAN FORM!
YOU'RE "CHARACTERS" NOW.
EBEKO?!
A SAILOR UNIFORM AND BRAIDS?!

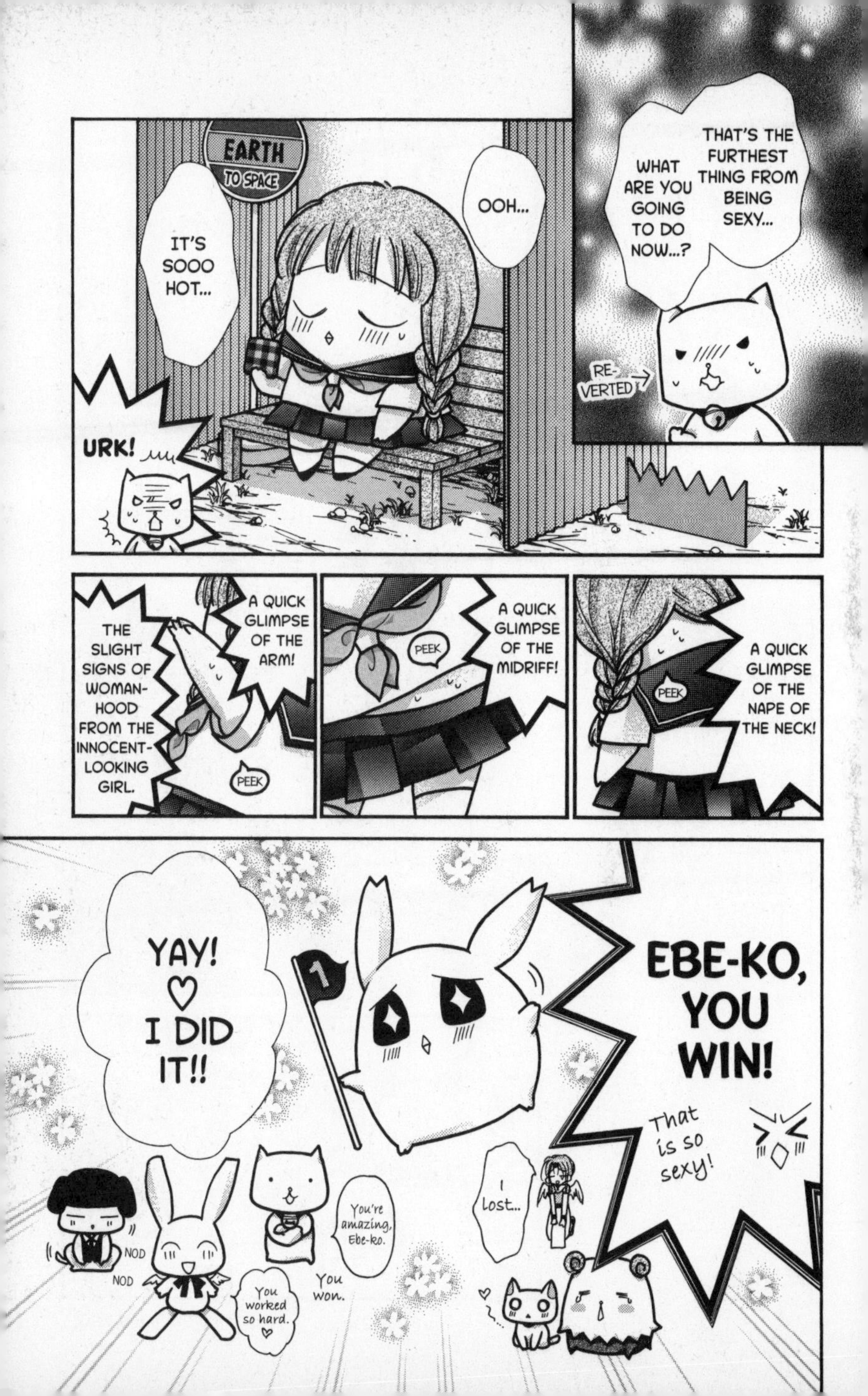
THAT'S THE FURTHEST THING FROM BEING SEXY...
WHAT ARE YOU GOING TO DO NOW...?
RE-VERTED
OOH...
IT'S SOOO HOT...
URK!
A QUICK GLIMPSE OF THE NAPE OF THE NECK!
PEEK
A QUICK GLIMPSE OF THE MIDRIFF!
PEEK
A QUICK GLIMPSE OF THE ARM!
THE SLIGHT SIGNS OF WOMAN-HOOD FROM THE INNOCENT-LOOKING GIRL.
PEEK
EBE-KO, YOU WIN!
YAY! ♡ I DID IT!!
That is so sexy!
I lost...
You're amazing, Ebe-ko.
You won.
You worked so hard. ♡
NOD
NOD

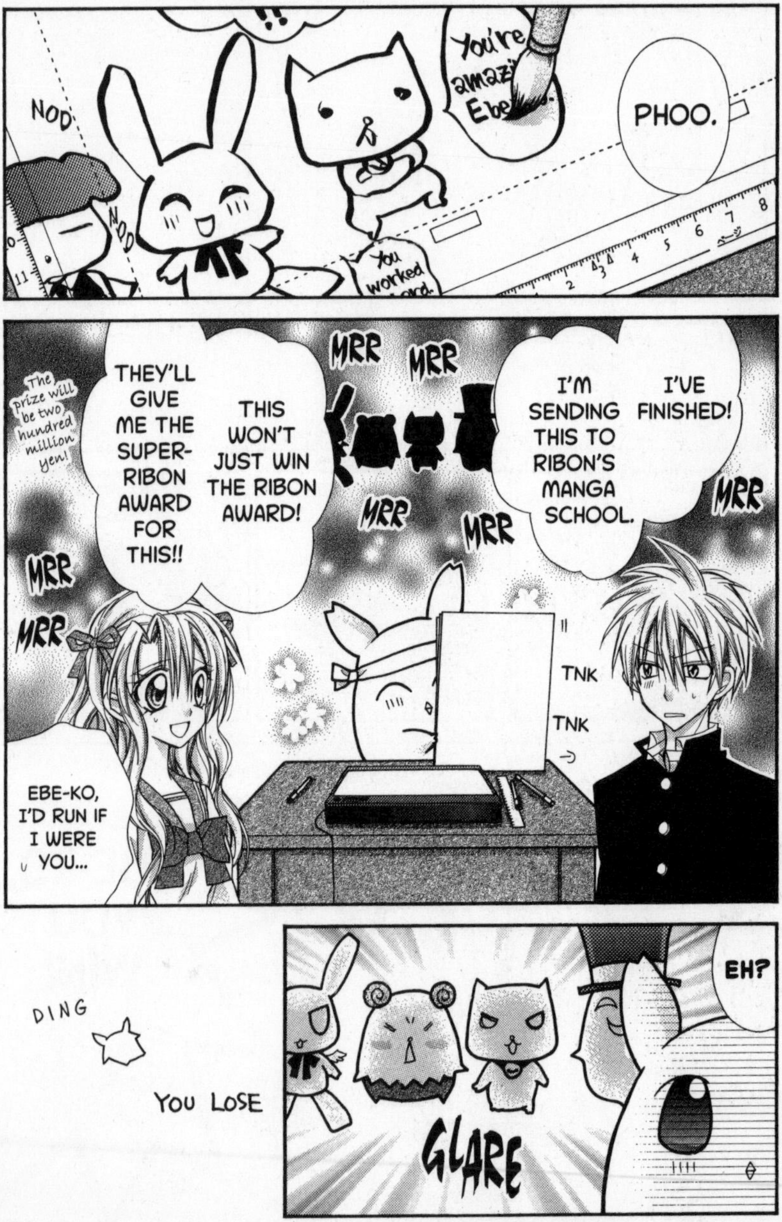

!!
PHOO.
You're
NOD
NOD
You worked
I'VE FINISHED!
I'M SENDING THIS TO RIBON'S MANGA SCHOOL.
MRR MRR
MRR MRR MRR
THIS WON'T JUST WIN THE RIBON AWARD!
THEY'LL GIVE ME THE SUPER-RIBON AWARD FOR THIS!!
The prize will be two hundred million yen!
MRR MRR
TNK TNK
EBE-KO, I'D RUN IF I WERE YOU...
EH?
GLARE
DING
YOU LOSE

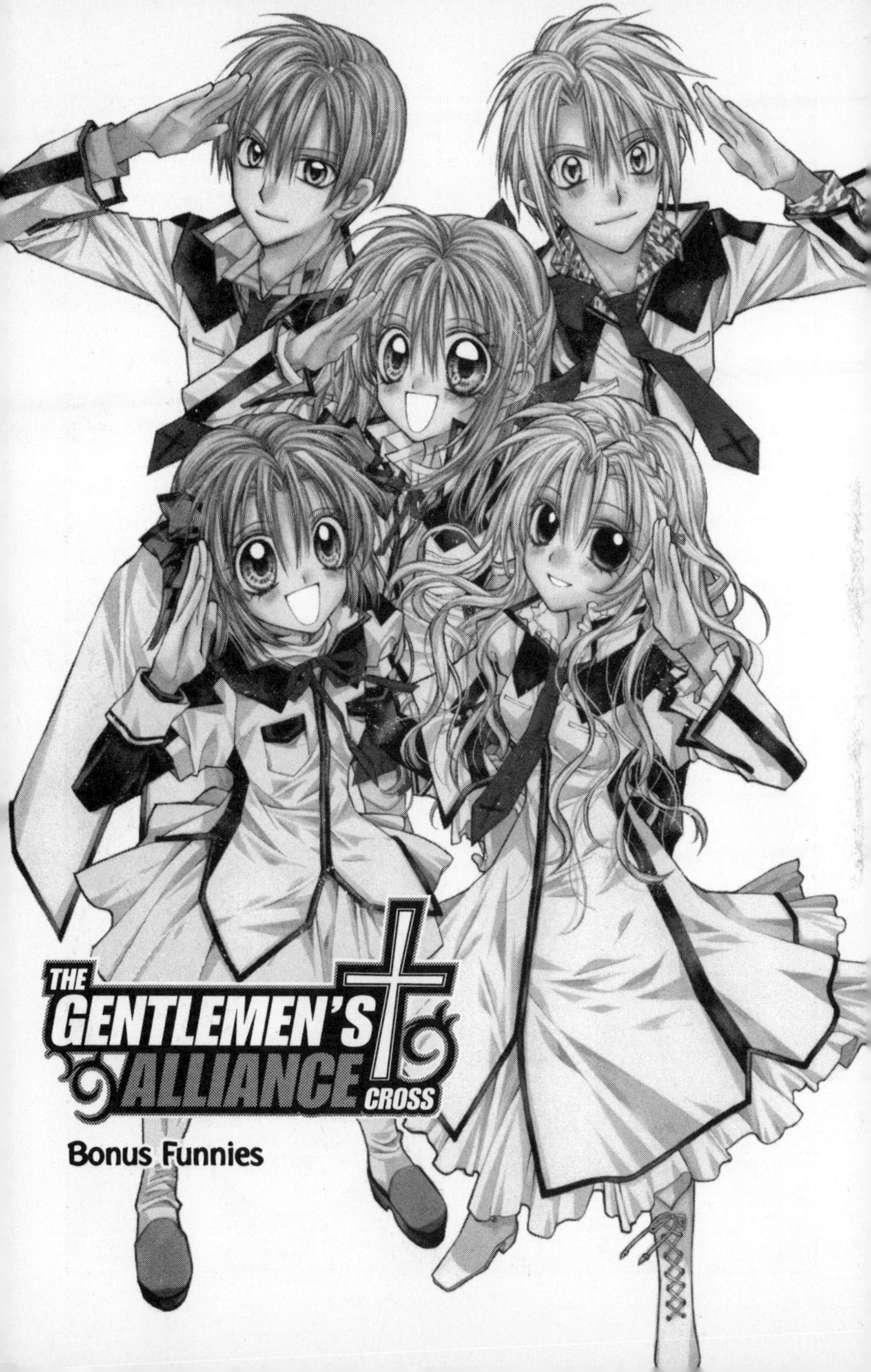
THE GENTLEMEN'S ALLIANCE CROSS
Bonus Funnies

MY CAMOUFLAGE LIFE

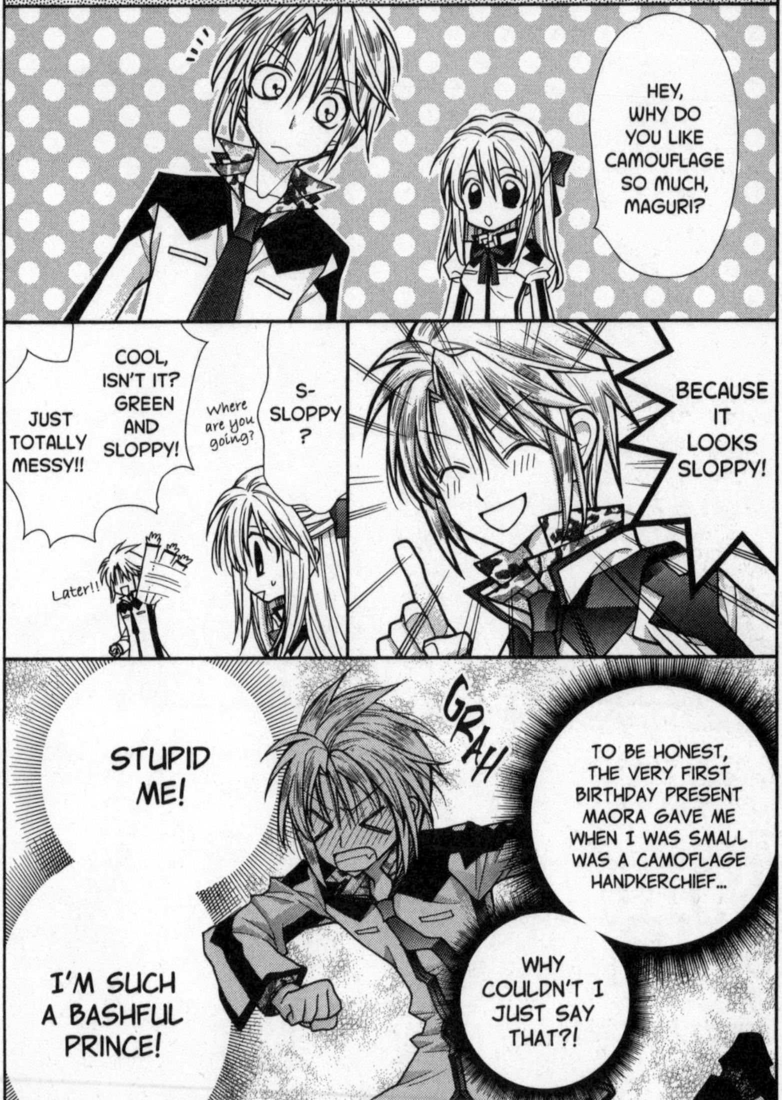
HEY, WHY DO YOU LIKE CAMOUFLAGE SO MUCH, MAGURI?
BECAUSE IT LOOKS SLOPPY!
S-SLOPPY?
Where are you going?
COOL, ISN'T IT? GREEN AND SLOPPY!
JUST TOTALLY MESSY!!
Later!!
GRAH
TO BE HONEST, THE VERY FIRST BIRTHDAY PRESENT MAORA GAVE ME WHEN I WAS SMALL WAS A CAMOFLAGE HANDKERCHIEF...
WHY COULDN'T I JUST SAY THAT?!
STUPID ME!
I'M SUCH A BASHFUL PRINCE!

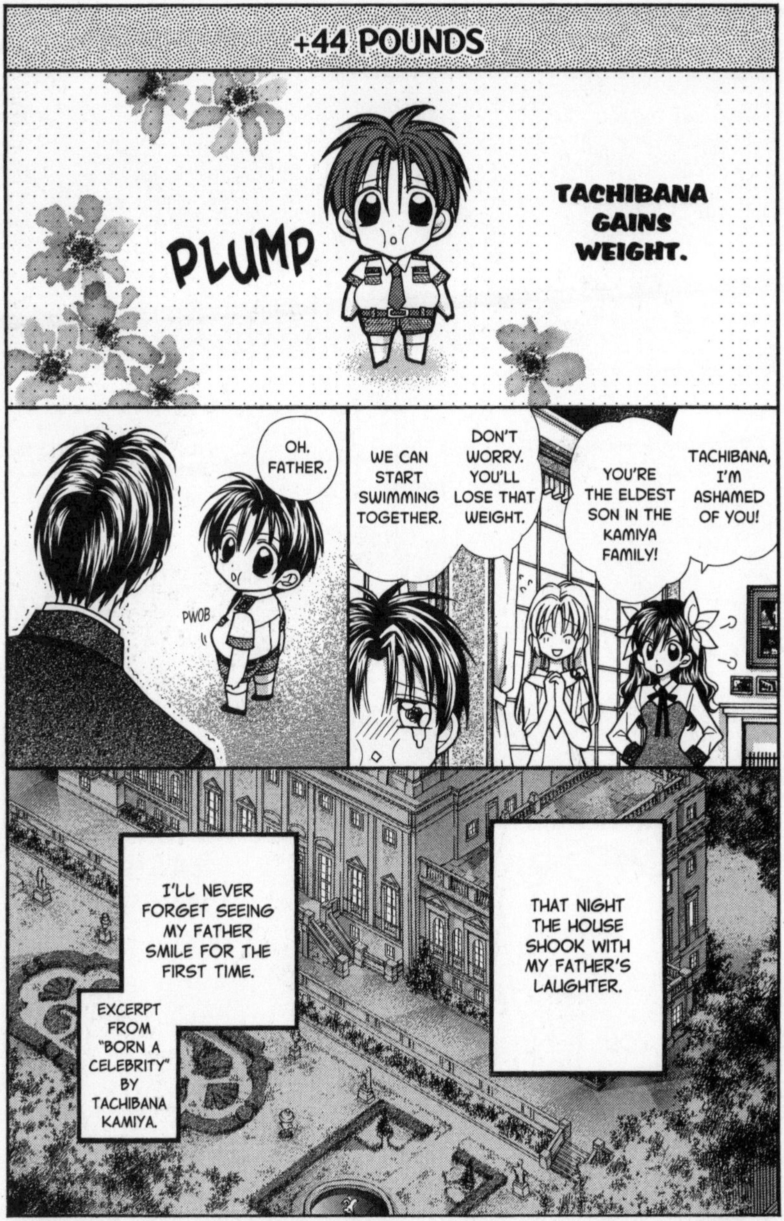
+44 POUNDS
TACHIBANA GAINS WEIGHT.
PLUMP
TACHIBANA, I'M ASHAMED OF YOU!
YOU'RE THE ELDEST SON IN THE KAMIYA FAMILY!
DON'T WORRY. YOU'LL LOSE THAT WEIGHT.
WE CAN START SWIMMING TOGETHER.
OH. FATHER.
PWOB
THAT NIGHT THE HOUSE SHOOK WITH MY FATHER'S LAUGHTER.
I'LL NEVER FORGET SEEING MY FATHER SMILE FOR THE FIRST TIME.
EXCERPT FROM "BORN A CELEBRITY" BY TACHIBANA KAMIYA.

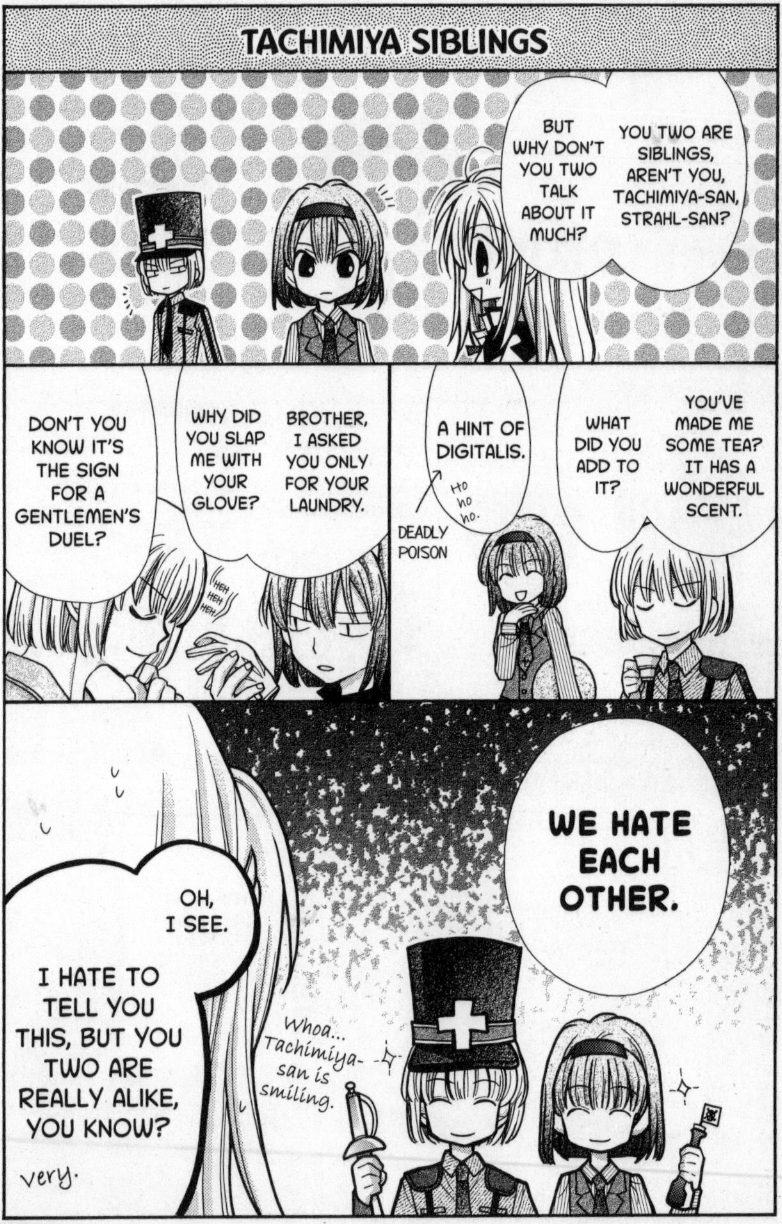
TACHIMIYA SIBLINGS
YOU TWO ARE SIBLINGS, AREN'T YOU, TACHIMIYA-SAN, STRAHL-SAN?
BUT WHY DON'T YOU TWO TALK ABOUT IT MUCH?
YOU'VE MADE ME SOME TEA? IT HAS A WONDERFUL SCENT.
WHAT DID YOU ADD TO IT?
A HINT OF DIGITALIS.
Ho ho ho.
DEADLY POISON
BROTHER, I ASKED YOU ONLY FOR YOUR LAUNDRY.
WHY DID YOU SLAP ME WITH YOUR GLOVE?
HEH HEH HEH
DON'T YOU KNOW IT'S THE SIGN FOR A GENTLEMEN'S DUEL?
WE HATE EACH OTHER.
Whoa... Tachimiya-san is smiling.
OH, I SEE.
I HATE TO TELL YOU THIS, BUT YOU TWO ARE REALLY ALIKE, YOU KNOW?
very.

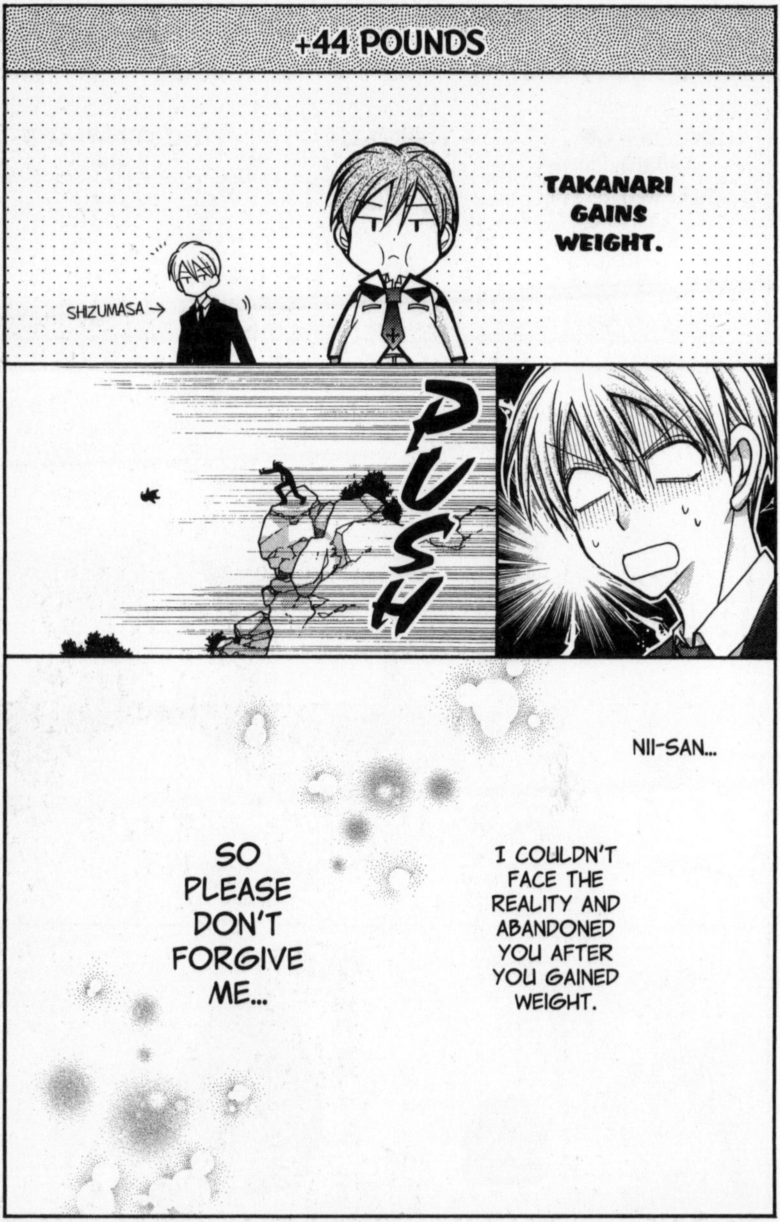
+44 POUNDS
TAKANARI GAINS WEIGHT.
SHIZUMASA →
PUSH
NII-SAN...
I COULDN'T FACE THE REALITY AND ABANDONED YOU AFTER YOU GAINED WEIGHT.
SO PLEASE DON'T FORGIVE ME...

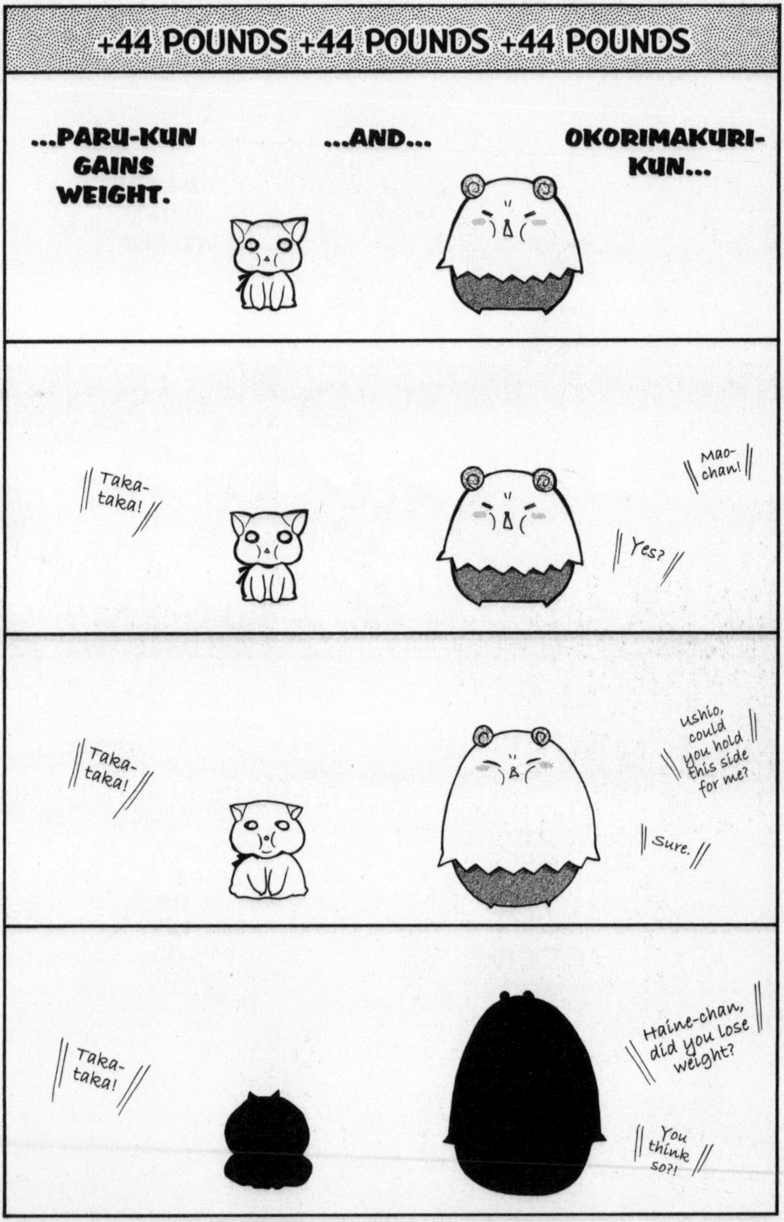
+44 POUNDS +44 POUNDS +44 POUNDS
OKORIMAKURI-KUN...
...AND...
...PARU-KUN GAINS WEIGHT.
Mao-chan!
Yes?
Taka-taka!
Ushio, could you hold this side for me?
Sure.
Taka-taka!
Haine-chan, did you lose weight?
You think so?!
Taka-taka!

IN LOVE WITH USHIO-SAN

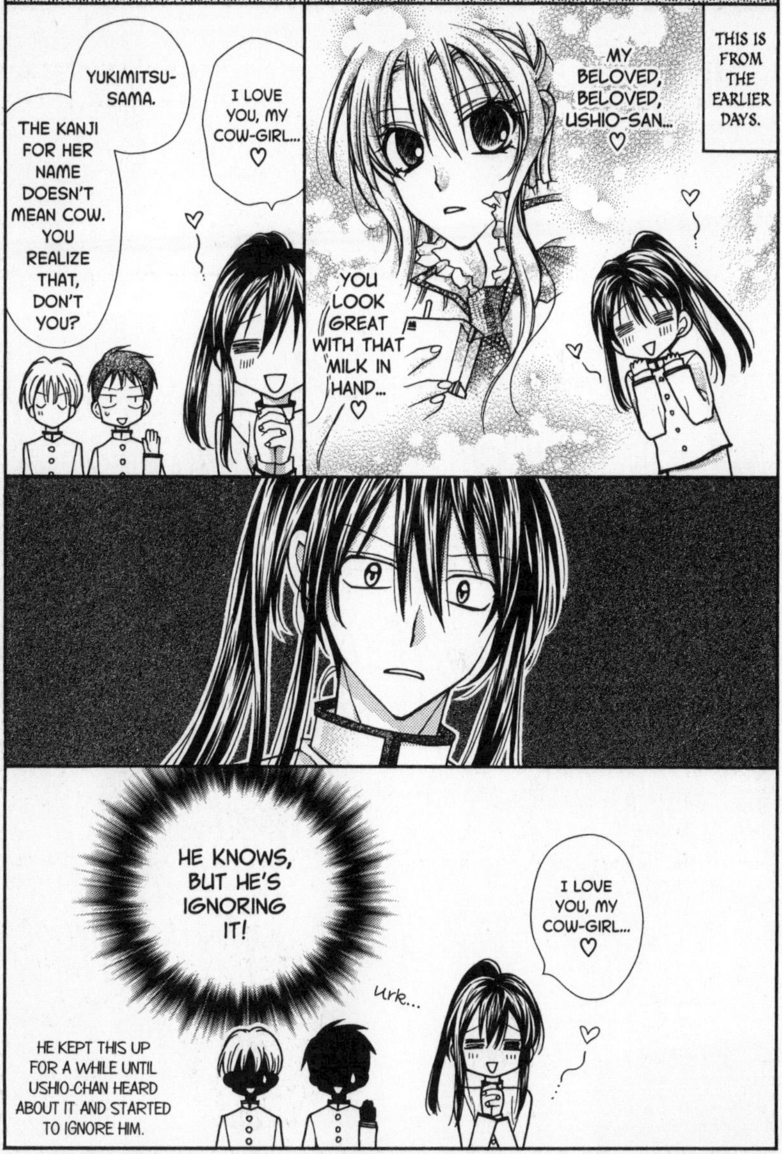

THIS IS FROM THE EARLIER DAYS.
MY BELOVED, BELOVED, USHIO-SAN... ♡
YOU LOOK GREAT WITH THAT MILK IN HAND... ♡
I LOVE YOU, MY COW-GIRL... ♡
YUKIMITSU-SAMA.
THE KANJI FOR HER NAME DOESN'T MEAN COW. YOU REALIZE THAT, DON'T YOU?
I LOVE YOU, MY COW-GIRL... ♡
urk...
HE KNOWS, BUT HE'S IGNORING IT!
HE KEPT THIS UP FOR A WHILE UNTIL USHIO-CHAN HEARD ABOUT IT AND STARTED TO IGNORE HIM.

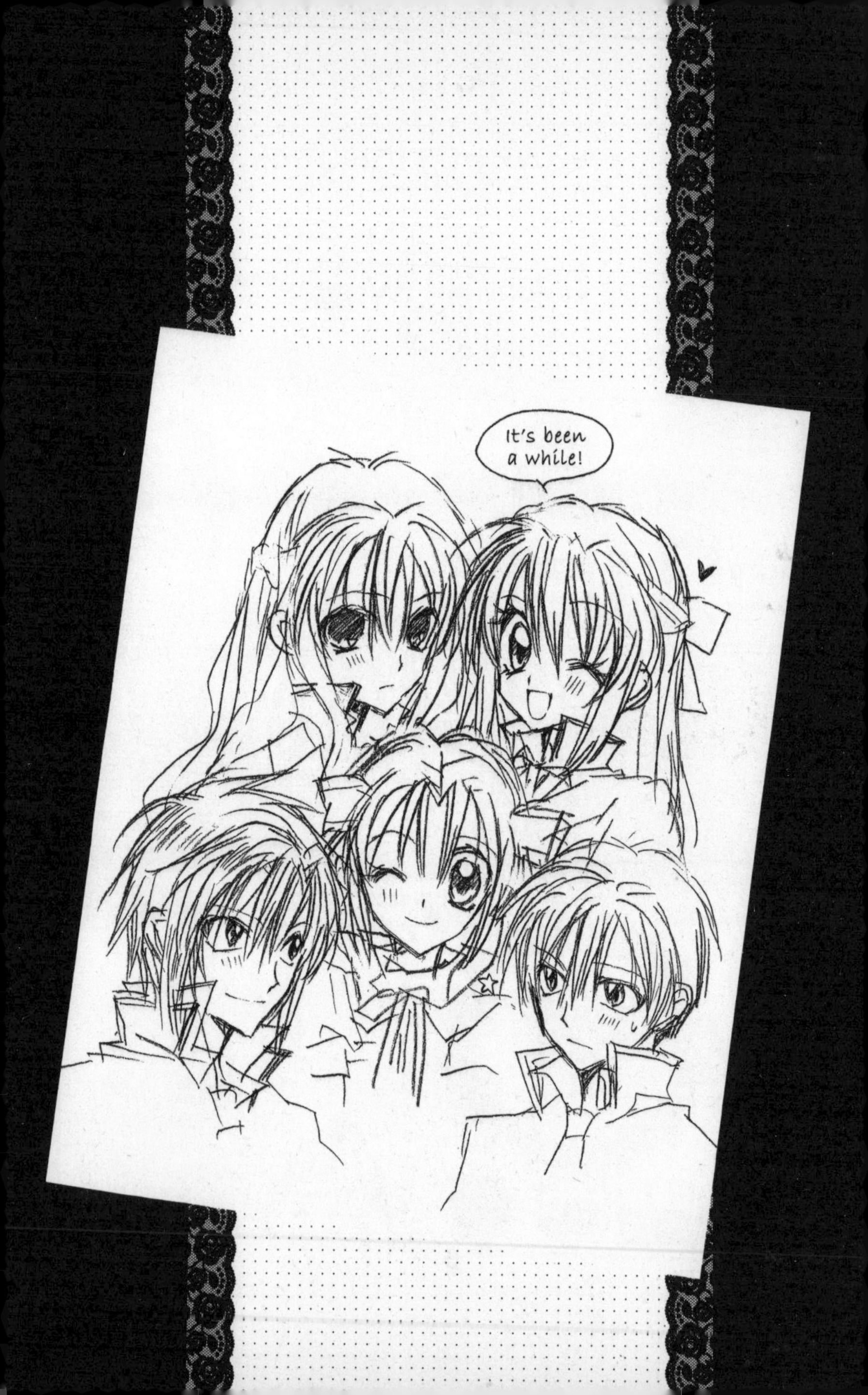
It's been a while!

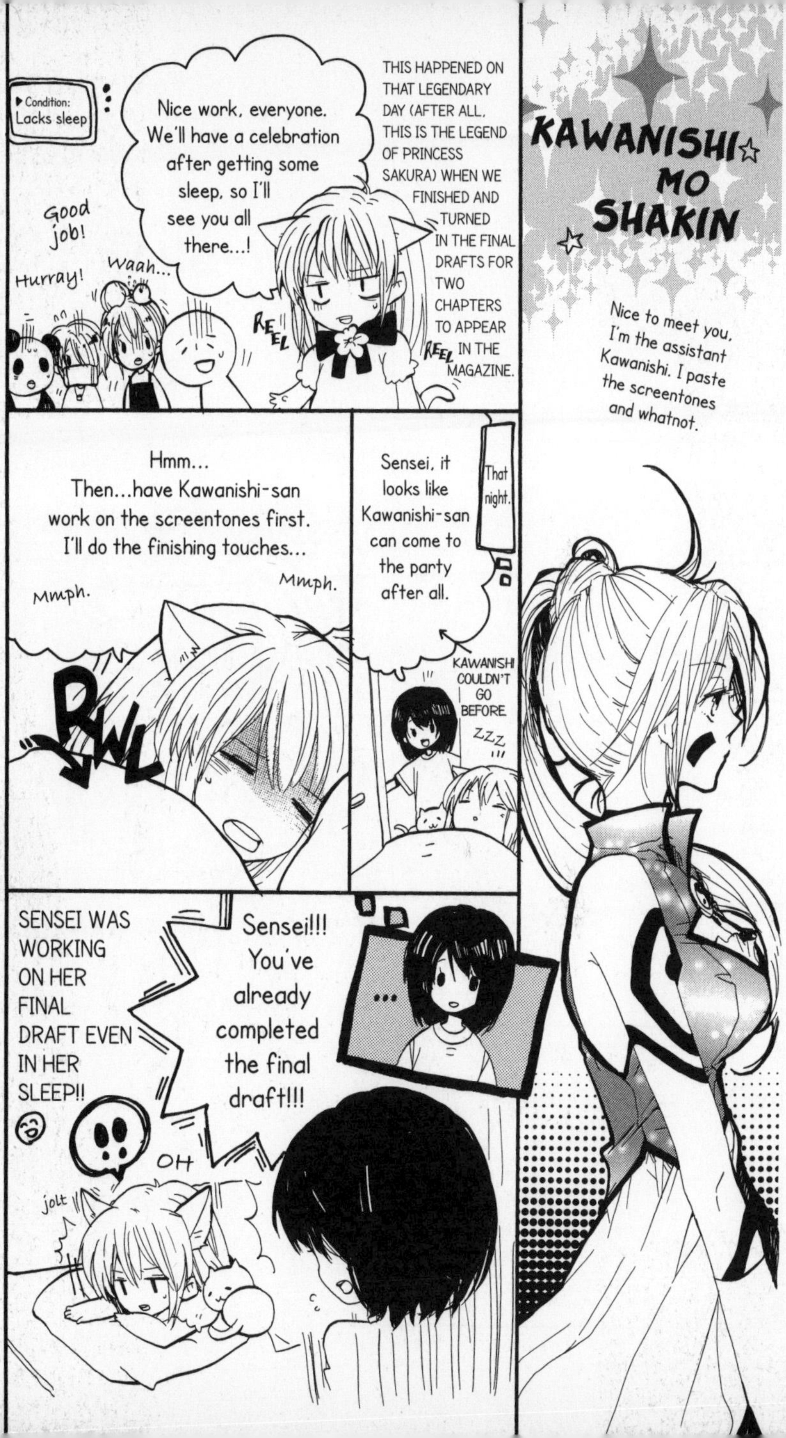
KAWANISHI☆ MO SHAKIN
Nice to meet you. I'm the assistant Kawanishi. I paste the screentones and whatnot.
THIS HAPPENED ON THAT LEGENDARY DAY (AFTER ALL, THIS IS THE LEGEND OF PRINCESS SAKURA) WHEN WE FINISHED AND TURNED IN THE FINAL DRAFTS FOR TWO CHAPTERS TO APPEAR IN THE MAGAZINE.
▶ Condition: Lacks sleep
Nice work, everyone. We'll have a celebration after getting some sleep, so I'll see you all there...!
REEL
REEL
Waah...
Good job!
Hurray!
That night.
Sensei, it looks like Kawanishi-san can come to the party after all.
KAWANISHI COULDN'T GO BEFORE
ZZZ
Hmm... Then...have Kawanishi-san work on the screentones first. I'll do the finishing touches...
Mmph.
Mmph.
RWL
Sensei!!! You've already completed the final draft!!!
...
SENSEI WAS WORKING ON HER FINAL DRAFT EVEN IN HER SLEEP!!
OH
jolt

MARI-SHAKI☆

Mari Endo

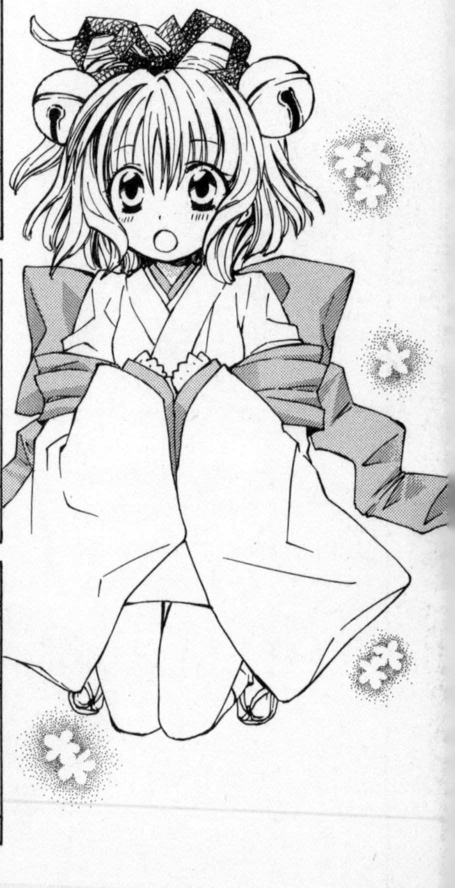

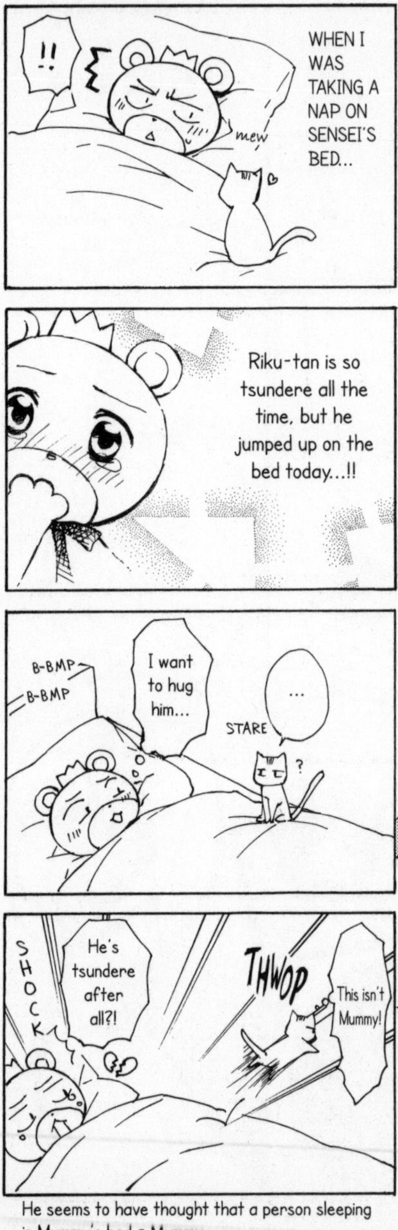

WHEN I WAS TAKING A NAP ON SENSEI'S BED...
!!
mew
Riku-tan is so tsundere all the time, but he jumped up on the bed today...!!
STARE
...
?
I want to hug him...
B-BMP
B-BMP
This isn't Mummy!
THWOP
He's tsundere after all?!
SHOCK

He seems to have thought that a person sleeping in Mummy's bed = Mummy...

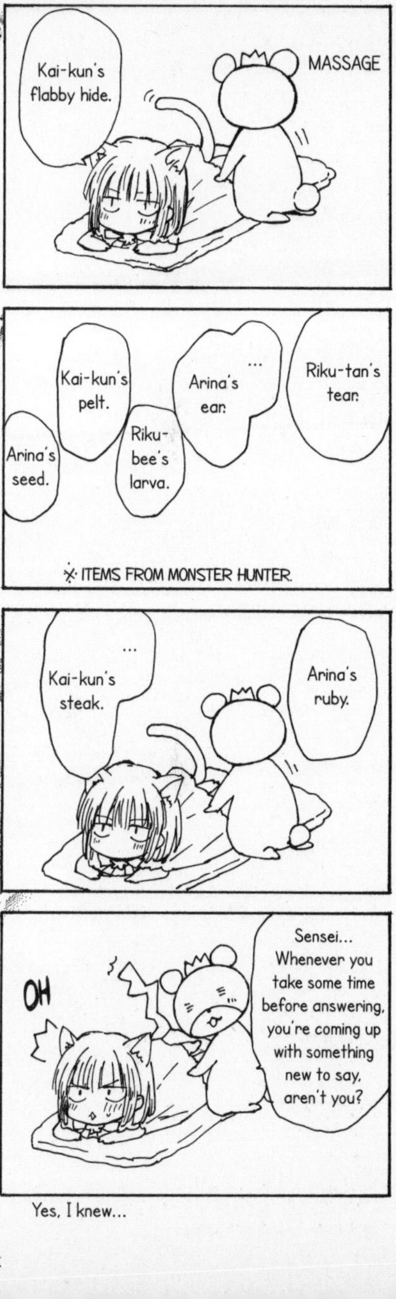

MASSAGE
Kai-kun's flabby hide.
Riku-tan's tear.
...
Arina's ear.
Kai-kun's pelt.
Riku-bee's larva.
Arina's seed.
※ ITEMS FROM MONSTER HUNTER.
Arina's ruby.
...
Kai-kun's steak.
Sensei... Whenever you take some time before answering, you're coming up with something new to say, aren't you?
OH

Yes, I knew...

Congratulations on publishing volume 6!
I'm always so excited to read this. ♥
Thank you very much for letting me
have a page for myself!

7/2010 Mari Endo

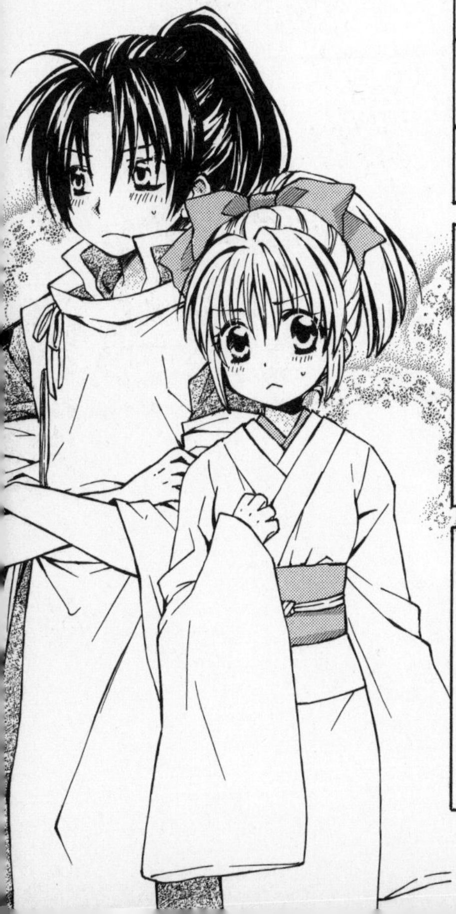

ARINA TANEMURA

As the author, I'm starting to get worried about overly earnest and hardheaded characters like Asagiri and Kohaku. I find it easier to create characters who tend to be a little too serious and awkward, so I end up creating many characters like that. (Ukyo is one too.) The daring, reckless bad boy—much to my surprise—is Enju. Aoba has mellowed, but he is basically a mischievous character who often lets his emotions get the best of him. Hayate is a cheerful guy who easily gets carried away. But if I were to consider everything, I guess Princess Sakura would be the character with whom I'd want to become friends. She's strong. And she's got Chizakura as well. (That's the reason?)

Arina Tanemura began her manga career in 1996 when her short stories debuted in *Ribon* magazine. She gained fame with the 1997 publication of *I·O·N*, and ever since her debut Tanemura has been a major force in shojo manga with popular series *Kamikaze Kaito Jeanne*, *Time Stranger Kyoko*, *Full Moon*, and *The Gentlemen's Alliance †*. Both *Kamikaze Kaito Jeanne* and *Full Moon* have been adapted into animated TV series.

Sakura Hime: The Legend of Princess Sakura
Volume 6
Shojo Beat Edition

STORY AND ART BY
Arina Tanemura

Translation & Adaptation/Tetsuichiro Miyaki
Touch-up Art & Lettering/Inori Fukuda Trant
Design/Sam Elzway
Editor/Nancy Thistlethwaite

SAKURA-HIME KADEN © 2008 by Arina Tanemura
All rights reserved.
First published in Japan in 2008 by SHUEISHA Inc., Tokyo.
English translation rights arranged by SHUEISHA Inc.

Printed in the U.S.A.

Published by VIZ Media, LLC
P.O. Box 77010
San Francisco, CA 94107

10 9 8 7 6 5 4 3 2 1
First printing, February 2012

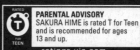

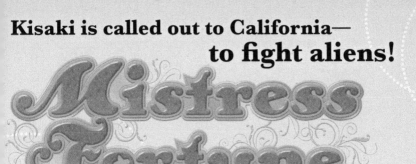

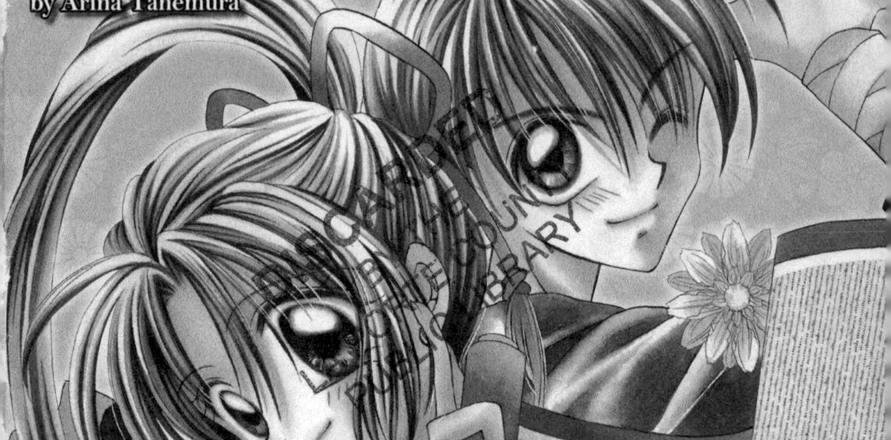

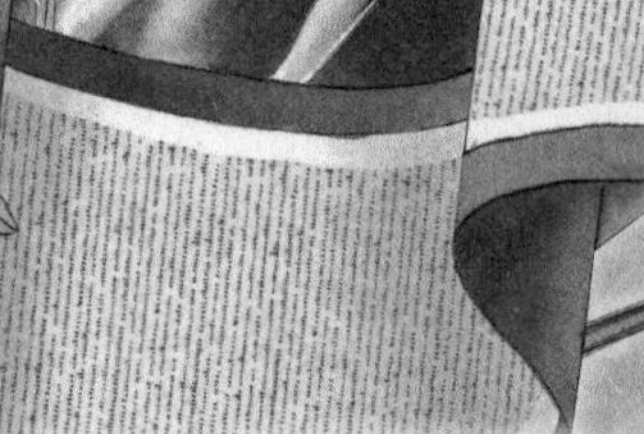
Shojo Beat Manga
Short-Tempered Melancholic and Other Stories
Short-Tempered Melancholic
Arina Tanemura
Story & Art by
Arina Tanemura